THE IDEAS OF RICHARD WAGNER

An Examination and Analysis of His Major Aesthetic, Political, Economic, Social, and Religious Thoughts

Alan David Aberbach

UNIVERSITY
PRESS OF
AMERICA

LANHAM • NEW YORK • LONDON

Copyright © 1984 by Alan David Aberbach

University Press of America,™ Inc.

4720 Boston Way
Lanham. MD 20706

3 Henrietta Street
London WC2E 8LU England

Library of Congress Cataloging in Publication Data

Aberbach, Alan David.
  The ideas of Richard Wagner.

  Bibliography: p.
  Includes index.
  1. Wagner, Richard, 1813-1883. I. Title.
ML410.W13A22 1984   782.1'092'4   84-13029
ISBN 0-8191-4145-3 (alk. paper)
ISBN 0-8191-4146-1 (pbk. : alk. paper)

All University Press of America books are produced on acid-free
paper which exceeds the minimum standards set by the National
Historical Publications and Records Commission.

DEDICATION

There is an old saying that there are three partners in the making of a human being: the Holy One, blessed be his name, the father, and the mother. It is a good saying.

This work is dedicated with love to Sydna Aberbach.

iv

ACKNOWLEDGEMENTS

The author wishes to acknowledge, with grateful appreciation, a major research Grant-in-Aid from the Social Sciences and Humanities Research Council of Canada, without whose aid this book could not have become a reality. Appreciation is also extended to Dean Robert Brown of the Faculty of Arts and Dean Tom Calvert of the Faculty of Interdisciplinary Studies, Simon Fraser University, for financial assistance.

Several friends and colleagues have read this manuscript and tendered valuable suggestions. The author is particularly indepted to Keith L. Johnson and David Lemon for their painstaking concern for every detail. In the early stages of the writing Henry Ewert offered invaluable grammatical and textual suggestions.

The author would like to thank the more than eight hundred members of The Opera Club of The Western Canadian Opera Society, for permitting him to try out-- over a period of ten years--various sections of this manuscript in lecture form.

Finally, to my students. Since beginning to teach a course on Wagner's **Ring of the Nibelung,** I have been constantly encouraged by their enthusiasm and insights.

Simon Fraser University
Department of History
April 1984

TABLE OF CONTENTS

PREFACE

"If my works do not speak out clearly for themselves--those of my art, by correct performances, and those of my literary labour, by being properly understood--it does not really make much difference whether folk think necessary to lay my weakness in the one direction or in the other."
Richard Wagner, "Introduction to the Collected Edition of his Writings."

A few recent studies of Richard Wagner begin with a question: can one justify another work on Wagner? The answer would have to be a qualified "yes" to the extent that a monograph covers material that is new, or presents an approach that can add to our already considerable knowledge of this much-discussed, much analyzed, multifaceted and ubiquitous individual.

Many major works have appeared since his death in 1883 and there is no lack of books on Wagner's life, musical and otherwise. There is, however, one curious void: not one full-length examination has yet to appear which presents and analyzes the evolution of Wagner's major ideas.

Wagner was concerned with history, politics, society, religion, economics, literature, philosophy, aesthetics, and psychology, as well as music. His ideas developed over more than forty years during which time he was actively involved in an attempt to synthesize his thoughts. Wagner's son-in-law, the historian and biographer Houston Stewart Chamberlain, commented in his study **Wagner**: "Wagner's writings, with his letters and his works, will always be the most important, I might more properly say, the **only** source from which we shall be able to derive a deeper knowledge of this extraordinary man."

This work fills a void by following Chamberlain's suggestion. It seeks to examine the evolution of Wagner's major ideas as reflected in his prose, poetry, letters, and music-dramas and it deals with these ideas as a manifestation and reflection of several major concerns and themes in mid-nineteenth century European thought and culture. This study is not designed as a collection of plot summaries nor does it discuss the development of Wagner's musical ideas.

ix

Richard Wagner lived during the height of the Romantic movement but unlike the age of the Enlightenment which preceded it, romanticism tended to be less rationally-optimistic about the ability of man to understand or control his circumstances. The mind of the Enlightenment era tended to believe that through the use of reason man could understand and control his world, and come to grips with it; but romanticism had a more colorful subjective outlook. Viewing man and his institutions with great skepticism, Wagner grew increasingly disturbed over what was happening in Western Europe: man's spontaneity, creativity, and initiative were being frustrated or rejected while at the same time he was becoming enslaved to outworn institutions and archaic principles.

Developing a profound understanding of the problems of his age, Wagner desired to articulate its fears and aspirations. In so doing he actively participated in its historical, political, economic, social, and philosophical conflicts. Wagner wanted to find his niche in society but became an alienated outsider because he rejected its values. Alienation created conflicts within him which found expression in his literary and musical career.

CHAPTER 1

THE SEARCH FOR A CULTURAL NICHE

By writing on a wide-range of subjects which affected man and his universe, Richard Wagner achieved some degree of success in his non-musical prose works. He sought, with mixed success and some notoriety, to add to the thoughts of Western civilization. Eclectic and catholic in his reading taste, Wagner possessed an almost insatiable compulsion to write on political, economic, social, and religious subjects. Some view his rhetoric as pretentious, cumbersome, and even trivial; others believe him to be an original thinker although opinions vary on the depth of his originality.

Of course, it was not Wagner's prose works but his musical and aesthetic ideas which ultimately earned him the attention of the world. Having commented on many of the great issues affecting European thought and culture, in thousands of pages of prose, he is usually remembered today not for his prose, but as the originator of a unique musical art-form improperly called "music-drama" yet incapable of being called by any better name. Music-drama, in its broadest definition, was Wagner's unique legacy to Western thought, and for this alone, he achieved immortality.

Until the time Wagner completed the second act of **Rienzi** in 1838 his interest was in becoming an opera composer. His first effort occurred in 1833-4 when he composed **Die Feen.** A casual examination of this opera reveals how closely Wagner tried to relate to the German world of Mozart, Beethoven, and Weber. His style was so similar to that of his predecessors that one could point to all three as his quotable models. Indeed, one critic who examined that opera believed that Mozart's style had been refined by Gluck and **Die Feen** therefore represented a backward step. Wagner responded to this criticism: "You accuse me of total ignorance of how to handle my medium, ignorance of harmony, ignorance of the rudiments of study. You think that none of my work has genuine emotion behind it. You will allow me no inspiration anywhere."[1]

----

[1] Wagner to Franz Hauser, March 1834, **Letters of Richard Wagner**, selected and edited by Wilhelm Altmann, M. M. Bozman, trans., London and Toronto, 1927, 2 volumes, 1: 13. Hereafter cited as Altmann.

Since **Die Feen** did not achieve the success that Wagner had sought, two years later he tried a second musical idiom. In composing **Das Liebesverbot** Wagner modeled the opera after the Italian bel canto school of Bellini and Rossini. Once again, he failed to achieve a success: "The thing is unsuitable, on German soil, both subject and music, and even if I wished to adapt it particularly to Germany, what gigantic difficulties has not the unknown German composer to face in order to find favor in Germany! That is indeed the curse under which all German opera labors!"[2]

Wagner's third attempt to carve a niche in the opera firmament and to find a meaning to his life, as well as economic survival, came with **Rienzi**, begun in 1838 when he was twenty-five years old. Here Wagner tried a third opera idiom, French 'grand opera', "which owes its conception and ultimate form to the desire of emulation woken by my earliest impressions of the Heroic Operas of Spontini, as also of the dazzling genre of Grand Opera ... the Opera of Auber, Meyerbeer, and Halévy."[3] The premiere of **Rienzi** took place in Dresden. It went well: "I must tell you that **never**, as they all assure me, has any opera been received for the first time in Dresden with such enthusiasm as my **Rienzi**. There was an uproar, a **revolution**, throughout the town. I was called tumultuously **four** times."[4]

Although he achieved a good success with **Rienzi**, Wagner soon recoiled when some critics began to point out the not so subtle musical influence of Meyerbeer on that composition. Clearly upset by this not incorrect allegation, Wagner tried to respond: "Only one thing startles me and--I admit it--incenses me, and that is that you calmly tell me that I often have a flavour of **Meyerbeer**! Really, I simply cannot conceive what in this wide world **could** be called 'Meyerbeerish' except, perhaps, the artful attempt to win a shallow

---

[2] Wagner to Robert Schumann, 3 December 1836, Altmann, 1: 44.

[3] "Zukunftsmusik," **Richard Wagner's Prose Works**, William Ashton Ellis, trans., 8 volumes, Broude Brothers, 1892-99, 3: 327. Hereafter cited as **PW**.

[4] Wagner to Edward and Cecilie Avenarius, 21 Oct.1842 Altmann, 84. Since Wagner had a tendency to underline key words in his prose all such cases appear in bold print.

popularity. ... It is no more nor less than a death sentence upon my creative power."[5]

Despite his protest, Wagner's attempt to imitate clearly recognizable models was deliberate: "In Italy I shall then compose an Italian opera. ... [Then] we shall go on to France. In Paris I shall compose a French opera--and God knows where I shall be then! And **who** I shall be--certainly no longer a German Philistine."[6]

For each of his works from **Rienzi** through **Parsifal** Wagner wrote a prose sketch and then later the poem, composing the music only after the poem had been completed. One of the earliest of an infinitely small number of composers who also wrote their own librettos, Wagner found it impossible to compose music to the words of others:

> I really lay no claim to a poet's reputation... I at first took to writing for myself of necessity, since no good librettos were offered me. I could not now however, compose on another's operatic text for the following reasons. It is not my way to choose some story or other at pleasure, get it versified and then begin to consider how to make suitable music for it. For this mode of procedure I should need to be twice inspired, which is impossible. The way I set to work is quite different. In the first place I am only attracted to matter the poetic and musical significance of which strike me simultaneously. ... Subject matter ought to be selected which is capable of musical treatment only. I would never take a subject which might be used just as well by an able playwright for spoken drama.[7]

Wagner develops an aesthetic theory that is destined to govern all his future compositions: "to the

----

[5] Wagner to Robert Schumann, 25 February 1843, Altmann, 1: 91-2.

[6] Wagner to Theodor Apel, 27 October 1834, **Letters of Richard Wagner** (The Burrell Collection), John N. Burk, ed., New York, 1950, 32n. Hereafter cited as Burrell.

[7] Wagner to Karl Gaillard, 30 January 1844, Altmann, 1: 107-8.

operatic poet and composer falls the task of conjuring up the holy spirit of poetry as it comes down to us in the sagas and legends of past ages. For music affords a medium of synthesis which the poet alone, particularly in association with the stage, has not at command. Here is a way to raise opera to a higher level from the debasement into which it has fallen...." Several years later when commenting on the particularly successful popular reaction to the song contest in the second act of **Tannhäuser**, Wagner wrote:

> Very few could be sure whether they had the musician or the poet to thank... I naturally have no special ambition to see my poetry cast into the shade by my music, but I would certainly be guilty of a lie were I to pretend that my music was at the mercy of my poetry. I cannot make use of any poetic matter which is not first conditioned by music. My Song Contest, even though the poetic element predominates in it, could not have expressed my higher intentions without music.[8]

In actuality Wagner remained inconsistent regarding whether to assign the priority to words or music. The argument may have been academic but it obviously gave him much thought. At times he clearly preferred to assert that the music served as the means for the enhancement of drama, while at other times he declared that the music came to him even before he wrote any of the prose. Only gradually did he come to realize that "word-tone-drama" were inseparable. But the relationship between word and music, whether coming from the same or from different hands, represented more than a mere collaboration:

> For the poet it is impossible to render in words all that passes at the bottom of this stanchless fount, which responds in turn to the breath of God and of the Devil; he may speak to you of hate, of love, of fanaticism and frenzy; he will set before your eyes the outward acts engendered on the surface of those depths: but never can he take you down into them, unveil them to your look. It is reserved for Music alone, to reveal the primal elements of this marvellous nature; in her mysterious charm our

---

[8] Wagner to Edward Hanslick, 1 January 1847, Altmann, 1: 125.

soul is shewn this great, unutterable secret. And the musician who exerts his art in this direction, alone can boast of mastering all its resources.[9]

In a newspaper article which appeared in the **Gazette Musicale** Wagner asked, "Is it really so terribly difficult to write a good opera libretto?" He answered his own question: "The main thing is to have **poetry** inside you and your **heart** in the right place."[10]

Wagner wrote **Rienzi** and completed most of the musical composition of the first two acts while serving as a conductor in Riga. As a result of a variety of intrigues and problems, and as a consequence of his current Meyerbeerian experiment, the Wagners decided to try France as their new home and in the summer of 1839 set out from Riga to Paris by way of London.

Wagner's autobiography **Mein Leben** contains a vivid (albeit romanticized and possibly even fictionalized in spots) description of his sea voyage on the **Thetis**. The Baltic sea journey was expected to last eight days. A violent storm erupted and on July 27 "the captain was compelled by the violence of the west wind to seek a harbour on the Norwegian coast." The seminal idea for **The Flying Dutchman** is well-documented: "The idea of this opera was, even at that time, ever present in my mind, and it now took on a definite poetic and musical colour under the influence of my recent impressions."[11] The experience of his adventure on the **Thetis** was destined to have a lasting influence.

Since all the elements of the trip were strong in imagery, or fancy, they were indelibly imprinted on Wagner's mind. Many of these experiences were to be reflected in **Der fliegende Holländer** and Wagner often related them to friends:

----
[9] "Halévy and **La Reine de Chypre**," **PW**, 8: 179.

[10] Wagner, "A First Night at the Opera," 31 December 1841, **Wagner Writes from Paris**, edited and translated by Robert L. Jacobs and Geoffrey Skelton, London, 1973, 166.

[11] Richard Wagner, **My Life**, in two volumes, New York, 1911, 1: 200.

...he told us--in his own way of speaking, where the words came pouring out like driven snow--the story of his adventures on the journey here, how he had set sail in a little boat and had been driven off course to Norway by the gales. Then how the whistling of the wind in the frozen rigging had made such a strangely demonic impression on him, indeed had sounded to him like pure driven music, so that once, when a second ship had suddenly appeared before them in the storm and then vanished again in the darkness as quickly as it had come, he immediately thought of **The Flying Dutchman** and had since constantly been thinking of the story and composing music to it.[12]

One can immediately recognize that Wagner's dramatic nature was as vital to the realization of his dramatic work as the music. In this illustration one can find perhaps the earliest example of Wagner's total conception of an integrated work of art.

After completing **Rienzi**, Wagner terminated his imitation of the three opera musical models. With the **Dutchman** he began to break new ground. Not only did it contain major personal and philosophical contentions, a characteristic of all his subsequent works, but it was not structured on musically imitative forms. A fateful personal episode had intruded to make him veer from the field of opera to create something entirely new and as yet undefined--music-drama, although Wagner would call it simply, drama: "From my own plight he won a psychic force; from the storms, the billows, the sailors' shouts and the rock-bound Northern shore, a physiognomy and colour."[13] This "psychic force" would have far-reaching ramifications.

The phrase music-drama is, at best, one of convenience. Wagner later objected to the unhyphenated German word "musikdrama" because its connotations seemed erroneous: "the word 'music' denotes an **art**,

----

[12] "Friedrich Pecht on his acquaintance with Wagner," **Allegemeine Musik-Zeitung**, Berlin, 20 and 27 July 1894, as quoted and translated in **Wagner: A Documentary Study**, compiled and edited by Herbert Barth, Dietrich Mack, Egon Voss, New York, 1975, 160-1. Hereafter cited as Barth.

[13] **My Life**, 1: 301.

originally the whole assemblage of the arts, whilst
'drama' strictly denotes a **deed** of art."[14] Clarifying
his view, Wagner assumed that music "must neither stand
before nor behind the Drama: she is no rival, but its
mother. She sounds, and what she sounds ye see upon the
stage." In actuality, the phrase "show-play" might be
even more appropriate since his works were "deeds of
Music brought to sight." But this phrase was just too
cumbersome. Unable to find any totally acceptable term
to fit his conception of the intimate relationship
between music and drama, Wagner eventually settled on
"Bühnenfestpiel", or "stage-festival-play."

Regardless of what Wagner called it, his purpose
was clear: "the raising of the dramatic dialogue itself
to the main object of musical treatment."[15] As his
works evolved Wagner saw as part of his unique destiny,
"the longing to raise the Opera to the dignity of
genuine Drama" which would ultimately succeed in
"uniting Music so completely with the Drama's action,
that this very marriage enables the action itself to
gain that ideal freedom." **The Flying Dutchman**
represented the beginning of the development of this
concept.

Each of Wagner's ten music-dramas from **The Flying
Dutchman** to **Parsifal** contained autobiographical
elements. Through them Wagner related to the world of
man and nature, and to the cosmos of which earth is a
part. Wagner's music-dramas were unique. In them he
expressed his thoughts, ideas, and feelings on history,
politics, economics, society, aesthetics, religion,
philosophy, and psychology. Encompassed within music-
drama would also be found Wagner's ideas relating to
man's relationship with his fellow man and with God.
The uniqueness of music-drama was that Wagner presented
ideas and developed paradoxes in the prose which were
then conveyed through music. Unlike opera, Wagner's
music-dramas deliberately expressed the eternal
questions of existence. In the librettos Wagner often
used the world of mythology and romance in order to
employ allegory and metaphor as the devices for
expressing archetypes. These, in turn, would express
universals.

----

[14] "On the Name 'Musikdrama,'" **PW**, 5: 301.

[15] "Prologue to a Reading of **Götterdämmerung** Before a
Select Audience in Berlin," 18 February 1873, **PW**, 5:
305.

Wagner arrived in Paris in August 1839. By early 1840 he was involved not only with completing **Rienzi** but with the embryonic poem of the **Dutchman**. The intrusive nature of the Dutchman on Wagner's psyche made him anxious to devote his energies in that direction, but to earn a living he began to write short stories and articles, first for the **National Gazette** of Paris (run by Maurice Schlesinger, a Jewish German who befriended Wagner), later for several German newspapers.

The two and one-half years spent in France and the friendships that Wagner made there were decisive in shaping his future direction. This pivotal period of time did not provide material rewards and successes but it did permit him to rethink the direction in which he was going. As a consequence, Wagner changed his fundamental approach to music. The "psychic force" of which he often spoke intruded more and more into his outlook. Wagner soon underwent a transformation which completed the process by which a potential opera composer became a seminal thinker whose ideas would create a new art form.

Wagner clearly recognized the evolutionary changes that were occurring although he seemed unaware of the forces behind them. "So far as my knowledge extends, in no artist's life can I point to so startling a change, accomplished in so brief a time, as here comes to light in the author of those two operas ... for the first was scarcely ended ere the second lay almost ready."[16]

Therefore 1840 turned out to be decisive as two interrelated events occurred: he wrote his poem of **The Flying Dutchman** and shortly thereafter a short story entitled "A Pilgrimage to Beethoven." "A Pilgrimage

----

16 "Author's Introduction," **PW**, 7:3. Years later Wagner all but disowned **Rienzi**. Yet it held historical importance and wasn't totally worthless: "**Rienzi** is very repugnant to me, but they should at least recognize the fire in it; I was a music director and I wrote a grand opera; the fact that it was the same music director who later gave them such hard nuts to crack--that's what should astonish them." See **Cosima Wagner's Diaries**, edited and annotated by Martin Gregor-Dellin and Dietrich Mack, translated by Geoffrey Skelton, Vol. 1, 1869-1877, Volume 2, 1878-1883, New York, 1978, 1980, 20 June 1871, Vol. 1, 379. Hereafter cited as **CW's Diaries**.

to Beethoven" appeared in the **Musical Gazette** on November 19, 22, 29, and December 3, 1840. The nature of the fictionalized story is not particularly significant; however, Wagner has Beethoven discuss a theory of music and opera that was of seminal importance: "All that stuff operas are patched together out of nowadays--arias, duets, terzettos and what have you--I'd get rid of and put in its place what no singer would want to sing and no public to hear. Glittering lies, boring sugary trash: that's all they understand. Anyone who composed a true musical drama would be written off as a fool."[17] Toward the end of the story Wagner became more reflective as Beethoven clearly articulated future possibilities: "The human voice, a far nobler and more beautiful organ than any orchestral instrument, is **there** a fact of life. Why should it be handled any less independently? What new results might not be achieved? Develop the very thing which sets the voice apart and you throw open fresh possibilities of combination."

Wagner had Beethoven's Ninth in mind. The powerful new force of the last movement--the combination of Beethoven's sublime music with Schiller's "Ode to Joy"--had an impact which if rightly exploited might open opera and drama to new experiments undreamt of up to this time. Wagner now began to articulate his formative ideas: "Instruments represent the primal organs of Creation and Nature; their expression can never be clearly defined and formulated since they convey the primal feelings as they first issued forth from the chaos of the Creation, perhaps even before there was any human heart to hear and feel." Aside from a theory of music, one sees here Wagner's deeply felt religious nature and his assimilation of the Genesis concept of creation, order out of chaos, with music: "The genius of the voice is completely different: this represents the human heart, the separate individual sensibility, limited but clear and definite."

An inner drive to succeed despite the likelihood of failure found expression in the prose and the music of the **Dutchman**. Obviously Wagner could not totally discard the influences of the past, but neither would he be restricted by them. One additional point needs to be mentioned here, although it will be discussed more

---

[17] "A Pilgrimage to Beethoven," **Wagner Writes from Paris**, 79.

fully later. At this time Wagner was just beginning to be aware of the mystical and transcendental influences determining his actions.

Several factors influenced the writing of the poem and prose of the **Dutchman**. First, Wagner was frustrated over his place in life. The move to Paris was totally unproductive, both financially and artistically. Second, the artistic world appeared too conservative with an entrenched inner circle who seemed to frown on originality. Tried and true artistic models were sought and expected and the role of the creative artist seemed to be destined for nothing better than to pander to the whims of society. Third, a new inner resolution was in the process of being shaped. Gradually, and for no tangible reason, Wagner was beginning to have confidence in his own ideas, and this would permit him to emerge as a creative artist regardless of whether he would succeed or fail.

The revolt he was fighting was one in which his ego needed to break through what he assumed to be the conservative artistic milieu of his day. Once this battle was fought, and won, it would become possible for Wagner to exploit his developing concepts regarding the relationship of music to the voice. His growing perceptions that music and the voice might pursue two independent but interrelated roles would ultimately create a new art-form. He would gradually come to recognize that the voice could express the more serious elements of drama thereby leaving it to music to establish the psychological and spatial characteristics of the design. Full-scale music-drama would then emerge.

Gradually Wagner began to perceive that music represented something mystical that was not easily definable. Although he hypothesized that music existed prior to and independent of man, he never explained how he arrived at this contention nor what it means. With the creation of man human sound was added to the already preexisting music. Man became joined with God. Although "all is perishable, only God's world remains for ever, and God's work is revealed in the creations of genius."[18] Music represented the spiritual element

----

[18] Wagner to Franz Liszt, 27 December 1852, **Correspondence of Wagner and Liszt**, Francis Hueffer, trans., second ed. rev., William Ashton Ellis, Vienna House, 1973, Vol. 1, 239. Hereafter cited as **Wagner-**

within the world while the voice represented the spiritual element within the human creation. When God created order out of chaos, music descended from the world of chaos to be made more meaningful when combined with the voice of man. The human voice, combined with music, could conceivably be the linkage between the physical and the spiritual. Music, ennobled and spiritualized, could rise to a wholly new level:

> Imagine, now, these two elements brought together and united! Imagine the instruments [of the orchestra] that convey the primal feelings--those raw wild feelings encompassing the infinite--united with the voice that represents the limited, but clear, definite sensibility of the human heart. That second element, the voice, would have a beneficial effect upon the instruments' expression of the struggle of primal feeling in that it would set it within the framework of a definite, unifying course; on the other hand, the human heart itself, represented by the voice, would be infinitely strengthened and expanded by gathering to itself those primal feelings: for now its former vague awareness of the Highest would be transformed into a God-like consciousness.[19]

Expressing not only a unique theory of music and drama but more importantly his growing awareness of mysticism, Wagner assumed that man could somehow elevate the physical into the spiritual.

The **Dutchman** contains all the ingredients of music-drama although each of the elements is not as integrated into the whole as would be found in his later works. There are still musical set-pieces which are numbered parts of the whole, and in this respect it is still more "opera" than music-drama. But in the interplay of voice and prose, Wagner created the very innovations previously discussed by him in "A Pilgrimage to Beethoven."

Despite his new inner security, Wagner was faced with a crucial problem. Psychologically he might have become satisfied with his newly-found confidence and a

----

Liszt Correspondence.

[19] "A Pilgrimage," 80-1.

willingness to revolt in the name of art; but the artist is not an outsider nor can he exist independently of society. What then was the role of the artist? Was alienation the price that one must pay for creativity? How does one develop the strength to endure? Must the artist be forced to come to an accommodation with society, and if so, on what terms?

As Wagner failed to fit into the model expected of an opera composer, these questions became all the more relevant. It led to a lifetime battle for it appeared to him as if his values were evolving while those of society remained stagnant. Given this belief accommodation seemed all but impossible.

While Wagner searched for answers he transferred his quest to the Dutchman, making him the archetype of the alienated man. The popular meaning of the fable and the Dutchman's actions prior to the beginning of the music-drama were not crucial to Wagner's purpose. They merely served as pegs on which to hang his intent. To become meaningful the Dutchman had to embody all humanity. The Dutchman had to be elevated beyond the myth so that he would be an archetype, a type of universal man who was being pitted against society but one who desperately tried to relate to it.

Artistically concerned with how his work would be presented to the public, Wagner became one of the earliest stage directors. Since the right psychological conditioning was necessary to make the arrival of the Dutchman's ship so eventful, Wagner had to create a mental setting in his audience. So successfully is this done, by the music and stage direction, that when the Dutchman's ship arrives and the Dutchman makes his first appearance, the audience is riveted to his every movement, action, and word:

> His first entry is most solemn and earnest:
> the measured slowness of his landing should
> offer a marked contrast with his vessel's
> weirdly rapid passage through the seas. ... his
> rolling gait, proper to sea-folk on first
> treading dry land after a long voyage, is
> accompanied by a wave-like figure for the
> violins, ... the actor must never let himself
> be betrayed into exaggerated stridings to and
> fro: a certain terrible repose in his outward
> demeanour, even amid the most passionate
> expression of inward anguish and despair, will

give the characteristic stamp to this impersonation.[20]

So concerned was Wagner with the impact of the opening monologue that he found it necessary to explain, in vivid detail, exactly how the singer must look, act, and think in order that the audience might retain its psychological conditioning. Emphasizing how the drama is as important as the music, Wagner left nothing to chance. One must be aware of the sense of action as well as the internal agony of the Dutchman. The Dutchman's opening lines, "The term is up, the seven years are ended yet again" are "to be sung without a trace of passion, as though the man were tired out. ... he bows his head once more, as though in utter weariness." Later, as the Dutchman reflects on "how often in the sea's most deep abyss have I with desperate longing cast myself", Wagner remarked: "I do not wish the singer to cramp too much his outer motion, yet he still must abide by my prime maxim, namely however deep the passion, however agonised the feeling which he has to breathe into the voice-part, he must for the present keep to the utmost calm in his outer bearing: a movement of the arm or hand, but not too sweeping, will suffice to mark the single more emphatic accents."[21]

Clearly Wagner's intent as composer, librettist, and stage director was to gradually build up the personality and the mental state of the Dutchman and to instruct the actor on how to develop the right characterization so as to more effectively portray the meaning behind the role. After the Dutchman hears about and meets Senta he becomes vulnerable to the emotion of utter despair. If the audience itself felt compassion for him too early in the work it would become more difficult to maintain this high level of intensity. The work must proceed gradually, and build.

Having written his own libretto, Wagner knew exactly what he wanted expressed through the words of the drama. His theatrical sense of staging, added to a sharp psychological understanding of motivation, gave him the added interest in personally directing his works. At one point in the action, just when the

---

[20] "Remarks on Performing the opera: **The Flying Dutchman**," PW, 3:210.

[21] Ibid., 211.

Dutchman again feels the intense pessimism that he had experienced throughout his years of wandering, Wagner commented: "This whole, almost direct address to 'God's angel,' for all the terrible expression with which it is to be sung, must yet be delivered ... without any marked change beyond what the execution necessarily demands at certain places: we must see before us a 'fallen angel' himself, whose fearful torment drives him to proclaim his wrath against Eternal Justice."

In one case Wagner's dramatic conception and sense of timing made him consider expunging some music that might inhibit the action. Toward the end of the work Eric exclaims that Senta's obedience to the Dutchman is "blind" and that she had promised herself to him. At this point Wagner gave Eric a beautiful cavatina to sing but warned that it ought not be sung in a "sugery rendering." It "ought to breathe distress and heartache." Nevertheless, coming at this point in the drama wrongly interfered with the action of the scene and Wagner decided that it might be better left out.[22]

One additional aesthetic conception related to this psychological imperative: the work should be done without a break, in one act, so that both the intensity and meaning could be maintained right to the crucial ending.

The use of archetypal figures represented Wagner's first great departure from the field of opera writing. Music could be used to illustrate unconscious psychological states of mind and to express what is needed to create the right mood, while the words represent perceived conscious states of the mind. The interaction of word and music could depict the known, the unknown, or the myriad worlds between.

In some respects Wagner developed the manner and means by which the audience as well as the archetypal characters can be manipulated. His understanding of psychological forces was partially drawn from his knowledge and love of the works of ancient Greek writers, and partly from a sharp perception of the world around him. When psychological characterization was important, Wagner willingly reduced both the action and the music to the barest level, leaving nothing to detract from the words: "The form of the poem of **The**

---
[22] Wagner to Hans von Bülow, 30 October 1851, Altmann, 1:214.

Flying Dutchman, however, as that of my later poems, down even to the minutiae of their musical setting, was dictated to me by the subject matter alone, insomuch as that had become absorbed into a definite colouring of my life, and in so far as I had gained by practice and experience on my own adopted path any general aptitude for artistic construction."[23]

That Wagner was breaking new ground was obvious to him. He had expected success with **Rienzi,** not with the **Dutchman;** but it was with the **Dutchman** that the public first recognized that an unusual creative artist had emerged on the musical scene. Whether he realized how far he had come is difficult to say but a few years later he reflected upon that moment in his life:

> This was the first Folk-poem that forced its way into my heart, and called on me as man and artist to point its meaning, and mold it into a work of art.
>
> From here begins my career as a poet, and my farewell to the mere concoctor of opera-texts. And yet I took no sudden leap. In no wise was I influenced by reflection. ... My course was new; it was bidden me by my inner mood, and forced upon me by the pressing need to impart this mood to others.[24]

Written ten years after Wagner completed **The Flying Dutchman,** this statement is significant on several levels. First, it contained his recognition that the impetus for the **Dutchman** was an internal one stemming from his own perceptions and consciousness. Second, Wagner found a meaning to the fable that was unique. Third, he recognized that his artistic and aesthetic conceptions were not final products but the beginning of a new approach to art, music, and drama. It was not his intention to greet the world with a "fixed and finished entity." Had this been the case it is doubtful if the work would have had such a lasting impact. It was a seminal work and a significant beginning.

---

[23] "Remarks on ... Dutchman," **PW,** 3:217.

[24] **A Communication to my Friends,** **PW,** 1:308. Hereafter cited as **Communication.**

As can be seen, Wagner's aesthetic ideas went beyond his concepts of music and drama. But would the public accept them? Italian opera with its stress on voice, and the prevalent public fad for the bel canto operas, was the fashion of the day: "the singer's voice--its kind and quality--is the public's main concern; **how** he sings is less important and **what** he sings is to most people of no importance whatsoever."[25] Could the opera-going public accept an entirely new and totally differing concept?

More and more it became obvious to Wagner that as a creative artist he should try to convey to society the values which he saw and understood. That only certain elements in society would understand, should not deter him. He was therefore surprised when the **Dutchman** became successful: "it seemed peculiar to me that this difficult music, not quickly or easily understandable, and which I ought to offer to an enlightened audience only, has become most popular so far."[26] When the **Dutchman** was first produced in Dresden in 1843 Wagner wrote Robert Schumann: "I yesterday achieved a triumphant success with my opera, **The Flying Dutchman,** of which I am prouder than of the success of **Rienzi,** because in this new opera I strike out a way markedly different from anything to which the public is at present accustomed."[27] Wagner's euphoria after the opening night dissipated quickly when it appeared that the **Dutchman** would enjoy a relatively short immediate success. He used less hyperbole in his autobiography:

> The performance took place on 2nd January, in the year 1843. Its result was extremely instructive to me, and led to the turning point of my career. The ill-success of the performance taught me how much care and forethought were essential to secure the adequate dramatic interpretation of my latest works. ... The audience fell to wondering how I could have produced this crude, meagre, and gloomy work after **Rienzi.** ... **The Flying**

----
25 "The Virtuoso and the Artist," **Gazette Musicale,** 18 October 1840, **Wagner Writes from Paris,** 56.

26 Wagner to Karl Gaillard, 30 January 1844, Burrell, Letters, 109.

27 Wagner to Robert Schumann, 3 January 1843, Altmann, 1:87.

Dutchman saw only four performances, at which the diminishing audiences made it plain[28] that I had not pleased Dresden taste with it.

Even before Wagner left Paris in 1842 for Dresden he had become acquainted with the broad outlines for his next two music-dramas, **Tannhäuser** and **Lohengrin**. The impetus for his deepening interest in philosophical subjects, and in the Greek classics, came as the result of a friendship with Samuel Lehrs which he had cultivated in Paris. Lehrs, like his fellow compatriot Heinrich Heine, was a German Jew who had come to Paris to earn a livelihood. According to Wagner their relationship developed into "one of the most beautiful friendships of my life." Lehrs dropped in almost every night and the two friends discussed a variety of subjects which influenced Wagner's way of thinking: "My intercourse with Lehrs had, on the whole given a decided spur to my former tendency to grapple seriously with my subjects. ... This desire now furnished a basis for closer study of philosophical questions."[29]

The background to Wagner's involvement with **Tannhäuser** came about by several seemingly inconsequential events. He had acquired a pamphlet in which the Tannhäuser and the Venusberg legends were discussed, but in the same pamphlet he came across a reference to the legend of "The Minstrel's War on the Wartburg": "At this juncture Lehrs brought me the annual report of the proceedings of the Königsberg German Society [probably sent to Lehrs by his brother who taught philosophy there] in which the Wartburg contest was criticized with a fair amount of detail. ... Here I also found the original text."[30]

As Wagner indicated in his autobiography, reading the three legends gave him a hitherto unknown appreciation for Germany in the middle ages and a "whole new world opened to me." Shortly after moving back to Germany in April 1842 Wagner took a trip to Teplitz and in June wrote a scenic draft which

----

[28] **My Life**, 1:293-4.

[29] **Ibid.**, 210.

[30] **Ibid.**, 260. In addition, the German Society report also included a critical study of the legend of **Lohengrin** giving Wagner some ideas for his third music-drama.

ultimately combined several legends under the title
Tannhäuser, and the Tournament of Song at Wartburg. By
May 1843 the poem had also been completed. Wagner used
little of the original setting, for it was of minor
concern to him, but the myths were a means to an end.
Myths emerge as part of a people's past but they belong
to all, and could be perceived as part of any culture's
inheritance; therefore they were universal because they
were understandable to all. Myth well served Wagner's
purpose. He manipulated them into music-dramas which
carried forward both the archetypes and the
philosophical and aesthetic questions that he had
raised earlier.

Once again Wagner tried to get the public to
understand his work by concentrating on how it was to
be performed. The words were crucial. Unless the
audience clearly understood what he was trying to say
they could never appreciate the proper relationship
between the words and the music. It was the content of
the drama, and not the music, which occupied his first
interest although it would be incorrect to assume that
the music was merely the hand-maid of the text. But the
audience needed to understand the message. Wagner
concentrated on getting the performers, the directors,
and the conductor, to recognize that he did not write
an opera but a "Staged Festival Play."

Before the music director even looked at the
orchestration he should "read through my score with the
closest attention to the poem", and then meet with all
the performers; but the "so-called 'vocal rehearsals'
should not begin until the players have become
acquainted with the poem itself, in its whole extent
and context."[31] Wagner suggested that they all meet
together "at which [time] the poem shall be gone
through in the fashion usual with a spoken play, each
individual performer reading the role aloud." This was
a radical innovation and Wagner knew it. But if the
public were to gain a true understanding behind the
meaning of the drama then the players themselves must
first understand it. Rehearsals were to be repeated
until this point was achieved so that the words could
be conveyed in their proper musical setting: "My work

----
[31] "On the Performing of **Tannhäuser** (An Address to the
Directors and Performers of this Opera)", **Neue
Zeitschrift,** Dec. 3 and 24, 1852, January 1, 7, 14,
1853, **PW,** 3:172.

demands a method of performance directly opposite to the customary."

Intelligent though they may be, Wagner believed that most opera singers paid only minimal attention to the text they were voicing. Opera performances which he had observed tended to be dull and, even worse, poor theatre: "Mere 'singers' have never been any use to me. I want good actresses who can sing, and while I cannot get them, the performance of my works will always be only a shadow."[32] But if the singers could appreciate that what he was offering them was not an ordinary opera, then they might fully accept the novelty of the situation. Unlike customary operas **Tannhäuser** contained no recitatives or arias. The work should be viewed as a seamless whole with the singers approaching the work as a unity. Wagner was certainly not trying to minimize the importance of the music and there was not even a hint that the work could just as easily be performed as a play without music. But it was his contention that words and music were coequal and each should receive the fullest attention.

Wagner's final instruction would probably dismay many contemporary conductors. Not only was he flexible to musical timings, thereby permitting almost unlimited variations, but he assigned the conductor to a seemingly subsidiary role:

> From the moment when the singer has taken into his fullest knowledge my intentions for the rendering, let him give the freest play to his natural sensibility, nay, even to the physical necessities of his breath in the more agitated phrases; and the more creative he can become, through the fullest freedom of Feeling, the more will he pledge me to delighted thanks. The conductor will then have only to follow the singer, to keep untorn the bond which binds the vocal rendering with the orchestral accompaniment.[33]

Wagner offered one parting word. There were singular moments in the drama where the text was so urgent that the performer of the title role must be in total

----
[32] Wagner to Francisca Wagner, 21 March 1852, Altmann, 1:222.

[33] "On the Performing of **Tannhäuser**," 175.

19

control of the "dramatic as well as the musical situation." The performer "will not get through as a merely well-trained singer; no, the highest dramatic art must yield him all the energy of grief and desperation, for tones which must seem to break from the very bottom of a heart distraught by fearful suffering, like an outcry for redemption. It must be the conductor's duty, to see to it that the desired effect be made possible to the chief performer through the most discreet accompaniment, on part alike of the other singers and the orchestra."

When Wagner presented the revised version of **Tannhäuser** in Paris he was concerned with ensuring that his singers portray the dramatic ending to the second act with an intensity that would overwhelm the audience. Quite obviously he concentrated on the performer of the title role: "Give me a good finale to the second act. **There** is the dramatic crisis, **there** is the moment when Tannhäuser must claim and compel the most intense interest. If he fails in this, the whole third act becomes a mere piece of staginess for which I would not give a snap of the fingers. ... It is **the** decisive moment **for the whole evening!** ... Sing the second act finale as if it was your last note for the evening, and be assured that only **then** will you sing the third act to my entire satisfaction."[34]

In moments of despair Wagner wondered if he would ever see his intentions fully realized: "I know that the work will never be performed as I mean that it should be. Possibly performers and public may appreciate the softer more emotional parts of the work, but they will never realize the energy of passion that underlies it."[35] He was right. Just how correct his perception turned out to be was revealed at the premiere in Dresden:

> They left the theatre, after the first performance of **Tannhäuser**, in a confused and discontented mood.--The feeling of the utter loneliness in which I now found myself, quite unmanned me. The few friends who gave me hearty

----
[34] Wagner to Albert Niemann, 21 February 1861, Altmann, 2:120.

[35] Wagner to August Röckel, 12 September 1852, **Richard Wagner's Letters to August Roeckel,** Eleanor C. Sellar, trans., Bristol, 1897, 58. Hereafter cited as Röckel.

sympathy, felt so depressed by the painfulness of my situation, that the involuntary exhibition of their own disappointment was the only sign of friendly life around me. ... Not wounded vanity, but the shock of utter disillusionment, chilled my very marrow. It became clear to me that my **Tannhäuser** had appealed to a handful of intimate friends alone.[36]

The close bond that Wagner felt toward the character of Tannhäuser reflected a man whose entire being was manifested in his artistic creation. He yearned for public approval and understanding but it was still too early for either. Years later, in his autobiography, he expressed these thoughts more directly:

My real intention was, if possible, to force the listener, for the first time in the history of opera, to take an interest in a poetical idea, by making him follow all the necessary developments. For it was only by virtue of this interest that he could be made to understand the catastrophe, which in this instance was not to be brought about by any outside influence, but must be the outcome simply of the natural spiritual processes at work. Hence the need of great moderation and breadth in the conception of the music; ... in order that according to my principle it might prove helpful rather than the reverse to the understanding of the poetical line.[37]

In asking that the audience become an active rather than passive observer, Wagner was breaking with tradition and the going was rough: "I had straightaway to suffer myself to be instructed by an otherwise highly intelligent friend that I had no right to wish to have **Tannhäuser** performed my way, as the audience, like my friend who had everywhere received this work favourably, had obviously thereby stated that the more comfortable, more subdued interpretation of hitherto was basically the correct one, even if unsatisfactory to me."[38]

---

[36] **Communication**, 336-7.

[37] **My Life**, 1:369.

Shortly after completing **Tannhäuser** Wagner was ready to proceed with his next project but decided, at first, to give himself some time: "a new subject has captured me completely. However I mean to restrain myself forcibly, firstly because there are things that I would like to learn, and secondly because I am convinced that if a dramatic work is to have intense significance and originality it must come as the result of a definite upward step, a real cultural advance in the life of the composer. Such a step, such a new period, is not to be marked off every half-year; it takes years to produce this stored ripeness."[38]

Wagner originally came into contact with the story of **Lohengrin** at approximately the same time that he began **Tannhäuser**, but the legend of the swan knight was both unappealing and as he considered it at the time, inappropriate for his consideration: "The medieval poem presented Lohengrin in a mystic twilight, that filled me with suspicion and that haunting feeling of repugnance with which we look upon the carved and painted saints and martyrs on the highways, or in the churches of Catholic lands."[40] However, after completing **Tannhäuser** he saw **Lohengrin** in an entirely new light.

Less than two months later the preliminary prose sketch of **Lohengrin** had been completed. What prompted him to embark on this work so much earlier than anticipated?

> I finished yesterday the writing down of a very complete and detailed plan for Lohengrin which gives me a great deal of delight, nay I frankly confess it, fills me with complacent pride.

> My invention and modeling have the lion's share in this creation: the old German poem which has handed this high-poetic legend down to us is

----

[38] Wagner, "Recollections of Ludwig Schnorr," **The Diary of Richard Wagner, 1865-1882, The Brown Book,** presented and annotated by Joachim Bergfeld, translated by George Bird, London, 1980, 138. Hereafter cited as **The Brown Book.**

[39] Wagner to Karl Gaillard, 5 June 1845, Altmann, 1:116.

[40] **Communication,** 333.

the most threadbare and mawkish of all its class, and I consider myself very fortunate to have yielded to the fascination of rescuing this almost unrecognizable legend from the rubble of its poor, prosaic treatment by the ancient poet, and restored it through my own invention and remolding to its native worth.[41]

In both letters Wagner revealed the genesis and the thoughts which influenced him to deal with this subject. He was not interested in writing a drama as an end in itself, nor was he influenced by epic or heroic subjects in terms of story-telling; on the contrary, he was prepared to deal with a subject only if it could become an instrument for advancing man's knowledge of himself. That he began **Lohengrin** many months earlier than anticipated attests to the immensely significant thoughts that suddenly came to him shortly after he had completed **Tannhäuser**.

When Wagner completed **Tannhäuser** it became obvious to him that he was reintroducing a style of theatre not seen since the days of ancient Greece. Traditional opera demanded little public understanding of the ideas behind the words, but Wagner was now insisting that his audience immerse themselves in the drama. His style placed a new emphasis on the drama as being coequal with the music. But "if we consider honestly and unselfishly the essence of music, we must own that it is in large measure a means to an end, that end being in rational opera the **drama**."[42]

No longer doubting his course of action, Wagner approached **Lohengrin** prepared to see it through regardless of the consequences: "My true nature--which, in my loathing of the modern world and ardour to discover something nobler and beyond-all noblest, had quite returned to me--now seized, as in a passionate embrace, the opposing channels of my being ...--With this work I penned my death-warrant: before the world of Modern Art, I now could hope no more for life. This I felt; but as yet I knew it not with full

----
[41] Wagner to Albert Wagner, 4 August 1845, **Family Letters of Richard Wagner**, William Ashton Ellis, trans., Vienna House, 1971, 133. Hereafter cited as Ellis, **Family Letters**.

[42] **Wagner-Liszt Correspondence**, 8 Sept., 1850, 1:92.

distinctness:--that knowledge I was not to gain till later."[43]

The innovation which he began in **Tannhäuser** was continued in **Lohengrin**. Music and word would henceforth form an inseparable continuity: "Nowhere in my score of **Lohengrin** have I put the word 'recitative' over a vocal phrase--the singers are not to know that there are recitatives in it. On the other hand I have taken care to weigh and to indicate the spoken emphasis on the words so closely and exactly that it ought only to be necessary for the singers to sing the roles exactly according to their value in the tempo indicated in order to arrive at the correct speaking expression through that means alone."[44]

But Wagner was also renewing and intensifying the part to be played by the singer. No longer was he merely to be a singer, in the Italian manner, but a "singing-actor." This would be relatively easy for Germans to do as their language and temperament being less colorful than the Italian, would lend itself better to this approach: "What the German needs, to fit him for a dramatic style of singing in keeping with his natural parts, consists in something altogether different from the teaching-apparatus there [in Italy] in vogue. For all that the German singing-actor (as I may call him) requires, besides recovery of his scandalously neglected naturalism in speaking, as in singing, lies solely on the **mental** plane."[45]

Wagner had accomplished a major innovation in the evolution of his dramas, and a departure from **Tannhäuser** and **The Flying Dutchman**. **Lohengrin** could not be categorized as myth, nor could it be stated unequivocally that the words should be taken literally. Some would assume that the drama originated in mythology whereby anything could happen, even the absurd arrival of a knight in shining armor in a skiff drawn by a swan. Others would speculate more deeply about this rather novel, if not bizarre, spectacle, wondering how its meaning was derived from the literal dramatic events in the story. Allegory rests in not making everything obvious, but opera audiences had

----
[43] **Communication**, 323.

[44] Wagner to Liszt, 8 September 1850, Altmann, 1:189.

[45] "Actors and Singing," **PW**, Vol. 5, 204.

24

little experience dealing with a non-literal, and sometimes intentionally vague story-line. Wagner solved this rather handily. He developed and refined the dramatic qualities so that the story could be accepted literally, allegorically, or mythologically. This strategy in fact would see him through the remainder of his music-dramas.

Perhaps unintentionally at first, it soon became apparent to Wagner that his music-dramas contained a series of layers that may conveniently be classified as literal, allegorical, and esoteric. Later in life he commented that occasionally he did not always realize the depth of all of his thoughts until they had been pointed out by others. Not every reader or listener would understand all that he was trying to say, but each could take for himself something of value. Not everyone could delve below the surface and peel back each of the layers of the drama. Differences in intelligence, temperament, and perceptiveness applied to the comprehension of any work of art.

All layers and meanings are valid. **Lohengrin** both complemented and supplemented **Tannhäuser.** Whereas **Tannhäuser** was a male-centered drama in which the female forces of Venus and Elisabeth battled within Tannhäuser's psyche, in **Lohengrin** the perspective is widened and the archetypal creation more closely parallels the human mind where the polarities of male-female exist together.

Wagner had asked that the public not try to view **Tannhäuser** and **Lohengrin** as operas but as dramas. In this respect he was unsuccessful. It was painfully obvious that most of those who criticized the drama tended to view it as an opera and were unaware of and/or unconcerned with its inner thoughts and meanings. It was equally obvious that he could not hope to answer all the criticism nor could he adequately explain meanings that could only be understood by those who possessed the "feeling" for self-understanding. He did try to deal with a few points of dissension, perhaps more for himself than for those to whom his answer was directed: "Criticism had proved itself unequal to alter the denouement of my **Lohengrin,** and by the victorious issue of the encounter between my instinctive artistic Feeling and the modern Critical conscience, my zeal for its artistic completion was kindled to a yet brighter flame. In this completion, I felt, would lie the demonstration of the rightness of my feeling."[46]

Wagner completed the autograph score of **Lohengrin** in April 1848. But from that moment, until November 1853, he did not compose any new music for too many other things were on his mind: his uncertain artistic standing and where his career may or may not be going; indifference on the part of the public regarding new and untried art-forms and in particular his innovative enterprises that appeared to them not to be true opera; finally, his conducting position at Dresden. Complicating these matters was Wagner's growing fascination for political subjects which ultimately got him into great difficulty when he found himself not only advocating revolution but actually working with the insurrectionists against the King of Saxony, his benefactor and employer. Finding himself on the losing side Wagner fled to Switzerland where he lived, off and on, for the next twelve years.

When Wagner left Dresden he was a psychologically disturbed man, and for good reason. Confiding to a friend he discussed the "disintegration of my whole artistic nature. The despair at my official position, the crushing burdens which it imposes on me, the worthlessness of every undertaking within the sphere of this official contract--have for years now been dragging me into a deep depression, which can only increase as time goes by."[47] Wagner had lost confidence in himself and even questioned his right to exist. Previously he had believed that his artistic ability was "the very purpose of my existence" but now even that was questionable for he could no longer find "pleasure in composing any more."

It became imperative that Wagner reassess his life and this he did through his prose works. During the first five years in exile his prose output was prodigious as he tried, often desperately, to come to grips with himself, intellectually and emotionally, and with the world. Two major prose works emerged during 1849, **Art and Revolution,** and **The Art-Work of the Future. Opera and Drama** appeared in 1851 whereas **A Communication to my Friends** appeared two years later. Finally, in 1853, the completed poem **The Ring of the**

_____

[46] **Communication**, 345.

[47] Wagner to Eduard Devrient, 17 May 1849, Barth, 177.

Nibelung. Later that year Wagner began to compose music once more.

In **Art and Revolution** Wagner sought "to discover the meaning of Art as a factor in the life of the State, and to make ourselves acquainted with it as a social product."[48] There were several personal elements contained within the work, namely his query about why the artist who, desiring no profit, but only to create, can not exist in society? Related to this was the attempt to illustrate how a revolution would be of substantial benefit not only to the artist but to all society. Wagner intended to prove that revolution was an indispensable instrument, the best means whereby a new society, one conducive to the development of art, can be created. Political radicalism was the means, the catalyst, for the transformation of art and society.

From ancient Greece to the present, Wagner saw the evolution of art as one continuous link. The greatness of Greek culture rested upon tragedy which they viewed as a religious experience. The expression of tragedy in Greek drama represented "the highest conceivable form of art", one in which "the noble part of his own nature united with the noblest characteristics of the whole nation." But as the State declined so too did drama and art. Try as it might, from that period of time and later throughout the Roman world and to the present, art was "never more the expression of a free community." Philosophy ascended in its place and "To **Philosophy** and not to Art, belong the two thousand years which, since the decadence of Grecian Tragedy, have passed till our own day." After the decline of Greece, art itself declined: "For Art is pleasure in itself, in existence, in community; but the condition of that period, at the close of the Roman mastery of the world, was self-contempt, disgust with existence, horror of community. Thus **Art** could never be the true expression of this condition: its only possible expression was **Christianity**."[49]

By bringing Christianity into his analysis Wagner now sought to discover whether or not it had contributed to the decline of European artistic values. Since Christianity represented the institutionalization of a set of values, Wagner sought to examine what those

---

[48] **Art and Revolution, PW,** 1:31.

[49] **Ibid.,** 37.

27

values were, and what they represented, in order to determine the influence that Christianity had on the cultivation of art. This led to one significant observation: "The poetry of Chivalry was thus the honourable hypocrisy of fanaticism, the parody of heroism: in place of Nature, it offered a convention."

Wagner concluded that the Church sought an accommodation with the artist whereby as the patron of the arts--through its financial power--it would be in the position of controlling the kind of art being created. After the Renaissance, the rise of a wealthy class further debased the cultural milieu; now art "preferred to sell her soul and body to a far worse mistress [than Christian hypocrisy]--**Commerce**." Wagner brought his survey of two thousand years up to date: "This is Art, as it now fills the entire civilised world! Its true essence is industry; its ethical aim, the gathering of gold; its aesthetic purpose, the entertainment[50] of those whose time hangs heavily on their hands." Gold bought fame and "self-seeking passions." This observation would lead to the **Ring**.

Contemporary society's perverse values, especially the Christian's perceived antipathy between physical beauty and nature, were an outgrowth of years of decline, and it would be folly to presume that a two thousand year trend could be reversed. Therefore, as is now the case, drama, music, and opera, to name but three aspects of art, produced little but "civilised corruption and modern Christian dulness [sic]!" At this point Wagner reintroduced some of his earliest aesthetic ideals by indicating that in the process opera had become a one dimensional experience, a "chaos of sensuous impressions jostling one another without rhyme or reason" while in the earlier Greek model music was a multidimensional aesthetic experience involving all aspects of drama and the attendant arts. But Wagner was not a reactionary who merely desired to return to the past. Far from it. Seeing the decline of Greece as emanating from slavery and man's inhumanity to man, Wagner's new model sought through revolution to create a new form of art which would lead to the regeneration of man. The two would work together: "Art is **revolutionary** because its very essence is opposed to the ruling spirit of the community."

---
[50] **Ibid.**, 42.

Art and Revolution was written at a critical juncture in Wagner's life. Temporarily living in Paris, without a real home or even a country where he could establish himself, his writing came immediately in the aftermath of the Dresden experience. It perhaps served to reinforce a belief that all his political actions were really done only in the name of art. Writing this relatively short article may have been a useful psychological crutch for it served to exonerate the radicalism of a civil servant who had been unable to get his way. By calling on man to "lift up Art to its true dignity", Wagner sought to elevate himself. All that he did in Dresden was done for altruistic and not egotistic reasons. Man could be regenerated and Wagner sensed that he knew how it could best be done!

In **Art and Revolution** Wagner forged the first link in the symbiotic relationship between aesthetics and man's political, economic, and social world. Although the ultimate synthesis would be found in **The Ring of the Nibelung,** the genesis began in Paris in 1849.

After finally settling in Zurich Wagner produced his longest prose work, **The Art-Work of the Future,** before the end of 1850. As explained to a friend, "this will be my last literary work. If I have been understood, and if I have convinced others--even if few in number --others must and will fulfil that portion of the task which is the work of many, not of one."[51]

The Art-Work of the Future was dedicated "with great esteem" to Ludwig Feuerbach (1804-72), a well-known and influential German philosopher and critic of religion. Undoubtedly Wagner had been influenced by many of Feuerbach's philosophical ideas, especially the importance of man as the key in the man-nature relationship. Many of the same ideas were implicit in **Tannhäuser** and **Lohengrin** but it was Feuerbach's works which actualized what Wagner was trying to say. The primacy which Feuerbach gave to man's activism played a significant role in helping Wagner find himself. In the dedication Wagner explained why he felt it necessary to express himself in prose: "No personal conceit, but a need too great for silencing, has made of me--for a brief period--a writer."[52] Wagner was concerned with

---

[51] Wagner to Uhlig, 26 October 1849. Quote appears in **PW**, 1:68.

[52] "Dedication of the Original Edition," **PW**, Appendix,

the "thinking artist", which doesn't necessarily mean
the creative personality. Since "thinking artists"
represented a collection of entities greater than the
sum of their individual parts it was as part of a
community that their importance became paramount: "it
is not the individual, but only the community, that can
bring artistic deeds to actual accomplishment." By
expressing himself through prose Wagner was attempting
to reach similarly-minded "thinking artists" and not
just the exceptional creative man or woman. All should
join the revolt against the contemporary state of art.

In the first part, "Man and Art, in General",
Wagner provided the key to the work. He established,
albeit sometimes in a convoluted manner, the
definitions and philosophy that infuse the remainder of
the piece. Wagner used the terms "Art" and "Science" in
their broadest sense. Through science man could
understand the objects of his experience, "but the
activation of the consciousness attained by Science,
the portrayal of the Life that it has learnt to know,
the impress of this life's Necessity and Truth, is--
Art."[53] It appears that Wagner conceived art to be the
subjective reflection of all that is brought to man's
objective attention by science. Art could enable man to
make nature conscious and if man sought to make his
life "a true mirror of Nature" then the realization of
life would transcend time and place. By "mirror of
Nature" Wagner seemed to be expressing some kabbalistic
ideas about life as an inverse earthly reflection of
the heavenly world. Using the mirror-image symbolism
Wagner reinforced his transcendental and mystical
perceptions which led him to conclude that through man
the true nature of art can be revealed. Art, and
therefore life, is "a conscious following of the only
real Necessity, the inner natural necessity."

Within the first few pages Wagner elevated man
above religion, class, race, and country. He
universalized man, enabling art without religion to
become the only important connecting link between man
and God, bypassing obstacles which for centuries had
prevented people from fulfilling their destinies. The
liberation of humanity came as a result of "the birth

1:394.

[53] **The Art-Work of the Future, PW,** 1:71. In a footnote
Wagner explains this to mean "Art in general, of the
Art of the Future."

of Knowledge out of error", the result being: "Then first will Man become a living man; whereas till now he carries on a mere existence, dictated by the maxims of this or that Religion, Nationality, or State."[54] A human would become a man in the sense of full humanity upon attaining true "oneness with Nature."

The creation of art by the thinking artist could be the "perfect reconcilement of Science with Life", a reflection of what the future might bring for humanity. A good part of **The Art-Work of the Future** described how various art-forms contributed to the final mosaic. It illustrated, in particular, how dance, poetry, and music added to an understanding of nature, thereby revealing the humanistic scope of the arts.

Wagner was promulgating a philosophy of art which sought to reconcile, unify, and synthesize, his assessment of two thousand years of history. Although believing that he was dispassionately removed from his subject matter, it is obvious that Wagner saw himself as merely one thinking artist whose love of truth and concern for humanity was leading him to suggest a new system through which humanity as a whole could create and enjoy a better life-style; it promised a true reward on earth, if not elsewhere. Man, through the focal point of art, was capable of devising and enjoying a new set of institutions which would permit the fullest realization of humanity's highest ideals.

Having had his entire world shattered, Wagner may have been trying inadvertently to rationalize a set of beliefs which could validate his identity. The European milieu of 1849 did not willingly embrace any of his ideas, musical or otherwise, but **The Art-Work of the Future** provided a rational defense for these beliefs. Its objective: public acceptance of his ideas on poetry, drama, and music.

Since Wagner was now coming to a clearer understanding of himself, out of this awareness would emerge a fundamental conviction that he was on the right track after all. In the early 1840's he might not have fully understood the implication of the words which he so eloquently placed in Beethoven's mouth about the combination of drama and music, and he may have only glimpsed its embryonic realization in **The Flying Dutchman**, **Tannhäuser**, and **Lohengrin**; but in **The**

---
[54] Ibid., 71.

31

Art-Work of the Future his ideas combined the intellect with "feeling." Wagner was now coming to an understanding of several forces at work which would enable him to approach the poetic and dramatic conception of **The Ring:** first, that as a thinking artist he had revealed certain basic truths in his first three music-dramas even if he did not fully realize or understand them at the time; second, that the combination of music and drama provided the right vehicle for the understanding and expression of transcendental and mystical truths. Music represented the "heart of man. But the organ of the heart is tone; its conscious speech the **art of Tone.**" Since Beethoven formed an invincible partnership between music and drama in the fourth movement of the Ninth Symphony, it was no wonder that throughout Wagner's life Beethoven represented his one consuming musical passion: "The Last Symphony of Beethoven is the redemption of Music from out her peculiar element into the realm of **universal Art.** It is the human Evangel of the Art of the Future. Beyond it no forward step is possible; for upon it the perfect Art-work of the Future alone can follow, the **universal Drama** to which Beethoven has forged for us the key."[55]

Wagner had first conducted the Ninth in 1846. To enhance its enjoyment for the audience he prepared a program guide explaining how he viewed the essence of each of the four movements. The guide may express more of Wagner's feelings than those of Beethoven but it reveals some of the thoughts that Wagner later refined in **The Art-Work of the Future.** The first movement portrayed "a titanic struggle of the soul, athirst for Joy, against the veto of that hostile power which rears itself between us and earthly happiness. ... at the movements close this gloomy, joyless mood, expanding to colossal form, appears to span the All, in awful majesty to take possession of a world that God has made for--Joy."[56] The second movement portrayed man's entrance into a new world "as if, in our flight from despair, we rushed in breathless haste to snatch a new and unknown happiness." The third movement was designed "to calm our wrath, allay the soul's despairing anguish, and turn its turbulence to gentle melancholy!"; but toward the end of the movement a second theme "appears as the yearning of love", and by

=====================
[55] **Ibid.,** 126.

[56] "Jottings on the Ninth Symphony," **PW,** 8:247-8.

the end of the movement "Love and Hope came arm-in-arm to wield their whole persuasive force upon our troubled spirit."

However, it was the mighty fourth movement, incorporating part of Schiller's "Ode to Joy" that captured Wagner's poetic imagination:

> the musical poem is urging toward a crisis, a crisis only to be voiced in human speech. ... And now it is as if a revelation had confirmed us in the blest belief that **every human soul is made for Joy.** ... we clasp the whole world to our breast; shouts of laughter fill the air, like thunder from the clouds, the roaring of the sea; whose everlasting tides and healing shocks lend life to earth, and keep life sweet, for the joy of Man to whom God gave the earth as home for happiness.[57]

Wagner's fascination with the Ninth went well-beyond musical boundaries. In it Wagner glimpsed both Beethoven's and his own feelings for man, God, and the world. Beethoven represented the thinking artist, one who was able to bridge the gap between the individual and the community. It was through the Ninth Symphony that Wagner discovered himself. Beethoven had dramatically expanded the symphonic form. Through the addition of words music entered into a new dimension.

But words, belonging to the poet and the dramatist, became the final link in the evolution of music-drama. Poetry represented life because "Poetry turned to Science, to Philosophy. To the struggle for a deeper knowledge of Nature and of Man, we stand indebted for that copious store of literature whose kernel is the poetic musing which speaks to us in Human- and in Natural- History, and in Philosophy."[58] If poetry would be combined with drama these two arts would work in intimate connection with each other, providing mankind with the "consummation of knowledge."

---

[57] **Ibid.,** 254-5. An interesting kabbalistic viewpoint which sees the happiness of man on earth as parallel to the happiness of man in heaven, an idea not particularly prevalent in Christian theology.

[58] **The Art-Work of the Future,** 139.

Since Wagner placed so high an emphasis on poetry and drama it was not surprising that he saw in Shakespeare the single most important force in the development of these arts. The Bard saw "unadulterated Life" and in his works brought literature to its finest perfection, just as Beethoven was the epitome of the musician and had brought the art-form of music to its highest perfection. But Beethoven and Shakespeare represented only the beginning of the road which led forward toward the art-work of the future, for "the literary Drama can only redeem itself from this state of misery by becoming the actual living Drama." This could be accomplished by uniting these arts into one effective combination, but not in the form of opera! Opera represented egoism, not community; it is a "shameful compact" in which the arts were merely a "counterfeit" combination, not one reflecting life.

By making a clear distinction between traditional opera and his new concept, Wagner clarified exactly what he intended to do: to express in music-drama not fiction, nor myth, but a depiction of "elemental reality", a life-force which would focus on reality. Although myth and story might be fancifully used, they would serve as a means for exploring--through allegory and metaphor--the reality beneath the surface. Here is Wagner's fundamental point: life itself must be portrayed in music-drama. Within three years Wagner completed the poetry and prose of **The Ring.** It would represent the force of the thinking artist and his depiction of life. When Wagner added the musical component to the prose, over a period of twenty-three years, it was not opera that he created, but an entirely new art-form, one consistent with his philosophy. It was "The Art-work of the Future."

Because Wagner was not indifferent to the other arts he gave each its due; but it is clear that poetry, drama, and music represented the new trinity while the other arts were supplemental. This should not be construed as diminishing their importance for they too were necessary for the emergence of the final product: "Not one rich faculty of the separate arts will remain unused in the United Artwork of the Future; in it will each attain its first complete appraisement."

It is clear how Wagner visualized the Art-work of the Future, but the "artist of the future" would be both poet and performer and would represent the "Fellowship of all the Artists": "Who then, will be the **Artist of the Future**? The poet? The performer? The musician? The plastician? --Let us say it in one word: the **Folk**. That selfsame Folk to whom we owe the only genuine Art-work, still living even in our modern memory, however much distorted by our restorations; to whom alone we owe all Art itself."[59]

In summary, Wagner called for a revolution in order that man's cultural needs might be satisfied and fulfilled. The Jews as they fled ancient Egypt and crossed the Red Sea served as his model of inspiration for the new revolt, so that the contemporary Pharaohs might perish. As "the Folk, the chosen people passed scathless through the sea towards the Land of Promise: and reached it when the desert sand had washed its body of the last remaining stain of slavery" so too shall the new revolution come from a similar "inner, free Necessity" to liberate the modern world. Years later, when Wagner's romanticism would be mellowed by age, he would begin to see the enormous gap which existed between his faith in man and the reality of man's inclination toward passivity. To assume that the "folk" could, or would, actively work to usher in a new millenia--a new culture with its innovative art-forms--remained but a utopian dream. That the folk never rallied to Wagnerian music-drama as the new cultural entity for the future ultimately revealed to him the limitations of the German spirit!

Both **Art and Revolution** and **The Art-Work of the Future** lead in a natural progression to Wagner's final massive work **Opera and Drama,** his last major theoretical prose work before commencing **The Ring.** Why was it necessary that he write yet another prose work? At this time it was simply impossible for Wagner to compose music while he was still in the process of coming to grips with the most intimate questions of his life. Shortly before his current round of problems, Wagner had written a poem entitled "Siegfried's Death" (which after many modifications was later incorporated in **The Ring**). Franz Liszt tried to persuade him to begin composing its music but it was a premature request. Writing to a friend, Wagner declared that "the choice of what I should take next in hand has tortured me; was it to be a poem, a book, or an essay?"[60] Music was not one of his options. Wagner still felt it

---

[59] **Ibid.,** 204-5.

[60] Wagner to Theodor Uhlig, August 1850, **PW**, 2:v.

necessary to continue his study and exploration of man and civilization.

After completing **The Art-Work of the Future** Wagner realized that it contained too many vagaries. For the sake of intellectual honesty he had to clarify some of the generalities. **Opera and Drama** was written with unbelievable speed, in about four months. Although its five hundred pages are often rambling and circuitous, the work as a whole has unity and serves to round-out Wagner's philosophical approach to music and drama. Once it was out of the way he would be able to resume composing music. By the middle of February 1851 it had been completed: "Here you have my testament: I may as well die now --anything further that I could do, seems to me a useless piece of luxury!"[61]

Wagner quickly established his thesis in the introduction: "that the error in the art-genre of Opera consists herein: that a Means of Expression (Music) has been made the end, while the End of expression (the Drama) has been made the means."[62] Opera therefore contained one fatal flaw: "The aim of Opera has thus ever been, and still is today, confined to Music." As a result it had become a "monstrosity" and not a vital art-form. Wagner proclaimed that the purpose of his writing was "to prove that by a collaboration of precisely **our** Music with dramatic Poetry a heretofore undreamt significance not only can but must be given to Drama."

For the most part **Opera and Drama** consists of Wagner's attempt to prove his thesis. In Part One, "Opera and the Nature of Music", he illustrated what he liked to call the "absurdity" of opera, and with a vengeance: it was artificial, frivolous, lacked dramatic necessity, and was boring!: "Opera was thus the premature bloom on an unripe fruit, grown from an unnatural, artificial soil." Most opera composers were not true musicians, although there were, of course, some notable exceptions, in particular, Spontini, Gluck, and--at times--Mozart; nevertheless, composers should express "the Feeling of the characters conversing on the stage" and since Gluck all compositions had been deficient in providing real

---

[61] Wagner to Uhlig, Feb. 1850, **PW**, 2:viii.

[62] **Opera and Drama, PW**, 2:17.

36

drama. Even Weber was more concerned with melody than with music which was expressive of real drama.

Wagner concluded Part One by asserting: "we have reached the end; -- for we have followed Music's powers in Opera to the proclamation of her utter impotence." How had this happened? Part of the blame was the fault of religion: "Christianity had choked the organic impulse of the Folk's artistic life." Excessive concern only for the soul, and not with the body, enabled the Church to exert a harmful influence over music. In referring to an "organic impulse" Wagner again used sexual symbolism to characterize the feminine aspect of music: "But every musical organism is by its nature--a womanly; it is merely a bearing, and not a begetting factor; the begetting-factor [drama] lies clean outside it, and without fecundation by this force it positively cannot bear.--Here lies the whole secret of the barrenness of modern Music!"[63]

Wagner continued his analogy by describing music [female] as the passive agent, the one who surrenders herself, through love, to the drama [male]. She must not be wanton (Italian music), nor a coquette (French music), nor a prude (German music)! "What kind of woman most **true music** be?" he asked.

> A woman **who really loves,** who sets her virtue in her **pride,** her pride, however, in her **sacrifice;** that sacrifice whereby she surrenders, not one portion of her being, but **her whole being** in the amplest fulness of its faculty--when she conceives. But in joy and gladness to **bear** the thing conceived, this is **the** deed of Woman,- and to work deeds the woman only needs to be entirely what she is, but in no way to will something: for she can will but one thing--**to be a woman!**[64]

Wagner raised the obvious leading question: "Who then must be **the Man,** whom this Woman is to love so unreservedly?" The answer forms Part Two, "The Play and the Nature of Dramatic Poetry."

----

63 **Ibid.,** 109.

64 **Ibid.,** 115. Wagner is, of course, writing in metaphoric terms. In no way does this represent his attitude toward women.

Wagner traced the evolution of poetry in much the same way as he had earlier traced the development of music, momentarily stopping at Shakespeare who "condensed the narrative Romance into the Drama." But modern drama represented its "unnatural, mongrel shape, and Germany was the soil on which this fruit was reared." Wagner blamed part of Germany's problems on its predominantly Catholic outlook. Although there had been a Luther, there was as yet no Shakespeare. Goethe and Schiller were significant as poets and dramatists but neither had been concerned with "modern life" and both had avoided criticizing contemporary society.

Wagner's focal point was narrow but clear: he was concerned with ultimate values, those capable of becoming universal; he eliminated from his consideration all factors other than those which concern man's life and purpose on earth. He did not seek to examine literature as an end, but only as a means to an end. Using different criteria, Schiller and Goethe would be proclaimed dramatists akin to Shakespeare; indeed, Wagner later believed this to be the case! That he was genuinely fond of both may be demonstrated by their portraits which adorned his living room wall when he moved into Wahnfried. But at this time he was concerned with a rigidly prescribed perception of literature which had validity only to the extent that it permitted man to understand himself, and then only if it resulted in some positive social action. As long as Schiller was concerned with history he traveled the right path, but when fanciful romance was introduced into his stories his writing became distorted. Since Schiller's time, drama has become impotent.

The drama of the future would have to break from the limitations imposed by man's artificial institutions, especially those of religion. Christianity was so preoccupied with death that it all but ignored life: "This dying, with the yearning after it, is the sole true content of the Art which issued from the Christian myth; it utters itself as dread and loathing of actual life, as flight before it,--as longing for death." This was both unnatural and untrue. In addition, the Christian religious view is alien to literature because it "inculcated a life of contemplation and inaction." Its purpose was but "to flee from an un-understood reality, to gain contentment in a world of fancy."[65] If drama was to remain valid then it would have to concern itself with humanity and play a dynamic role "to shape it--this is the trend of humankind since ever it wrested to itself the outward faculty of knowing the phenomena of Nature in their genuine essence; for from this knowledge have we won the measure for the knowledge, also, of the essence of Mankind."

The true poet was able to express the "phenomena of human society" which represented the "soil of history", but "unvarnished" and without distortion. But there could be a considerable difference between the poet and the politician. The poet would have to become the politician because the politician was incapable of becoming a poet. The poet of the future had a formidable task--to organize a new society:

> But to bring the unconscious part of human nature to consciousness within society, and in this consciousness to know nothing other than the necessity common to every member of Society, namely of the Individual's own free self-determining,--this is as good as to say, annul the State; for through Society has the State marched on to a denial of the free self-determining of the Individual,--upon the death of **that**, has it lived.[66]

The poet had an awesome responsibility for it was from him that society would gain an understanding of transcendental values. The poet became the receptacle for truth and it was to him that one must turn to construct a new political, social, and religious system. In his attack upon the state Wagner developed a litany of crimes for which the state must assume primary responsibility: it determined one's thoughts, feelings, and place in the world; it determined one's education and how one is brought up; finally, the state regulated the religious, social, and cultural order. But the poet would turn the state into a means for the betterment of society. One of his first reforms would be to separate religion from the narrow confines of the political structure: "But religious Conscience means a universal conscience; and conscience cannot be universal, until it knows the Unconscious, the

---
[65] **Ibid.**, 159-65.

[66] **Ibid.**, 193-4.

Instinctive, and Purely-human, as the only true and necessary thing, and vindicates it by that knowledge." Universal conscience is the "social Religion of the Future."

Wagner explained only vaguely how these processes would work. Somehow the poet would be able to clarify life by explaining his experiences to society: "His aim he can only reach by physically presenting to our eyes the things of Life in their fullest spontaneity; and thus, by vindicating Life itself out of the mouth of its own Necessity; for the Feeling, to which he addresses himself, can understand this Necessity alone." Through the drama the poet expressed both the "Understanding" and the "Feeling", culminating in the "emotionalising of the intellect." Wagner seemed to know what the poet would do but never answered the question of how or why the poet became the receptacle for the so-called "higher values."

Intuiting "the utterly peculiar nature of the poet, of the artist", Wagner often found himself to be "unintelligible to the world." His source of knowledge appeared to be unlike that of most people: "Then I plainly recognise herein the wonder of it, its total opposition to the usual view of life: whereas that view turns ever on the pivot of experience, poetic intuition, preceding all experience, embraces altogether of its own potency what first lends all experience a sense and a meaning."[67] Perhaps that explains why they became poets in the first place.

If this were actually Wagner's rationale it could conceivably complicate his belief in free will. Perhaps what was significant for his own development was the assumption that it was the poet who was best qualified to deal with the knowledge once it was acquired. Unlike a contemplative philosopher, the poet must act: "His Idea then will take great part in this experience's shaping: the purer and higher that, the more unworldlike and incomparable this; it will purge his will, his aesthetic interest will become a moral one, and to the highest poetic idea will link itself the highest moral consciousness. Then will it be his task to prove it in the moral world; the same

----
[67] Wagner to Mathilde Wesendonck, 19 January 1859, **Richard Wagner to Mathilde Wesendonck,** William Ashton Ellis, trans., London, 1905, 95. Hereafter cited as **Wagner-Wesendonck Correspondence.**

foreknowledge will guide him, that, as cognition of the aesthetic idea, had moved him to present that idea in his artwork and qualified him for the experience."[68] This assumption enabled Wagner, as poet, to exercise in his work a bold approach that did not exist earlier.

The poet would establish the proper relationships between man and God and nature: "The Judaeo-Christian Wonder tore the connexion of natural phenomena asunder, to allow the Divine Will to appear over Nature." And here Wagner came to the fullest appreciation of the role of the poet; the poet, almost alone in the world, had the capacity to understand nature, and through his understanding the world could be enlightened. "It is just the fullest understanding of Nature, that first enables the poet to set her phenomena before us in wondrous shaping; for only in such shaping, do they become intelligible to us as **the conditionments of human actions intensified.**"[69] Through the "Understanding" one sees all the parts which comprise nature. The poet restores man's relationship with nature which had been broken by the beliefs of the Judeo-Christian tradition. Later, when Wagner wrote **The Ring,** his design, purpose, and intention was to depict nature and reality in its elemental forms.

But, as Wagner hypothesized, if music could be the woman, and the poet the man, then the symbolic act of union through love would produce an "act of birth" from which would emerge Part Three, "The Arts of Poetry and Tone in the Drama of the Future"--the aesthetic god-father of music-drama.

In Part Three Wagner developed the ideas that he had first discussed in "A Pilgrimage to Beethoven", written ten years earlier. A new art-form could emerge by linking music and drama in a way never before anticipated. Neither music nor drama could achieve by itself the dimensions to be realized when joined. For the "tone-poet" the final result should express an understanding of the values and ideals emanating from man's oneness with God. Drama would utilize the prose of the poet to express reality. Through music both the Feeling and the Understanding would be fully integrated: "that the Poetic Aim can only be realised through its complete transmission from the

---

[68] **Ibid.,** 96.

[69] **Opera and Drama,** 218.

Understanding to the Feeling" which provides "the breath that may ensoul it into living motion." Therefore the tone-poet through harmony and melody would take over and complete what the word-poet could only begin. To Wagner this reversed Christianity since the tone-poet provided a return to nature and with it a conceptual image of God and not a literal embodiment as in the form of Jesus.

Both the singer and the orchestra would play very novel roles in music-drama. The singer "is a human being artistically representing human beings, and the artistic outpours of his Feeling are ordered by the highest necessity of transforming a thought into a Man."[70] This idea is highly significant when one considers the characters who appear in **The Ring**. Although Wagner used myth and legend, the characters were all designed to represent real, not mythical beings. The orchestra would play a supporting role to that of the singer to "vindicate the inner sphere of Musical Harmony." It is through the orchestra that one could express "the faculty of uttering the **unspeakable**." In practical terms Wagner would come to utilize the orchestra to express significant thoughts whether or not they were expressed verbally. The orchestra would reveal conscious and/or unconscious thoughts of protagonists and antagonists. In addition to illustrating states of mind, emotion, and thought, the orchestra would provide the listener with knowledge that might not be obtained from the words: "That which Poetry could not speak out, however, is imparted to the ear by precisely the language of the Orchestra." But in all cases the orchestra would play a supporting role for it too could serve only as a means to an end, as a way to "develop into a messenger of the very **Thought** itself, transmitting it to Feeling"; its presence should never detract from the primacy of the words.

The orchestra therefore would establish a new dimension by going beyond what is verbalized. It could express known thoughts that one or more of the protagonists might not wish to reveal; or it could express intuitive states of mind. In addition, through the music, ideas or plans of action could be revealed that are either known or unknown to the actors involved in the drama; or emotions and feelings which are incapable of being verbalized could be expressed through the music alone. In all cases the music would

----
[70] **Ibid.**, 309.

42

have the "capability of awakening forebodings and remembrances"; therefore in its own unique way it would contribute to the dramatic thrust of the artistic enterprise. The idea that an orchestra could and should express both conscious and unconscious mental states and images was a major artistic innovation.

To successfully realize the totality of his unique conceptions Wagner was later forced to build his own theatre, one in which the orchestra and its conductor could be totally hidden from the view of those in the audience so as never to detract from the presentation of the drama.

Wagner's theoretical views were designed to provide a plan that would enable him to create a new art-form integrating all the elements presented in **Opera and Drama.** Although there had been a partial integration of the arts in ancient Greece, it had never developed, then or since, in the way anticipated by Wagner.

Rather defensive and certain that he was likely to be misunderstood (or perhaps understood all too correctly), Wagner found it important to reject, in advance, the charge that he was expressing arbitrary and self-serving ideas and views:

> The New that I may have said, is nothing other than the Unconscious in the nature of the thing, and has become conscious to me, as a thinking artist, merely because I have grasped in its continuity a thing which artists heretofore have taken only in its severance. I thus have invented nothing new, but merely found that continuity.

The success of Wagner's artistic philosophy depended on the perfect relationship between the "poet's-Aim" and the "musician's Expression": "Let us tell the Musician then that every, even the tiniest moment of his Expression in which the poetic-aim is not contained, and which is not conditioned 'necessarily' by that Aim and its realisement,--that every such moment is superfluous, disturbing, bad." Likewise the poet had to be aware that his purpose would "be entirely realised in the Expression of his musician ally." The poet and the musician might be two people or two aspects of the same person, but insofar as artistic expression was concerned they had to be as one. It is in this new relationship between poetry and music that traditional opera became obsolete.

At the very end Wagner hinted at some of the ideas which had appeared slightly beneath the surface in his first three music-dramas: "The artist has the power of seeing beforehand a yet unshapen world, of tasting beforehand the joys of a world as yet unborn, through the stress of his desire for Growth." This idea was not developed any further perhaps out of fear that it might weaken his argument. Wagner was prepared to say that the priest and the politician should be replaced by the poet-musician; but he did not indicate that only in this way could God's purpose be revealed to human history.

Wagner's final words marked his new beginning: **"The begetter of the Artwork of the Future is none other than the Artist of the Present, who presages that Life of the Future, and yearns to be contained therein. He who cherishes this longing within the inmost chamber of his powers, he lives already in a better life;--but only One can do this thing:--the Artist."**[71]

Several decades later, as Wagner reread the second edition of **Opera and Drama,** it led him to reflect back on that formative period of his life: "It is a very curious work, and I was very excited when I wrote it, for it has no precedent in the history of art, and I was really pursuing a goal nobody had hitherto seen."[72]

From the summer of 1849 through all of 1850 and well into 1851 Wagner theorized about every subject of importance to him in an attempt to understand himself and the world in which he was living. While completing **Opera and Drama** he had gained fresh insights into the direction he had unwittingly and intuitively taken in his first three music-dramas. Determining that he was on the right course after all, Wagner wrote to Franz Liszt indicating that "when I have finished **Opera and Drama,** I intend, provided I can find a publisher, to bring out my three romantic opera-poems with a Preface introducing them and explaining their genesis."[73] By the end of December 1851 **A Communication to my Friends**

----
[71] **Ibid.,** 376.

[72] **CW's Diaries,** 13 January 1879, 2:253.

[73] Wagner to Liszt, 25 November 1850, **PW,** 1:268.

appeared in book form. "This Preface was really the most important message I had to deliver, for it was absolutely necessary in completion of **Opera and Drama**... What can I say, if now my friends do not clearly understand?"[74]

Art and Revolution, **The Art-Work of the Future**, and **Opera and Drama** are all theoretical works but **A Communication to my Friends** is a practical work, partly autobiographical and partly a device in which Wagner sought to explain his own previously-written musical poems and how the new art-form of music-drama will work in future compositions. The **Communication** was an attempt to indicate the direction that Wagner had taken in the early 1840's, his understanding of the present, and the nature of the new beginning that he would shortly commence.

In many ways the **Communication** is a remarkable personal document, but although it is centered around the genesis of Wagner's creativity he took special care not to make it appear self-serving. He wanted and needed to be understood:

> I must explain, once and for all, that whenever in the course of this Communication I speak of 'understanding me' or 'not understanding me,' it is not as though I fancied myself a shade too lofty, too deep-meaning, or too high-soaring; but I simply demand of whosoever may desire to understand me, that he will look upon me no otherwise than as I am, and in my communications upon Art will only regard as essential precisely what, in accordance with my general aim and as far as lay within my powers of exposition, has been put forth in them by myself.[75]

And those who would come to understand him should not think that he is a genius: "My faculties, taken separately, are not great, and I can only be and do something good when I concentrate all those faculties on one impulse and recklessly consume them and myself for its sake. Whatever part that impulse leads me to adopt, that I am as long as necessary, be it musician,

---

[74] Wagner to Uhlig, 1 January 1852, **PW**, 1:268.

[75] **Communication**, 269.

poet, conductor, author, reciter, or what not."[76]
Genius was the ability to take art and life and
"assimilate the kindred and the needful", an ability
that was available to many: "Yet if we look a little
closer, we shall find that these new openings are in no
wise arbitrary and private paths, but continuations of
a long-since-hewn causeway."[77]

Wagner importuned his friends not to make an
artificial distinction between himself as man and as
artist. Interest only in his artistic output would be a
serious error and would be as ludicrous as trying to
make a distinction between the soul and the body. This
"interest in the Man within the Artist" became
especially significant in the composition of **The Ring**.

The "Artist of the Present" should influence the
"Art-Work of the Future" to make it reflect "an inward
feeling of deepest discontent with the life of the
Present." Therefore, it is the essence of life,
involving both his understanding and reflection, that
the thinking artist should express in his art-work. Art
should be not only socially-based but the manifest
expression of man as a total human being. And what
would be required of the artist? "To recognize the
Life-stress of the Present, is to be impelled to put it
into action."

Wagner admitted that his earlier works were not
the kind of music-drama that he was now contemplating;
indeed they sometimes related more closely to the type
of traditional opera that he had recently criticized.
But while he was sometimes most critical of his music,
the dramatic perceptions were correct: "I speak chiefly
of my poems, not only because the bond between my art
and my life lies plainest shown in them, but also
because I have to call on them to witness that my
musical working-out, my method of operatic composition,
was conditioned by the very nature of those poems." He
admitted having made some major errors in his musical
style, particularly the unnecessary, dramatically wrong
inclusion of an Overture in **The Flying Dutchman** and
Tannhäuser, but the significant factor of the drama,
was the way of the future.

---

[76] Wagner to Liszt, 16 August 1853, **Wagner-Liszt
Correspondence**, 1:317.

[77] **Communication**, 289.

Once again Wagner found it necessary to flail Christianity for its extraordinarily significant contribution to the corruption of art, and he apologized lest anyone think that religion influenced his earlier work: "I denote the Christian principle as hostile to or incapable of Art." On the other hand, "I was a more honest Christian than any of those who now, with smug impertinence, upbraid me for my lapse from Christianity."[78]

Since much of the **Communication** is autobiographical it sheds light on both his career and the ideas contained in his musical compositions. In the **Communication** Wagner brought his musical and dramatic theories up to date, giving himself the opportunity to reexamine the past so that he might begin anew.

Recognizing how the drama and the music were both to serve as means to an end, he arrived at a fresh perspective: "Now, however, I had completely learnt this speech of Music ... Yet that which is utterable in the speech of Music, is limited to feelings and emotions: it expresses in abundance, that which has been cast adrift from our Word-speech at its conversion into a mere organ of the Intellect, namely, the emotional contents of Purely-human speech."

Having surveyed both his life and the world in which he was living Wagner concluded by reaffirming his radicalism: "I deemed we must either remain completely rooted in the Old, or completely bring the New to burst its swathings." This commitment drove him to proceed to wherever it will take him: "now I had to direct my blows against the whole art-system, **in its coherence with the whole politico-social status of the modern world.**"

Wagner's career as a theoretical writer (or "art-philosopher" as he called it) was coming to an end. **Art and Revolution, The Art-Work of the Future, Opera and Drama,** and **A Communication to my Friends** brought to completion his major theories and ideas. Henceforth he would resume his work as a poet, an artist, and a musician, but all three were as one.

---

[78] **Ibid.,** 350. Wagner's religious ideas are covered in Chapters 6, 7, and 8.

CHAPTER 2

THE THINKING-ARTIST

In November 1851 Wagner completed his **Communication** with these words: "So now I give you time and ease to think it out:--for only with my work will ye see me again." The past had been integrated into the present and all that remained was the future. After a period of six years of turmoil, revolutionary activities, personal and artistic dislocation, and theoretical musings spanning thousands of years of history, Wagner's blueprint for the future lay outlined before him.

While Wagner was still in the midst of his involvement in theoretical and political concerns, between the summer of 1848 and the spring of 1850, his mind still entertained numerous topics which might become suitable for poetic and musical treatment. As early as 1848 his perception relating to the integration of the political and social evolution of mankind with drama was reflected in a sketch (he called it a prelude) entitled, "The Wibelungen. World-History as Told in Saga." This sketch revealed Wagner's fascination with the early political development of the West when clans from the East, under patriarchal domination, spread throughout Europe. The "Saga of the Nibelung" evolved as part of man's "religio-mythic nature" but as Wagner reflected on it his concern was not with "Siegfried as God of Light or Sun-god" but with the saga's "connection with history."

Clearly Wagner's artistic development went hand in hand with his non-musical thought-processes to the extent that subjects he envisioned as suitable for musical development had to relate to the larger picture involving human history: "we now will merely take the saga where it clothes$_1$ itself with the more human garb of ancient hero-dom."[1] Saga, even as myth, was a reflection of humanity but its non-objective method of presenting stories, as a form of knowledge, enabled it to operate on man in a way quite unlike historical fact. Since saga often went into dimensions that lay outside the bounds of history it offered both an enlarged parameter and an even greater perspective:

----
[1] "The Wibelungen. World-History as Told in Saga (Summer 1848)," **PW**, 7:263.

49

bare History scarcely ever offers us, and always incompletely, the material for a judgment of the inmost (so to say, instinctive) motives of the ceaseless struggles of whole folks and races; that we must seek in Religion and Saga, where we mostly shall find it with convincing clearness.

Religion and Saga are the pregnant products of the peoples insight into the nature of things and men. ... The Gods and Heroes of its religion and sagas are the concrete personalities in which the spirit of the Folk portrays its essence to itself ... Hence the Folk is thoroughly sincere and truthful in its stories and inventions, whereas the learned historian who holds by the mere pragmatic surface of events, without regard to the direct expression of the people's bond of solidarity, is pedantically untrue because unable to understand the very subject of his work with mind and heart, and therefore is driven, without his knowing it, to arbitrary subjective speculations.[2]

Believing that by studying religion and saga man could glean a knowledge of events beyond what he learnt from history, Wagner treated the common man, the folk, in a way then traditionally ignored. Calling for a "Folk-history", he gradually became more deeply involved with the realm of saga, seeing history as more representative of the folk than of the limited concerns of the privileged classes.

----

[2] **Ibid.**, 266-7. Wagner's criticism of history has a degree of validity to it. Many mid-nineteenth century European historians saw and described events largely in political terms centering around power struggles. As viewed by the most distinguished German historian, Leopold von Ranke, the discipline of history was not designed to reflect man's "inmost motives" to quote Wagner, but to be as objective about recording the past as the evidence permitted. Nevertheless, Wagner's point of view reveals some of the limitations of the so-called school of scientific history. Although Wagner's criticism of history was perhaps self-serving he had a point of view that would find greater congeniality in the twentieth century.

Since history may be expressed by myths, Wagner came to the conclusion that myths can be universalized since they express all of man's inmost motives. The popularly-known Nibelungen saga depicted elements of nature and creation. The term "Nibelheim" came down from the Scandinavian myths and referred to "the Home of Haze", or "Night-spirits." These are, by tradition, black-elves, "children of Night and Death [who] burrow the earth, find out its inner treasures, smelt and smith its ore." The name Nibelungen refers to their "treasures, arms and trinkets, again in the Frankish stem-saga, but with the distinction that the idea originally shared by all the German stems has here evolved to ethical historic import."[3]

When myth evolved to the point where it treated human history in ethical terms, then value judgments entered the realm of history. The treasure of the Nibelungen, or its hoard, contained evil ingredients, thus giving it an ethical base. The nature of the evil is that whoever possesses the hoard "increases his might beyond all measure", and unlimited power is in itself evil. But the idea of the hoard also becomes a convenient metaphor for Wagner: "For in the Hoard there lies withal the secret of all earthly might: it is the **Earth itself with all its splendour, which in joyous shining of the Sun at dawn of day we recognise as our possession to enjoy, when Night, that held its ghostly, gloomy, dragon's wings spread fearsomely above the world's rich stores, has finally been routed."** The hoard is therefore "the means of gaining and insuring mastery", and whoever obtains it, through whatever means, brings death, destruction, and the perversion of ethical values.

Since myths and sagas transcend nations and tribes, their evolution provided one further reasonable tool for understanding the past: "In its earliest form, the stem-saga of the Nibelungen went back to the memory of a divine Ur-father, not only of the Franks, but perhaps of all nations issued from the Asiatic home." Jesus was but the latest of the "stem-gods."

Whoever is historically thought to be in possession of the hoard is both feared and envied. War is usually fought over the desire to seize the hoard whether it is analogous to wealth, territory, power, or "mastery of the world." However, in his reading of

----

[3] **Ibid.**, 276.

history Wagner perceived that from the time of Julius Caesar to Frederick 1, the spirit of freedom will always challenge whoever possesses the hoard: "The world-ruler recognised from whence his deepest wound had come, and who it was that cried his world-plan final halt. **It was the spirit of free Manhood loosed from the nature-soil of race.**" Mankind will fight against unnatural and arbitrary power.

While the Nibelungen-hoard was analogous to man's more animalistic urges (however part of the human condition it might be) for power or territoriality, its opposite metaphor is the legend of "the spiritual ascension of the Hoard into the Grail." Wagner sees much of history as a battle between man's twin-halfed soul whereby the animalistic (the physical part) is opposed to the divine (the spiritual part). He applied both of these metaphors allegorically to mid-nineteenth century Europe:

> blood, passion, love, hate, in short--both physically and spiritually--purely-human springs and motives at work in the winning of the Hoard; man restless and suffering, man doomed to conscious death by his own deed, his victory, and most by his possession, at the head of all ideas of the root-relation of acquirement. ...

> So--after the fall of the heroic-human Wibelungen--this hereditary ownership, then property in general, de facto possession, became the title for all rights existing or to be acquired; and Property gave Man that right which man had theretofore conveyed to property. ... Possession now was consequently Right.[4]

Wagner had not only updated ancient myth and saga but he applied it to the present. Almost inadvertently he has begun the process by which he would create a music-drama of monumental proportions which would depict the very forces at work that he had been describing. But he went even further. He also gave it a religious dimension by accepting the Old Testament tradition whereby God created first the night and then the day; but he sees this as representing an upward progression from "joyless" and "unfriendly" darkness to "Light, the Day, the Sun." Wagner used an interesting

----
4 **Ibid.**, 296-7.

52

analogy: as day always then succumbs to night, and "Summer in the end must yield to Winter", so must man create a life-image of the incorporeal force. Based largely on nature, man created religion, and with it the eventual arrival in human form of the gods.

The thoughts expressed in "The Wibelungen" were immediately followed by another short essay entitled, "The Nibelungen-Myth. As Sketch for a Drama", which Wagner also wrote in the summer of 1848. With but a few exceptions this short outline contained the entire scenario for what would eventually become **The Ring of the Nibelung.** Between the summer of 1848 and March 1850 The **Nibelungen-Myth** was followed by **Siegfried's Death** (based largely on the last part of his Nibelungen sketch), **Jesus of Nazareth,** and **Wiland the Smith.** While each contained some important commentary relating to the contemporary scene none were viewed as totally satisfactory for musical development. **Siegfried's Death** and **Wiland the Smith** were finished in verse form and both contain much completed dialogue. Wagner considered **Wiland** the more likely subject for musical treatment rather than the Siegfried saga because he felt the latter contained little of contemporary importance. At that time the one aspect of Siegfried that Wagner found most interesting and appealing was as the personification of the "human being in the most natural and blithest fulness of his physical life" unencumbered by personal or historic relationships.[5] It is amazing to see how far Wagner would change his conception of this hero within the next two years.

Wagner's intense involvement in Dresden's political affairs, his exile from Germany, and the entire dislocation of his life eventually made it impossible for him to work on **Wiland.** In writing to Franz Liszt's mistress Wagner cajoled: "I beg you to persuade Liszt to undertake the musical execution of Wiland in my stead. ... It takes me back to a time to which I do not want to be taken back. I cannot finish the poem now, either in words or in music."[6]

As Wagner settled into life in Zurich and completed his major theoretical prose works, several forces began to fuse. By 1851 he had completed **A**

----

[5] **Communication,** 375.

[6] Wagner to Princess Wittgenstein, 8 October 1850, **PW,** 1:216.

Communication to my Friends, his final summation of the life he had led and the music he had composed in the 1840's. By this time he understood his responsibility as a "Thinking Artist" and had some clearer ideas as to his future development. To be true to himself, whatever he would now do had to relate to the political, social, and artistic considerations he had spent the previous few years developing. Now the time had come to integrate theory with practice.

When Wagner wrote **Siegfried's Death** it contained an ethical dimension--that one became a Nibelung when in possession of the hoard, an allegory for supreme power. Wagner now saw in his earlier sketches new opportunities consistent with his concern for contemporary man: "I had set forth this wide-ranging purpose in a sketch of the Nibelungen-mythos, such as it had become my own poetic property. **Siegfried's Death** was, as I now recognize, only the first attempt to bring a most important feature of this myth to dramatic portrayal."[7] While sketching **Young Siegfried** Wagner expanded these developments but even here "Connexions of the most vital importance had been left unrealised, and relegated to the reflective and co-ordinating powers of the beholder." Finally in completing the full poem of the **Ring** Wagner enlarged his perspective to include a cosmology embracing what he considered to be the ethical, political, economic, and social issues of prime importance to man in mid-nineteenth century Europe. If he could successfully portray these issues, verbally, musically, and dramatically, he would create one enlarged music-drama capable of depicting man's social and moral evolution to the present. It was an ambitious task over unchartered waters.

After completing the poems of **Die Walküre** and **Das Rheingold** he reworked **Young Siegfried** and **Siegfried's Death,** renamed them **Siegfried** and **Götterdämmerung,** and harmonized the poems so that they became part of the unity of The Ring. By late 1852 the **Ring** poem was complete, although Wagner would modify certain parts of it over the next twenty-five years. In Zurich, on February 16, 17, 18, and 19, 1853 Wagner read the completed poem to some of his friends and in August, while on a trip to Italy, the inspiration came to begin the musical composition:

---

[7] **Communication,** 390. Written for Weimar, **Young Siegfried** was originally designed as a comedy.

I fell into a kind of somnolent state, in
which I suddenly felt as though I were sinking
in swiftly flowing water. The rushing sound
formed itself in my brain into a musical sound,
the chord of E flat major which continually
re-echoed in broken forms; these broken chords
seemed to be melodic passages of increasing
motion... I awoke in sudden terror from my
doze, feeling as though the waves were rushing
high above my head. I at once recognized that
the orchestral overture to the **Rheingold**, which
must have lain latent within me, though it had
been unable to find definite form, had at last
been revealed to me. I then quickly realised
my own nature; the stream of life was not to
flow to me from without, but from within. I
decided to return to Zürich immediately, and
begin the composition of my great poem.[8]

This happening is not easily explainable but it
was not a singular occurrence. Wagner's inventiveness
and the mental state necessary for this to occur,
remains one of the more fascinating unstudied aspects
of his creative genius. Writing to a close friend,
Wagner once revealed part of the way in which his saw
his creativity working: "My illness then is of
transcendental nature, and all other medical measures
can have no decisive effect if I'm not cured up there.
From my brain the affection [sic] spread to my entire
nervous system and manifested itself in complete
exhaustion with fever symptoms."[9] Describing his
nervousness over not being able to be present when
Tannhäuser was to be done in Berlin, and bitter over
the political circumstances preventing his supervision
of the production (he was in exile at the time), Wagner
wrote out elaborate instructions regarding its
presentation. This caused a further recurrence of his
mental problems:

I lapsed into a condition similar to the one
after the **Walküre**, and I still am in this
condition as I write you today. Feverish
excitement and exhaustion, sickeningly uneasy
numbness of the brain, melancholy, fear of all
work; I am often so tired that I can walk only

---

[8] **My Life**, 2:603.

[9] Wagner to Ernst Kietz, 7 September 1852, Burrell,
191.

very slowly; then again a little better, but with the tendency toward excitability. That I cannot get well again, in the sense that you imagine it, is as clear as day: I'm mentally ill--and mental illness is incurable. ... The world has escaped my heart; I loathe it; I cannot love it: this way it is no longer an object of sentiment for me, but only of fantasy; only through the activity of my brain can I communicate with it. I'm too genuine to be able to lie to myself; too experienced to be ignorant.[10]

After more than five and one-half years Richard Wagner resumed his musical career in November 1853: "this return to my work can best be compared to a reincarnation of my soul after it had been wandering in other spheres."[11]

Much has been written about **The Ring of the Nibelung,** but in its simplest guise--and it is far less complex than commonly believed--the **Ring** is an allegory depicting the birth, development, disintegration, and destruction of one civilization. It is an allegory which, as Shaw correctly perceived, related directly to the major forces and processes at work in mid-nineteenth century Europe. Wagner's intent, concern, and--as he saw it--his responsibility was to demonstrate how and where man went wrong! What Gibbon did in prose with **The Rise and the Fall of the Roman Empire** Wagner would do in music-drama with the rise and fall of Western man: "**World disintegration** is the only good thing I can see in recent European developments." The **Ring** is an intensely pessimistic means by which Wagner hopes to achieve an optimistic end. Illustrating what went wrong in the rise and fall of one model of civilization, albeit a mythical pre-Christian one, Wagner's design was to permit man to learn from the past, recognize his failings and short-comings, replace the old system of corrupted values with a new spiritual one, and finally create a better life-style for future generations to enjoy.

Like most nineteenth century romantics Wagner seemed convinced that man can learn from the past, would he but try. Although this required self-

---
[10] **Ibid.,** 192-3.

[11] **My Life,** 2:610.

examination the time was opportune. The age of progress coupled with a spiritual infusion could presumably enable man to see what he had created with the universe that was given to him by God. The **Ring** is a composite of life; it is a multidimensional multi-faceted way of incorporating all of man's musical and cultural development up to the mid-nineteenth century, in combination with his political, economic, and social experiences. If Wagner were successful he will have created a unique art-form and one designed to accomplish a novel end, the regeneration of mankind.

Whether music can and should be used for this purposes is a question which never entered his mind. He was writing prose and music in the only way that he could, and for reasons that were important to him. He had a philosophical statement to make about the world, and music would contribute to the way in which it was presented. Wagner's aesthetic philosophy was becoming realized in the form of an innovative artistic endeavor that would be breaking new ground. Even the way the cycle begins reflects his new development. Previously his works began with an independent overture. But from the time of the composition of the **Ring,** through the remainder of his works, Wagner eliminated the overture. Later, when modifying **The Flying Dutchman** and after rethinking **Tannhäuser** for Paris he changed each overture into a prelude.

The **Ring** is not designed to be examined only on a literal level for Wagner was concerned with depicting archetypes, each illustrative of some significant aspect of history and the erosion of man's values. It is man's total condition that is being portrayed and often Wagner doesn't seem to care about loose ends. Wagner provides only the amount of information which he considers important and necessary for one to know. He is not concerned with presenting a total picture and was deliberately vague exactly when it suited him. He sometimes leaves unanswered questions that can be raised regarding the text simply because they are irrelevant to him. An unwillingness to deal with certain specifics still causes concern for some who on first approaching the **Ring** look only for a literal plot. And yet, at one time, Wagner took the exact opposite stance:

> a work of art, and especially a drama, can have
> its true effect only when the poetic intention
> in all its more important motives speaks fully

to the senses. ... and I am compelled therefore to communicate my entire myth in its deepest and widest significance with the greatest artistic precision so as to be fully understood. Nothing in it must in any sense be left to be supplied by thought or reflection; the unsophisticated human mind must be enabled by its artistic receptivity to comprehend the whole because by that means only may the most detached parts be rightly understood.[12]

On the other hand, replying to a friend who had complained that the **Ring** poem lacked "lucidity and distinctness of statement," Wagner commented: "I believe that a true instinct has kept me from a too great definiteness; for it has been borne in on me, that an absolute disclosing of the intention disturbs true insight. What you want in drama--as indeed in all works of Art--is to achieve your end, not by statement of the artist's intentions, but by the presentment of life as the resultant, not of arbitrary forces, but of eternal laws."[13]

The **Ring** gradually builds on Wagner's designed model until it can illustrate the total corruption of the established world order: "Consider well my new poem; it contains the beginning and the end of the world."[14] At the end of the cycle the order is destroyed, but not by God! One of Wagner's major concerns was to illustrate that through the use of free will man, and not God, was responsible for all actions. It was man who must destroy the old system, replacing it with a new one which would offer better opportunities for the enjoyment of life and the creative forces at work within the universe. No Armageddon is acceptable. God granted man the gift of life and with it the free will to construct his own system of values based on biblical standards. Wagner was forever hopeful that man would see what he had done with the universe and then create a new model and a new system. He presented his listeners and readers with an

----

[12] Wagner to Liszt, 20 November 1851, **Wagner-Liszt Correspondence**, 1:171-2.

[13] Wagner to August Röckel, 25 January 1854, Roeckel, 100.

[14] Wagner to Liszt, 11 February 1853, **Wagner-Liszt Correspondence**, 1:257.

optimistic world-view, although perhaps a very romantic naive one.

Illustrating forces at work that were both contemporary and of immediate consequence to nineteenth century man required a method of presentation never attempted before. Twenty-five years before the **Ring** was completed and performed, and even before he had composed one note of the music, Wagner knew how it must be done: "Its purpose is the complete representation of all the circumstances of the theft, the origin of the hoard of the Nibelungs, its seizure by Wotan, and Alberich's curse. I cannot contemplate the separation of the component parts of this giant whole without wrecking my intention from the first. All the complex drama must be represented on the stage in rapid sequence."[15]

Even without the musical setting, Wagner was so pleased with the intrinsic value of the poem that he arranged to have it published privately, although it was not yet to be made available for public sale. Writing to his publisher, Wagner proudly declared: "it is the completest, ripest work of my life, and I believe that even in the poem, I have presented the nation with a gift which will be held to have value in the future, as well as in the present."[16] The poem alone was "rooted and grounded in itself, in the life and the view of life of the poet, bringing to the musician a new subject to which, and in which, he must discover new music--that is music suited to this subject and to this subject alone."[17] This was the art philosophy that Wagner had articulated in **Opera and Drama**. It remained now to accomplish the task.

It is at this point that Wagner specifically used the word "drama" while referring to his composition: "I shall never write an **Opera** more. As I have no wish to invent an arbitrary title for my works, I will call them **Dramas**, since hereby will at least be clearest indicated the standpoint whence the thing I offer should be accepted":

----
[15] Wagner to Liszt, 20 November 1851, Altmann, 1:216.

[16] Wagner to Breitkopf and Härtel, 10 July 1856, Altmann, 1:305.

[17] Wagner to Louis Schindelmeisser, 13 August 1853, Altmann, 1:253-4.

I propose to produce my myth in **three complete dramas** preceded by a lengthy Prelude. ... At a specially-appointed Festival, I propose, some future time, to produce those three Dramas with their Prelude, **in the course of three days and a fore-evening.** The object of this production I shall consider thoroughly attained, if I and my artistic comrades, the actual performers, shall within these four evenings succeed in **artistically conveying my purpose to the true Emotional** (not the Critical) **Understanding** of spectators who shall have gathered together expressly to learn it.[18]

Wagner continues to emphasize two points: first, that knowledge is obtained by the "Feeling" which involved an emotional understanding, while a "Critical Understanding" was but a partial means for obtaining knowledge; second, that his listeners should come to learn and not just to hear the **Ring**, for it contained important messages that listening alone could not convey.

But how does one perform such a work? Wagner recognized the horrendous problems associated with the undertaking "which every man of practical experience was bound to deem inexecutable at any of our opera houses."[19] These problems were later compounded by his determination not to have the cycle broken up, especially after **Das Rheingold** and **Die Walküre** received individual performances in Munich before the remainder of the work had been composed. This greatly upset Wagner and he tried desperately to prevent it from happening. But Ludwig II (who in actuality was by then Wagner's patron and the owner of these works) was determined that both should be performed.

Das Rheingold received less than a satisfactory debut performance, with not even the full orchestra being used. Wagner was, at first, stoic upon hearing news of the performance: "He [the King] cannot kill the work, I am the only one who can kill it, by breaking with him and not completing it. The fact that he is ruining things now will not detract from the impression when they are one day presented in the way I

---

[18] **Communication**, 391.

[19] "Epilogue to the **Nibelung's Ring**, 1871," PW, 3:257.

60

want. ... All this is in the hands of Fate."[20]   In the future the complete unit would have to be performed whole and as one entity: "True, ... I was completely turning my back on the modern opera-houses ... [but] was I the man to give up all notion of a live performance of such a work, when I was doing my utmost to put life into its smallest features?"[21]

Knowing the impossibility of presenting the cycle exactly as he wanted it to be done at any currently existing theatre, Wagner finally decided to publish the **Ring,** indicating his belief that even without its completed musical setting the work could stand on its own. There was also an important practical reason for its publication: "to ascertain whether my work, regarded from this side [the poetic], could rouse sufficient attention to wake among the educated of the nation a fancy for entertaining the wider-reaching plan of execution which I coupled it with."[22]

The first public edition of **The Ring of the Nibelung** appeared in 1865. Wagner appended a preface to it in which he indicated where and how the work ideally ought to be performed: in a small town, "free from all the influence of the daily repertory of our standing theatres", during a summer festival of four sequential days. Wagner himself supplied the "acoustic-architectonic plan." The choice of Bayreuth as the site was dictated by both political and artistic reasons: "I did not want a capital city with a permanent theatre, nor a watering place which, in summer particularly, would furnish an utterly unsuitable public; it had to be not far from the heart of Germany and a Bavarian town."[23]   The story of the building of the festival-house at Bayreuth is familiar.

----

[20] **CW's Diaries,** 25 October 1869, 1:157-8.

[21] "Epilogue to the **Nibelung's Ring,"** 257.   Ten years earlier, before completing the third act of **Siegfried** or any of **Götterdämmerung,** Wagner did plan to produce **Das Rheingold** in Vienna when the new Royal Opera House was completed. See Wagner to B. Schott and Sons, 17 October 1861, Altmann, 2:133.

[22] **Ibid.,** 265.

[23] Wagner to Friedrich Feustel, 1 November 1871, Altmann, 2:248.

Determined that nothing should mar the impact of
the drama itself Wagner's architectural proposals
greatly modernized performing concepts: "I next should
lay especial stress on the invisibility of the
orchestra--to be effected by an architectural illusion
quite feasible with an amphitheatric plan of
auditorium."[24] The reason for this unusual departure
was to obtain "the true impression of a work of
dramatic art." No acoustic or dramatic barrier must
exist between the expression of the words and their
being heard and understood by the audience.

Wagner had a lot to say and it was crucial that
his meaning be understood: "But I meant in the
presentment of the whole Nibelung myth to express my
meaning even more clearly, by showing how from the
first wrongdoing a whole world of evil arose, and
consequently fell to pieces in order to teach us the
lesson, that we must recognize evil and tear it up by
the roots, and raise in its stead a righteous world."[25]
A philosophical point of view which took four nights to
perform was a radical departure from the traditional
world of opera. By calling **Das Rheingold** a Prelude,
Wagner clearly differentiated its purpose from that of
the remainder of the cycle. It was designed to show the
beginning of the world order that was to be portrayed,
as it emerged slowly out of the void, to eventually
embrace the four cosmic elements of water, air, earth,
and fire. Wagner needed four days to show time-
perspective. Man's problems evolved over thousands of
years. It was therefore necessary that the
complications arising in **Rheingold** needed the
perspective of time, evolution, and descent, before the
final catastrophe at the end of **Götterdämmerung.**

The cycle stresses main ideas, leaving out
incidentals: "It reveals nature in her undisguised
truth, with all those inconsistencies which, in their
endless multiplicity, embrace even directly,
conflicting elements."[26] The musical rendering was
made to enhance the words and to create a clear aura of
understanding. Prose alone could not illustrate the

----

[24] "Preface to the Public Issue of the Poem of the
Bühnenfestspiel **Der Ring des Nibelungen**," PW, 3:276.

[25] Wagner to August Röckel, 23 August 1856, Roeckel,
149-50.

[26] Wagner to Röckel, 25 January 1854, Roeckel, 96.

process of creation and the emergence of life, but the
musical opening to **Rheingold** does exactly that. In
countless ways the music supports thoughts, feelings,
and emotions unaided by words. Perhaps even more
perceptively the music is sometimes used to express
unconscious and or secret thoughts of the participants
thereby enabling the audience to understand both their
words and their thoughts. Only in music-drama can this
be accomplished for in a prose soliloquy an actor can
express only his conscious thoughts.

In **Das Rheingold** Wagner presented and demonstrated
all that needed to be said regarding the issues of
primary importance in the cycle: the use, misuse, and
abuse of power by both Wotan and Alberich; the
deceptiveness and chilling intellect of Loge; the
vulnerability of brotherhood as exemplified by both
Mime and Fafner; the frequent way that love is
compromised; and finally, a warning that fate can
somehow appear to influence, control, or interfere with
destiny. In no way could Wagner have resolved all the
complications and the permutations of the tragedy in
one single presentation. He, and the audience, needed
time to let the cycle develop and unfold. To illustrate
how deeply entrenched and corrupt the old order had
become in its desperate struggle to survive beyond its
logical end point would take Wagner three additional
days of exploration beyond the Prelude. In Days One,
Two, and Three he expands the perceptions of his
audience by means of a prolonged time sequence designed
to demonstrate the future dilemmas facing Wotan and
Alberich. Each gets further entrapped by self-made
machinations until at the end of Day Three Brünnhilde
passes "final judgment on the gods" and through free
will becomes the agent of their destruction thus
serving as a regenerative power for man's redemption.

In purely musical terms, Wagner was not always
certain just what he had composed. The musical
rendering of **Das Rheingold** seemed to take on a life of
its own, sometimes to Wagner's surprise, and even
uncertainty: "I went to this music with so much faith,
so much joy; and with a true fury of despair I
continued, and have at last finished it. Alas! the need
of gold held me too in its net. Believe me, no one ever
has composed in this manner; my music, it seems to me,
must be terrible; it is a slough of horrors and
sublimities."[27]

---

[27] Wagner to Liszt, 15 January 1854, **Wagner-Liszt**

One of Wagner's most successful innovations occurs in the second scene of the second act of **Die Walküre** (Day One). In a monologue of remarkable psychological perceptiveness Wotan's introspective analysis is presented in a bold and dramatic manner. The words of this scene are so important that the musical accompaniment for a good part of the time is virtually nonexistent. Nothing is permitted to interfere with Wotan's words which are conveyed in a deep and solemn intonation so sparse of music that the impact is shattering. Wagner was understandably nervous over how this scene would be accepted. He viewed it as "the most important scene of all!" But would the audience understand it? Revealing his fears to Franz Liszt, Wagner commented:

> if my intentions are perfectly understood, the effect must be beyond anything that has hitherto been in existence. Of course, it is written only for people who can stand something (perhaps in reality for nobody). That incapable and weak persons will complain, cannot in any way move me. You must decide whether everything has succeeded according to my own intentions. I cannot do it otherwise. ... I was once on the point of rejecting the whole scene. In order to come to a decision, I took up the sketch, and recited the scene with proper expression, when, fortunately, I discovered ... that if properly represented, the scene would have a grand effect even in a purely musical sense... For the development of the great tetralogy, this is the most important scene of all...[28]

Wagner completed the poem **Der Ring des Nibelungen** in November 1852 and began its musical composition one year later. The autograph score of **Das Rheingold** was completed in September 1854, **Die Walküre** in March 1856, and the first act of **Siegfried** in March 1857. In August Wagner finished the compositional sketch for the second act but did not resume further work on this part of the **Ring** until March 1869, an extraordinary twelve year interruption. Finally, on 25 August 1872 Wagner completed the final act of **Götterdämmerung** and to

---

Correspondence, 2:7.

[28] Wagner to Liszt, 3 October 1855, **Wagner-Liszt Correspondence**, 2:116-7.

commemorate the event sent a copy of it, together with a short poem to the King.

On Dispatching Act III of Götterdämmerung to King Ludwig II

'The immortal work is complete!
Borne by me as in a dream,
as my will did direct,--
what for years of anxiety,
the maturing breast has concealed,
out of winter-night woes
the forces of love and of spring
have impelled toward light of day:
proudly on view may it stand,
like a bold edifice of the King's,
its splendour show to the world!'[29]

The circumstances which led Wagner to consider **Tristan and Isolde** as a music-drama have been adequately described by others. Suffice to say, there were two major reasons: in the first place, the intensity of his emotional involvement with and passion for Mathilde Wesendonck finally made it impossible for him to concentrate on orchestrating **Siegfried**. For the moment his musical inspiration to continue working on the **Ring** had been seriously compromised.[30]

A second reason, but a legitimate concern in its own right, Wagner had not produced a work for the theatre since **Lohengrin** was premiered at Weimar in 1850. Although **Das Rheingold** and **Die Walküre** had been completed, he was not inclined to see any parts of the cycle produced until the entire project had been completed. Therefore, "in the summer of 1857 I decided to break off the musical setting of my Nibelungen-work and undertake a shorter labour, which I meant to bring me into contact with the Theatre once more."[31]

---

[29] **The Brown Book**, 192.

[30] The impact of this emotional attachment and Wagner's attitude toward love and sexuality is covered in Chapter 5.

[31] "An Open Letter to Friedrich Uhl, Editor of the Wiener Botschafter," 1865, printed in **Bayreuther Blätter**, June 1890, entitled, "Invitation to the Production of Tristan in Munich," **PW**, 8:239.

Wagner was still in exile and therefore unable to hear any German production of **Lohengrin:** "Only under the greatest difficulty had it been possible for me, from time to time, to hear even the sound of an orchestra. Germany, where people were giving my **Lohengrin** which I myself had never heard, remained shut against me."[32] Desperately in need of money and anxious to again have his name before the public, Wagner seemed to need a plausible excuse for temporarily abandoning the **Ring.** His passion for Mathilde Wesendonck could not be made public but an acceptable rationalization for beginning a new project was forthcoming after Wagner determined that Tristan was really related to Siegfried: "Their intrinsic parity consists in this: both Tristan and Siegfried, in bondage to an illusion makes this deed of theirs unfree, woo for another their own eternally pre-destined bride, and in the false relation hence-arising their doom."[33] The one basic difference which is to be found in Tristan and not Siegfried is "death through stress of love", although this too, in a lesser way, "finds expression in Brünnhilde."

While Wagner was sincere in describing some of the reasons prompting him to abandon the **Ring,** it was only part of the story. The power of love is a theme to be found in all of Wagner's works, but when he personally came under its sway it made his work both a joy and a chore. He may have been able to interject thoughts about Mathilde in **Die Walküre** ("the short prelude bears the letters: G.S.M. [Gesegnet sei Mathilde--Blessed by Mathilde]!") but this did not permit him to concentrate on the awakening of Brünnhilde by Siegfried.[34]

Shortly before Wagner met Mathilde he wrote Liszt: "Of real enjoyment of life I know nothing; to me enjoyment of life, of love, is a matter of imagination, not of experience."[35] But after the beginning of Wagner's emotional involvement, the theme of love began

----

[32] "Epilogue to the **Nibelung's Ring,**" PW, 3:267.

[33] **Ibid.,** 268.

[34] Mathilde Wesendonck, **Allgemeine Musik-Zeitung,** Berlin, 14 February 1896, "Mathilde Wesendonck reminiscences of Wagner's time in Zurich," Barth, 188.

[35] Wagner to Liszt, 9 November 1852, **Wagner-Liszt Correspondence,** 1:236.

to appear in many of his letters. Although his marriage to Minna had been compromised for some time, they lived together in a reasonably amicable relationship. Mathilde, however, offered him what he most needed-- empathy, compassion, and understanding. The very themes that so many of his characters had searched for in vain, and the one characteristic most lacking in Minna, Mathilde now supplied. Its effect was overwhelming not only personally but professionally. He was in love and **Tristan** was the monument erected to love.

For the first and only time in his musical career Wagner composed music to someone else's words. The five poems that Mathilde wrote for Wagner, and presented to him while he was working on **Tristan,** made such an impact on him emotionally that he momentarily dropped his own work so that he might immediately begin to set them to music. Three of them bear the subtitle, "Study for Tristan and Isolde", with Wagner carrying over parts of their musical setting into the music-drama. "Träume" contains some of the music to be heard in the "liebesnacht" scene in act two, but when first composed Wagner commented: "The pencilling of the song ... has pleased me better than the whole proud scene! Heavens, it's finer than all I have made! It thrills me to my deepest nerve, to hear it."[36] This song was the only one of the five which Wagner orchestrated, having it played under Mathilde's window in celebration of her twenty-ninth birthday on 23 December 1857.

Tristan and Isolde has been analyzed and dissected since its first hearing. It has been portrayed as the paragon of erotic love and as the depiction of a destructive life-force which could undermine the value of honor and decency in the name of egoism. It has also been viewed as a mystical and transcendental series of allegories and metaphors. Musicologists consider the work as a representation of an innovative musical idiom which helped usher in the atonalities of the twentieth century. On a variety of levels this work does indeed reflect virtually all of these elements.

The mystical and spiritual ingredients and the deep psychological layers surrounding the drama represent aspects of the work clearly envisioned by Wagner:

---

[36] Wagner to Mathilde Wesendonck, 28 September 1861, Wesendonck, **Letters,** 283.

67

> Here, in perfect trustfulness, I plunged into
> the inner depths of soul-events, and from out
> this inmost centre of the world I fearlessly
> built up its outer form. ... Life and death,
> the whole import and existence of the outer
> world, here hang on nothing but the inner
> movements of the soul. The whole affecting
> Action comes about for reason only that the
> inmost soul demands it, and steps to light with
> the very shape foretokened in the inner
> shrine.[37]

Despite the fact that God is never mentioned within
this work, it is obvious that mystical and spiritual
elements occupy a critical axis.

Although the action is confined to a minimum in
order to reveal states of the soul, the musical
treatment is broader and perhaps more important than in
his earlier works. Up to **Tristan** Wagner had a tendency
to place the greater stress on words, with music often
serving as the means by which the thoughts were
expressed and conveyed. But in **Tristan** the music plays
a more vital role.

Wagner usually printed each of his poems before
beginning their musical treatment, but after **Tristan**
was published he began to entertain second thoughts:
"Between a poem altogether built for music and a purely
poetic stage-play the difference in plan and execution
must be so fundamental, that, if the former is viewed
with the same eye as the latter, its true import must
stay entirely lost,--that is, until completed by its
music. ... When the music is furnished to my work: then
melodic phrases enter into play and inter-play, engross
and incite."[38]

The relationship between poetry and music became
more vexing in **Tristan** than in the other music-dramas,
possibly because the circumstances under which the work
was written and composed affected Wagner more
personally than any other work. After completing the
final orchestration Mathilde called him a sage to which
he replied: "what has put it into your heart to want to
think me--or wish me--a 'sage'?" Claiming that a sage

---
[37] "Zukunftsmusik," **PW**, 3:330-1.

[38] Wagner to Mathilde Wesendonck, 15 April 1859,
Wesendonck, **Letters**, 121.

is usually devoid of humor, Wagner preferred to think of himself as "a poet and--what is much worse--a musician. Just consider my music, with its delicate, secretly flowing sap, penetrating through the subtlest pores of perception to the very marrow of life, there overpowering conscious pride, the carefully constructed fortifications of the self, sweeping away all that belongs to the mirage of personality, leaving nothing but the marvellous exaltation of avowed impotency. How can I be a wise man, when it is only in such raving madness that I am at home?"[39]

Recognizing that **Tristan** marked a noticeable progression in the course of his aesthetic development, Wagner called this work an "action", one in which would be found "a far more intimate amalgamation of poem and music." Emphasizing that the musical treatment "brought a wealth and inexhaustibility such as one could not so much as form a notion without it", Wagner was later dismayed at how "nobody really--no musician--has recognized what kind of music it is."[40] This is not quite accurate: when Vienna tried to produce the world premiere of this music-drama it was abandoned after countless rehearsals, as unplayable! Recognizing that in terms of this music-drama the music was actually more important than the words, Wagner tried to communicate these feelings. Emotional and mystical states of mind could more easily be conveyed through music. Unlike the **Ring**, **Tristan** was not rooted on significant political, economic, and social values: "Here, in Music's own most unrestricted element, the musician who chose this theme as introduction to his love-drama could have but one care: how to restrain himself, since exhaustion of the theme is quite impossible."[41]

Tristan also represented Wagner's first use of a new type of internal musical structure. When he expressed amazement that professional musicians had not recognized what he had actually accomplished in this work, it was probably due to their lack of response to this innovation. Wagner called it the "art of transition":

----

[39] Wagner to Mathilde Wesendonck, 24 August 1859, Altmann, 2:61-2.

[40] **CW's Diaries**, 17 January 1880, 2:429.

[41] "Prelude to **Tristan und Isolde**," **PW**, 8:387.

I now realize that the special fabric of my
music ... owes its construction above all to
the highly sensitive feeling which directs me
to interlink and interrelate every element of
transition between the most extreme moods. I
should now like to call my deepest and most
subtle art the art of transition, for the whole
fabric of my art is built up on such
transitions: sharp and sudden changes I have
come to dislike; they are often unavoidable and
necessary, but even then they may not occur
unless the atmosphere has been so carefully
prepared for the sudden change that it seems
inevitable. My greatest masterpiece of the art
of the most subtle, most gradual transition is
certainly the big scene of the second act of
Tristan und Isolde. This scene begins with
pulsating life at its most passionate--and ends
with the most mystical, innermost longing for
death. Those are the pillars: now my child,
just look how I have connected these pillars,
how it leads across from one to the other! Now
there you have the secret of my musical form,
of which I am bold enough to assert that such a
degree of consistency and clarity in a
structure which embraces every detail has never
before even been dreamed of.[42]

Six years after he had completed the music-drama,
and after aborted attempts to stage the work elsewhere,
the world premiere finally took place in Munich in
June, 1865. Giving his opinion of the performance King
Ludwig did not mince words: "Only One!--Hallowed One!
What rapture!--Perfect. Overwhelmed by delight!--... To
drown...sink down--unconscious--highest bliss.--Divine
work!-- Eternally true--till death and beyond!--"[43]
Pro-Wagner papers praised the work, anti-Wagner papers
damned the work: "it is the glorification of sensual
pleasure, tricked out with every titillating device, it
is unremitting materialism... In the service of this
end, music has been enslaved to the word." One
newspaper reported that the pro-Wagner claque filled
the theatre ensuring wild and enthusiastic but biased

----

[42] Wagner to Mathilde Wesendonck, 29 October 1859,
Barth, 189.

[43] **König Ludwig II und Richard Wagner, Briefwechsel,**
compiled by Otto Strobel, 5 vols, Karlsruhe 1936-9,
1:105, as translated in Barth, 208.

applause. Nevertheless, although three performances were scheduled, a fourth had to be added just for the king.

The musical innovations and poetic ideas that Wagner introduced into **Tristan** were slow in gaining recognition: "Nobody takes Tristan as seriously as I do, neither poets nor musicians." Wagner was fortunate in having a superb singing actor portray the title role. Ludwig Schnorr von Carolsfeld was, according to Wagner, the perfect Tristan:"the unforgettable greatness of my friend's artistic triumph" was a source of personal happiness. Commenting on the long and difficult third act Wagner stated: "From the first bar to the last all attention and interest were directed towards, riveted on the singer alone, and that there was not a single moment, not a single word of the text that was met with inattention or distraction, rather that the orchestra completely disappeared beside him, or--more accurately--appeared to be subsumed by his delivery."[44]

Aside from Schnorr, Wagner soon became depressed at the thought of finding any other singer who would be capable of both understanding the words and singing the music of the title role: "I shall have to pay terribly for this work one day if I mean to have it performed to perfection. I can see that most incredible sufferings lie before me. For I do not disguise from myself that I have far overstepped the limits of our capacity for performance."[45]

Wagner frequently made changes in his works after they first appeared. When Schnorr suddenly died, shortly after the premiere of the work, Wagner talked of cutting chunks out of both the second and third acts for he came to the realization that the orchestration was too strong for "the insignificant singers of today." He never got around to making the changes but commented to Cosima, less than one year before he died: "At supper he told us very emphatically that he would have to make cuts in the third act of **Tristan** since no one will ever again do it in the way Schnorr did, and even then it was so shattering that it went beyond what

----

[44] "Wagner's recollection of Ludwig Schnorr," Barth, 209.

[45] Wagner to Mathilde Wesendonck, early August 1860, Altmann, 2:108-9.

71

one should be allowed to experience on stage. Also in the second act, where the 'artificial metaphysical wit,' though always full of emotion, cannot be followed by a large audience."[46]

The extent to which Mathilde Wesendonck inspired Wagner to write **Tristan** yet remains conjectural. Upset when the German emperor claimed that Wagner must have been in love when he wrote Tristan, he categorically denied the accusation although probably out of deference toward Cosima: "Yet anyone familiar with my life well knows how insipid and trivial it was, and it is quite impossible to write a work like that in a state of infatuation. Yet probably it was due to my longing to escape from my wretched existence into a sea of love. It is this kind of unfulfilled longing which inspires a work, not experience."[47] Several years earlier when Wagner first mentioned this remark made by the emperor he commented to Cosima: "but when the German Emperor exclaims, 'How deeply Wagner must have been in love at that time,' it is really quite ridiculous.--If that were so, I should now be writing **Parsifal** on account of my connections with the Christian church, and you would be Kundry! No, I just felt the need to go to the very limit musically, as if I had been writing a symphony."[48] Nevertheless, Wagner so frequently mentioned **Tristan** that its importance appears to be deeper than his comments to Cosima: It was a work which "lay so near my heart"; Tristan is "a being utterly consumed by love"; In it, it is "Eros who holds sway."

Musically-speaking, nothing that Wagner composed prior to **Tristan** meant so much to him: "How a glance into this last completed work revived, filled, strengthened, and inspired me ... This joy, I should say, a father can scarcely experience at sight of his child! ... Thou shalt not end yet; thou still must achieve! A man who has only just made **such** a thing, is full to overflowing still!"[49] On the day that Wagner completed **Tristan** he was joyful but reflective:

----
[46] **CW's Diaries**, 5 March 1882, 2:820.

[47] **Ibid.**, 2 June 1882, 863-4.

[48] **Ibid.**, 28 September 1878, 158.

[49] Wagner to Mathilde Wesendonck, 11 November 1859, Wesendonck, **Letters**, 191.

72

I have finished The Rhinegold, The Valkyrie, most of Siegfried, and now Tristan and Isolde. I cannot tell what the general verdict on these works may be; but they will certainly be reproached with being too full, too continuously charged with wealth of subject-matter, too persistent in the unvarying powerful expression of burning passion, of profound meanings. It will be clear at a glance that these scores are far richer, more delicately woven, more lavishly equipped than all my earlier scores put together.[50]

The work is all too easily dismissed, in non-musical terms, as an illustration of erotic love. Wagner himself recognized that "half-castes will understand it in their own sensual way", but he frequently called it a transcendental work, implying that the true meaning is reflected only in the internal longing that the lovers have for each other whereby each becomes part of the personality of the other. Even the emotional intensity of the second act was to be expressed by thoughts rather than actions. At the height of their passion the actors were to lie on their backs, head to head, but not physically touching.

Wagner's initial contact with **Die Meistersinger** occurred in 1845, at the time he was working on **Lohengrin** and well-before his political and economic interests had developed. Living in Dresden, and relatively happy, the comedic aspects of the story appealed to him, especially since they portrayed a slice of life high in romantic imagery in an earlier pre-industrialized Germany. But it was the character of Hans Sachs that most fascinated Wagner. Reading through Gervinus's **History of Germanic Literature** Wagner came across both the story of the mastersingers of sixteenth-century Nürnberg and their ever-popular "artisan-poet" Hans Sachs. Wagner thought of several cheery episodes to make the prose sketch a light comedy but ultimately **Lohengrin**'s grip on his thoughts delayed any possibility of continuing with **Die Meistersinger** at that time. But two humorous episodes were vividly implanted in his mind and both were later incorporated into the drama. In one episode Sachs "gives the Marker a practical lesson by making him sing, thereby taking revenge on him for his conventional misdeeds." A

---

[50] Wagner to Princess Marie Wittgenstein, 8 August 1859, Altmann, 2:60.

second episode ends the second act: "I added a scene consisting of a narrow crooked little street in Nuremberg, with the people running about in great excitement."[51]

When Wagner next returned to the story in 1861, sixteen years had passed. Desiring to establish a close historical perspective, Wagner read through all the reference works available to him so that his depiction of sixteenth-century Nürnberg might be accurate. Much of the information came from Wagenseil's **Nürnberg Chronicle**, especially those parts which relate to the rules (tabulatur) of the singing contest, the kinds and types of singing faults, and the method by which one rose from level to level in the process of becoming a master singer. In his autobiography Wagner commented: "I remained at my hotel, eagerly making extracts of portions of the Chronicle, which to the astonishment of the ignorant I appropriated for my libretto."[52] Finally, in November 1861 Wagner totally rewrote his earlier prose sketch, completed the poem in 1862, and immediately commenced its musical rendering.

Ultimately **Die Meistersinger** is only tangentially related to the real-life story of Hans Sachs. Wagner was not really concerned with depicting the workings of the guilds and crafts that dominated life in Nürnberg, although both of these subjects were prominently featured in the drama. It is Wagner's conception of the character of Sachs which dominates the work. He is made into the embodiment of the "thinking artist", a status denied to all the characters in the **Ring**. The drama therefore became rather personal for in it he presented his first real portrayal of a mature human being. Illustrating the cobbler-poet in an historical setting, Wagner offered an idealized archetypal conception of what may be called "the artist of the future." The libretto excited him to the point where he could exclaim with confidence: "I am clear now that this is my most perfect masterpiece."[53]

His timing for rethinking the subject matter could not have been better. By 1861 Wagner knew and

---

[51] **My Life**, 1:366.

[52] Ibid., 2:802.

[53] Wagner to Mathilde Wesendonck, 22 May 1862, Altmann, 2:158.

understood all the non-musical points that he was making in the **Ring,** and having completed the music for **Das Rheingold** and **Die Walküre** he began to think more positively about the workability of his musical theories. Although **Die Meistersinger,** like **Tristan,** was viewed as a temporary diversion from the **Ring,** it is clear that Wagner intended to interrelate some tangents from the **Ring** into his new work, although not on the same intricate level. In the cycle Wagner was attempting to illustrate how the world got into its current political and economic predicaments, but in **Die Meistersinger** he would be able to portray, on a smaller scale, the way in which a pre-industrial society dealt with several similar issues. By ranging through a variety of value structures Wagner could still raise some of the more significant questions even though the sixteenth century was far simpler than the society being illustrated in the **Ring.**

Wagner returned to the mastersingers theme shortly after a political amnesty permitted his return to Germany. Both occurrences came at a fortuitous time for while he was living in Switzerland Wagner became too personally and artistically involved in **Tristan und Isolde,** ultimately becoming distracted from continuing work on the **Ring.**

Shortly after returning to Germany he was summoned to Munich where for the next eighteen months Wagner lived comfortably under the patronage of the eighteen year-old King, Ludwig II. As his friendship with the king intensified Wagner willingly offered many suggestions regarding both political and artistic matters. Had Wagner been content only with his personal needs and goals he might have been able to concentrate exclusively on completing the **Ring,** especially now that the king offered not only financial security while Wagner was still composing the cycle, but further agreed to help in the design and construction of the special theatre needed for its presentation. For the first time in his life he had everything that he could personally want. But other thoughts kept intruding and none of greater importance than one which could work to his benefit as well as to Germany's. Ludwig seemed pliable to Wagner's suggestions and with proper direction the impressionable young king might take the initiative to enhance cultural and artistic matters as a counterbalance to the militarism rampant in other parts of Germany, Prussia in particular.

Remedying the truly deplorable state of musical education in Germany was a matter of the highest priority. To accomplish this task as well as to promote a truly German cultural identity, Wagner prepared, at the king's request, a "Report to His Majesty King Ludwig II of Bavaria upon a German Music-School to be Founded in Munich." Wagner may have had certain personal ends in mind while preparing this memorandum in March 1865, mainly that the lack of professionalism among the German singers and musicians would make it difficult if not impossible to properly perform his own works. But in a larger perspective the ends that were so vital for his own personal success were also vital to the future course of music in Germany. If Germany were to attain eminence in the field of music, then a cultural identity was the necessary means for achieving this end. "We have Classical works but as yet no Classic rendering for them."[54]

Although several Royal Conservatories existed in Germany, what was taught in them, according to Wagner, could not be called professional. Great conservatories as in Naples, Milan, and Paris, maintain the best techniques and traditions of the past, but "in our German schools it is impossible to maintain and nurse a classic style, because it is either totally unknown, or else unadvocated, at our public art-institutes." Calling German musical standards notoriously backward in "evolving a Style in harmony," he went on to flail music schools for an even worse offense: "the Germans have not as yet advanced beyond a mere aping and imitating the stylistic idiosyncrasies of the French and Italians." Since each country had a unique musical style which should be encouraged, Wagner urged that attention be given to that which is truly German: "to call into life, in some suitable centre of German life and German culture, a standard institution for the mode of performing works of German style."

In advocating the establishment of a pan-Germanic cultural identity, Wagner maintained that music, as with poetry and drama, could serve as a catalyst for the emergence and flowering of a dormant entity which he called the "German spirit." His ends were clear: "to give the nation's musical taste a more earnest and a nobler trend", even though a German nation did not yet exist. Thwarting his plan was the persistent Germanic infighting which too often had shattered the

----

[54] "A Music-School for Munich," **PW**, 4:191.

peace. Predictably enough, within a year of Wagner's report, Bavaria would be at war with Prussia.

It is difficult to ascertain exactly what Wagner envisioned as the problem that needed to be corrected. At one point he commented on the existence of classic works, but criticized the inability of Germans to play them correctly; at another point he commented on the lack of a classical style. Previous to this report Ludwig had already promised Wagner the necessary aid for the completion and performance of the **Ring,** including the construction of a suitable theatre and the canvassing of singers and musicians throughout Germany. But Wagner either wanted to go beyond what was needed for his own projects or he was convinced that the current standards were so low that his artistic requirements would not be met. The development and successful performing of German music required the creation of new music institutions, and none was more desperately needed that a "preparatory Music-School." If German works were to be properly performed, a proper regard for professional musicianship had to be created. German composers from Bach to Mozart to Beethoven (to Wagner?) had been creating and developing new musical forms that were quite unlike the works of French and Italian composers. Now it was incumbent on Germany to correctly present these works.

Despite his criticism of current musical deficiencies, Wagner had some positive words to say. German musical culture was unique in several important ways: first, Germans were more "reflective" as musicians than those of Italy or France; second, they were capable of integrating foreign elements, assimilating the best that was to be found in other cultures into a uniquely Germanic style. Rather than merely copying national traits and characteristics the German absorbed the best while molding a new artistic creation. In this way German musicianship may continue to develop and hopefully the classic works of Mozart and Beethoven might yet be correctly performed. But at the present time "Let anyone name me the school in Germany where the authentic rendering of Mozart's music has been established and preserved!"[55] To truly understand Bach and other great German composers one needed to be reflective in musical matters, and to learn this required training. The proper place to begin was by first establishing a preparatory music school.

---
[55] **Ibid.,** 192.

Wagner's concern was not a new one. In 1834, at the age of twenty-one, he first expressed criticism of non-symphonic German music and the lack of schools of musical training for singers. Although his aesthetic philosophy of art was not even in its embryonic stage, he speculated on the question of why opera appeared to be so foreign to the German mind. Coming to the conclusion that German composers were too erudite, "too intellectual and much too learned to create warm human figures", Wagner appealed to the public to recognize that both the German folk and the German composer must begin to look at the voice, not as an instrument in the orchestra, but as an adjunct[56] to the orchestra which required a new musical form. But singers must be trained for "where, in all our German fatherland, are there training-schools for higher vocal culture?" Lamenting on the inability of Germans to sing correctly, Wagner urged that this defect be remedied in order to create "not only a well-trained organ, but also a good delivery, correct declamation, pure enunciation, sympathetic expression and thorough knowledge of music."[57]

Wagner's contempt for French and Italian music was relatively new. Several years earlier he had maintained that music should be "neither Italian nor French--nor even German." But as early as 1845 he tended to deny that one could be a "European composer", emphasizing his belief that since German music was intrinsically better it should be non-imitative. But too often German composers "despair of a specifically German spirit and think they must set about being cosmopolitan. They think they can blend Auber-ish spiciness with Donizetti-ish tunefulness, in a flux compounded of Teuton profundity, and so make sure of producing something universally acceptable. Practically all modern German opera seems to me to suffer from this objectionable quest for superficial success."[58]

----
[56] On German Opera," 10 June 1834, **Zeitung für die elegante Welt**, PW, 8:55.

[57] "Pasticcio," Nov. 6, 10, 1834, **Neue Zeitschrift für Musik, PW,** 8:60.

[58] Wagner to Louis Spohr, 4 February 1845, Altmann, 1:113. Only a few years earlier Wagner was guilty of doing exactly what he now criticizes others for doing. Perhaps he was now trying to bolster German self-confidence.

Fifteen years later Wagner's criticism of French music was still uppermost in his mind: "Reflect how starved is all French art... But then, you see, neither is the Frenchman constitutionally musical, and all his music he has gotten from abroad. From of old the French musical style has been formed by mere contact with Italian and German music, and strictly speaking is nothing but a cross twixt these two styles."[59]

Establishing a music school was but the first step in Wagner's plan. Ever since the appearance of the works of Goethe and Schiller, German prose and dramatic speech had also been undergoing a significant evolutionary change in style. Schools of acting were as necessary for poetry as were music schools for the training of singing: "it would be difficult, well-nigh impossible, to recommend from among our actors of to-day even the teacher of correct pronunciation and declamation in classic modes of verse..." However, the music school was his first immediate priority.

By-passing the already existent Royal Conservatory which Wagner believed to be inept both in organization and curricula, he urged the king to appoint a Royal Commission to be charged with making recommendations for the creation of a new preparatory music school in Munich. The functions of the new school would be clear: "they would consist in a continual testing of instruction, coupled with efficiently-conducted practice in common", the end result being "to cherish and preserve the classical works of the past by establishing and putting in practice their correct mode-of-rendering, in such a way that not only shall the artists themselves acquire the sense of true and beautiful expression, a fine artistic taste, but the general sense of Art (among the public) shall also reach its highest power and cultivation,[60] upon the only groundwork proper to the German spirit."

Throughout the lengthy report and contained within every aspect of the discussion relating to the development and cultivation of artistic matters, one finds Wagner's intense concern with matters "German." The development of a cultural identity was perhaps the single most important aspect of his romantic

----

[59] Wagner to Mathilde Wesendonck, 10 April 1860, Wesendonck, **Letters**, 216-7.

[60] "A Music School for Munich," 212.

nationalism. Although Wagner appreciated the relationship between a music school and a greater awareness of dramatics to successfully realize the finest presentation of his own works, the ideas expressed to the king were not actually new, although some of the particulars were.

Even before he returned to Germany from France, in 1840, Wagner often talked about and wrote on the subject of German music, well before he conceived and theorized on his new dramatic art-form and wrote his first music drama. Music was a "divine art" and the German had a special disposition--he didn't say what it was or where it came from, but it existed--which enabled him to understand its qualities in a way that was unique: "A German learns all the difficult part of musical theory in his childhood along with his school studies, with the result that when he reaches the stage of being able to think and feel for himself nothing is more natural than that music should be part of his thinking and feeling, and that far from regarding it as mere entertainment he should approach it in a religious spirit as one of the holiest things in his life."[61] At the time this was written the fractured nature of the German States seemed to prevent German musicians from becoming better known within the Germanic-speaking countries, but in the international scene as Wagner glibly declared, Germans displayed a musicianship that made them qualitatively different from the French or the Italians.

Wagner's belief in the exceptionalism of German musicians and composers enabled him to say, with unabashed pride: "the German more than any other possesses the power to go to another country, develop its art to its highest peak and raise it to the plane of universal validity. Handel and Gluck abundantly proved this, and in our time another German, Meyerbeer, has provided a fresh example."[62]

Undoubtedly Wagner's immediate concern now was to prepare for the **Ring**; but his nationalistic tendencies were of longer duration, and just as intense to him as his own musical interests. Often hypercritical of

----

[61] "German Music," **Wagner Writes from Paris**, 40.

[62] **Ibid.**, 50. After deciding that Meyerbeer was a Jew and therefore not a German, Wagner removed this flattering remark from the article.

Germans and the non-existence of a country called Germany, Wagner never doubted one point: "a great mission lies prefigured in the whole temper of the German, and a mission scarce within the cognisance of other nations."

Wagner cajoled the king to recognize those inherent qualities of greatness that remained submerged only because of the inadequate political structures of the Germanic states. Ultimately a Germanic spirit would flower. It awaited only the truly enlightened leader: Ludwig was the one to do it! Bavaria had the ability and power to set an artistic and a cultural example which would be admired and emulated by the rest of Germany. This might then serve as a catalyst for the emergence of one united Germany, culturally preeminent in Europe, and no longer an artistic underling of France and Italy. Wagner rhapsodized in poetic grandeur: "not only that Beethoven and Goethe have issued from our loins, but also that their works, despite our present inability to conceive and represent them quite distinctly, are yet remotely grasped and loved by us,--bears witness to our natural capabilities."[63]

Admitting that he was often driven by an "inner compulsion" to search for the meaning of creativity, and was sometimes derided for his visionary artistic efforts, Wagner always felt it necessary to speak out in the name of art: "We are what we are only while we create; all the other functions of life have no meaning for us, and are at bottom concessions to the vulgarity of ordinary human existence, which can give us no satisfaction."[64]

Sixteen years earlier he tried to interest the King of Saxony in a series of reforms which would have permitted the theatre to be upgraded. In his "Plan of Organisation of a German National Theatre for the Kingdom of Saxony", Wagner sought to end the conception of theatre as mere entertainment for a bored citizenry. Calling for the elevation of theatre into the realm of serious art, supported directly by the State, Wagner presented an elaborate and detailed blueprint for its total reorganization, complete with particulars over

----

[63] "A Music School for Munich," 214.

[64] Wagner to Liszt, 7 June 1855, **Wagner-Liszt Correspondence**, 2:92.

what was to be taught, to whom, and how; he further elaborated on how the theatre was to be funded and its responsibilities to the other cities and towns in Saxony.

Wagner's focal point was clear. Theatre "combines all the arts with the object of ennobling taste and manners. This interest of the public's must be active, energetic,--not slack and superficially attracted."[65] As part of this plan, Wagner called for the establishment of "The Musical Institute" allied with the theatre, and designed "to be of service to the cause of Music in the entire Saxon fatherland." A professional and permanent well-trained orchestra, the development of the vocal arts, and the establishment of dramatic classes, would all be incorporated into one overall plan for the Theatre. Saxony would thereby take the lead among the German States in the cultivation of the arts. "A Union of all the composers" together with "all the active members of the orchestra" would elect the Director, who must be acceptable to the Minister of State.

Wagner had tried to continue the work initiated in Dresden by Weber. Through his efforts a truly German musical idiom slowly began to develop, replacing the preponderant influence of Italian opera. Shortly after establishing himself in Dresden Wagner wrote: "I have now set myself the glorious task of carrying on Weber's work, that is to say, of helping to emancipate Dresden musically, of smitting the Philistines hip and thigh, of ennobling the public taste here and of thereby making its voice one to be considered."[66] Before anything could come of the plan Saxony was embroiled in revolutionary and insurrectional political violence. As Wagner was a direct participant in the fighting his departure and later exile from Saxony permanently ended his cultural reforms.

---

[65] "Plan of Organization of a German National Theatre for the Kingdom of Saxony," **PW**, 7:335.

[66] Wagner to Karl Gaillard, 5 June 1845, Altmann, 1:115. Just how successful he was may be gleaned by the printed **Tagebuch** of the Royal Saxon opera for the previous year. The company produced twenty-nine different operas totaling one hundred and six performances. Italian operas consisted of less than fifty percent of the total. See Burrell, Appendix A, 476.

While living in Switzerland, two years later, Wagner again tried to encourage a new approach to theatre: "Let us sum in a word the whole ailment wherewith almost every theatre of Europe is striken, even unto death: it consists in this, that with very few exceptions, among which only the first opera-houses of Italy can be included, **there is no Original-theatre but that of Paris, and all the rest are merely its copies."**[67] By now Wagner had become obsessed not only with the belief in a "German spirit" but in the idea of German exceptionalism in musical and artistic matters. Arbitrarily but with supreme self-confidence, he stated as fact that differences exist between German and Italian audiences. The German treats opera and theatre seriously while the Italian displays little but grossness "while they treat all the opera's groundwork, namely the choruses and roles of so-called minor personages, with the most deliberate negligence, filling it out with banal, everlastingly repeated, absolutely nothing-saying stopgaps, intended just to make a bustle during the public conversation."[68] On the other hand, a German audience concentrates on the totality of an artistic work.

Wagner's plan for Zurich was designed to encourage the development and presentation of original works for the theatre, which by this time would even include his own: "Our artist-personnel must therefore leave its pure concernment with the Play, and step into the realm of Musical Drama." Quite unashamedly Wagner asked, "Let us keep Zurich in eye, and particularly in its weighty bearing on the whole of German Switzerland. Are there no creative forces here? Unknown they may be, but surely not un-existing." Of course Wagner was fairly well-known by this time, even notorious, so it is indeed possible that he was being altruistic, thinking only of rising young composers who were unknown to the public. Once again he proposed that a Commission for Theatrical Affairs be established, under the State, to investigate the possibility of establishing a program for innovative theatrical reforms. Stressing the intimate relationship between civilization and art, Wagner saw art as the fulcrum for humanizing civilization.

---

[67] "A Theatre at Zurich," **Neue Zeitschrift**, June 27, July 4, 11, 1851, **PW**, 3:29.

[68] **Ibid.**, 31.

In more recent years with the building of the new opera house in 1863, Wagner tried to encourage theatre reform in Vienna. Re-echoing the words of Kaiser Joseph II when he called for the Imperial court-theatres "to contribute to the ennobling of the nation's manners and taste", Wagner went one step further. Concerned with style as well as content he proposed: "that the Opera-house should be an art-institute whose duty it is to contribute to the ennobling of public taste through constantly good[69] and correct performances of musico-dramatic works." True artistry in Vienna was being discouraged by a conspicuous lack of standards and through the absence of an artistic structure which would encourage distinction. The waltzes of Strauss were thoroughly enjoyable and "if you don't wish for higher things, then be content with this." In his reorganization plan Wagner suggested implementing the bureaucratic structure of the Paris Opera, whereby several distinguished personalities assumed the major positions of vocal director, orchestra director, and stage director, under one overall chief director. Performances should then be reduced in quantity but increased in quality. Through these measures a new creativity would be established while frivolity in the arts would be abolished. Little came from Wagner's suggestions and even an appeal to the nation's honor went unheeded.

Now it was up to Ludwig to decide "whether attainment of the suggested goal would, or would not, contribute alike to the welfare of Art and to the fame of Bavaria and its noble King." Ludwig created a Royal Commission and Wagner was one of its appointed members. But after a few preliminary meetings the scheme was considered too costly and nothing came of it at that time. A few months later the conflict between Wagner and the king's cabinet came out into the open, thereby putting the final end to the proposal although "not a single critical vote of any significance was raised when this report was published."

In actuality Munich was not Wagner's first choice for the location of his proposed music school. Nürnberg seemed a more suitable locale: "It is remarkably significant that this very genuine and unique 'German art centre' Protestant Nürnberg, should have come to the Bavarian Crown and consequently into the domain of my ardently Catholic royal friend. It is **there** that the

---
[69] "The Vienna Opera House," **PW**, 3:372.

future 'German Academy' belongs, and so do all those other things which can never flourish in the superannuated un-German capital of our little Louis Quatorze."[70] Ludwig might have enjoyed reading what else Wagner had to say: "There, too, is the place for our school, around which there must ultimately grow up a general School of Art and Science, German and non-Jewish. I should like the King to give me a lodge of the castle of Bayreuth for my retreat--Nürnberg near by--all Germany about me.--Only for heaven's sake don't let a word of this get abroad. Even the King would not understand it in the least as yet. To him--and for the matter of that, to the world as well--I must convey the idea empirically, and little by little. 'Hans Sachs' belongs to Nürnberg..."

Two years later, after Wagner was out of Munich and ensconced safely in Switzerland, some form of music school was established in Munich under the direction of Wagner's disciple Hans von Bülow. But within a short period of time Bülow's known close association with Wagner provoked renewed antagonism. Eventually he too was forced to resign the post and leave Munich.

Wagner fought long and hard for the reforms he envisioned as necessary to bring music, drama, and art up to date. Many times he thought of abandoning his efforts, especially during the long years of exile: "If there were such a thing as a will capable of overruling the necessity of one's own being, I should assuredly will **not** to be an artist any longer; and how I long to be able to forget all about art and have done with feeling life a perpetual burden! Unhappily, though, there is no way of escape for me, and any thing I could do to flee from art would be more artificial than art itself. When you see me staggering on under my burden, though, don't imagine I see before me a clear goal .[71] It all goes on involuntarily simply because I **must."**

The nature of Wagner's artistic creativity has been traced to many sources but in one moment of deep depression Wagner himself provided an unusually fascinating answer: "If I now turn to my great work, it

----

[70] Wagner to Hans von Bülow, 20 February 1866, Altmann, 2:223.

[71] Wagner to Robert Franz, 25 September 1852, Altmann, 1:233.

85

is done for the purpose of seeking salvation from my misery, forgetfulness of my life. I have no other aim, and shall think myself happy when I am no longer conscious of my existence. In such circumstances my only joy is to know at least that I may benefit my friends by my art; in their sympathy with my works lies the only enjoyment I find in them."[72]

----
[72] Wagner to Liszt, 30 January 1852, **Wagner-Liszt Correspondence**, 1:189.

CHAPTER 3

THE QUEST FOR A NEW WORLD ORDER

In the decade of the 1840's Wagner's creativity emerged and flowered but to mixed popular acclaim. Within one decade, between 1840-1848, he had written the opera **Rienzi,** and the three music-dramas, **The Flying Dutchman, Tannhäuser,** and **Lohengrin.** In the latter he revealed the depth of his reflections on spiritual questions, his deepening involvement with mystical and transcendental thoughts, and a growing recognition of the problems inimical to man in society. He had questioned matters relating to the meaning of life, the role of free will, the nature of evil, the interrelationship between God and man, the origin of values, the role of religion, the essence of human nature, and the interaction between man and society. By the time **Lohengrin** had been completed Wagner's mystical bent was clearly evident. Since he pondered man's struggle to find the meaning of life, it was natural that he be concerned with man's so-called higher and lower natures and the perpetual battle between the forces of light and the forces of darkness.

Taken as a totality Wagner's first three music-dramas carried him along on a spiritual odyssey that was not resolved even when he completed **Parsifal,** in 1882, one year before his death. Yet in the meantime new thoughts began to emerge and the year 1848 became a watershed.

Between 1848 and 1853 Wagner's creativity would be found exclusively in prose and poetry. Although not one note of music was composed during this period, other perceptions expanded dramatically. A reawakened interest in political matters included a fundamental reexamination of man in society, an investigation which soon involved him more deeply in economic, social, and cultural issues than ever before. Ultimately Wagner became radicalized, a revolutionary figure who examined society, found it wanting, and embarked on an active course designed to change the conception, structure, and organization of society.

Just as Wagner was working on the final orchestration for **Lohengrin,** in February 1848, word arrived from Paris describing the abrupt departure of King Louis Phillipe and the proclamation of the Republic of France. Wagner became absorbed with this historical phenomenon and it revived his earlier political interests. After completing **Lohengrin**, in April, his involvement with politics intensified: "I too caught the fever of excitement which had spread everywhere."[1]

Wagner's awareness of political forces and issues did not come about suddenly in 1848. It was during his student days at Leipzig, in 1830, that the seventeen year-old Wagner first sensed the excitement and importance of political man. In the aftermath of the Napoleonic wars European nations led by Austria and Prussia had embarked on a conservative program designed to restore order and the status quo which had existed prior to the expansion of France under Napoleon. Dominated by Austria's Prince Metternich, the Congress of Vienna in 1815 redesigned the political map of Europe. By 1819, through the imposition of the Carlsbad decrees, political liberty, freedom of the press, and freedom of assembly had been sharply curtailed throughout most of Western Europe. Universities and other institutions of learning were especially vulnerable to censure lest a potentially radicalized student body attempt to promulgate revolutionary, liberal, or national ideas.

The year 1830, despite all attempts at political control, proved to be a forerunner of a radicalism that would become more widespread over the next two decades: Charles X, the restored Bourbon King of France, was forced to flee; political outbreaks also took place in Belgium, Poland, Hesse, Brunswick, and Wagner's state of Saxony. He was far from indifferent to these developments: "The King of France had been driven from his throne; Lafayette who a moment before had seemed a myth to me, was again riding through a cheering crowd in the streets of Paris. ... Suddenly to become conscious of living at a time in which such things took place could not fail to have a startling effect on a boy of seventeen. The world as a historic phenomenon began from that day in my eyes..."[2]

The events of 1789 had produced in their aftermath a reign of terror, but Wagner viewed the 1830 political outbreak in France as an "heroic popular struggle crowned with victory, and free from the blemish of the

----

[1] **My Life,** 1:435.

[2] **Ibid.,** 47.

terrible excesses that stained the French Revolution."
Violence and radicalism had broken out in Saxony too,
and reports reached Wagner in Leipzig indicating that
street fighting had erupted in Dresden, near his home:
"At a stroke I became a revolutionary, and acquired the
conviction that any tolerably resolute man should
concern himself exclusively with politics. I now felt
at ease only in the company of political writers."[3] In
the wake of the Saxon uprising Frederick Augustus had
been proclaimed regent and a new constitution was
granted to the Saxon people.

These occurrences affected Wagner to such an
extent that he felt it necessary to express himself
through music: "I composed a political overture [not
extant], the prelude of which depicted dark oppression
in the midst of which a strain was at last heard under
which, to make my meaning clearer, I wrote the words
Friedrich und Freiheit."[4] Political circumstances soon
produced an acute reaction in Wagner: "now [I] began to
read the papers and cultivate politics
enthusiastically." But events in France and Saxony were
soon eclipsed by news of the desperate struggle of the
Poles to free themselves from Russian political
control: "The victories which the Poles obtained for a
short period during May 1831, aroused my enthusiastic
admiration; it seemed to me as though the world had,
by some miracle, been created anew." During the year
that Russia was trying to subdue Poland many refugees
arrived in Leipzig with further news of Russian
atrocities. "I felt the siege and capture of Warsaw as
a personal calamity. My excitement when the remains of
the Polish army began to pass through Leipzig on their
way to France was indescribable..."

These early incidents tend to reflect a degree of
romanticism hardly unusual in a boy of seventeen.
Inspired by the work of the Leipzig Polish Committee
Wagner wrote an overture which he simply called
Polonia. Once again, historical forces prompted Wagner
to express himself in music. "I was confronted by the
Revolution of July 1830. The effect upon me was both
violent and stimulating; especially keen was my
enthusiasm for the struggling, my sorrow for the
vanquished, Poles. But these impressions were not as

---

[3] "Autobiographical Sketch," Winter, 1842, Barth, 12.

[4] **My Life,** 48.

yet of any perceptible formative influence upon my artistic evolution."[5]

Nine years later while struggling to make a name for himself in Paris, Wagner was hired by Moritz (Maurice) Schlesinger, a music publisher and fellow German, to write short stories and articles for the **Gazette Musicale.** Several of the stories reveal "in a fictitious garb and with a dash of humour, my personal fate. ... Every line that I wrote was a cry of revolt against the conditions of our modern art."[6] But a close mental link soon developed between Wagner's artistic fate and the political status of the weak and fragmented Germanic peoples. It was in Paris that one could identify Wagner's evolution into a romantic nationalist. Wagner's romanticism blended with his developing nationalistic outlook for a united Germany, forced him to take a more searching interest in political matters. By the end of the decade Wagner's correlation of romanticism with nationalism flowered into revolutionary activism.

Wagner's involvement in political matters appears to be closely related to his perception of cultural and especially aesthetic problems. It was his inability to achieve recognition within Saxony that prompted him to set his sights elsewhere. A disunited Germany meant that few artists could become known beyond the boundary of any one State. This was an intolerable situation for the development of art, his or others. While in Paris Wagner became an avid reader of German history. "Even at this time it delighted me to find in the German mind the capacity of appreciating beyond the narrow bounds of nationality all purely human qualities..."[7]

The connection between cultural matters and politics may be observed in Wagner's first article "De la musique allemande (On German Music)" which appeared in the **Gazette Musicale** on July 12 and 26, 1840. Somewhat facetiously and "with the enthusiastic exaggeration characteristic of me at that time", Wagner made a determination that music was too often a misguided reflection of national values and attitudes. "It has been said that whereas the Italians use music

---

[5] **Communication, PW,** 1:292.

[6] **Ibid.,** 304.

[7] **My Life,** 257.

for lovemaking and the French for social reasons, the Germans cultivate it as a form of science. It would be better perhaps to say that the Italian is a singer, the Frenchman a virtuoso and the German--a musician."[8]

Some of these remarks may be dismissed as hyperbole, but Wagner did attach himself to a theme which would appear with regular consistency throughout his life, namely, that art--in its broadest sense-- should not be a reflection of any country, race, or people, but should encompass the whole of humanity. The German artist can and should take the lead to demonstrate this truth. It was only the German who worshiped music as a "divine art" and not as a means for making money: "It is almost as though the German genius were destined to seek from its neighbours what it did not inherit from its motherland and to lift what it takes out of its narrow boundaries and provide something universal for the whole world. Naturally this can only be achieved by one who is not content merely to counterfeit a foreign nationality but who preserves pure and uncorrupted the endowment of his Germanic birth, namely genuineness of expression and purity of invention."[9]

Wagner was beginning to develop a theme which would become increasingly more important to his artistic and political career--that the German genius had the potential to offer humanity a higher and more noble perception of cultural values. The one inhibiting factor preventing the flowering of German genius was the lack of German political unity: "His fatherland is divided into a number of kingdoms, electorates, duchies, and free cities. ... the composer who brings out his works in Berlin is ... completely unknown in Vienna or Munich: it is only from abroad that he can make his name known all over Germany."

Wagner's thesis clearly reveals both his romantic nationalism and his own sense of destiny--the fate of Germany and the fate of music are intertwined. While Germany remains divided music will remain localized: "thus we have Prussian, Swabian and Austrian folksongs but no truly German one. This lack of centralisation

----

[8] "German Music," **Wagner Writes from Paris,** 37.

[9] **Ibid.,** 45.

... explains why no great musical piece of nation-wide significance will ever appear..."[10]

After being appointed principal conductor at the Royal Saxon opera in Dresden, Wagner returned to Germany: "and so I left in the spring of 1842; for the first time in my life I saw the Rhine, - and with tears in my eyes I, a poor artist, swore eternal faith to my German fatherland."[11] But what exactly did the German fatherland mean to the twenty-nine year old Wagner? "An ardent yearning patriotism awoke within me, such as I had never dreamt before. This patriotism was free from any political tinge; for I was alive, at any rate, to the fact that political Germany had not the slightest attraction to offer me, as compared with, say, political France."[12]

If German politics held so little interest for him what was the nature of his nationalism? Wagner's interest lay in seeking more than a unified political state. He apparently visualized a new kind of country, a Germany which had never existed before: "Yet this longing was not directed to any old familiar haunt that I must win my way back to, but onward to a country pictured in my dreams, an unknown and still-to-be-discovered haven..." In this statement one finds the essence of Wagner's romantic nationalism. He envisioned a currently nonexistent country but one which might become the model for the ideal political state of the future. And this new state would apparently somehow benefit humanity. But in concrete specific terms which applied to the people of the cities and towns of Germany as he found them now, upon his return, his description was less than flattering: "as for my Fatherland, apart from its lovely ranges of hills, vales and woods, I rather dislike it than otherwise. They are an accursed people, these Saxons, greasy, paunchy, ill-bred, lazy and coarse--what have I to do with them?"[13]

---

[10] Ibid., 39. Wagner was not suggesting that Bach and Mozart were provincial composers but that their music would be better known if the country were united.

[11] "Autobiographical Sketch," Barth, 16.

[12] Communication, 310.

[13] Wagner to Samuel Lehrs, 12 June 1842, Altmann, 1:81.

From 1842 until 1848 Wagner read deeply in German history "in order to assure myself of what it was, in particular, that I held dear in the German Home for which I was yearning", but as far back as his studies carried him it became obvious that the past offered few glimpses of his ideal society, and no blueprint for the present or the future. Ultimately it was not in the history of the past that Wagner would discover the traits of an ennobled mankind but only in the yet to be created future.

What was Wagner searching for? Why did he turn to a study of history and what answers did he fail to find there? Part of the answer is to be found in Wagner himself. That he was restlessly trying to find his niche in life is clear. He found society exasperating partially because he seemed ill-equipped to fit comfortably into it, and partially, perhaps, because he and his works were not accepted unequivocally by his peers. Part of Wagner's unhappiness seemed to be related to his lack of success. Therefore it is possible to view his study of the past as self-serving: what caused the development of a Germany which would be indifferent to people like Beethoven and Wagner? But this is an incomplete answer.

Wagner fits in with other mid-nineteenth century romantics who tended to view man's recorded history with suspicion and concern. Since romanticism hypothesized that man was capable of resolving the major existential questions of the day, it was incumbent that the thinker play an active role in history. The middle decades of the nineteenth century seemed to offer what centuries of European life had denied, the centrality of man as a force in shaping his own historical destiny. Wagner, like others, postulated endless questions on why history so often reflected man's timidity and passivity. But now that the temporal power of the Roman Catholic Church had been curtailed in much of Western Europe, man was no longer restricted by the exclusivity of powerful religious forces. In addition, enlightenment science had postulated an orderly, mechanistic, and law-governing cosmos capable of being understood by man, while romanticism went one step further by assuming that once man understood his cosmos he might even be able to tamper with it. Man's role had never been more important.

This was the element that Wagner found missing in man's past history: the dynamic thrust of man himself.

The connection between culture and politics and their symbiotic relationship dominated Wagner's thoughts and prompted his burgeoning political radicalism. By 1848 he became frustrated with life in Dresden: "It was here that a great self-delusion, forced upon me by circumstances, though not completely unawares to myself, became the cause of fresh development, painful but decisive, of my character both as an artist and as man."[14]

Wagner's unhappiness was rooted in several wide-ranging causes. His career was developing but not in any spectacular way, despite the initial success of **Rienzi,** and the completion of **The Flying Dutchman, Tannhäuser,** and **Lohengrin.** In personal terms, his marriage was not conducive either to happiness or even tranquility.[15] Finally, life in Dresden was artistically, socially, and politically debilitating. The combination of these factors undoubtedly helped produce his agitated mental state. But Wagner singled out culture, and especially the indifference of the public toward artistic matters, for his special concern:

> Our theatrical institutions have, in general, no other end in view than to cater for a nightly entertainment, never energetically demanded, but forced down people's throats by the spirit of Speculation, and lazily swallowed by the social Ennui of the dwellers in our larger cities. Whatever, from a purely artistic standpoint, has rebelled against this mission of the stage, has always shown itself too weak for any good. The only regulator of

----

[14] **Communication,** 317.

[15] Wagner had married Minna Planer, an actress, in 1836. Within six months she had run off with a wealthy merchant. Although preparations were made for a divorce, the couple were ultimately reunited; but not before Wagner had traveled considerable distances to find and persuade her to return to him. Although the start of their marriage was rocky both displayed much affection toward each other before later events led to their permanent separation after twenty-five years of marriage. There is considerable evidence to suggest that before meeting Wagner Minna had given birth to an illegitimate daughter, Natalie, whom she tried passing off as her sister.

distinctions, has been the **section** for whom this entertainment was to be provided: for the **rabble,** brought up in tutored grossness, coarse farces and crass monstrosities were served; the decorous **Philistines** of our bourgeoisie were treated to moral family-pieces; for the more delicately cultured, and art-spoilt **higher** and **highest classes,** only the most elegant art-viands were dished up, often garnished with aesthetic quips.[16]

And what is the result?: "The Opera has thus succeeded in fining down the mob, in vulgarising the genteel, and finally in turning the whole conglomerate audience into a superfinely-mobbish Philistine; who now, in the shape of the Theatre-public, flings his confused demands into the face of every man who undertakes the guidance of an Art-institute."

Here is the heart of Wagner's prognosis of popular cultural values. The artistic scene, including the predictable response to it by the public, was intrinsically bound up with the political and social attitudes of the day: "While pondering on the possibility of a thorough change in our theatrical relations, I was insensibly driven to a full perception of the worthlessness of that social and political system, which of its very nature, could beget no other public art-conditions than precisely those I then was grappling with--This knowledge was of decisive consequence for the further development of my whole life."

By 1848 Wagner's political ideas had coalesced, and he perceived that society had to be radically changed and the old ways overthrown. If humanity were to be served then man had to be awakened to the worthlessness of his cultural, social, and political values. Since each of these elements was related to Saxony's political and social structure, Wagner approached the political scene as the hub from which all else radiated. Because he was aware that some would argue that his radicalism was brought about because of a determination to see his own artistic ideas prevail, Wagner acknowledged that he could be viewed as "a revolutionary for the sake of the theatre." He was prepared to accept this and there is, of course, some truth in it: "the stronger my artistic enthusiasm, the

---
[16] **Communication,** 351.

sincerer and more imperious is my feeling of revolt against the vulgarity, philistinism, effrontery and contemptibleness in our whole blessed round of circumstances. Of far more weight than writing operas, and fresh supplies of operas which no one cares a rap for, do I now hold it to express myself in public on our art-conditions; and I am doing it by addressing my words to **thinking artists**."[17]

Wagner had made several attempts to improve performances while also restructuring the nature of the theatre; but it was obvious that no theatrical reform could ever accomplish all that needed to be done, unless society itself changed its values. But what precisely did Wagner envisage? A rebellion against the current "politico-juristic Formalism" and the creation of a new society. Society changed by art and art reformed by an enlightened society. He was now determined to bring this about, to create "a new physical mold which should correspond to the true essence of humanity--a mold which is only to be gained through the destruction of the physical form of the present, and therefore through Revolution."[18] The existence of an entrenched, conservative aristocracy prevented man's essence from being realized while a new model--to be achieved through revolution--would permit the development and fulfillment of man's destiny.

Political events in Germany helped to further Wagner's ideas. In 1848 various German states experienced outbreaks of violence as inflamed activists called for both a unified country and more representative institutions. When demonstrations broke out in Vienna Wagner became so excited that he wrote a poem to commemorate the occasion and to encourage similar responses among other Germanic-speaking peoples:

GREETING FROM SAXONY TO THE VIENNESE

Now is my heart from care set free,
No longer need I sorrow;
Since rescued whole is Germany,
With joy I greet the morrow.
What evil of ourselves we thought,

----
[17] Wagner to Clara Wolfram, 1 December 1849, Ellis, **Family Letters**, 153.

[18] **Communication**, 355.

It now has turned to good;
Who once to shame our honour brought,
Them have ye well withstood.
                    . . .

"The German Folk might suffer harm
From what does others good;
A little bondage--no alarm!--
Beseems the German mood."

They talk behind, they talk before,
Bid men not be too bold here;
Say quiet fits the burgher more,
And valour more the soldier:
"You see how bad this is for trade;
Much mischief has it brought.
The son gets what his father made,--
What then, if he made nought?"

Accursed traps are all they set us!
And into them we run?
The day whose dawn had scarcely met us,
Already pale its sun?
The moment for decision bades,
The answer's in our power:
How far the Germans courage strides?[19]
And shall we do, or cower?

In March riots in Berlin prompted King Frederick
William IV to declare his "willingness" to merge
Prussia with other German states into a German
federation, but by the end of the year with the
restoration of royal authority the idea dissipated
quickly. Nevertheless, a quasi-legal political system
for the German states had been established by the
Frankfurt Parliament which met from May 1848 through
June 1849. During the time that it met the German
National Assembly hoped to introduce a written
constitution, and the Assembly elected King Frederick
William as Emperor. His refusal to accept the title
ended this early attempt at unity but it did pave the
way for the creation of the North German Federation in
1867.

Wagner was far from indifferent to the results
that might be accomplished by the Assembly in
Frankfurt. Since it was largely composed of
----
[19] "Greeting from Saxony to the Viennese," **Allgemeine
Osterreichische Zeitung,** 1 June 1848, **PW,** 8:215-17.

representatives of the middle-class, rather than of the aristocracy, and as it contained many well-educated members, he saw its potential. Writing to one of its representatives, Wagner revealed his keen interest in what the Assembly could accomplish if only it would boldly tackle key problems in the proper order.

Resolving the question of the territoriality of the German states of the federation was the item of the highest priority. Indeed, before the Assembly even began to work on a constitution it must "set up a commission to work out proposals for a rational and natural distribution of the territories of the constituent German states, on the principle of no longer tolerating states with a population of less than three or more than six million."[20] Because of his study of history Wagner was concerned that no political structure should be comprised of weak and fragmented states; conversely, having a few powerful states would be equally dangerous. Once the questions relating to territoriality had been resolved then "should the Assembly get down to the constitutional task, for this cannot be undertaken until we have **clear ground** beneath our feet. How useless a constitution would be in this present state of Germany! **The Parliament must first completely revolutionize the individual states.**"

While the Frankfurt Assembly was meeting Wagner continued his political activities. His first overt move was to join the Vaterlandsverein, a radical organization composed principally of workers seeking fundamental changes in society, as well as in the form and structure of government. Although an active member Wagner would later try to underplay his role in the organization, insisting that "this party particularly needs intellect and moderation of sentiment to restrain its wild excesses."[21]

On 16 June 1848 the **Dresdener Anzeiger** published Wagner's article entitled, "The Relationship of Republican Aspirations to the Monarchy." On the day before, Wagner had read his impassioned address to the members of the Vaterlandsverein. By now his radicalism had evolved from a passive philosophical position to

----

[20] Wagner to Franz Jacob Wigard, 19 May 1848, Barth, 170.

[21] Wagner to Baron von Lüttichau, 18 June 1848, Altmann, 1:136.

that of an active political agitator. Wagner's romantic nationalism now emerged with clarity and eloquence, despite its fundamentally naive viewpoint. He called for the creation of a republican government in Saxony, headed by a king!: "I accordingly felt it incumbent on me to show the public quite clearly that, while we might strive to achieve all that is attainable, the monarchy does not in itself stand in direct opposition to our aspirations--in fact that our ideal would accord well with and be more desirable under the monarchy."[22]

Wagner argued that this unique political arrangement would be attainable once the king himself really understood the nature of republican government. Then King Frederick Augustus II would himself announce to his subjects: "I declare Saxony a Free State."[23] By this proclamation the king would become the first free man in Saxony and the process of republicanism would have begun. The monarch would have freed the king and "at head of the Free State (the republic) the hereditary King will be exactly what he should be, in the noblest meaning of the title: the First of the Folk, the Freest of the Free!" Wagner argued passionately that his ideas were attainable, and not visionary, but they were conditional on both the king and society acting together.

Wagner's attitude displayed both the grandeur of romanticism and its limitations. That his ideas were visionary does not necessarily detract from the possibility that they were attainable. But the question that Wagner and perhaps many other political romantics fail to realize relates to the practicality of an idea when it runs contrary to entrenched power. Wagner would learn about the dynamics of power the hard way, in the upcoming political revolution; its consequences would later be reflected in **The Ring of the Nibelung.**

Wagner's belief that the king of Saxony would be willing and able to act in a manner suggested by this speech, ludicrous or naive as it might appear, was based on several events which had occurred two months earlier. In March some concerned citizens had sent

----

[22] **Ibid.,** 137.

[23] "Fatherland Speech," Appendix to "German Art and German Policy," **PW,** 4:143. Two years later, in a letter written to Julie Ritter Wagner asked, "Can a prince decree a republic?"

petitions to the king calling for certain political reforms. These petitions were then followed by overt radical activities which threatened the stability of the monarchy to the point where Frederick Augustus II agreed to make some concessions. "The King dismissed his ministry and elected a new one, consisting partly of Liberals and partly of really enthusiastic Democrats. ... I was really touched by this result, and by the heartfelt joy which was evident among the whole population."[24] However, these reforms polarized society and rival political factions developed. Wagner's Fatherland speech had been delivered before the Patriotic Union, the more democratic faction, but one which would tolerate a restricted kingship.

Not only did Wagner require that the king cooperate in the creation of a new society but the nobility too must see the necessity for "the extinction of the last glimmer of aristocratism; as our gentlemen of the nobility no longer are feudal lords with power to enslave and clout us as they please." Wagner required of the nobility that "they should give up the last remnant of a distinction. ... if ye forget your fathers, we promise to be generous..."[25] So, in addition to having the king declare Saxony free, the nobles too should willingly renounce their past actions and policies, assume an enlightened attitude, and work with the people for the creation of a new society. The aristocratic Parliament should be abolished and in its place a new "House of the People's Deputies" created.

After Wagner publicly expressed his thoughts, reaction was immediate. It might be understandable that the king would not be personally amused by the idealism and supposed political innocence of his musical director, but the obvious public stance taken by Wagner skirted treason. Nothing could have been further from Wagner's intentions. He, like most of the populace, supported the king. When informed of the king's intense displeasure Wagner was startled: "The King can't really be angry about it! In my letter I put him high above all the others. How could a King be shown greater than by relinquishing his throne and living among his people as the first nobleman of the liberated nation?" Wagner's faith and belief in the common man, the Volk, is unmistakable and as one of his

----

[24] **My Life**, 436-7.

[25] "Fatherland speech," 137.

reforms Wagner insisted that women too should have the right to vote. But in the Fatherland speech Wagner went beyond a discussion of political and social matters; indeed, by bringing in the nature of the prevailing economic system he not only anticipated a primary focal point for **The Ring** but also extended his radicalism.

The idea of the "people" was important to Wagner. He saw them collectively, not belonging to any particular state or place. They represented "all the units which made up the total of a commonality." This idea of a collective people, the volk, was the antithesis to the egoism of the individual, whether as person or state. Wagner called for necessity not luxury, the group not the individual, communism not egoism. He used the term "communism" briefly and in a very restrictive sense as the antithesis to the "I", the single unit; communism represented the passing over from the "I" to the collective "you." It was a "socio-political ideal which I conceived as embodied in a 'Volk' that should represent the incomparable productivity of antique brotherhood, while I looked forward to the perfect evolution of this principle as the very essence of the associate Manhood of the Future."[26] But egoism can become a useful aspect of communism if there is "genuine egoism in which each isolated art-variety would give itself the airs of universal Art."[27] Egoism need not be selfish if its object becomes the community.

Even before the emergence of Darwin's theories Wagner talked about the "great evolutionary process of Nature in **Man himself.**" He saw in human evolution "the rational and natural progress from the unconscious to the conscious, from un-knowledge to knowledge, from need to satisfying."

While man's political and social structure was being transformed from the old to the new mold, it was time to address the true origin of the difficulties: "For then must be taken firmly and deedfully in eye **the question of the root of all the misery in our present social state,**--then must be decided whether Man, that crown of the Creation, whether his lofty spiritual, his artistically stirring bodily powers and forces, were meant by God to serve in menial bondage to the

----
[26] "Introduction to Art and Revolution," **PW**, 1:28.

[27] **The Art-Work of the Future, PW**, 1:99.

stubbornest, the most lifeless product in all Nature, to sallow metal?"[28] Wagner now came to see man's burning passion for wealth and power as the dominant forces of his day: "Everything strives to its freedom, towards its god--and our god is Gold, our religion the Pursuit of Wealth."[29]

Gold, in its lifeless but innocent state, dominates the first scene of **Das Rheingold**, and precipitates the action of the drama. Wagner did not mince words: money cripples "the fair free Will of Man to the most repulsive passion, to avarice, to usury" and the "demoniac" power of money was the basis for the artificiality and corruption of society.

Wagner did not offer an economic blueprint for the future, but in the first scene of **Das Rheingold** he illustrated how the lure for gold, or economic power, corrupts: "He who from the Rhinegold fashioned the ring, that would confer on him immeasurable might, could win the world's wealth for his own." That enigmatic but tempting proposition set into motion a series of events that began when Alberich willingly forsook even love to secure the wealth of the world. But once he obtained it, what would he do with the power? Portraying the answer with an awesome intensity that depicted his aversion toward all who possessed money, Wagner assumed that power meant domination, exploitation, and ruthless behavior toward underlings. Because one had to be on guard against those who would try to take economic power away, money caused anxiety. Man's behavioral patterns even changed, until it finally resulted in the manipulation of man by his fellow man. Alberich personified such a being in the third scene of **Rheingold** when he called his workers "stupid", intimidating them in a brutal, uncivil manner:

> Nibelungs all, bow down to Alberich!
> Now he is watching you everywhere:
> repose and rest is refused you:
> you must work for him though he is unseen;
> expect him when you do not perceive him;
> you are his vassals for ever!
> Hoho! Hoho! Listen for him, he is near,

---

[28] "Fatherland Speech," 138.

[29] "Art and Revolution," **PW**, 1:51.

the Lord of the Nibelungs![30]

This scene is a frightening display of naked power and what Wagner perceived to be the attitude of the factory owners and those in control of man's economic fortunes. Alberich cracks the whip over his workers, calls then "despicable dogs" before forcing them back to the mines: "Find me gold from the new veins! My whip waits for those that don't dig deep!"

Even in later years Wagner talked about his "instinctive dislike of the rich. ... I have searched my heart and find that ... nothing seriously touches me save in so far as it awakes my fellow-feeling--that is: fellow-suffering. This compassion I recognize as the strongest feature of my moral being, and presumably it also is the wellspring of my art."[31] On the other hand, wealth would permit him to devote his full energies to prose and music, giving the kind of freedom he desperately needed. While in Paris in 1860 he reflected on what money would be able to do: "I need to be **rich**; I need thousands and thousands [of francs] to sacrifice regardlessly, to buy myself space, time, and willingness. As I am not rich--well, I must endeavour to make myself so; I must let my older operas be given here in French, so as to devote the considerable proceeds to disclosing my new works to the world.-- That's what stands before me; I have no other choice, so--here's to death and extinction."[32]

Wagner's attack on the financial concepts of his day were rooted in two elements: first, that the "full emancipation of the human race" and the "fulfillment of Christ's pure teaching" could never come about as long as man permitted "usury, paper-juggling, [and] percentage and bankers' speculations";[33] secondly, that

---

[30] **Das Rheingold,** Scene 3, translation by Lionel Salter which accompanies the Deutsche Grammophon and Phillips recordings of the complete work. All subsequent unnumbered citations from the **Ring** are from this work although, on a few occasions, the author has substituted his own translations.

[31] Wagner to Mathilde Wesendonck, 1 October 1858, Wesendonck, **Letters,** 47-8.

[32] Wagner to Mathilde Wesendonck, 28 January 1860, 203.

[33] "Fatherland Speech," 139.

communism did not provide an attractive alternative model. Wagner called communism "preposterous" and "senseless." Categorically rejecting the idea of a "mathematically-equal division of property" Wagner instead called for a more positive change in values, as he issued a clarion call for a "fresh young Germany" to take upon itself the cause of "the complete rebirth of man"s Society ... when thence there springs a free new race, brought up to fullest exercise of all its energies."

Concerned with his own position as an employee of the government, Wagner denied that his speech espoused ideas against the king. In a private letter to the Intendant of the Court Theatre, Wagner argued that he was the only speaker to address the Patriotic Union who tried to demonstrate how the king could be united with a republican form of government. "Hence it was natural that the wish should rise in me, to convince both parties, alike Monarchists and Republicans, of the truth of the opinion to which I had come, and, if I succeeded in that, to incline both parties to one common goal: the maintenance of the Kingship,[34] and therewith of the land's internal peace."

Rather than pleasing both sides and affording a reconciliation of potentially conflicting viewpoints, Wagner succeeded in alienating both sides: "I admit that I now am heartily perturbed to see from various tokens that, as a matter of fact, I have been misunderstood: therein I recognize the danger, in these times, of speaking out an independent thought...."

During the later part of 1848 Wagner commenced work on two prose sketches, one of which, "Siegfried's Death", ultimately became incorporated into **The Ring.** The second prose work may never have been intended as a music-drama but the subject matter not only related to Wagner's political interests but also attempted to bring religion into his attack on man's existing institutions. "Jesus of Nazareth" was written sometime between November 1848 and the early part of 1849. Wagner saw Jesus as a "**solitary** One--who, fronted with a materialism so honourless, so hollow, and so pitiful as that of the Roman world, and still more of the world subjected to the Romans, could not demolish it and build upon its wrack an order answering to his soul's

----

[34] Wagner to Baron von Lüttichau, 18 June 1848, **PW**, 4:146.

desire. ... So the thought attracted me, to present the nature of Jesus--such as it has gained a meaning for **our**, for the consciousness directed to the stir of Life..."[35] Jesus would become self-serving to Wagner's ends; he would become the social revolutionary who would usher in a new romantic age of political and economic reforms.

After completing the sketch Wagner came to the conclusion that by re-introducing the older Judaic-Christian value system he might be compromising his argument that man should seek a new model for his future. "I deemed we must either remain completely rooted in the Old, or completely bring the New to burst its swathings. A clear glimpse upon the outer world, freed from all illusions, taught me conclusively that I must altogether give up my **Jesus of Nazareth**."[36]

Nevertheless, in terms of the Dresden of 1848 and the land of Israel at the time of Jesus, one finds that in both places a love of money, property, and possessions were dominant values; as Jesus sought to drive the money-changers out of the Temple, so too should man in mid-nineteenth century Germany drive away crass and selfish economic interests. If man would recognize that love is more important than material possessions perhaps man's enlightened nature could then elevate his spiritual as well as his physical happiness. It is here that Wagner was at his most eloquent:

> Every creature loves, and Love is the law of life for all creation; so if Man made a law to shackle love, to reach a goal that lies outside of human nature (--namely, power, dominion-- above all: the **protection of property**), he sinned against the law of his own existence, and therewith slew himself; but in that we acknowledge Love, and vindicate it from the law of the false spirit, we raise ourselves above the brute creation, since we arrive at knowledge of the everlasting law which has been sole power since the ur-beginning.[37]

---

35 **Communication**, 379.

36 **Ibid.**, 380.

37 "Jesus of Nazareth," **PW**, 8:301.

The absence of love in man's relationships with his fellow man was the great social problem of the day. As Fricka points out in **Rheingold**: "Loveless light-heartedness! ... What do you harsh men hold sacred and valuable when you thirst for power?" Criticizing her husband's quest for power, she offers a searing indictment that Wagner would like to apply to the current political scene: "Unloving, most unpleasant man! For the idle toys of might and dominion would you in blasphemous scorn, stake love and a woman's worth?"

Wagner's premise that love and power are irreconcilable may be dismissed as another illusion of mid-nineteenth century romanticism. The assumption that any power drive, whether economic or political, has to be at the expense of love says more for his limited perspective than for reality. Nevertheless, it is a viewpoint that he maintained for many years, and it found its way into the second scene of **Das Rheingold** when Loge philosophized: "In vain I searched, and see now full well that in the whole wide world nothing is so rich that a man will accept it in lieu of woman's beauty and delight." That any creature should renounce love for either gold, or property, would represent a spiritual abomination. That this appeared to be taking place in the late 1840's was proof that society had degenerated to the point where only revolution could usher in a new set of values.

A new society was needed, one which will devalue materialism and replace it with laws conducive to man's freedom. Freedom, not enslavement to property, was the heritage of the enlightened man. Man was told not to steal, and to love his neighbor; this meant: "Lay not up for thyself treasures, whereby thou stealest from thy neighbour and makest him to starve: for when thou has thy goods safeguarded by the law of men, thou provokest thy neighbour to sin against the law. Lay not up treasures of this world, and heap not Mammon, for thieves to dig at."[38] The exact embodiment of these thoughts is contained in several parts of **The Ring.**

At first it appeared as if Wagner looked back to the simpler pre-industrial days with its less complicated economic life-style. Mime in the third scene of **Das Rheingold** ruminated back to those days: "Carefree smiths, once we created ornaments for our women, wondrous trinkets, dainty trifles for Nibelungs,

----
[38] **Ibid.,** 304.

and lightly laughed at our work." The simplicity of the
domestic system had been destroyed by the introduction
of the factory system. But Wagner does not leave it
here for it is not simply a case of factory owners
dominating workers.The problem went deeper. The values
of society had been so undermined that even a simple
honest worker would turn against his fellow man if
given the opportunity. Mime, who bewailed the loss of
simplicity, appeared at first to be an unfortunate
victim of economic exploitation, but soon revealed
another aspect of his personality: "perhaps, yes
perhaps outwit the tyrant himself, and get him in my
power, snatch the ring from him, so that as I now am a
menial to this bully, I might be free and he my slave!"
Where power is to be found, it is exercised, and man's
humanity is either compromised or in jeopardy.

Wagner's ideas now emerge with unmistakable
clarity. An appeal to spirituality might be the way to
deal with the pernicious economic power corrupting the
world. God exists within all individuals but man has
the free will to turn against both God and one's fellow
man. When this happens evil enters the world. Man is
holy because "ye all descend from God and are in him
through Love, which is the only law."[39] Man must
respect the law of love and not the law of possession.

Wagner ultimately came to the conclusion that an
appeal to organized institutional religion and to man's
higher nature was not the most practical or even the
most relevant way of dealing with Germany in the late
1840's. Abandoning his work on "Jesus of Nazareth",
Wagner began forming contacts with liberal and
radically-minded individuals. One friendship, and one
acquaintanceship, proved to be of prime importance.
August Röckel came to Dresden in 1843 as Assistant
Conductor, but by 1848 had lost his court position
because of his radical political activities. He
thereupon began to publish the **Volksblätter,** a paper
calling for political agitation.

> First and foremost, he had planned a drastic
> social reform of the middle classes--as at
> present constituted--by aiming at a complete
> alteration of the basis of their condition. He
> constructed a totally new moral order of
> things, founded on the teaching of Proudhon and
> other socialists regarding the annihilation of

---

[39] **Ibid.,** 305.

the power of capital, by immediately productive labour, dispensing with the middleman. Little by little he converted me, by most seductive arguments, to such an extent that I began to rebuild my hopes for the realisation of my ideal in art upon them.[40]

Wagner wrote two major articles for Röckel. The **Volksblätter** offered him an opportunity to express his ideas and "led me to further reflection, and gave birth to new plans upon which, to my mind, a possible organisation of the human race, which would correspond to my highest ideals in art, could alone be based."[41]

It was during this time that Wagner also made the acquaintance of Michael Bakunin. After fleeing Russia Bakunin had become involved in revolutionary activities in Poland, Bohemia, Austria, and Prussia. Wagner met him at Röckel's home: "Everything about him was colossal, and he was full of a primitive exuberance and strength." Bakunin was a Hegalian, and a communist, and "democracy, republicanism, and anything else of the kind he regarded as unworthy of serious consideration." Friendship between them was difficult for their beliefs were dissimilar, even incompatible: "I, with my hopes of a future artistic remodeling of human society, appeared to him to be floating in the barren air; yet it soon became obvious to me that his assumptions as to the unavoidable demolition of all the institutions of culture were at least equally visionary."[42]

Nevertheless, meetings held between Wagner, Röckel, and Bakunin, with their interaction of views, helped Wagner synthesize his thoughts and precipitated the emergence of a more consistently thought-out focal point. Marie Schmole, the daughter of Ferdinand Heine, Wagner's closest friend at this time, later expressed her belief that both Bakunin and Röckel "made him believe that the overthrow of the existing government"

----

[40] **My Life**, 452. Wagner may have been less than candid. Since his autobiography was being dictated to Cosima, at the request of King Ludwig II, he may have been trying to disguise his political radicalism by indicating that it had sprung from artistic rather than from social and political causes.

[41] **Ibid.**, 453.

[42] **Ibid.**, 471.

was the best way to further his artistic plans. Convinced that Wagner acted only in the best interests of art and not for any political motives, Mrs. Schmole concluded that Wagner was duped into revolutionary activities by those who had nothing themselves to lose. While there is great advantage in blaming others for the emergence of Wagner's radicalism, this denies him the opportunity of having come to his own political conclusions. The first reflection of Wagner's more fully realized viewpoint appeared in an unsigned article entitled "Man and Established Society" in the 10 February 1849 issue of the **Volksblätter.**

In this short article Wagner's premises were articulated with considerable clarity and passion: "the battle of **Man** against existing **Society** has begun. Now, this is true if it be proved that our existing **Society** is an assault on **Man**, that the ordering of established Society runs counter to the **destiny**, the **right** of man."[43] He arrived at the conclusion that, "It is the destiny of **mankind**, through the ever higher perfecting of its mental, moral, and corporeal forces, to attain an ever higher, purer happiness. The individual is but a fraction of the whole; isolated, he is nothing; only as part of the whole, does he find his mission, right, his happiness." As Wagner surveyed contemporary society he was forced to the conclusion that, "Our established Society is without knowledge, without consciousness of her task; she fulfils it not." What then is expected of man? "The fight of Man against existing Society has begun. This fight, it is the holiest, the sublimest ever fought, for 'tis the war of consciousness with chance, of mind with mindlessness, morality with evil, of strength against weakness: 'tis the fight for our destiny, our right, our happiness."

Once man recognized that problems existed which were not being resolved, then the battle commenced. Since society was a creation of man, it was a means to an end; society was man's instrument for his betterment, for the guarantee of his happiness. To achieve these objectives Wagner became a revolutionary.

Two months later, on 8 April 1849, Wagner published a major article, "The Revolution." Contained within this article were many of the political, economic, and social points that appear more fully in **The Ring.** As such these thoughts represent Wagner's

---
[43] "Man and Established Society," **PW**, 8:228.

final statement of an historical nature until the prose sketch of **The Ring** five years later.

Taking an overview of the current scene in which revolts had already broken out from Belgium to Italy, not to mention Hesse, Brunswick, and Saxony, Wagner compared all of Europe to a volcano that was ready to erupt: "A supernatural force seems to be about to seize our continent, to lift it from its well-tried course and hurl it off on to another track."[44] He took delight in believing that the time was imminent for the destruction of the old order and the birth of a new one: "Yes, the old world, we can see, is about to collapse; from it a **new** world will arise, for the sublime Goddess of **Revolution** comes thundering in on the wings of the storm..." Despite the many attempts that were made by conservatives entrenched in power to stifle the emergence of the new order, they ultimately were unable to contain or prevent the liberalization of Europe. European statesmen, led as they had been for the past thirty-four years by Austria's Prince Metternich, tried to mobilize the upper classes to crush the revolutionary outbreaks as they had done so successfully in the past, but these efforts proved futile. No matter how hard the old order might try to preserve itself, its time had run out, and no reactionary policies can stem the time.

The role that politics played throughout the stormy course of European history convinced Wagner that political leadership seldom tolerated checks on its ability to control events. Metternich was merely the latest in a long series of major and minor tyrants eager to exert power through whatever means were available to them. Wagner reflected on Robespierre's role in the French Revolution: "The tragic element in Robespierre's character really consists in the spectacle he offers of utter helplessness, when, at the goal of his highest aspirations to power, he stands confronted by his own incapacity to make any sort of use of this power that he has attained. It is only in the confession of this helplessness that he becomes tragic, and in the fact that his own downfall is brought about by his inability to achieve anything towards the happiness of mankind."[45]

---

[44] "The Revolution," Barth, 170.

[45] Wagner to August Röckel, 26 January 1854, Roeckel, **Letters**, 92-3.

Wagner described Robespierre in words which made him the prototype for Wotan in the **Ring**: "He had no high end in view for the sake of which he condescended to unworthy means." That was Wotan's problem and it precipitated the events of the catastrophe which followed. Wotan is the paradigm of political power gone mad. He seeks legitimate power, attains it, devises a system to prevent anyone else from challenging his authority, and wields power in ways which betray his trust. Originally a constitutional ruler--the rules of law are written clearly on his spear, the visible symbol of legitimate rule--Wotan rules by a clearly-defined system of law, and not arbitrarily. As Fasolt tells him: "What you are, you are only by contracts: limited and well-defined is your power." Being transformed from a legitimate ruler to a leader who arbitrarily becomes a law-breaker, Wotan's downfall leads to the destruction of his entire society for not only did he have no noble ends for which his power was secured but he corrupted everything he touched. Valhalla was his vain attempt to institutionalize and entrench his strength by increasing his security, thereby hopefully thwarting all potential threats to his regime. It did not work.

Wagner was fascinated with political figures and the politics of force. But power begets power. Throughout history one finds well-intentioned leaders suddenly becoming arbitrary, perverting both themselves and their authority in the process of rule. Wotan was just such a being. A noble and decent leader is gradually, imperceptibly at first, transformed into a wielder of power who seeks to manipulate people and events, and ultimately betrays his trust, thereby precipitating his downfall. This was Robespierre: this is Metternich!

Wagner was clear-sighted enough to realize that the political destiny of any government affects the economic and social activities of its people. Any change in government, especially one as drastic as Wagner envisaged, would affect economic fortunes and some individuals would be reluctant to join a revolutionary cause for fear of financial ruin. Wagner not only appealed to all people to fearlessly join the revolt, but also had a compassionate understanding for those who were too afraid to side with the republicans.

> We see an anxious worried face, that of an honest and industrious citizen. He has worked

> and struggled his whole life, long and
> faithfully served the common weal, as far as
> his strength allowed him; no tears, no
> injustice taints the little sheaf which he has
> fathered through his fruitful efforts, to
> support **him** in his weak old age and **his**
> children as they enter a hostile world.
> Certainly he felt the approach of the storm,
> certainly he realizes no power can resist it,
> but his heart bleeds as he looks back on his
> arduous existence, the sole fruit of which is
> now destined to be destroyed. We must not
> condemn him if he clutches anxiously at his
> little nest-egg and in his blind fervour vainly
> resists the impending change[46] with all his
> strength. Harken unfortunate!

Wagner recognized the psychology of fear and the
nervous anticipation of economic dislocation but
appealed to the masses to look squarely at their
current financial problems. Neither the common man nor
even the majority of the middle class had a say in the
political and economic issues affecting them. As
industrialism intensified, the money paid to workers
and farmers had not kept pace with the vast profits
realized by the owners of the factories; consequently,
hardships were common. Conditions could be bettered
only by a radical transformation of the entire system.
Wagner called upon the most disenfranchised groups--the
factory workers and the farmers--to give their total
support to accomplish this goal. His poetic imagery had
seldom been as eloquent:

> Look, there come thousands pouring from the
> factories; they have labored and produced the
> finest cloths, but they themselves and their
> children are naked, they freeze and hunger for
> it is not to **them** that the fruits of their
> labour belong, they belong to the rich and
> mighty, who call the earth, and its inhabitants
> their **own**. See how they come from the farms and
> villages; they have tilled the soil and made
> of it a garden of plenty, and their efforts
> have produced crops in abundance, enough to
> feed every man alive--and yet they are poor and
> hungry and naked, for it is not to them and the
> others who are in need that the earth's gifts

----

[46] "The Revolution," 171.

belong, they belong to the rich and mighty, who call earth and its inhabitants their own."[47]

Wagner cajoled his readers into recognizing that through revolution not only would the old model be destroyed but through the same process a new model would be created. "All that exists must pass away, that is the eternal law of nature, the rule of life..."[48]

Fasolt and Fafner in **Rheingold** have many similarities to the workers who are being thwarted by conditions which they are impotent to change. Honest, hard-working, industrious, through the sweat of their brows they had faultlessly built the impregnable fortress for the gods. Having themselves acted in good faith, they suddenly, and unsuspectingly find themselves betrayed by the duplicity of their betters. The giants, like thousands of workers, are not as intellectual as their rulers but they represent honest and sincere workers who provide society with the labor needed to sustain life. They look to their rulers for fairness and for the protection of their interests, and believe in the sanctity of simple verbal agreements. Fasolt, speaking for any member of the working class, tells Wotan: "You have more wisdom that we have wits; you bound us, who were free, to keep peace: I will curse all your wisdom and flee from your place if openly, honorably and freely you do not know to keep faith in your bond!" It is a searing indictment. Both in the Fatherland speech and in the **Ring** Wagner illustrated the active role played by the leaders of society in fomenting the very political and economic power struggles facing mid-nineteenth century Europe.[49]

---

[47] **Ibid.**, 172.

[48] These words Wagner would later assign to Erda, the archetype of earth-mother, in **The Ring**.

[49] As early as **The Flying Dutchman** Wagner illustrated how tempting money is and what an avaricious man might be willing to sacrifice in order to obtain wealth. Having just met the Dutchman and after being shown his wealth, Daland is most willing to have him as a son-in-law. When the Dutchman proclaims that "all my riches would I offer you if with your people I could find a home", Daland immediately seizes upon the offer. His materialistic and shallow value system are sharply contrasted with those of the Dutchman who would willingly give it all away if only he could find

113

Having shown how the old order enslaved man to the political and economic domination of others, Wagner enlarged the scope of his argument. The old order "springs from sin, its flower is misery, and its fruit is crime", but the masses through no fault of their own had permitted materialism to eclipse even spiritual values; as a consequence all of society had become corrupted. The new society would have to introduce conditions permitting man's "creative power" to flourish so that one could take pleasure in all that might be created.

In the final paragraph Wagner summarized in poetic rapture his romantic perceptions of man, the German world of 1849, and what remained to be done:

> I will destroy the existing order of things which divides mankind into hostile nations, into strong and weak, into those with rights and those without, into rich and poor, for this order simply makes **wretches** of all. I will destroy the order of things which makes millions into slaves of the few, and these few into slaves of their own paper and their own wealth. I will destroy this order of things which divides work from enjoyment, which makes work a burden and enjoyment a vice, and renders **one** man miserable through want and **the other** miserable through excess. ... I will wipe from the face of the earth every trace of this crazy order of things, this compact of violence, lies, worry, hypocrisy, poverty, misery, suffering, tears, deceit and crime which fathers an occasional burst of impure lust, but almost never a ray of pure joy. Let there be an end to everything that oppresses you and makes you suffer, and from the ruins of this old world a new one shall arise, full of undreamed of happiness. ... you shall see yourselves as **brothers--all** you who live in it--and be free to recognize the value of life...[50]

Attempting to illustrate in music-drama all the problems previously discussed in his political writings, Wagner showed how moral standards had been
----
genuine love and compassion.

[50] "The Revolution," 172.

corrupted by political chicanery, how economic domination of the classes had gone unchecked by those eager to capitalize on the naivete of the masses, and how religion as an ethical force remained indifferent to the sufferings of the volk. At the end of the **Ring,** after the destruction of the gods and with them the old corrupt political and economic system, Brünnhilde in the original version declared: "Not goods, nor gold, nor greatness of gods; not house, nor land, nor lordly life; not burdensome bargains' treacherous bands, not want with the lying weight of the law; happy, in luck or need, holds you nothing but love."[51] His endlessly repetitious themes of love, brotherhood, and compassion would forever remain the new trinity upon which a new perfect order of society could be built: "What is to be the fate of this poem, the poem of my life and all that I am and feel, I cannot yet decide."[52]

Wagner knew that his radicalism meant trouble for him but he had now made a commitment and there was no turning back. "After what I have said, who can be so intentionally blind as not to see that I have there [in Dresden] no longer any choice, where I could only now determinately turn my back upon a world to which, in my inmost nature, I had long since ceased to belong?"[53] Within a month revolution broke out in Dresden and while it is impossible to say how much of a role Wagner played in the events leading up to it, his article certainly contributed to the radical climate of the day.

Shortly thereafter Wagner reinforced his ideas in **Art and Revolution.** The capitalistic system, through the veneration and power of wealth, could buy even fame, and with fame and power the upper classes became the patrons of the arts. Gold buys power, and power dictates taste. One can easily see here the origin of a theme brought out with exceptional clarity in **The Ring.** Wagner's conception of art would be to depict this reality: "Out of what can the artist **create** if he does not create **out of life,** and how can this life contain

----

[51] Richard Wagner, **Gesammelte Schriften und Dichtungen,** Vierte Auflage, 12 vols., Leipzig, 1907, Vol. 6, 254-6. English translation appears in Ernest Newman, **The Life of Richard Wagner,** London, 1946, Vol. 4, 481.

[52] Wagner to Liszt, 9 November 1852, Altmann, 1:238.

[53] **Communication,** 381.

an artistically productive essence unless it impels the Artist[54] continually to creations which correspond to life?"

The wealthy classes by controlling the economic system have power over the masses: "our modern factories afford us the sad picture of the deepest degradation of man,--constant labour, killing both body and soul, without joy or love, often almost without

---

[54] Wagner to Liszt, 8 September 1852, **Wagner-Liszt Correspondence,** 1:221. Never personally sympathetic toward the business and commercial elements in society, Wagner often considered them to be parasites and corrupters of taste. Yet several years later in **Die Meistersinger** he presented Pogner, a role "I read with special warmth", as an exception, perhaps even as the archetype of the truly enlightened businessman. Representing the Protestant and emerging capitalistic work-ethic, willing to assume a stewardship role as protector and defender of society and its institutions, Pogner automatically, and perhaps unthinkingly, assumed the need for institutions of political and social control. Thanking God for having provided him with his wealth, Pogner articulates the responsibilities incumbent upon him. Recognizing that he has been chosen for financial success not for his own glory but to serve as a means for the betterment of those less fortunate, Pogner willingly accepts the social contract by which he has a responsibility toward the people of Nürnberg. As a businessman he often hears criticism leveled against Protestants by some Catholics who accuse him, and others, of being too interested in business and financial matters, including the lending of money for interest. Subjected to the criticism that the newly-emergent and rising burgher class is interested primarily in financial acquisition, Pogner assures his attentive listeners that the accusation is untrue: "it has often vexed me that people honour the burgher so little, call him stingy and peevish: at courts and in meaner places I grew tired of the bitter reproach that only in usury and money was the burgher interested." Nürnberg, where the Protestant guilds were famous for their love of culture and refinement, enjoyed a reputation as one of the most famous free cities in Europe for "we alone in the broad German empire still cherish Art--by that they set little store. ... we treasure what is beautiful and good." Sixteenth-century Nürnberg, however, was not nineteenth century Dresden.

aim." Here Wagner returned to one of the themes to be found in his article "The Revolution", but this time he extended his analysis to include religion as an accomplice of business in the betrayal of humanity. Religion and monetary power formed an unholy partnership whereby man was further enslaved. By preaching that man's happiness should not be expected on earth but was to be found in some intangible future world, the church abrogated all social responsibility. Vested economic interests became the protectors and defenders of organized religion. They entrenched and perpetuated a relationship which debased the very dignity of man. "And thus we see with horror the spirit of modern Christianity embodied in a cotton-mill: to speed the rich, God has become our Industry, which only holds the wretched Christian labourer to life until the heavenly courses of the stars of commerce bring round the gracious dispensation that sends him to a better world."[55]

Where is the beauty and dignity of the honest, hard-working laborer, and what is his lot to be? For two thousand years man has been at the mercy of reactionary forces and these have "dragged down the fair, free man to itself, to slavery; the slave has not become a freeman, but the freeman a slave."

Throughout the course of history the ideal arrangement among power elites was to be able to combine political with economic power thereby consolidating control. Traditionally, when political and economic power were found in rival hands, the likelihood of conflict was ever present. During the 1840's the conservative entrenched political class viewed the rising power of the middle class with concern, just as the middle class saw, with some alarm, the untapped potential strength of the lower classes. How to obtain power while denying it to another represented one major theme brought out in the conflict between Wotan and Alberich. Each was jealous and intimidated by the power of his rival.

When Alberich points out that "envy led you to Nibelheim" a major idea is presented with alarming directness: those who wield political power will go to any length to entrench their power base by trying, if at all possible, to absorb the economic system; if this can not be done, the alternative was to form some

----
[55] "Art and Revolution," **PW**, 1:42.

acceptable accommodation with those who did wield economic power. On the other hand, those in control of the economic forces were just as likely to exert as much political influence and domination as they could, their goal being to make and control the political processes together with its decision-making apparatus. In both cases the stakes were high and neither position was likely to be compromised unless there was no alternative.

When Wotan asked Alberich a seemingly simple question, "But what help is the hoard to you since Nibelheim is joyless and treasures can buy nothing?", a gratuitous remark intimating that economic power alone was inconclusive, Alberich retorted: "I intend to work wonders: with it I will win the whole world for my own." He is to be taken seriously. Since economic power often has enough strength and power to take over, control, and manipulate political power, Wotan is determined not to permit this to happen. Later, when Wotan does secure Alberich's economic power, he feels less threatened: "Now I possess what will make me the mightiest of mighty lords!" During a moment of quiet introspection in the second act of **Die Walküre**, Wotan is finally able to admit to himself: "Impetuous wishes roused me to madness and I won the world for myself. With unwitting dishonesty I acted disloyally, by treaties I made alliances with powers concealing evil." He admits the trickery through which he acquired his power and "rises to the tragic height of **willing** his own destruction. This is the lesson that we have to learn from the history of mankind: to will what **necessity imposes**, and ourselves to bring it about."[56]

The attempt by the upper class to prevent others from securing any economic or political power prompted the radicalism of Wagner's day, giving him the crux for the **Ring**. But however much the upper and middle classes fought for control between themselves, it was traditionally at the expense of the lower class.

Wagner now came to the heart of his argument: only a full-scale revolution could change man's economy, society, political systems, culture, and religion. Revolution was the only means left to attain a new universality and a new set of values.

---

[56] Wagner to Röckel, **Letters**, 97.

In calling for universalism in art, Wagner's romanticism again emerged with clarity and eloquence. In some future day "the Art-work of the Future must embrace the spirit of a free mankind, delivered from every shackle of hampering nationality; its racial imprint must be no more than an embellishment, the individual charm of manifold diversity, and not a cramping barrier."[57] This statement expressed a visionary goal in which condition of nation, race, and class became superfluous; brotherhood was to be the driving force of the new society. Because traditional nationalism was concerned with one particular State it tended to shackle the rest of mankind. Revolution was the dynamic catalyst that would permit the emergence of a new unified, concept of internationalism: "If people cannot understand how to guard against the old (barbaric) abuses--such as unequal possession, etc., history will have to begin from the beginning again in order to teach us anew and still more forcibly."[58]

But if man's contemporary values were wrong and needed to be replaced, what would be the source of inspiration for a new set of values? Once again, although on this occasion he dealt with the question in a rather perfunctory manner, nature helped supply the answer. Within man, deeply buried, was to be found many of the true values which--if permitted to emerge--would form the building blocks for the future: "Nature, Human Nature, will proclaim this law to the twin sisters Culture and Civilisation: 'So far as I am contained in you, shall ye live and flourish; so far as I am not in you, shall ye rot and die!'"[59]

Although Wagner, at this time, did not explain the source of these values, they were undoubtedly related to the transcendental and mystical thoughts introduced in **Tannhäuser** and **Lohengrin**. In many ways the fate of Wagner, the creative artist, and that of society were obviously connected. In the first three music-dramas he was concerned with problems relating to alienation. Raising questions in **The Flying Dutchman**, **Tannhäuser**, and **Lohengrin** regarding whether certain individuals should or could be reconciled with society, Wagner

---

[57] **The Art-Work of the Future, PW,** 1:53-4.

[58] "Thoughts on the Regeneration of Mankind and of Culture," **The Brown Book,** 201.

[59] **The Art-Work of the Future,** 55.

answered the question in the negative. Now in 1849 he was seeking to produce a new social climate whereby he, as the embodiment of the personalities of his three music-dramas, could survive as an integral part of a new society whose values would permit the flourishing of the "Art-work of the Future." Wagner needed and wanted a home, a place within the right kind of society.

One must keep in mind the circumstances under which **Art and Revolution** had been written. Wagner had departed Germany for Zurich and had then gone on to Paris. The essay was written in Paris, before he finally established roots in Zurich. His interest in art became the key to a universalism of the future: "It is for Art therefore, and Art above all else, to teach this social impulse its noblest meaning, and guide it toward its true direction." The present offered man nothing, but the future offered hope. Was the goal attainable? Wagner argued forcefully in the affirmative.

Wagner realized that some would consider his ideas as visionary, or mere utopian rhetoric. He rejected this categorically:

> If history knows an actual Utopia, a truly unattainable ideal, it is that of Christianity; for it has clearly and plainly shown, and shows it still from day to day, that the dogmas are not realizable. How could these dogmas become really living, and pass over into actual life: when they were directed against life itself, and denied and cursed the principle of living? Christianity is of purely spiritual, and super-spiritual contents; it preaches humility, renunciation, contempt of every earthly thing; and amid this contempt--Brotherly Love! How does the fulfillment work out in the modern world, which calls itself, forsooth, a Christian world, and clutches to the Christian religion as its inexpugnable basis?[60]

Wagner concluded **Art and Revolution** by answering the statement which he posited in the introduction: "to discover the meaning of Art as a factor in the life of the State." The answer was unequivocal--not only

---

[60] **Ibid.**, 59-60.

would Art lead man to the better future, but it would
be the means of intercession between man and God:

> Fathom ye our purpose, and help us to lift up
> Art to its due dignity; that so we may show
> you how ye raise mechanical toil therewith to
> Art, and the serf of industry to the fair,
> self-knowing man who cries, with smiles
> begotten of intelligence, to sun and stars, to
> death and to eternity: 'Ye, too, are mine, and
> I am your lord!'
>
> Thus would **Jesus** have shown us that we all
> alike are men and brothers; while **Apollo** would
> have stamped this mighty bond of brotherhood
> with the seal of strength and beauty, and led
> mankind from doubt of its own worth to
> consciousness of its highest godlike might.
> Let us therefore erect the altar of the future,
> in Life as in the living Art, and to the
> sublimest teachers of mankind:--**Jesus, who
> suffered for all men;** and **Apollo, who raised
> them to their joyous dignity!**[61]

Art and Revolution not only emphasized the importance
of art to the destiny of mankind but it attempted to
provide a rational psychological justification for
Wagner's involvement in the Dresden revolution.

Wagner later tended to underplay his actual role
in the street fighting which broke out, and in **My Life**
vividly related how he saw or chose to see the events
which finally forced him to flee the city after
Prussian troops had been called in to quash the revolt.
The Dresden police issued a warrant calling for his
arrest on the grounds of treason, a crime punishable by
death. Rightly or wrongly, Wagner was considered one of
the principal ringleaders.[62]

Less than a week later Wagner wrote to a friend
describing the events that had transpired. He

----
[61] **Ibid.**, 63, 65.

[62] Röckel was arrested and condemned to death, but his
sentence was later commuted to life imprisonment. He
was finally released from jail in 1862. During the
period of his incarceration Wagner continued to write
to him but the censors prohibited any mention of
political matters.

categorically denied that the revolution had been premeditated; indeed, "the assault on the arsenal was the impulsive act of an unarmed populace, which after the ban on the parade of the citizens' militia, felt itself betrayed."[63] For his own part Wagner denied that he had ever addressed or encouraged the rioters; on the contrary, he claimed that he counseled them to end their violence. But the unexpected arrival of a foreign army precluded a peaceful accommodation. The radicals then saw their mission as a fight to release "the King from the oppressive Prussian influence. ... it was not the republic, red or blue, not Poland, nor Russia that from then inspired the most bitter and pitiless resistance in the struggles at the barricades, but simply the utterly subjective, personal fury of the citizens and the populace against the army..." As for his role, Wagner stated categorically that "at no point was I active, either with weapons or with public speeches: and I never had any kind of official position in the provisional government."

The true extent of Wagner's participation in the insurrection was neither as innocent as he would have others believe, nor as personally involved so as to indicate that he possessed a deeply-entrenched political or aesthetic ideology. Evidence suggests that he was more committed to its success than he was willing to admit in **My Life** although the reasons which underlay his commitment might have less to do with ideology than with other more personal factors.

The charge of opportunism is always a matter to be taken into consideration. Wagner had previously made suggestions to the king which would likely have enhanced his own artistic position within the Dresden musical scene, and at the expense of others. The king's unwillingness to reorganize the structure of the Court Theatre was both frustrating to Wagner personally and likely to prevent reforms that might enhance the prestige of the opera. Cultural frustration could have found its release by a more theatrical political revolution. That Wagner personally liked the king did not create any less of a desire to see done whatever had to be accomplished in the name of art. If revolution proved to be an instrument for the attainment of ends which he considered legitimate and important for the future, so be it. Nevertheless, while undoubtedly true that Wagner would personally benefit,

---

[63] Wagner to Eduard Devrient, 17 May 1849, Barth, 175.

his cultural and political stance clearly went beyond self-interest.

Five days after he fled Dresden, leaving his wife behind until he was able to find temporary living accommodations somewhere, Wagner wrote Minna and explained or rationalized his thoughts about the aborted coup: "wherever I trod I was hurt, with an inward fury I finally turned my back to my art which yielded me nothing but suffering. ... I was at variance with this world. I ceased to be an artist. I frittered away my creative powers, and became a mere revolutionary if not in deeds, at least in conviction; that is, I was seeking in a wholly transformed world the ground for some new art creations of my spirit."[64] These psychological insights are incisive. Wagner had recurring debt problems and his career, although developing slowly, was being stifled by an entrenched conservatism that brought him great impatience. Still close in time to the event, Wagner rationalized that his participation in the revolution was "in order to be able to **construct** something on fresh ground; it is not **destruction** which attracts us but the **formation of something new,** and that is why we are not the kind of men whom Destiny needs--these will arise from the lowest dregs of the people; we and our hearts cannot have anything in common with them. You see! **Thus I am parting with the Revolution."**

Whether Wagner's letter to his wife was sincere or not is conjectural. Minna disapproved of many of his activities and disliked several of his friends. She did not understand why Wagner should be engaged in any activity which could compromise his secure court position. His salary while not exceptionally high did permit a comfortable life-style and he seemed to have had few genuine worries at the time. Even his own works were being given a fair hearing and they had been achieving some degree of success. As far as she was concerned Wagner had little reason for radicalism. Wagner's letter could well have been designed to pacify her annoyance at his activities, and could even have been written because of his growing uncertainty over whether Minna would join him in exile. He tried to persuade her that "I have become an entire **artist** again. I **love** my art again."

----
[64] Wagner to Minna Wagner, 14 May 1849, Burrell, 227.

Several days later he again wrote, trying to reassure her that his friendship with Bakunin had little to do with politics but everything to do with "human and artistic interests." But when he found out that a warrant had been issued calling for his arrest, Wagner became less conciliatory: "Good, then! So be it. The measure of the torment of my soul is full: at last--I feel **free** once more."[65] Several months later while being interrogated by the police, Bakunin commented: "I soon saw that Wagner was a mere dreamer, and although I talked to him, even on politics, I never worked in common with him."[66]

Actually, both men were withholding information. In the police charge against Wagner seven points of evidence were brought forward, the most important ones being that Wagner knew and worked intimately with Bakunin and Röckel and that secret meetings took place at Wagner's house, and in the gardens. More seriously, during one of the garden meetings Wagner discussed the feasibility of "arming the populace..." If true, Wagner's involvement was infinitely more immediate than he admitted to anyone. Röckel, when brought to trial, stated: "Wagner, who was interested in arming the people, had lent me his garden for a discussion on this project...[67]

After fighting broke out Wagner was "attracted by surprise and interest in the drama, without feeling any desire to join the ranks of the combatants",[68] a charge flatly denied by others who saw him personally involved in manning the barricades. Wagner then climbed the church tower where he had a better view of the proceedings but "even from this elevation I could not see anything clearly." Several witnesses offered a fuller account of this incident which Wagner trivializes in **My Life**. According to them, Wagner climbed the church tower to "observe the positions of

----

[65] Wagner to Minna Wagner, 19 May 1849, Burrell, 234.

[66] Woldemar Lippert, **Wagner in Exile**, 1849-62, Paul England, trans., undated, 191. Lippert was keeper of the principal public archives of Saxony.

[67] **Ibid.**, 192. According to Lippert this information comes from the Wagner dossier presented at Röckel's trial.

[68] **My Life**, 1:476.

the troops and the approach of the insurgents from the country." Rather than being a mere observer he was responsible for "sending messages, [by] throwing down notes tied to stones from the tower gallery."[69] Some of the troops reportedly even went with Wagner! This charge was contained in the police indictment against him and was actually admitted by Röckel at his trial. It must be remembered, however, that this evidence came out later, and before the court. By that time Wagner had made good his escape and was therefore in no immediate danger. Damaging evidence against someone not present could have worked for the advantage of those on trial. The extent to which it can be proved true or false is based only on conjecture.

A few years later while reflecting back to this period of his life and on those political and economic happenings which would find some significant expression and meaning in the **Ring**, Wagner commented:

> my entire politics consists of nothing but the bloodiest hatred for our whole civilization, contempt for all things deriving from it, and a longing for nature. This, of course can't be understood by a man who felt so enchanted with the industrial exhibition. Well, now you have that exhibition an exhibition on the pillory, with all your industrial workers! I must now atone for thinking so highly of workers as workers. With all their clamor about labor, they are the most miserable of slaves whom anybody may pocket who promises them a lot of 'work' at the moment. ... Yet I don't despair of a better future, only the most terrific and destructive Revolution could make our civilized beasts 'human' again.[70]

On various occasions over the next few years Wagner tried unsuccessfully to obtain an amnesty. Once, in 1853, word reached Germany that Wagner might secretly attempt to reenter. Immediately the Saxon police issued a further warrant, complete with a picture of him, so that "anyone meeting with this man

---

[69] Lippert, 192.

[70] Wagner to Ernst Kietz, 30 December 1851, Burrell, 187.

must arrest him and hand him over to the Royal Court of Justice in Dresden."[71]

In 1854 King John the brother of Frederick Augustus II ascended the throne of Saxony. Shortly thereafter Wagner appealed directly to him for an amnesty. It was now seven years since the revolution. Hoping to convince the new king of his altruistic rather than political motives, Wagner stated that his previous political activities including his abrupt departure from Dresden "was moved not so much by the fear of not obtaining a favourable verdict as by my despair of ever finding sufficient scope for the realization of my artistic ideas..."[72] Stating that his involvement in political and economic affairs was conditioned only by a fundamental belief that a new world order would be more conducive to a new artistic order, Wagner declared: "Politics and the events of the day concerned me only in so far as I felt it my duty to try to bend my material aims to my artistic purposes." Now that he has had seven years to reflect on his past mistakes and his "reckless action", Wagner appealed to the new king to permit him to return "to my Fatherland. My art it is that binds me with indissoluble bonds to Germany, since only there can I hope to see my music dramas produced."

Wagner's appeal was rejected, but not before all the evidence was carefully examined by the Ministry of Justice and by the King who actually initialed the draft copy of the letter denying approval of his petition. It appears that the king was actually interested in seeing Wagner return, but the extent of the hard evidence against him precluded a favorable verdict. This might be viewed as a further indication of Wagner's active political participation in 1849.

One year later the Grand Duke of Baden wrote to King John requesting that Wagner be permitted to visit Baden for a period of four weeks. In refusing this royal request King John made an especial point of indicating that his late brother had agreed to amnesty for most of the participants who had stood trial, but Wagner had fled and the administration of justice, in

---

[71] **Allgemeiner Polizei-Anzeiger**, 11 June 1853, as quoted in Lippert, 39.

[72] Wagner to King John of Saxony, 16 May 1856, Lippert, 65.

his case, had been thwarted. Admitting that "circumstances are strongly against him" the king went further in expressing his current attitude toward Wagner:

> When he came to Dresden, a poor man, unknown, and burdened with debts, my brother, recognizing his genius, gave him an excellent appointment, such as he was hardly entitled to expect. These benefactions Wagner repaid with base ingratitude; he not only endeavoured to excite those under him to hostile demonstrations against the Government, but also--or so, at least, it is believed--took an active part in the traitorous attempts of May 1849. Your Royal Highness will therefore understand that, while something might be said for the other culprits, such a man as this deserves no more than the sternest justice.[73]

Year after year Wagner appealed to friends and influential rulers to intercede on his behalf. Most of his arguments were artistic and related to a desire to produce and hear his own musical compositions. Believing that his music-dramas were inherently German, he argued that as a German composer he needed and wished to return to Germany; yet, unlike the others who were involved with the insurrection he was unwilling to stand trial on the charges against him.

It would be twelve years before Wagner was finally able to return to Germany. By August 1860 the political climate had changed. But even then he did not receive a full pardon nor was the amnesty unconditional: "... I am neither amnestied nor has my sentence been remitted. All I have obtained is the promise that the claim to extradition will be abandoned whenever, for the purpose of performing my work, I wish to enter a German territory, the government of which has given its consent, and asked permission of the Saxon Government. ... Our German potentates cannot enter into direct communication with me for I am still a political outlaw..."[74] The pardon, but not political forgiveness, was declared by the king in 1860. Wagner replied: "The

----
[73] John, King of Saxony to Frederick, Grand Duke of Baden, 2 December 1857, Lippert, 78-9.

[74] Wagner to Liszt, 13 September 1860, **Wagner-Liszt Correspondence**, 2:324.

concession provides for all that is most important for the development of my artistic productions, and in return for this great favour I feel compelled to the present expression of my deepest and most sincere gratitude..."[75] Finally, in 1862 Wagner received a full amnesty and could now enter every part of Germany: "His Majesty, the King, in answer to the petition for pardon presented directly by you, is pleased to exempt you from any further prosecution on account of your participation in the treasonable enterprise of May 1849, and the criminal proceedings therewith connected, and to grant you the right of free reentry into Saxony."[76]

After fourteen years Wagner could now return to Dresden where his estranged wife had been living. Even though separated, Minna had played a significant role in obtaining Wagner's full pardon and he was grateful.

Strangely enough Wagner clearly had mixed feelings about the thought of reentering Germany: "With real horror I think of Germany and of my future enterprises in that country." For the many years that he has been involved in the ideas centering around the **Ring**, the degeneracy of contemporary Germanic life and thought has been paramount in his mental outlook. Whatever optimism did exist in Wagner's psyche would relate to a yet to be realized Germanic spirit which might emerge if conditions permitted; but how and when this might occur were still problematical. For the moment he was under no illusions: "... we have no Fatherland, and if I am 'German' it is because I carry my Germany along with me."[77] Having lived for so many years away from Germany, Wagner was both dubious and nervous about returning. Word of his initial amnesty reached him while in Paris but his feelings were mixed: "I feel too deplorably homeless, and ask myself: where dost thou, then belong? A question I can answer with no country's name, no town's, no hamlet's; all, all are foreign to me..."[78]

---

[75] Wagner to Most Serene Monarch, August King and Lord, 26 July 1860, Lippert, 144.

[76] The Ministry of Justice to the former Kapellmeister, Herr Richard Wagner, 28 March 1862, Lippert, 161.

[77] Wagner to Liszt, **op. cit.**, 327.

[78] Wagner to Mathilde Wesendonck, 3 March 1860,

As letters of congratulations and telegrams poured in, Wagner's uncertainty increased: "this is nothing to me but the opening of a new field of suffering, of suffering that certainly outweighs all chance of any kind of gratification, in measure as I see nothing in front of me but sacrifices on my own part." All he could feel at the moment was that the amnesty "left me utterly cold and indifferent."[79]

While in Paris in 1860 Wagner supervised a new production of **Tannhäuser**. Happy over the elaborate preparations being undertaken to ensure the success of the production, he expressed the hope that "some German prince would do the same for my new works." During the following year he returned to the subject matter of **Die Meistersinger**, completely rewrote the prose sketch, and by January 1862 completed the poem. Unexpectedly, two years later, Wagner got his wish when Ludwig II of Bavaria summoned him to Munich and assumed responsibility for his livelihood. Wagner had achieved his wish and was ecstatic over his first meeting with the young king: "He wants me to stay near him always, to work, to rest, to have my works performed; he wants to give me everything I shall need for that purpose; I must finish the 'Nibelungen' and he will have it performed as I want. I shall be completely my own master, not a court Kapellmeister, nothing but myself and his friend."[80] With profound gratitude Wagner wrote a short poem entitled, "To the Kingly Friend," and sent it to the king:

> My King, thou rarest shield of this my living!
> Of bounteous good, thou overbrimming hoard!
> I seek in vain, at goal of all my striving,
> To match thy favouring grace with fitting word!
> Both tongue and pen are hush'd in sore misgiving,
> And yet o'er many a record have I por'd
> To find the word, the only word, to bear thee

Wesendonck, **Letters**, 213.

[79] Wagner to Mathilde Wesendonck, 22 July 1860, **Letters**, 236.

[80] Wagner to Eliza Wille, 4 May 1864, Eliza Wille, **Fünfzehn Briefe von Richard Wagner mit Erinnerungen und Erläuterungen**, Munich-Berlin-Zurich, 1935, 64, quoted in Barth, 204.

The thanks that deep within my heart I wear
thee.
                    ...
So comes to blissful rest in thy good pleasure
My round of work fulfill'd and yet to be:
And since no shade of fearing thou hast left
me,
The very seed and root of Hope thou'st reft
me.

Thus am I poor, with but one sole possession,
The Faith whereto belief of thine is wed:
'Tis that, the bulwark of my proud confession,
'Tis that, whereby my Love is steel'd and fed;
Yet shared, lo! mine is but a half-possession,
And wholly lost to me, should thine have fled.
So but from thee my strength to thank is
taken,
Through thine own kingly Faith of strength
unshaken.[81]

After establishing his residence at Munich it was
not long before Wagner began to discuss political
matters with the king: "he already imagined himself
joint ruler of the whole kingdom of Bavaria."[82]
Whether or not Wagner initiated the political dialogues
is conjectural and there is evidence that he was
uncomfortable in his new position as confident of the
king. That Ludwig was infatuated with Wagner's music,
and in Wagner as a person, is clear enough. But Wagner
clearly recognized both the predicament he was in and
the delicate nature of his relationship to Ludwig's
court: "Why this cup? Why must I find, in the very
place where I sought peace and leisure to work, a
responsibility forced upon me..."[83] Despite his feigned
innocence it was a role Wagner enjoyed.

Living comfortably for the first time in his life,
Wagner returned to the musical sketch of **Siegfried**. But
ever desirous of putting into practice some of his
still-imprisoned thoughts, during the nineteen months
that Wagner spent in Munich he gradually began to
----
[81] "To the Kingly Friend," Summer, 1864, **PW**, 4:1-2.

[82] Friedrich Pecht, **Aus meiner Zeit**, Munich 1894, Vol.
2, 134, quoted in Barth, 205.

[83] Wagner to Eliza Wille, 26 February 1865, Altmann,
2:212.

assume a more aggressive political stance with the impressionable king. His timing was most inopportune. The premiere of **Tristan und Isolde** had not gone well. One Munich newspaper called it "the glorification of sensual pleasure." Although Wagner chose to see his influence on the king primarily as an opportunity to enlighten him on matters of artistic importance, others viewed it as a political scandal. A few were hopeful:

> Wagner is also playing politics with the king... The king is supposed to have asked what his views were on German affairs, and ever since Wagner has been sending him regular letters expounding his opinions.

> It's bound to lead to trouble, an artist getting any real influence in the running of the State... The circumstances are really quite extraordinary. Things are looking so bad everywhere in Germany--Bavaria is the most important of the Central States--it's just possible that someone like Wagner, an inspired, protean spirit, who broadly speaking always pursues a single, noble ideal, could provide the impulse[84] needed to start a favourable development.

Wagner was so overwhelmed with the king's persistent generosity, breadth of vision, and intelligence that he began to view their friendship as an opportunity to mold and create Ludwig into the archetypal thinking artist. The king's influence over Wagner was equally clear: "There is a secret that can only be revealed to my exalted, gracious friend in the hour of my death: then he will understand fully what must seem obscure at present--that he alone is the creator and author of everything that the world will from now on attribute to my name."[85] Ludwig's youth, energy, and intelligence gave Wagner hope for the political and cultural future of Germany, providing the

---

[84] Peter Cornelius, 15 November 1865, **Ausgewählte Briefe**, Vol. 2, Leipzig, 1905, 25, quoted in Barth, 210-12.

[85] Wagner to Ludwig II, 6 November 1864, quoted in Barth, 205. Wagner's use of hyperbole is viewed by some as both insincere and self-serving; it may be. On the other hand, in letters to friends he expressed views similar to these when referring to the king.

king could develop into an enlightened monarch. He even once referred to Ludwig as Germany's "Savior." There was only one potential source of difficulty—the ultraconservative and even reactionary members of the Court. These men, of closed minds, were stifling the king's natural intelligence and creativity. Wagner's attitude would cause friction and lead ultimately to his downfall; but never could he remain politically and culturally passive when new opportunities for action were present.

Wagner's romantic nationalism once more emerged when he urged the king to create a German College of Music in Munich. His "meddling" in Bavaria's internal affairs prompted the intercession by the Minister of State whose impassioned letter to the king attacked Wagner's friendship as "unprecedented effrontery":

> This man has dared to assert that the members of Your Majesty's Cabinet, men who have proved their loyalty, do not enjoy the least respect among the people of Bavaria, yet it is rather he himself who is despised by every class of the people. ...

> This is the view, not only of the nobility and the clergy, but also of the respectable middle class and the workers who laboriously earn their bread by the sweat of their brows, while arrogant foreigners luxuriate in the proceeds of royal generosity and show their gratitude by slandering and mocking the Bavarian people and their affairs.

> ... while the cultivation of the arts and of ideals is a noble cause to flower from a healthy body politic and one becoming to a prince, it is not the primary and certainly not the only objective, especially in times like the present, when the very existence of states and thrones is under serious threat from many quarters, and when, therefore, there is a far greater need for action in the real world than for dreaming in the ideal world.[86]

---

[86] Ludwig Freiherr von der Pfordten to Ludwig II, 1 December 1865, Sebastian Röckl, 'Von der Pfordten und Richard Wagner', **Süddeutsche Monatshefte**, Munich, April 1928, 539, quoted in Barth, 212.

By no coincidence of timing, a newspaper article viciously attacking Wagner appeared the next day. Wagner was accused of an egocentric love of power: "money, a lot of money, and ever more money is what he wants!" The article ranged over a wide list of accusations against Wagner, mostly fictitious, but it served its purpose. Wagner prepared a rebuttal and it appeared in a rival paper but, as he wished, without his name. Nevertheless, the damage had been done. Instead of aiding his cause it kept the matter before the public, and served to widen the breach between the king and his ministers. Public and private pressures forced the eighteen year-old king, less than one week later, to make a determination that Wagner should leave Munich: "Believe me--I had to act as I did ... I could do no other", was all that Ludwig could say.

The newspaper **Der Volksbote** played the decisive role in alienating the public against Wagner: "The wildest consternation now greeted my supposed interference with the structure of the Cabinet and revealed itself forthwith in the well-known **Volksboten** agitations, in the course of which the King was audaciously held up to scorn and mockery."[87]

Bowing to pressure from the Minister of State who threatened to resign and cause a scandal unless Wagner was sent from Court, the King wrote: "My dear Minister of State, My decision is made.--R. Wagner must leave Bavaria [sic Munich]. I will show my beloved people that their trust, their love, are worth more to me than anything else.--You will know that it was not altogether easy for me; but I have overcome;--"[88]

Although their friendship continued, Wagner's influence on the king in non-musical matters ended with his departure from Munich in December 1865. He had become a cause celebre:

> Munich, 9 December. The news that Richard Wagner has been ordered to leave Bavaria ran through the city the day before yesterday **like wildfire**, which is enough in itself to show the extent and the depth of the agitation that the

---

[87] Wagner to Dr. Med Schanzenbach, 17 January 1867, Altmann, 2:230.

[88] Sebastian Röckl, 'Von der Pfordten und Richard Wagner', **op. cit.**, Barth, 213.

133

man has aroused by his behaviour. Expressions of the liveliest satisfaction have been voiced everywhere ... but a patriotic joy, which only increases as gradually more and more is learned of how, in spite of all the previous denials, Wagner has tried to exploit our youthful monarch's favour, even going so far as attempting to influence him in matters of state.[89]

In numerous letters to friends Wagner denied his influence on the king, claiming that he asked for money not for himself but "to raise the salaries of his poor Court musicians." Whether or not he was unjustly accused depends on who one wishes to believe. Wagner categorically denied giving the king anything other than general advice, having nothing to do with politics, but "immediately there was a violent uproar in the public press, pointing to my extravagance and my influence over the King, misleading him into all kinds of wild projects..."[90]

Wagner returned to Switzerland and commenced composing the music to **Die Meistersinger von Nürnberg**. Once again he internalized his ideas. Now he made Hans Sachs the "thinking artist."

---

[89] **Der Volksbote**, Munich, 10 December 1865, Barth, 213.

[90] Wagner to Julius Fröbel, 28 November 1865, Altmann, 2:221.

CHAPTER 4

"THE GERMAN SPIRIT"

The first performance of **Die Meistersinger** took place in Munich in 1868. Despite the fact that the composer was no longer a welcomed member at court, King Ludwig II attended and Wagner was invited to share the royal box. After the performance Wagner again left Munich and saw the king but once again before the opening of the Bayreuth Festival eight years later.

Shortly after Wagner first met the king, just four years earlier, he had been asked to prepare a paper indicating whether or not he had rethought any of his major ideas since they appeared in his earlier prose writings. Ludwig had read everything published to date. Contained in a short paper entitled "On State and Religion", Wagner's response represented his first major theoretical prose writing in thirteen years. Although it was not published until 1873, the article offers an opportunity to examine the extent to which Wagner's ideas remained consistent or were modified by the passage of more than a dozen years.

Being asked by the king to prepare a written statement regarding his current political and religious attitudes presented obvious problems. If Wagner were too forthright it could conceivably endanger the beginning of his relationship with the eighteen year old monarch, and perhaps economically jeopardize both the completion of the **Ring** and the chances for its successful presentation. For the first time in his life Wagner was beginning to enjoy a degree of security and stability which might be threatened if he were not prudent. Expressing himself too bluntly might cool the interest of the king toward him, and yet a paper which could influence the king on political and cultural matters might be of inestimable importance.

Candidly admitting that with the passage of time "a definite utterance becomes more and more difficult the older and more experienced one grows", Wagner claimed that his fundamental axiom remained unchanged: it is not life which permitted one to judge art but the reverse--art permits one to judge life! As Art must find a basis in "Life, in State, and lastly in Religion", Wagner was drawn to matters pertaining to politics, society, and religion. Politics, as such, did not attract him as much as the broad outlines of political philosophy. He had not, so he claimed, become a revolutionary to implement a specific ideological viewpoint or to espouse a narrowly parochial or monistic political cause. On the contrary, drawn to political philosophy because he took "Art in such uncommon earnest", Wagner's radicalism emerged as an obvious means to secure artistic and social ends. Possessing little interest in politics as a power game, except when it impinged on man's social and economic relationships, Wagner claimed that Germany in 1864 was ripe for self-examination. The time had come for an enlightened king, the "thinking artist", to correlate politics with the needs of society. Undeniably the needs of society would be best served by an acceptance of Wagner's musical and dramatic theories, not to mention his political, social, and religious points of view. When first writing about political matters in the late 1840's Wagner had become convinced that "my world will never make its entry until the very moment when the present world has ceased--in other words, where Socialists and Politicians came to end, should **we** commence."[1]

Since political ideas and artistic interests interrelate, and as passion in belief is part of art, he now turned to an enlightened king as the ultimate last hope for mankind. A truly enlightened monarch could improve the world for his talents and abilities gave him opportunities beyond those of any other member of the kingdom: "blindness is the world's true essence, and not Knowledge prompts its movements..."

The "State" is achieved by "a contract whereby the units seek to save themselves from mutual violence, through a little mutual practice of restraint"; therefore, stability is essential to the security of the State and is necessary for "a freer evolution of spiritual attributes." To "attain its true **ideal**", required the presence of a monarch who was beyond party and factionalism.

At this point Wagner introduced an idea brought out more subtly in **Die Meistersinger**. Although a realistic approach to life and its uncertainties was highly desirable, the average person existed by maintaining a set of illusions [wahn], seeing only his or her immediate interests and needs, and seeking ways of satisfying them. This limited perspective was

----
[1] "On State and Religion," **PW**, 4:8.

completely understandable. But a king can not rule in
the realm of illusion; instead he was, above all,
required to have a broad viewpoint which would permit
him to cut across the peripheral vision held by others.
If his depth and insights were the same as his people,
he could not be an effective leader. While illusions
may be tolerable for the populace they were unthinkable
in a king for whom enlightenment was the prerequisite
for the welfare of his subjects. Drawing upon this
assumption Wagner seems to correlate the king with the
"thinking artist." It was a dubious assumption.[2]

The relationship between the ruler and his
subjects required a delicate balance so that the
preservation of society may be inviolably secured. To
foster the best relationship between ruler and ruled
may require the use of an artificial catalyst.
Patriotism might serve as a useful means, an example of
a necessary illusion, binding people together. A
romantic attachment to a homeland would foster a belief
"that any violent transmutation of the State must
affect him [the common man] altogether personally, must
crush him to a degree which he believes he never could
survive..." While many would tend to see patriotism as
the assertion of a collective ego, Wagner, curiously
enough, saw it as just the opposite. Patriotism was
"the positive renunciation of egoism", and its symbol
is the king for he was the "live embodiment" of the
value of the state. Seeing this illusion as a necessity
for the common man, although not for the king, Wagner's
nationalistic bent seems oblivious to the likelihood of
a self-indulgent aggrandizement of the nation-state.

While the burghers and the common people may feel
the emotional force of patriotism and see the king as
the representative of the highest ideals of a state, to
the truly enlightened king there is a higher ideal:
"the interest of mankind in general", should transcend
the role of power. Reversing one of the cardinal
principles promulgated by Machiavelli and maintained by
countless political rulers for decades, Wagner asserted
that the power of one state need not be at the expense
of another. Nor is it a logical necessity that one
state must be greater in size, population, or materials

----
[2] A few years later, after Wagner's son Siegfried was
born, he commented to Cosima that the boy must have a
proper education: "otherwise he will become a dreamer,
maybe an idiot, the sort of thing we see in the King of
Bavaria." See **CW's Diaries**, 5 November 1869, 1:162.

than its neighbor. Although "injustice and violence toward other States and people have therefore been the true dynamic law of Patriotism", perhaps the time had now come for a new approach, a new "state of International Law."[3] Traditional ideas of patriotism may no longer by valid or "pure" or useful to the human race. And if patriotism was an illusion then it could represent a "constant menace to public peace and equity."

By reasserting these views Wagner's romanticism emerged as perhaps more illusory than even the false sense of patriotism that he had talked about creating. Again implying that man can never be free while a member of a particular race or state, Wagner's cosmopolitan attitudes had not undergone any appreciable modification over the years; but neither did he develop any practical wisdom regarding the nature of power and the political process.

Hans Sachs and Ludwig II had similar problems when trying to relate to, and deal with, human nature and society. But Ludwig lives, and as king he had both a responsibility and an obligation not just to Bavaria but to all Germany, whereas Sachs lived only historically and within the rarefied atmosphere of an enlightened free city in which the guilds were answerable only to themselves. But the king, like Sachs, must recognize and appreciate the limitations of his people: "the weakness of the average human intellect" and the myopia and deceptiveness of "public opinion." Although man can not live without illusions, these sometimes resulted in an "insatiable egoism" where even public opinion was misled by a false sense of patriotism. Occasionally this produced great mischief as well as power confrontations among rival states. The king must be on guard not to let this happen.

Ludwig was faced with one additional problem which was provoking degrees of mischief within his kingdom, a fairly free press. Wagner raised a query: was a free press desirable or useful to a kingdom? The existence of an uncensored free press sometimes acted as an incentive for creating and manipulating public opinion, taking the public along a particularly narrow prejudice or course of action. Quite often the news, sometimes disguised under the illusion of patriotism, could be

----
[3] "On State and Religion," 16.

dangerous to the welfare of society. Because it can all too easily spread the spirit of hatred and militarism, and since it often posited a belief in the exceptionalism of one State at the expense of another, the press can often be a counterbalance to the broader and more noble ideals held by an enlightened monarch. Wagner accused the press of sometimes being guilty of "utter want of independence and truthful judgment, behind the lofty mission of her subservience to this sole representative of human dignity, this Public Opinion, which marvelously bids her stoop to every indignity, to every contradiction, to to-day's betrayal of what she dubbed right sacred yesterday."

Denying the ability of the press to always maintain objectivity, Wagner conjectured that too often those who wrote for newspapers were "a literary failure or [from] a bankrupt mercantile career", while the owners are greedy for gold and seek "the sublimation of public spirit, or practical human intellect. ... with the invention of the art of printing, and quite certainly with the rise of journalism, man has gradually lost much of its capacity for healthy judgment."[4]

This criticism of the press was somewhat harsh, but given the nature of newspaper publishing in Munich in the 1860's Wagner's defensive posture may not be entirely unwarranted. That Wagner held these ideas is no surprise especially since he was so often the favorite target of newspapers. Although he never openly advocated censorship--his liberalism would not permit such a thought--it is ironic that within the next eighteen months the press would play a major role in fomenting hostility between the king's cabinet and Wagner, serving as the major fulcrum in forcing the king to ask Wagner to depart Munich. Perhaps Ludwig did not always read Wagner's articles as thoroughly as he claimed.

Because Bavaria was a relatively free and liberal kingdom, "the vulgar egoism of the masses" could prove a problem for any monarch. On one side was to be found a crass public opinion emanating from certain illusions having been created by the press, on the other side stood the monarch who not only needed to understand how these thoughts had developed, but must be able to transcend all parochial viewpoints. The king's moral

----
4 Ibid., 20.

fiat extended to all Europe, for he had a continental responsibility to seek accommodation with the other states for the benefit of humanity. Enlightenment meant recognizing and accepting a broad perception of the world, a view unlikely to be shared by all the monarch's subjects. Disparity between the perceptive ability of the king and his subjects was fraught with dangers that could lead to political instability. But "the King desires the Ideal, he wishes justice and humanity; ... True justice and humanity are ideals irrealisable: to be bound to strive for them, nay, to recognize an unsilenceable summons to their carrying out, is to be condemned to misery."[5] But the attempt must be made!

Wagner presented Ludwig with many random speculations, a mish-mash of coherent and incoherent thoughts, a series of questions with virtually no practical answers, and the idealistic ruminations of a romantic nationalist who saw Bavaria as capable of playing a truly major role in Europe and the world at large in the cause of humanity. Although not blind to the reality of power, Wagner was deceiving himself if he thought that this particular king could serve as a catalyst for the new type of romantic nationalism that he envisioned. Convinced that, "if he but thrives and prospers! Then at last the German nation will have for once the example it needs--something different from Frederick II."[6] Wagner would be crudely awakened from his reverie not by the king, but by his conniving ministers. Ludwig was but eighteen and infatuated with the ideas and music of the composer. Perhaps Wagner thought he could make the king into a "thinking artist", a poet-politician, but this was not to be. Hans Sachs could mold and guide Walther, but Ludwig was not so pliable.

Toward the end of 1865, Wagner's last few months in Munich, his interest in the question of a German identity reawakened. Beginning with the question, "What is German?", Wagner sought to answer what seemed, at first, a straight forward question. He soon discovered that it was far more complicated than he had ever imagined. Part of his attempted answer came in an article with the same simple title as the original question, but after it was finished Wagner decided

----

[5] Ibid., 22.

[6] Wagner to Eliza Wille, 30 April 1865, Altmann, 2:215.

against its publication. It finally appeared in 1878 as an appendix to a printed edition of his later work, "German Art and German Policy."

In searching for a national identity, one common to all Germanic-speaking peoples, Wagner was confronted with one obvious glaring reality: Germany was not a nation. Part of his search for that elusive nationalism that he mentally envisioned was the need to ascertain what might legitimately be designated and called "German." Recognizing that no great nation entertained doubts regarding its own identity, the fact that one so often heard talk of "German depth", "German earnestness", and "German fidelity", betrayed an immaturity within people. So many seemed to be desperately searching for that unifying cement behind which an identity might coalesce. Added to this can be found a self-consciousness brought about by the reality of regional divisiveness. In searching for the meaning behind the word "deutsch", Wagner found that it referred to no particular people at all. When "deutschland" was first used it represented only a "collective-name for all the races who had stayed this side of the Rhine."[7] In the early days of the middle ages only common elements of speech, not common customs, ideas, or traditions, served to identify the people. Nevertheless, Wagner believed that a "German spirit" existed throughout the middle ages.

Consistent with Wagner's romantic nationalism was a penchant on his part for interesting-sounding phrases that beg definition. Somehow, without defining what lurked beneath the surface, Wagner found something noble lying buried deep in the teutonic past. "The nation was annihilated, but the German spirit has passed through." He does not say what the "German spirit" is except to state the obvious, it isn't to be found here and now. But although elements of this elusive mystical "spirit" were "reborn" after the Thirty Years' War it arrived in an undesirable form which produced a curious current phenomenon: "German poetry, German music, German philosophy, are nowadays esteemed and honoured by every nation in the world: but in his yearning after 'German glory' the German, as a rule, can dream of nothing but a sort of resurrection of the Romish Kaiser-Reich, and the thought inspires the most good-tempered German with an unmistakable lust of mastery, a longing for the upper hand over other

----
[7] "What is German?", **PW**, 4:152.

141

nations."[8] A false illusion of German exceptionalism, rooted on the ideas of strength and power, represented a fallacious and dangerous concept of nationalism. Expedient military and political considerations can not form the cultural and moral base upon which ennobled ideas will grow.

This was not the only negative characteristic: "The Germans possess other qualities, such as envy and the correspondingly mischievous spitefulness, allied to a degree of insincerity, which is all the more pernicious because it wears the mark of old-time sturdiness."[9]

For an identity to emerge Germans must search for and find from within themselves qualities that apply to all humanity. In this regard Wagner's romanticism was not limited to Germans as Germans. There was a uniqueness in the true, if elusive, German spirit that offered opportunities that transcend nationality. The human race was infinitely more significant than the German race. Wagner tried to make a parallel by discussing what was most unique about Christianity--its ability to transcend nations and peoples. Christianity was not bound by geography. It was as universal as humanity. The German too had the "spirit" capable of "restoring the Purely-human itself to its pristine freedom." But the unfortunate desire for power corrupted virtually every German prince or king thereby preventing the emergence of the true German spirit. The perversion of those special spiritual qualities was now further exacerbated by the "junkers, the lawyers, and the Jews" who were working together with conservative political leaders to take the German peoples along the road to political and economic power at the expense of art, philosophy, and culture. But although the German spirit may be lying dormant it can be reawakened to life.

Some notable positive characteristics were still to be found in Germans: the desire to conserve the best of the past--"he hoards the Old, and well knows how to use it"; the ability to assimilate what is good and

---

[8] Ibid., 154.

[9] Wagner to Friedrich Nietzsche, 12 June 1872, **The Nietzsche-Wagner Correspondence**, Elizabeth Foerster-Nietzsche, ed., Caroline V. Kerr, trans., New York, 1921, 132.

noble from other cultures without also taking that
which is harmful or not good; and in religious terms,
the "right to deal honestly and in earnest with the
Highest." If one desired to see the prototype of those
ideas which embody and give meaning to the phrase,
"German spirit", one need only look at Bach. In him one
quickly discovered the "individuality, the strength and
meaning of the German spirit ... **that the Beautiful and
Noble came not into the world for sake of profit, nay,
not for sake of even fame and recognition.** And
everything done in the sense of this teaching is
'deutsch' and therefore is the German great; and **only
what is done** in that sense, can lead Germany to
greatness."[10]

Wagner's conception of the pure, selfless, hard-
working, honest, and spiritual paradigm epitomized by
Bach was partially embodied in Hans Sachs. Toward the
conclusion of **Die Meistersinger**, Sachs peroration calls
for recognizing the existence of a German spirit which
is being endangered by foreign powers: "Beware! Evil
tricks threaten us: if the German people and kingdom
should one day decay ... what is German and true no one
would know any more, if it did not live in the honor of
the German Masters." The existence of a "German
spirit" transcended sixteenth century Nürnberg and
nineteenth century Bavaria: "Therefore, I say to you:
honor your German Masters, then you will conjure up
good spirits! And if you favor their endeavors, even
should the Holy Roman Empire dissolve in mist, for us
there would yet remain holy German Art."

The Holy Roman Empire was dissolved by Napoleon
but in its aftermath Wagner sought a political
structure which would permit the flowering of "holy
German Art." Entertaining the belief that only through
unification could the true "German spirit" emerge,
Wagner worked unceasingly toward accomplishing this
goal. As a loose disunited confederation of independent
states, this spirit could never hope to emerge. In the
north, militaristic but Protestant Prussia was
dominated by the mercantile Junker class ever bent on
business and conquest; in the south, Catholic and
conservative Bavaria, more refined and cultured than
other parts of the confederation, was being politically
emasculated by those seeking to keep the folk as mere
pawns of the State.

----
[10] "What is German?", 163.

143

Although Wagner's hypothesis seemed clear enough to him it was based on several convoluted assumptions: there was a universality in man that transcended race, religion, and nationality; to encourage this universality to emerge required the development of a selfless group of people united in one empire who would serve as a role model for the rest of Europe; a unified Germany, backed by enlightened leadership, would take the first steps along a path which would lead to a newly restructured economic and political order. When other national states emulated the "German spirit", nationalism itself would wither away, leaving only universal man. But a self-contained and destructive nationalism, as in France, represented a threat to universal goals because it was based on self-serving and provincial ends, while the "German spirit" was capable of transcending these limitations. Wagner's hypothesis of romantic nationalism would lead Germany and Europe to a new greatness based on morality, selfless dedication to art uncorrupted by money, and a permanent end to militarism: "Ah, how full of enthusiasm I am for the German Confederacy of the Teutonic Nation! God forbid that the villain Louis Napoleon should lay hands on the German Confederacy."[11]

Some of these sentiments were to be found in **Die Meistersinger** which Wagner considered "the most optimistic of my works. This is the form in which I visualized Germans in their true character, their best light, with a popular poet like Hans Sachs, an enthusiastic youth who, though not a mastersinger, feels poetically, and a respectable pedant. This is their level in life; everything else, elegance for instance, is affectation; but their feelings are of the highest."[12] At the end of this music-drama Wagner again raised the fundamental question relating to Germany's political future.

Once Germany's rulers learn to perceive the true nature of the German spirit, there was hope for its eventual emergence. But it required the leadership of enlightened kings and princes. At first Wagner thought

----

[11] Wagner to Liszt, 8 May 1859, Altmann, 2:44.

[12] **CW's Diaries**, 16 March 1873, 1:608-9. See also 14 March 1882, 2:826: "He reads the text of **Die Meistersinger** in his collected writings, is pleased with it, and says this is really his masterpiece." This was said one year before his death.

that Ludwig might play a pivotal role but he soon became pessimistic: "The immaturity of the young Prince [King Ludwig] in matters political has become so clear to me, that for the present I have abandoned any attempt to guide myself by his judgment in this respect. Through the impudent dealings of the **real** political rulers of Bavaria [Ludwig Freiherr von der Pfordten, the Minister of State] you will yourself have perceived how childish is the young man in these matters; but nevertheless, I regard him as promising in the highest degree."[13] Because too many Germans deluded themselves with false pride in who they were and what their destiny seemed to be, Wagner's view of Germany in 1865 was bleak. "Sloth and easygoingness" was producing a fiction, "to make the German Folk imagine it is something special and does not need to first endeavour to become it.--"[14]

Trying to answer the question "What is German?" ultimately proved an impossible task. Wagner quickly discovered that the question contained too many puzzles that could not be as immediately resolved as he thought possible. Instead of finding answers he only managed to discuss certain tendencies which he perceived as existing within the German psyche. He hoped to go further. He finished the article but dissatisfied with its incompleteness decided against its publication.

After his enforced departure from Munich, Wagner continued to find the question so important and intriguing that he decided to take time off from his musical work to further pursue its answer. At this time he was still putting the finishing touches on **Die Meistersinger,** while **Siegfried** still remained but partially complete: "I think more and more about 'What is German?' and my latest studies on this question have aroused the most remarkable degree of scepticism in my mind, so that I am beginning to believe that 'being German' is a purely metaphysical conception. As such, however, it is intensely interesting to me, and in any case is unique in the history of the world, and is to be compared only to Judaism, unless Hellenism can also be made to serve as an historical parallel."[15]

---

[13] Wagner to Julius Fröbel, 11 April 1866, Altmann, 2:224.

[14] "What is German," 167.

[15] Wagner to Nietzsche, 24 October 1872, **Nietzsche-**

145

Encouraging a friend, Julius Fröbel, to establish the **Suddeutsche Presse** as a paper for the dissemination of his political ideas and prose and "for advocating my views on art", Wagner informed him that: "Everything stands or falls with--Germany. ... Your recognition of the incomparable importance of Bavaria, is a challenge to you, as to me, to expect great decisions from this last great homeland of the German race. ... Well then, up with the standard! No compromises! Strict separation from all the base journalism of our day! Ah--if only you had found some other title than this South German Press!"[16]

Fifteen articles, later collected under the title "German Art and German Policy", were written by Wagner between 1865-67. In them he again posited questions concerning: the relationship between art and politics, in particular whether the struggle to produce "German art-endeavours" in any way related to "the struggle of the Germans for a higher political standing; his contempt for materialism; the belief that art should be an end in itself; the existence of an imprisoned German spirit just waiting to be released; the assumption that a German folk will emerge from the German spirit; and, of course, the grandeur and nobility of Germanic ideas which when universalized will uplift humanity and bring in a new millennium for the world. If there is a common denominator behind most of his ideas it is to be found in his romantic belief that traditional forms of nationalism narrowly restrict man's humanity, but if and when a German nationalism appeared it must go beyond parochial concerns by viewing man in universal terms.

True German nationalism will not become a veneration of the state as an end, but would only serve as a means for the liberation of mankind beyond the confines of state, time and place. If anchored on his artistic and philosophical ideals, rather than on

----

Wagner Correspondence, 143.

[16] Wagner to Julius Fröbel, 2 September 1867, Altmann, 2:236. Shortly thereafter Fröbel resigned as editor and launched a personal attack on Wagner. He "calmly denounces me to the Bavarian Government as founder of a sect that proposes to do away with State and Religion and replace it all by Opera and Theatre whence to reign." See Wagner, "Appendix to Judaism in Music," **PW**, 3:115n.

contemporary bourgeois economics or politics, Germany will succeed in its spiritual task. But the central problem is procedural and not substantive. How does one bring about the so-called German spirit if princes and kings of a disunited Germany were so indifferent to it? Wagner phrased it well: "the German Reich itself [is] in an almost inexplicable state of suspended animation." Curiously enough Prussia provided Wagner with a good illustration of a State in the process of discovering which unifying elements could provide it with a vitality for growth. But in this case militarism supplied the cement, the bond of union among the people. Although disapproving of these means, it proved that a cohesive unity could be deliberately created. If instead of militarism, "true culture and civilisation" could be substituted, how much nobler the state would become. Wagner's analogy went further--what militarism was doing for Prussia, theatre could do for Germany: **"there lies the spiritual seed and kernel of all national-poetic and national-ethical culture, there no other art-branch can ever truly flourish, or ever aid in cultivating the Folk, until the Theatre's all-powerful assistance has been completely recognized and guaranteed."**[17] The theatre is to the German what the opera is to the Italian, the bullfight to the Spanish, the can-can to the French, the gladiator games to the Romans, the tragedies to the Greeks, and the "buffooneries of his clowns" and the "searching-dramas of his Shakespeare" to the English.

Having discussed means, ends, and goals Wagner was realistic enough to perceive that there was a danger and a dilemma intrinsic in his assumptions. The "German spirit" and "high German Art" should provide the framework for the emergence of his idealized political state. But if the state proceeded only out of political self-interest, then its goals may not relate to the purity of the vision perceived by Wagner. The creation of a united German empire might prove to be a useful political expedient, but how does one ensure that political unification would be a useful catalyst for attaining desirable cultural goals? As he warned when talking about the baneful influence of the French in **Die Meistersinger,** sometimes the mere existence of a state is viewed as its legitimate end in which case much mischief could occur.

---
[17] "German Art and German Policy," **PW,** 4:69.

There are dangers, to be sure, but the State of Bavaria had taken a significant lead which augers well for the future by recognizing that potential government leaders needed to be educated to their responsibilities. By establishing a "school for higher State-officials where an education directed purely to the ends of usefulness would reach its hand already to the only truly humanistic, i.e. the ideal education, an end unto itself. And the State which builds itself from below upwards, in this project, will also shew us finally the ideal meaning of the Kingship. ... that Kingship which must set the ideal crown upon the new true Folk-State now in course of building."[18]

If a proper political relationship can be established between the crown and the common people, and if the leaders of government used the financial power of the State to encourage freedom and independence in the arts thereby permitting new art-forms to emerge while preserving the best of the past, unencumbered by the need to find money for its cultivation and preservation, Bavaria could create "a model German State." Prussia may have the military might but Bavaria could achieve distinction by "a high Ideal." Wagner was sometimes criticized for the vagaries implicit in the term he was so fond of using. When the **Norddeutsche Allgemeine Zeitung** once commented negatively "to the effect that I must not consider myself the sole lessee of the 'German spirit.' I took the hint, and surrendered the lease." Despite a feigned humor Wagner never tired of this subject. It remained an ideal goal, elusive though it may be, throughout his life.

In the five years between the time Wagner wrote "What is German?" and 1870, political events within the loose conglomeration of States, duchies, free cities, and kingdoms, collectively known as the German Confederation changed almost yearly. Prussia successfully maneuvered a confrontation with Austria its major rival. Fearing too many irreconcilable differences with Prussia in economics, culture, military strength, and religion, Catholic Bavaria decided to cast its lot with Catholic Austria. Prussia's military and diplomatic strength was prodigious and after emerging victoriously a new political structure was formed which permanently excluded Austria. Also excluded from the newly-created

----

[18] **Ibid.**, 116-7.

North German Confederation, largely on the insistence of Napoleon III, Bavaria and other south German states were militarily and economically drawn into a special economic relationship with Prussia but were politically able to keep their own State structures. Skillfully uniting all of North Germany into a political unit with King Wilhelm I of Prussia as President, Otto von Bismarck held the more important post of Chancellor.

By 1870 through his remarkable skills at leadership and diplomacy, Bismarck had successfully consolidated the power of the North German Confederation. But fearful of Prussian military strength and suspicious of Prussian interests in Spain, France declared war. After the outbreak of war and seemingly with France as the aggressor, sentiment quickly broke out everywhere, including Bavaria, in favor of the political unification of all Germany. On November 30, 1870 the king, acting in consort with his cabinet, agreed that Bavaria should become part of the Empire. The Upper Chamber approved on 31 December and the Lower Chamber on 21 January 1871, thereby prompting Ludwig II to ask Bismarck to draw up a letter to the King of Prussia asking Wilhelm I to assume the imperial title.

Wagner was surprised at first but then delighted by the outbreak of war: "War has been declared. The French are the putrefaction of the Renaissance."[19] His unexpected bluntness and hostility toward the French apparently caught even Cosima by surprise. Since he had long been an ardent pacifist she was curious at his change in attitude, but Wagner's answer was less than satisfactory: war is sometimes noble, "it shows the unimportance of the individual."

Part of the reason why Wagner was elated when war broke out was pleasure that the intellectual and cultural arrogance of the French would finally be checked. It was a self-serving and grossly unfair criticism but one that appears psychologically determined. Ever since the fiasco of the revised version of **Tannhäuser** which he had written for Paris ten years earlier, Wagner seems to have harbored pent-up feelings of hostility toward the French. Tired of what he perceived to be French cultural domination and supremacy within the German-speaking lands, he somehow assumed that it was unlikely that the German spirit

---

[19] **CW's Diaries**, 17 July 1870, 1:246.

could emerge while French cultural imperialism was
stifling creativity within German thought and culture.
When Ludwig ordered the mobilization of the Bavarian
army, even before the actual outbreak of war, placing
it at the disposal of Prussia after war erupted, Wagner
was very pleased. The king had acted with great
courage.

As part of a present to celebrate the king's
twenty-sixth birthday Wagner sent him a poem. It bore
the simple title, "August 25th, 1870."

> Spoken has been the kingly word
> wherefrom Germany anew is risen,
> the nations' noble bastion of glory,
> released from ignominious bands;
> what wise counsel never could effect
> a Kingly word has transformed into deed:
> in all the German lands
> that one word sounds forth and resounds.
>
> And its deep sense I did understand
> as no other person understood it;
> if for the people it meant victory,
> for me that word brought a forgetting;
> and I could inter many a grief
> that had long been gnawing at my heart,
> and the suffering that had possessed me
> as often as I gazed on Germany's shame.
>
> And the meaning that lay in that word
> also did not stay concealed from you:
> he who staunchly kept the noble hoard,
> was participator in my sorrows.
> By Wotan, in anxiety, sent forth,
> tidings his raven found him that were good:
> the dawn of humanity sends out its beams;[20]
> shine now brightly forth, you Godly Day!

By August 1870 the alliance between North and
South Germany became solidified by the creation of one
German army. Much of the credit went to Bismarck, the
hero of the moment: "He is a true German; that is why
the French hate him."

----

[20] "For the King's Birthday, 25 August 1870," **The Brown
Book,** 178-9.

During the war Wagner's attitude toward the French gradually became more and more bitter. Referring to Paris as "this kept woman of the world" he went so far as to secretly confess that "the burning of Paris would be a symbol of the world's liberation at last from the pressure of all that is bad." Cosima commented in her Diary that Wagner even wanted to write Bismarck "requesting him to shoot all of Paris down."[21] When Napoleon III surrendered to King Wilhelm, Wagner was ecstatic, and even thought of writing some music for the occasion--not a victory march for the Germans--but a funeral dirge for the French! Flushed with excitement he forgot all the negative remarks he has made so often against the Prussians: "what would Europe be without this Prussian strength. Without this despised little corner, from which no one expected anything, but which has been getting itself prepared, so to speak, ever since the fall of the Hohenstaufens ... Where would Germany be without Prussia? For that reason it is understandable that they do not wish to give up their Prussianness, for they can really say they do not know what Germany means."[22] On 18 January 1871 King Wilhelm I of Prussia was proclaimed Emperor of Germany.

Wagner's entire stance over the Franco-Prussian war reveals considerable inconsistencies between his philosophical position and the reality of historical events: he disliked war, but this one was more than acceptable because it would produce ends that he favored; he distrusted the Prussians, but this time they were the saviors of a united Germany; he called for a "German spirit" which idealized universality among people, but considered the French the scum of Europe. Few romantics were this naive, or so egocentric.

The new German reich was comprised of twenty-five states, including the four kingdoms of Prussia, Bavaria, Saxony, and Württemberg. Bismarck's power and prestige, which had grown steadily since 1848, quickly usurped the center of attention from Wilhelm. For many years Wagner had distrusted the Prussians, fearful of their military attitudes, suspicious of their cultural values, and convinced that the economic power of the Junkers worked negatively as far as the German volk was concerned. In commenting to Cosima on the Prussian

---

21 **CW's Diaries**, 18 August 1870, 1:258.

22 **CW's Diaries**, 18 October 1870, 285.

character Wagner declared: "In the Prussian officers 'what the king commands, I obey,' which must certainly seem terribly stupid and narrow-minded to the French, there lies a deep meaning and a deep realization that there are certain matters one cannot discuss with semi-morons. I have lived through all these illusions myself and have now got to the point of understanding the meaning of a limited sense of duty."[23]

But unification produced a political reality that had to be accepted, one which might yet prove culturally significant. In addition, it marked the triumph of Protestant religious power over Catholicism. Wagner could not help but wonder whether Bismarck himself might become the "thinking artist" and a cultured man. Could Bismarck be the man who would free the German spirit? Only time would tell. For the moment, however, Wagner was bewildered: "What German could have lived through the year 1870 without amazement at the forces manifested here, as also at the courage and determination with which the man [Bismarck] who palpably knew something that we others did not know, brought those forces into action?"[24]

Although he had previously asserted that a poet might become a politician but no politician could become a poet, Wagner was clearly drawn to people of authority--first the King of Saxony, then Ludwig II, and finally now Bismarck. Maintaining for years how the German spirit must emerge from the ideals and values of the folk, Wagner suddenly compromised the very core of his belief by himself seeking an accommodation with those in power. There are endless possibilities that may explain Wagner's unparalleled reversal between thought and action. One can be charitable and attribute it to his romanticism, or his artistic nature and temperament, or even his lack of depth when approaching certain complex issues. Perhaps Wagner was just being pragmatic, recognizing that Bismarck represented reality, and it was better to work with a known quantity in power, than wallow in the murky never-land of philosophical assumptions regarding the nature of the ideal society. Yet, beneath every possibility rests a suspicion that Wagner clearly perceived where his best interests might lay.

---

[23] **CW's Diaries**, December 1870, 304.

[24] Postscript to "What is German," 167.

152

To celebrate the end of the war and the unification of Germany Wagner offered to write a musical piece for Berlin, but was dissuaded. To accompany the German troops home from France he offered to compose a march. That too met with indifference! Finally, on his own volition he wrote a short musical piece dedicating it to the Emperor. He was informed that it was not really necessary and would not be performed. He wrote it anyway and at the end of the march added an Imperial Song which he hoped would be sung by the general populace, perhaps as a national anthem:

> Hail! Hail to the Emperor!
>   King Wilhelm!
> Shield and bulwark of all Germans' freedom!
>   Loftiest of crowns,
> how augustly it adorns your brow!
>   Gloriously won,
>   peace shall be your reward.
> Like the newly verdant oak,
> through you has risen up the German Reich:
>   Hail to its forebears,
>   to its banners
> bearing your device, which we carried
> when with you we defeated France!
>   Defiance to the foe,
>   protection for the friend,
> the German Reich for all peoples'
>   advantage and salvation![25]

Somewhat stoically, Wagner later reflected on that moment: "I ought not to have expected the 'German spirit,' new-risen on the field of battle, to trouble itself with the musical fancies of a presumably conceited opera-composer."

Wagner's euphoria was clearly evident in the energetic way in which he expressed himself in prose, poetry, and music. Clearly he was exhilarated at the new German reich and in his hope that unification would provide the means for establishing a German identity and spirit. When Wilhelm I was crowned Emperor at Versailles in January 1871, Wagner again felt compelled to express himself in poetic terms. This time he wrote a poem, "To the German Army."

---

[25] **The Brown Book,** 188-9.

Why is the grove of German poets
   silent?
Is 'Germany, hurra' so quickly sung to death?
Has,   at   the   sign   to   strike   up   'Watch on
Rhine',
'dear   Fatherland',   lulled   sweetly,   fallen
asleep?
   That German watch
now stands in France's empty heart;
   in battle after battle
sheds blood in searing agony:
   with quiet weight
   and pious discipline
performs undreamt-of deeds,
too great for you to guess but their import.

Plain words, they were at no loss
as feelingly they marched on in the rut;
the noise and singing of the German songs
would, one fancied, scare even the French.
   Faithful Army,
have you by your victories done some crime
   to be no more spoken of
in Chamber speeches only?
   The song of praise
   to victory's peace
sing timidly now diplomats
at one with angry democrats!

                  ...

Therefore shall a German only still be
   Emperor;
on foreign soil you were to consecrate him:
to him who with true courage laboured as
   recruiter,
be now revealed the value of his feats.
   Once stolen from us,
the worthiest of earthly crowns
   upon his head,
it shall reward the sacred deeds of faith.
   That is the song
   of victory's peace,
   as set down by the German Army's deeds:
The Emperor draws near: in peace be
   judgement done![26]

----

[26] "To the German Army," **The Brown Book,** 187-8. The
"Watch on Rhine" in the first verse refers to a battle
song which became popular with the army. When it was

Debating what to do with the poem Wagner finally decided to send it directly to Bismarck. A few weeks later he received a reply:

> I thank you for having dedicated a poem to the German army and for sending me the text of it. Greatly honoured as I feel, that you address the poem to me alone, as I learn, it would give me equal pleasure to see it published. You, too, have overcome the resistance of the Parisians after a long struggle, with your works, in which I have always had the keenest interest, although at time inclining toward the opposition party; it is my belief and my hope that many more victories will be granted them, at home and abroad. Please accept the assurance of my most profound respect.[27]

Seldom had circumstances and events looked more promising.

Two other prose works are associated with this period in which Wagner's romantic nationalism was at its fullest flowering. Just prior to war Wagner jotted down two pages of notes as an outline for an essay on Beethoven. He called it "Beethoven and the German Nation." The notes are sketchy and ambiguous but it appears that Wagner was interested in one major question: was there a relationship between Beethoven's music and the German spirit? He raised a subsidiary question regarding the origin and nature of Beethoven's musical inspiration, and found its answer to lie, in part, within the interpretation of dreams: "Music the direct dream image ... Sculptors and poets give nation what it would like to seem,--the musician--what it

----

printed in the **Illustrirte Zeitung,** Wagner at first became so angry that he blurted out to Cosima, "'I hope the French win. It is too pitiful!' He further commented: 'If a witty Frenchman were to see it,' he says, 'he would regard our German fatherland with a mild ironical smile for going into battle with such a melody.' We have sunk too low. Only our troops will rescue us, they are great, and Bismarck. With a smile he adds, 'He won't sing the Wacht am Rhein!'" See **CW's Diaries**, 26 September 1870, 1:276.

[27] Otto von Bismarck to Wagner, Versailles, 21 February 1871, Barth. 218.

really is."[28]   It   is difficult to know precisely what
Wagner meant by this enigmatic statement unless it is
assumed   that   somehow   national   traits   and
characteristics are revealed through music. It would be
extremely difficult   to know   what definitions   of
nationhood   are   revealed   in   Mozart's   operas.
Nevertheless,   several   months later he completed   the
essay publishing it under the title "Beethoven."

Wagner was concerned that the German nation ought
to recognize as its heroes not just those who fought on
the battlefield. In the preface he explained why he
wrote the essay: "...may it also enjoy the advantage
of bringing the German heart, in its present state of
higher tension,   into closer touch with the depths of
the German Spirit than could ever be effaced in the
national life of everyday."[29]

One   aspect   of   Beethoven's   genius   that   most
impressed   Wagner   was   his   ability   to   transcend
ethnicity. Beethoven was an example of that rare
individual who though born a German reflected no local
or   provincial   attitudes: "...   in   this   musician
Beethoven, who spoke the purest speech of every nation,
the German spirit redeemed the spirit of mankind from
deep disgrace." It was Beethoven's capacity to capture
the essence of humanity which made him the exemplar of
what Germany might become: "he has set open for us the
understanding of that art which explains the world to
everyone as surely as the proudest philosophy could
ever explain it to the abstract thinker."[30] Wagner
concluded the essay with an important statement, one
which most clearly represented his truest feelings.
Beethoven should be celebrated "no less worthily than
the victories of German valour: for the benefactor of a
world may claim still higher rank than the world
conqueror."

Twenty-five years earlier when Wagner first
conducted Beethoven's Ninth Symphony he decided to
write an annotated program guide for the benefit of the
audience. Wagner found all of Beethoven's concerns for
humanity reflected in this symphony, particularly in
its last movement which incorporated part of Schiller's

---

[28] **The Brown Book,** 176-7.

[29] "Beethoven," **PW,** 5:60.

[30] **Ibid.,** 84.

156

"Ode to Joy." Clearly captivated by its message Wagner's imagination roamed freely: "And now it is as if a revelation had confirmed us in the blest belief that **every human soul is made for Joy. ...** we clasp the whole world to our breast; shouts of laughter fill the air, like thunder from the clouds, the roaring of the seas; whose everlasting tides and healing shocks lend life to earth, and keep life sweet, for the **joy** of Man to whom God gave the earth as home for **happiness.**"[31]

The final prose work relating to the period of the Franco-Prussian war was a pseudo-comedy entitled, "The Capitulation. Comedy by Aristop. Hanes." Although containing political overtones it was written before the final German occupation of Paris, and was not meant as anything other than a broad comedy; indeed, it often poked fun more at the Germans, who were all too willing to absorb French culture at the expense of their own, than at the expense of the French, who were in the process of being defeated at the hands of the Germans. As Wagner declared in the preface: "If I now give my friends the text of this farce, it is quite certainly not to ridicule the Parisians in retrospect. My subject brings to light no facet of the French other than that, in the reflected light of whose illumination, we Germans cut indeed figures more ridiculous than those who, in all their acts of folly, show themselves ever original, whereas we, in disgusting emulation of the same, sink far below being ridiculous even."[32]

---

[31] "Jottings on the Ninth Symphony," **PW**, 8:203.

[32] **The Brown Book,** 181. It is an absurd farce, one which includes Victor Hugo and Offenbach among its list of characters (much to the former's later annoyance). In addition to being the saviour of French civilization because of his great familiarity with the sewers of Paris, Hugo at the end of the ditty welcomes everyone to Paris: "Now you've taken your beating, please accept our entreating: as foes you can't seize our **Paris,** but we'll give it you free as **amis.** Why knock at our forts? We open our **portes;** whatever you wished, it's all ready-dished ... Then come quick and get yourselves **frisés, parfumés, civilisés!** The great **nation** will lend you its tone, and its terms are so foolishly easy! Send your soldiers away, while the diplomats stay! **Diners, soupers!** we receive **attachés.**" See Wagner, "A Capitulation," **PW,** 5:32-3. Wagner hoped that the little play might be performed in some of the smaller theatres in Germany. His friend, the conductor Karl Richter was

With German unification accomplished, it remained only for time to tell what leadership would be provided by Wilhelm as Emperor and Bismarck as Chancellor. The basic question remained: would they prove responsive toward the encouragement of cultural and artistic matters? Continually stressing the cultural and artistic backwardness of the Germanic peoples, Wagner tried to get them to appreciate the need to undertake steps to mitigate against a perpetuation of this predicament. Installed as a member of the Royal Academy of the Arts in Berlin in April 1871, his address pointed out some of the more serious deficiencies within the German theatre: "To name in one word what on German soil has shewn, and goes on proving itself least worthy of the fame of our great victories of to-day, we have only to point to this Theatre, whose tendence avows itself aloud and brazen the betrayer of German honour."[33] Trying to encourage action by members of the Academy, Wagner cajoled them into recognizing that they too can and must play their role: "But to help forward from without, as well, that restoration of Art by the artists, would be the fitting national expiation for the national sin of our present German theatre." At every opportunity Wagner continued to press forward for all Germans to take a meaningful part in the encouragement of cultural matters: "We should merely have to constitute the German Theatre in a truly German-political sense, according to which there are many German States but only one Reich, a body called upon to execute the Great and the Uncommon, beyond the individual capacity of its component parts."[34]

Shortly after this occasion Wagner had his first opportunity to meet Bismarck. He was "utterly enchanted with the genuine charm of his character, not a trace of reticence, all of it arousing trust and sympathy. ... But we can only observe each other, each in his own sphere; to have anything to do with him, to win him over, to ask him to support my cause, would not occur

----

asked to compose the music. Richter began the task but never completed it.

[33] "The Destiny of Opera: An Academic Lecture by Richard Wagner," **PW**, 5:155.

[34] "On Actors and Singers," **PW**, 5:187. Later on, in frustration, Wagner would comment, "We might in a pinch have a German Reich, but we have no German nation." See **CW's Diaries**, 1 April 1874, 1:747.

to me. But this meeting remains very precious to me."[35]
But even after unification Bismarck seemed capable of
making an artificial distinction between Germans and
Prussians, much to Wagner's annoyance but not to his
surprise: "Who could be proud of being a Württemberger,
or a Bavarian, or a Saxon? But a Prussian, yes!"

The building of the Festival-Playhouse (Wagner's
name for his anticipated theatre at Bayreuth) was
planned just a few months before the outbreak of war
with France. After the establishment of the Second
Reich the Playhouse quickly assumed an importance of
the first magnitude not only for Wagner but, as he
believed, for Germany as a whole. Bayreuth was "near
the center of Germany" and not being in a capital city,
nor possessing an established theatre where his works
could be performed, gave it distinct advantages over
most other cities or towns. A new idea needs a new
building and "'Tis the essence of the German spirit, to
build from within: the eternal God lives in him, of a
truth, before he builds a temple to His glory."[36]

When the foundation stone was laid Wagner clearly
envisioned the possibility that the Bayreuth enterprise
might become the prototype for the establishment of a
national theatre, although he was astute enough to
recognize that if he had tried to make a financial
appeal for his endeavour on this basis he would
probably have had little hope for success.
Nevertheless, after finances were arranged and
construction began on the theatre, Wagner expressed his
thoughts about a national theatre to those who had
assembled at the laying of the cornerstone: "Through
you I to-day am placed in a position surely never
occupied before by any artist. You believe in my
promise to found for the Germans a Theatre of their
own, and give me the means to set before you a plain
delineation of that Theatre. ... I trust in the German
Spirit, and hope for its manifestation in those very

----

[35] *CW's Diaries*, 3 May 1871, 1:362.

[36] "The Festival-Playhouse at Bayreuth," **PW**, 5:327.
Prior to unification Wagner was more pessimistic: "We
will try once more with the German fatherland, with
Bayreuth; if it doesn't succeed, then farewell the
North, and art, and cold, we shall move to Italy and
forget everything." See **CW's Diaries**, 26 September
1870, 1zzz;276.

regions of our life in which, as in our public Art, it has languished in the sorriest travesty."[37]

Acting in support of Wagner, his close friend Friedrich Nietzsche wrote "An Appeal to the German Nation", in which he eloquently articulated the need to promote the "well-being and honor of the German spirit and the German name." Nietzsche's appeal was sent to over four thousand book and music dealers throughout Germany, but according to his sister it had virtually no influence and "not one response was forthcoming." Nietzsche considered the Bayreuth experiment crucial to Germany's future, "to establish a fitting temple for the national spirit... we regard it as our duty to remind you of our duty as Germans at a time when we are called upon to rally to the support of the great art-work of a German genius."[38]

Wagner's theatre was but the "delineation" of a German national theatre, and a temporary wooden one at that. Eventually he hoped a permanent building would be constructed, one displaying a distinctive German style of architecture, a monumental building that would become the center for German theatrical works, his and others. This idea so fascinated and excited him that he tried to persuade Bismarck to take an active interest in it. Sending him a letter in June 1873, together with a copy of the preliminary report from Bayreuth, and his speech at the laying of the foundation stone, Wagner hoped "to acquaint the great restorer of German hopes with the cultural idea that inspires me, and that I feel myself compelled to express in terms the nation will understand, devoting the greatest exertions of which I am capable to the task."[39] Whether Bismarck ever replied to Wagner's letter is unknown, but no active support, financial or otherwise, was forthcoming from Berlin. The Emperor did agree to give 30,000 thalers to the Festival but on 18 December 1875 Wagner discovered that Bismarck canceled the appropriation without any word of explanation.

----

[37] **Ibid.**, 324-5.

[38] Friedrich Nietzsche, "An Appeal to the German Nation," **Nietzsche-Wagner Correspondence**, 194.

[39] Wagner to Bismarck, 26 June 1873, **Richard Wagner an Freunde und Zeitgenossen**, 2nd ed., Berlin, 1909, 560, as quoted in Barth, 222.

Wagner tried to discover the reasons for this action but Bismarck's secretary could only recommend that he apply directly to the Reichstag for funds, indicating that the Chancellor would "try" to help the project along. Feeling this to be inappropriate, especially since the Emperor had originally come to his aid, Wagner declined to press the matter. However, in August 1876 when the Bayreuth Festival opened with the first performance of **Der Ring des Nibelungen,** Emperor Wilhelm I did attend, as did royal representatives from most of Germany's States. His presence at Bayreuth was well-noted: "All heads turn to the Royal Box. The emperor has just entered the theatre. Emperor Wilhelm in civilian clothes is certainly an unfamiliar sight to us Berliners and probably to most Germans. We really cannot imagine him in anything other than a General's uniform. In fact several seconds passed before the crowd recognized the emperor. But then a storm of applause broke out, suddenly filling the great room like a hurricane. 'Long live Kaiser Wilhelm', again and again--it seemed as if the cheers would never cease."[40]

The extent to which the **Ring** truly reflected qualities that can be called inherently Germanic is yet conjectural. Even German critics argue the case both ways, depending on whether their personal views are pro or anti-Wagner. One critic from Berlin did attempt to make an "objective" assessment of both the **Ring** and Wagner's concern for expressing his Germanness. His evaluation represents one of the many attempts to understand the composer while being critical of some major points:

> Wagner has three qualities as a musician which redound to the credit of the German nation. ... he knows how to avoid triviality. ... This is a German quality, for a German endeavours to possess a personality. Secondly: Wagner is concerned with absolute truth of expression; ... Thirdly: Wagner always strives for profundity, for exhaustive exposition. ... his deliberate intention is to overthrow the kind of swift-moving entertainment that is based on nothing more than a request for diversion,

---

[40] **Berliner Tageblatt,** 16 August 1876, Barth, 233. This was not the first Wagnerian music-drama that Wilhelm had seen. He attended a performance of **Die Meistersinger** in Berlin in February 1870.

reflecting a mere frivolous view of art. He demands a serious, collected attitude in his listeners, a kind of reverence for art--and he is right to do so, only he goes too far...

And that is why I say: Wagner's fundamental Germanness is un-German; he is representative of only one thread in the life of the nation, the obstinate German-at-all-costs side: the striving for depth without clarity, for truth without beauty, absolute subjectivity without any objective restraints. In a word: Wagner's work has about it something Gothic, barbarian--in the sense which Goethe used to give the words--and we must try to rid ourselves of this kind of Gothicism and barbarianism.[41]

This critic, tantalizing though his review may be, appears to be unfamiliar with Wagner's major thesis: that he was creating a new art-form and employing a new style. That Wagner was a German who wrote music-drama did not make his composition a Germanic music-drama. Wagner, however, contributed to the confusion by his persistent use of the phrase "German spirit."

After the initial three cycles **The Ring** would not be performed in Bayreuth for another twenty years. Five years later, in 1881, the Emperor did attend its first Berlin performance, and this time accompanied by Bismarck. Between the time that the German Empire was formed in 1871 and Wagner's death in 1883, little direct governmental encouragement was ever extended toward any general interest in the cultivation of the arts, or toward making the Bayreuth Festival Theatre into a national theatre. The expenses involved in the first cycles were so enormously high that without financial support from Berlin there was little likelihood that Ludwig would be able to secure enough funds from the Bavarian treasury to pay for a second season. But this did not deter Wagner, nor was he deflected from his obsession with the idea of the German spirit. He knew what it meant even if few others did.

Since he was totally disinterested in receiving any salary, payment, or royalties for **The Ring,** and even tried to insist that the performances should be

----
[41] Gustav Engel, **Vossische Zeitung,** Berlin, 9 September 1876, Barth, 235-6.

free, Wagner was uncompromising in the name of art: "Singers, and musicians will only get their expenses covered, they will **not** get fees from me. Those who will not come for the honour and love of the thing can stay where they are in so far as I am concerned. A man or woman who would only come to me for the sake of a wretched **wage**--Such a person could never satisfy my artistic demands."[42] Wagner got his way, as he had expected. All of the singer and musicians were paid out-of-pocket expenses only. He had appealed to them on artistic and patriotic grounds: "perhaps for the first time in your artistic career--to devote your powers simply and solely to the attainment of an artistic ideal, namely that of showing the German public what the German can do in a domain most peculiarly his own, and of placing before the foreigner on whose learnings we have for the most part existed hitherto, something which he can not possibly imitate."[43]

But it was not Germanness that he was after, only what might be done in its name. Illusion or not, Wagner still viewed art as universal but believed that German art, rather than French or Italian art, could better achieve true universality. Two months after the last **Ring** cycle Wagner was already importuning Ludwig for continued support of his project: "Bayreuth must remain an absolutely free foundation, with the sole objective of serving as the model for the establishment and development of an original, German, musico-dramatic art. ... please note, the irrevocable proviso that the undertaking itself is never exploited for financial gain, and in particular that its director never claims any compensation for his labours."[44]

Wagner now suggested three methods for trying to obtain support from Berlin. First, he could appeal to one of the members of the Reichstag to introduce a bill for the direct financial aid of the Festival House. Since he did not personally know any of the members this option would not likely lead to success. A second possibility was to make a direct appeal to Bismarck. As

----

[42] Wagner to Friedrich Feustel, 12 April 1872, Altmann, 2:252.

[43] "To the Singers Taking Part in the Dramatic Festival," 14 January 1875, Altmann, 2:265-6.

[44] Wagner to Ludwig II, 21 October 1876, **Königsbriefe**, Vol. 3, 95, as quoted in Barth, 238.

this would have to be done through the intermediary of the Emperor, Wagner was pessimistic that he would get any further funds now than before. Wagner had grown fond of Wilhelm I. Although the Emperor was "less talented" than Frederick the Great who stood "above Fate and literally direct it themselves", he did "possess certain qualities which the Universal Spirit needs in order to achieve great things." Among these qualities are "decency and trustworthiness", the very traits necessary "to bring about the downfall of the French."[45] The third way would be for Ludwig "as guardian and protector of the interests of higher German culture" to intercede. An appeal coming from the Bavarian Reichstag to the Berlin Reichstag for the support of the Festival House might carry weight. To save Ludwig time in preparing a draft document, Wagner drew up a model proposal that could be sent directly from the King of Bavaria to the Chancellor of Germany.

Several aspects of Wagner's proposals are revealing, but quite consistent with his earlier ideas. The opening resolution is direct: "'The Imperial Government takes possession of the Festival Theatre in Bayreuth with all its appurtenances ... and transfers it, as a property of the nation, to the town council of Bayreuth, to be administered by it.'"[46] One thousand tickets should be sold for each performance but a further six hundred seats should be offered "free to indigent German nationals, whereby the whole institution will best assume a 'national' character in its external constitution as well as its artistic purpose." Wagner waited for a reply. It never came.

After almost a year of waiting Wagner knew that he had received his answer: "We are in a terrible position. Help from the Reichstag is out of the question. There is not **one** single person in the Reichstag who understands what is at stake for us. Bismarck would say in all probability, if we asked for assistance: 'Wagner has had enough; a lot of princes, the emperor himself was there at his performances; what else does the man want?' We will get no support from that quarter."[47] Undeterred, Wagner called for renewed

---

[45] **CW's Diaries**, 26 January, 1871, 1:328.

[46] **Idem.**

[47] "Address to the Delegates of the Bayreuth Patrons' Association," made by Wagner on 15 September 1877,

164

individual support of the Festival idea and proposed a rededication to an important goal: "a style and an art of a kind that cannot be cultivated in the wretched theatres of the present day." Even if funds can not be obtained to produce **The Ring** a new music school should be started immediately at Bayreuth, "for training singers, players and conductors in the correct performance of musico-dramatic works of the truly German style." Neither the proposed music school at Bayreuth nor a second festival season were forthcoming: "Learn to know Germany and the German public! There all, all is lost! Believe me! Our achievement last year was a miracle ... But we cannot go beyond it."[48]

Wagner was dejected. It appeared that his Festival Theatre idea would die in the year of its birth: "I have shown what I can do, and now feel that I have a right--as indeed I am compelled--to close my public career as an artist."[49] He tried to find consolation from his intimate friends but nothing could relieve his bitter frustration: "What I have accomplished so far was in the nature of a question to the German people, 'Do you want this?' Now I take it that people do **not** want it and that ends it for me."[50]

For many years after the Franco-German war Wagner never lost hope that a nation might yet evolve from the structure of the unified political state, but by 1877 there were too many unresolved problems being ignored. The Empire was too busily involved with military matters, border disputes, religious conflicts between Protestants and Catholics, and trade arrangements, while cultural matters were being relegated to the States. And Wagner knew what that meant!

Blaming Germans again for bringing their troubles on themselves, Wagner again seriously considered emigrating to the United States. The thought of

----

Reported by Franz Muncker, **Richard Wagner Jahrbuch**, Vol. 1, Stuttgart, 1866, 205, as quoted in Barth, 239.

[48] Wagner to Emil Heckel, 11 February 1877, Altmann, 2:282.

[49] Wagner to Friedrich Feustel, 23 November 1876, Altmann, 2:279.

[50] Wagner to Emil Heckel, 9 December 1876, Altmann, 2:282.

transplanting his entire family loomed in his mind ever since he had been commissioned to write a short musical piece to help commemorate the Centennial Anniversary in 1876. To celebrate the one hundredth anniversary of the Declaration of Independence and to receive five thousand dollars which would be highly useful to the Festival, Wagner wrote a Centennial March. Privately expressing serious reservations about the quality of this piece, it was successfully played before President Grant and thousands of visitors to Philadelphia.

In moments of extreme frustration Wagner often talked about moving to the United States. Writing, in confidence, to the editor of the Bayreuth **Blätter** he commented: "If I am not successful I shall go to America and provide for my family--and never dream of returning to Germany."[51] Even as he approached his late sixties Wagner's frame of mind seriously entertained the idea of a permanent separation from Germany: "I must tell you in confidence that a notion of settling permanently in America with my family, my ideas, and my works, is taking deep root in me. I can only regret that I did not long ago choose a fresh and vital soil for the future of my works and of my family, and my deep conviction of the decay of European culture makes me all the more determined now to take this way out."[52] Thoughts of America persisted and shortly before his death Wagner told Cosima that America would "one day become the dominating world power", a thought he seemed to welcome.[53]

In the last years of his life politics figured heavily in Wagner's conversations, despite his growing and intensifying disgust with the Germans. Continuing to support some of Bismarck's ideas he gradually perceived the reality that the "Pomeranian Junker" was "a cultural barbarian": "The clumsy organization of the German Reich, the destruction of the small states, the failure, in order to help them adapt to the new organization, to look into the damage done, the petty lies .... All this is regrettable, for despite everything Bismarck is still one of the most

---

[51] Wagner to Hans von Wolzogen, 2 July 1877, Altmann, 2:288.

[52] Wagner to Friedrich Feustel, 4 March 1880, Altmann, 2:294.

[53] **CW's Diaries**, 3 November 1882, 2:943.

significant men in our history."[54] It was Germany's misfortune that Bismarck knew little about and cared nothing for German culture. He was a Prussian and not a German, and to Wagner that represented the fundamental nature of the problem. In the final analysis Bismarck had his priorities. He was interested primarily in the politics of power, and the strength of the army was the means for his conception of a viable nation. To Wagner this was shallow: "The Prussians are there just in order to beat the French from time to time when they get too arrogant, but the French remain the world's gods and rulers. We Germans are now like Bismarck's body, puffed up and in a constant state of agitation."[55] That Wagner's priorities were clearly related to his romantic perspective of nationalism is evident; if Bismarck supported the arts, especially Wagner's projects, that would qualify him to be considered a German. But if the Empire did not support the arts then Bismarck remained nothing else but a provincial Prussian.

For forty-two years Wagner talked, wrote, and pleaded for the re-emergence of the dormant "German Spirit." It always seemed to be an unattainable ideal goal. Perhaps one of the great problems of Wagner's romantic nationalism was his lack of concreteness. He knew in his mind what Germany could become and was just as certain that the answers to her greatness would be found in art, poetry, and drama. But Wagner was a visionary whose vision was so romantically elusive as to be all but unattainable; yet he still possessed great faith in human nature, despite all the negative remarks he made about the average German. Regrettably, Wagner could not translate thoughts into action.

Wagner's one-time friend, the philosopher Friedrich Nietzsche, came closer than anyone to an understanding of both the strength and weakness of Wagner's romantic nationalism:

> There is not a shadow of doubt in my mind but that Wagner would have succeeded had he been an Italian. The German has not the faintest conception of opera, and has always regarded it as something imported and un-German. In fact,

----
[54] CW's Diaries, 2 March 1878, 2:33-4.

[55] CW's Diaries, 2 February 1880, 2:435.

the entire stage is not taken seriously by Germans.

There is something comical about the whole situation. Wagner cannot persuade the Germans to take the theatre seriously. They remain cold and unresponsive--he becomes impassioned as if the whole salvation of Germany depended upon this one thing. Now all at once, when the Germans believe that they are occupied with graver matters, they regard anyone who devotes himself so seriously to art as a cheerful fanatic.

Wagner is not a reformer, for so far, everything remains as it always was. In Germany each one is inclined to take his own cause seriously, and therefore laughs at any one who claims a monopoly of seriousness....

Chief thing: the significance of an art such as Wagner represents does not fit into our present social and economic conditions. Hence the instinctive aversion to an undertaking that is considered untimely.

Wagner's chief problem: Why am I not able to make others feel what I feel myself? This leads to a criticism of the audience, the state and society at large. He places the artists and the audience in the relation[56] of subject and object--this is most naive.

The last word belongs to Wagner: "I wanted, with the support of the nation, to create something entirely new and original in a place to which that creation should first bring fame. I thought better of our upper classes than they deserved."[57]

---

[56] Nietzsche-Wagner Correspondence, 201.

[57] Wagner to Friedrich Feustel, 14 June 1877, Altmann, 2:285.

CHAPTER 5

SOCIETY, AND THE SEARCH FOR SOCIAL ACCOMMODATION

In his music-dramas and prose works Wagner's concerns went beyond political, economic, and religious issues. Fascinated with those aspects of life relating to man in his social setting, he seemed intrigued with exploring how and why certain individuals became alienated from society. Several basic questions were posited, the more important ones being: what causes social alienation? whose fault is it? is social accommodation always desirable? on whose terms?

There were also several important secondary questions: How far should society be willing to go to accommodate differences between or among its members? How should society deal with so-called antisocial behavior? Concerned with these questions and thoughts, Wagner's dramas often reflected situations representing or involving divergent behavioral problems. In some cases he attributed social alienation as a response, a reaction from specific political, economic, or religious problems. Often it was related to power. At other times the causes were psychological or sexual. One elemental question seems to form the nucleus for Wagner's historical approach to society: What factors are responsible for producing both a craving and a lust for power?

Whether or not his sociological theories were valid, Wagner made one major assumption: the absence of love was an effective catalyst in fomenting antisocial behavior and this factor alone was a major ingredient behind society's problems. This formidable conclusion, and its attendant questions, figured prominently in his thoughts and prose. In terms of social interaction no problem affecting society is of greater importance than that involving the relationship between the sexes. Since the foundation of society is traditionally based on the family unit, the way Wagner conceived the male-female unit was one basic element in the establishment of his social outlook.

In each of the music-dramas and in several prose articles, Wagner discussed topics relating to love, sexual involvement, and frustration. At times he juxtaposed sexuality with his spiritual thoughts, as in **Tannhäuser** where the sexual cravings and desires became pitted against spirituality. At other times, sexuality was portrayed as uninhibited lust and passion which involved, as in the case of Tristan and Isolde, a lack of concern for either society, its values, or even honor.

Wagner's attitude toward women may be observed by the roles they were made to play in his music-dramas, in prose articles where he discussed their nature, by a lifelong obsession to define and then find the ideal "woman of the future", and through his personal life as a man strongly attracted to women. Starting with Senta in the **Dutchman**, each female character related in some way to Wagner's conception of what the "quintessence of femininity" was meant to be.

Senta occupied a pivotal role and was almost equal in importance to the Dutchman. Heine's discussion of the fable offered Wagner remarkably little: "It seems as if she has penetrated his secret; and when he afterwards asks: 'Katherine, [Senta in Wagner's drama] wilt thou be true to me?' she answers: 'True till death.'" However it was the ending of Heine's story which most impressed Wagner. As Heine described it:

> When I reentered the theatre, I came in time to see the last scene of the play, where the wife of **The Flying Dutchman** on a high cliff wrings her hands in despair, while her unhappy husband is seen on the deck of his unearthly ship, tossing on the waves. He loves her, and will leave her lest she be lost with him, and he tells her all his dreadful destiny, and the cruel curse which hangs over his head. But she cries aloud: 'I was ever true to thee, and I know how to be true unto death!' Saying this she throws herself into the waves, and then the enchantment is ended. **The Flying Dutchman** is saved, and we see the ghostly ship slowly sink into the abyss of the sea.[1]

Heine's version of the fable ended with this theme of redemption.

Wagner wanted Senta to be a multidimensional woman. Epitomizing compassion and empathy, two characteristics of supreme importance to Wagner, she

---

[1] Heinrich Heine, **Memoir of Herr von Schnabelwopski**, quoted in libretto accompanying the Angel Records recording of **Der fliegende Holländer** (3616), 2.

must be willing to place life in a different perspective from that of her friends and other members of society. Viewing even death as preferable to compromising truth, genuine love, or empathy, she is willing to sacrifice her life for that of another, if this were necessary to redeem the value of life.

So strong is her empathy for the pain of the Dutchman, that even before she meets him she is able to penetrate beyond his portrait which hangs on the wall, much to the amusement and puzzlement of her friends. As in the play, Senta's words seem simple and clear: "But to the pallid man redemption would be granted were he to find a woman who would keep faith with him on earth until the end." But it is equally clear that Wagner had already significantly modified both the fable and Heine's treatment of it. Senta's words indicate not just a willingness to be true until death but in a more positive sense she will be one who "would keep faith with him on earth until the end."

It is in these words that Wagner went beyond legend. Senta was to bring redemption and life, rather than redemption and death. It is the life force and life situation which will permit values to be acted upon, while death simply resolves a situation in a negative manner. The Dutchman "never found a woman true", but "let me that woman be whose constancy redeems you! May the angel lead you to me! Through me shall you achieve salvation."

Several mental images of Senta's personality and Wagner's conception of her are troubling. Does Wagner really expect her to be taken seriously? Is his depiction of Senta and her conception of love really related to his ideal woman? Are her words and deeds an expression of Wagner's concept of love? If so, and he does seem to be quite serious in the way she should be viewed, it raises many obvious questions regarding Wagner's psychological image of women. Why is her personality to be so undifferentiated except in terms of the Dutchman? Is he of the opinion that a woman's primary role in life is to redeem man by a single-minded devotion involving self-sacrifice?

Senta can easily be viewed as neurotic, perhaps even verging on the psychotic, and with an unhealthy fixation on the Dutchman; or, she can be a psychologically healthy person driven by feelings of love, empathy, and compassion, one who can intuitively understand the loneliness and suffering of another. If one accepts this latter view, and this is clearly the focal point for Wagner, then it may follow that Senta recognizes that the Dutchman represents a human being alienated from society, a man who longs desperately to find someone to share and understand him. Senta recognizes not the fable of the Dutchman but the reality of the man who, in sailing alone on the sea of life, looks for a companion to help shoulder some of the burdens. If Senta could assume this role in the Dutchman's life, she would be well on the way toward becoming the "woman of the future." But she must not betray him!

The element of betrayal figures prominently in several of Wagner's works, almost as if the woman of the future represented one whose consistency and constancy were unbending. It may well be that Wagner's perceptions of women related to events in his life. At the age of twenty-two he had fallen passionately in love with an actress several years older and not indifferent to men's attentions who agreed to marry him. Even before Wagner married Minna Planer he sounded the ominous theme of betrayal: "O my life, don't forget, don't betray me ever, faithfully cling to me ... Do you hear? Do you hear? Don't ever betray me."[2] Minna did betray him and on several occasions; so too did Elsa, Brünnhilde, and several of his other fictional characters betray their trust.

Wagner's attitude toward women, love, and the relationship between the sexes evolved from Senta to her successors, Elisabeth, Elsa, Brünnhilde, and Kundry. Whether or not it is a healthy conception is debatable; it appears to postulate a very one-sided purpose for women, although in one sense with a biblically-oriented perspective. Woman was made from man to be his help-mate. Man was created first and only later did God decide that man needed a companion. Equality between the sexes was not ordained by God.

Perhaps Wagner was not trying to be quite so egocentric in his attitude toward women and love as it might appear at first glance. In an idealistic way Senta's feelings transcend the earthly nature of love. Indeed, she raises love to a lofty spiritual dimension never attained by Tristan and Isolde who glorify the sensual, erotic and animalistic nature of man. Senta

---

2 Wagner to Minna Planer, 6 May 1835, Burrell, 25.

doesn't reject love, or even passion, but she seeks a meaningful relationship beyond her physical and emotional needs.

As the relationship between the Dutchman and Senta begins to develop Wagner finds it imperative to indicate that love does not involve pity, but compassion. Were Senta merely to feel sorry for the Dutchman it would debase rather than ennoble the character of the drama. While under the right circumstances pity can be a distinguishing trait, it will not bring a meaningful relationship between them: "But Senta's passionate interjection: 'Ah! Such sufferings! Could I solace bring you!' stirs him to the depths of his being: filled with astonished admiration, he stammers out the half-hushed words: 'What sweet sounds to hear above Hell's discord.'"[3]

A human drama unfolds between two individuals who recognize the beginning of a relationship. But so protective is he that "his love for Senta displays itself at once in terror of the danger she herself incurs by reaching out a rescuing hand to him. It comes over him as a hideous crime, and in his passionate remonstrance against her sharing in his fate he **becomes a human being through and through**." When Senta responds, "I well know woman's holy duties, be therefore comforted, unhappy man!", Wagner envisions the ideal relationship between the sexes to be based on clearly defined ways of satisfying the others needs. But it is unmistakably obvious, and not altogether typical of mid-nineteenth century European thought, that woman's role is seen as almost exclusively in support of the man.

In **Tannhäuser**, Elisabeth pursues a more socially-acceptable approach in her relationships. Deeply in love with Tannhäuser, she became morose when he left to venture out on his own. When he attempts to reenter society it is because Elisabeth is paramount in his mind: "This one, this nameless thing, that alone can satisfy his present longing, is suddenly named for him with the name 'Elisabeth': Past and Future stream together, with lightning quickness, at mention of this name."[4]

----
[3] "Remarks on Performing the Opera: **The Flying Dutchman**," PW, 3:215.

[4] "On the Performing of **Tannhäuser**," PW, 3:199.

173

Explaining how the role of Elisabeth ought to be performed, Wagner commented that the singer should "give the impression of the most youthful and virginal unconstraint, without betraying how experienced, how refined a womanly feeling it is, that alone could fit her for the task." What the task is, he does not explain! A further aspect of her personality emerges in the initial meeting with Tannhäuser upon his return. Many times had she listened to the words and music of singers, but "what a strange new life your song aroused in my breast! ... Emotions I had never felt! Longings I had never known!" In actuality Wagner opened the second act with Elisabeth ecstatically proclaiming the reawakening of her awareness of her own feelings for Tannhäuser. Without this crucial awareness of her own emotions she could not have summoned the empathy she displays for Tannhäuser.

During the singing contest three major philosophical and psychological points of view are expressed regarding the nature of love and the role of sexuality. This scene is designed as a companion piece to the many philosophic discussions that have taken place, since the days of ancient Greece, over the meaning of love. Wagner was determined that the singing should not detract from the importance of the words: "it is clear that to precipitate the catastrophe by means of this scene in particular, the dramatist's or poet's aspect must, and indeed alone **could**, be the predominating aspect. To allow the singers to predominate by the arts of song, grace notes and cadenzas would have produced the impression of song competition, but not of a dramatic contest of thought and emotion."[5]

In the contest over the nature of love, three points of view are presented with Tannhäuser serving as both participant and commentator. Wolfram presents the first and in his utterances one sees "the whole evolution of Wolfram's life-views both as artist and as man." Both through words and the melody which accompanies them, Wolfram appears to be infatuated with the ethereal image of love, and visualizes Elisabeth as the star of heaven itself. Through allegory and metaphor he romanticizes on "the essence of love", implying that it is so divine as to be untarnished by any thought of sensuality: "O never may I sully that

----
[5] Wagner to Baron von Biedenfeld, 17 January 1849, Altmann, 1:142.

174

fountain or cloud its limpid waters with impure thoughts." His ode to romantic as opposed to sensual love reveals the poet but denies the reality of human nature. Yet, through him, Wagner deliberately captures the illusions of love.

The actor portraying Wolfram "needs little more than to address himself to the sympathy of the finer-feeling of our public, to be sure of winning its interest." The contrast in personality between Wolfram and Tannhäuser is clear in Wagner's mind: "The lesser vehemence of his directly physical instincts has allowed him to make the impression of life a matter of meditation; he is thus preeminently Poet and Artist, whereas Tannhäuser is before all Man. His standing toward Elisabeth, which a nobly manly pride enables him to bear so worthily, no less than his final deep fellow-feeling for Tannhäuser--whom he can never comprehend--will make him one of the most prepossessing figures."[6]

No sooner is Wolfram finished then Tannhäuser is forced to interject an opposing point of view, "and yet his heart is simply fighting for his love to Elisabeth." He tries to discuss the "true nature of love" and in his metaphoric commentary stresses the presence of the sexual nature of love, asking that its existence be recognized and accepted.

The second philosophical argument is presented when Walter tries to hide man's nature under a veil of hypocrisy and illusion. To him the fountain of love is "true virtue" and it must be found "through your heart, nor your lips." By focusing on the spiritual element alone, the balance between man's spiritual and animal desires is all but ignored. Listening to him the public is clearly impressed, for illusion seems so much more beautiful than reality. Tannhäuser again attempts to place love in a wider perspective by arguing that Walter's timidity pretends to ignore that God gave man his sexual nature. This statement appears to be the heart of Wagner's argument: God is the creator of man's urges. The enjoyment of "soft flesh" is normal and has an urgency "which lies near to the heart and thought." Tannhäuser's final line, "in enjoyment alone do I recognize love!" may have gone further than he had intended, but in any case Wolfram, Walter, and the

----
[6] "On the Performing of **Tannhäuser**," 204.

public were unwilling to acknowledge the existence of passion and the reality of man's biological nature.

The last contestant, Biterolf immediately joins in on behalf of the arguments of his friends. Accusing Tannhäuser of being a "blasphemer", and of defiling the chivalric code of honor toward women, he declares as his purpose in life "to preserve it in its purity for ever I would proudly shed my lifeblood. Woman's virtue and honor will I, as a knight, defend with my sword; but those delights that captured your immaturity are shoddy, not worth a blow." Recoiling from this argument, Tannhäuser lashes out at Biterolf: "What, poor wretch have you known of pleasure? Your life was lacking in love."

In trying to deal with the time-old question of love, Wagner makes Tannhäuser the spokesman for acknowledging the power of sensuality. Unless the sexual impulse is accepted as normal, one can never have any true idea what love is all about nor can a proper perspective be achieved between the physical and the spiritual aspects of man's personality. Indeed, not until the sexual side of man is recognized to be as powerful as it is, can man appreciate how sexuality can be controlled and united with the spiritual element, in the service of God.

Although it appears as if Tannhäuser lost the philosophical argument and was even in danger of losing his life, the ultimate answer to the question relating to the meaning of love is not provided by him, but by Elisabeth. Fearful for his life, she intercedes on his behalf. But Elisabeth's shock at Tannhäuser's admission of sexual indulgence awakens within him a strong sense of guilt. Her empathy and concern makes him sorrowful over having inflicted pain and suffering on her: "it is here that his love for Elisabeth proclaims the vastness of its difference from that of Venus: her whose gaze he can no longer bear, whose words pierce his breast like a sword--to her must he atone, and expiate by fearsome tortures the torture of her love for him. ...[7] Where is the suffering that he would not gladly bear?"

Wagner wishes to convey in **Tannhäuser** the nature and power of love in all its dimensions: romantic, illusionary, and erotic. He does this by exploiting the

----
[7] **Ibid.**, 200.

unique differences among the personalities. In the intense inner feelings but outward calm that Wolfram exhibits toward Elisabeth, he expresses his strong desire for her. But he is concerned for her happiness and is chivalrous enough to be just as concerned over Tannhäuser's soul. By recognizing, "O blessed love, how great thy power", Wolfram is accepting reality. But despite his nobility, perhaps even because of it, one can see why Elisabeth never took him seriously. Wolfram is the incomplete man, one so perfect that he never thinks of himself first, whereas Tannhäuser is, as Wagner indicated clearly, above all else--Man! When Elisabeth prays for Tannhäuser, Wagner reveals her to be more than merely a supplement to the action. She too acknowledges, as did none but Tannhäuser, the existence of sexual urges. Innocent in deed, she is normal in thought, whereas Wolfram is unable or unwilling to acknowledge the existence of the sensual within him: "if ever, engrossed in vain fancies, my heart turned away from thee, if ever a sinful desire or earthly longing rose within me, I strove with untold anguish to stifle my heart." Neither Elisabeth nor Tannhäuser were so troubled.

This drama, coming so early in his career, presented Wagner with a dilemma for he was at a loss in knowing how to reconcile either Tannhäuser or Elisabeth with society. However God's intervention provides the way out. Tannhäuser is saved, giving Wagner the benefit of having made clear than an acknowledgement and an enjoyment of sexuality is not tantamount to eternal damnation. It is a subject he will take up again.

In **Lohengrin** Wagner goes one step further in trying to develop his elusive but persistent theme relating to the "woman of the future." At least in this music-drama, for the first time, the major female role is alive at the end. Having seen her lover depart, Elsa returns to society, sadder but wiser. Despite a major religious allegory in this drama, the importance of love was one of the preeminent reasons for Wagner's initial interest in the subject. In discussing the "instrumental introduction" which precedes the drama, Wagner clearly enunciated his thesis: "From out a world of hate and haggling, Love seemed to have vanished clean away: in no community of men did it longer shew itself as law-giver."[8]

----
[8] "Prelude to **Lohengrin**," **Neue Zeitschrift**, 17 June 1853, **PW**, 3:231.

One is immediately struck with the source of Wagner's motivation--the absence of love--but what has caused this? Part of the answer is to be found in Wagner's conviction that society was in danger of destroying itself by its worship of materialism. Nevertheless, the essence of love is still to be found within man's soul, although it may be submerged. Through an elaboration of this idea Wagner progressed greatly beyond **Tannhäuser**. The action is no longer just a question involving the spiritual and the animal souls, but is enlarged to include the battle between the spirituality of love and the animalism of greed. The animal soul is not limited to sexuality for that is only one of its facets. In its entirety the animal soul also involves the aggressive and violent instincts within man, and these emerge whenever man tries to get an unfair advantage over his fellow man. The protagonists are the love of economic gain in contradistinction to the value of human love.

But what is needed to awaken man's recognition of love and how is mankind to reestablish the proper balance between a desire for economic power and the animalism of greed? These questions occupied Wagner for the next thirty years, but in **Lohengrin** he attempted its earliest answer. Man must recognize the transcendental nature of Godliness, and have enough faith in its message to live by it, without questioning its nature. It is an unrealistic and an immature premise. Elsa ultimately pays for it by her inability to measure up to this ideal.

In this drama Wagner further develops and makes use of polarities for differentiating personalities. It is an effective innovation both artistically and dramatically. Ortrud is the prototype of the political woman. She is powerful, cunning, and determined. Relying on cool detached logic to implement her designs, she enjoys manipulating individuals as means to her ends. A few years after he had completed **Lohengrin** Wagner provided Liszt with several insights regarding her behavior. Through an inability to love, her personality had undergone a transformation. In frustration she became politically-oriented; but while "a political **man** is repulsive, a political **woman** is horrible."[9] Ortrud lives in the past, among relics of her ancestors, with but hatred for those living in the

---

[9] Wagner to Liszt, 30 January 1852, **Wagner-Liszt Correspondence**, 1:192-3.

present. Because she is psychologically crippled, Ortrud turns to "murderous fanaticism", making enemies of all who live. Taking an overview of the situation Wagner speculated that "in history there is no more cruel phenomenon than political woman." Lovelessness makes her evil in the same way that it will make Alberich evil in **The Ring.**

Ortrud is the antithesis to Elsa who represents her darker underside. But the closer one examines the two women throughout the course of the drama, the more striking are their dual natures. If they are combined into a single personality, with each side in conflict with the other, one can see a remarkable unity. Similarly, this technique is employed with equal effectiveness by the way Wagner presents Lohengrin and Telramund. They too appear as opposites whereas, in actuality, they exist in a complementary and supplementary fashion. The four major characters are interrelated to a fascinating degree. In general, but with the possible exception of Telramund, each seems to know considerably more about the other than is warranted by the action.

When combined, Lohengrin and Telramund make up the personality of the average man who is possessed with both strength and weakness together with spiritual and demonic drives. Wagner depicted each as embodying the force of conflicting religious values, while they are also in political conflict with each other. If Lohengrin and Telramund, when combined, represent an average man, Elsa and Ortrud together constitute the average female. Elsa, unlike Ortrud, is capable of loving, but not without question. When she questions, she becomes the political Ortrud. The four together represent the vital life-force of creation, and in this respect Wagner has depicted the essence of life and the unity of the soul.

Although infinitely more sympathetic to Elsa, Wagner makes Ortrud into a totally convincing archetype. In commenting upon her as political woman, he offered some penetrating insights:

> She is a reactionary person who thinks only of the old and hates everything new in the most ferocious meaning of the word; she would exterminate the world and nature to give new life to her decayed gods. But there is not merely an obstinate, morbid mood to Ortrud;

her passion holds her with the full weight of a misguided, undeveloped, objectless feminine desire for love: for that reason she is terribly grand. She must never appear simply malicious or annoyed, and every utterance of her irony, her treachery, must transparently show the full force of the terrible madness which can be satisfied alone by the destruction of others or by her own destruction.[10]

In **Tannhäuser** Wagner had created the archetype of the ideal male while in **Lohengrin** he illustrated why Elsa was not the archetype of the complete female. The fault is to be found in Elsa: "this glorious woman, before whom Lohengrin must vanish, for reason that his own specific nature could not understand her,--I had found her **now**: and the random shaft that I had shot towards the treasure dreamt but hitherto **unknown**, was my own Lohengrin, whom now I must give up as lost; to track more certainly the footsteps of that **true Woman-hood**, which should one day bring to me and all the world redemption, after Man-hood's egoism, even in the noblest form, had shivered into self-crushed dust before her."[11] Being somehow incomplete, Elsa precipitated the entire resolution to the tragedy of lost love by her own actions. Asking the questions that she had previously agreed not to ask represented both free will and her own undoing and led to Lohengrin's subsequent departure.

Exiled and living in Switzerland, Wagner was unable to attend the world premiere in Weimar, but wrote Liszt regarding the feelings which must exist on the part of the audience by the end of the second act: "the public should feel that Elsa violently forces herself to conquer her doubt, and we should in reality fear, that having once indulged in brooding over Lohengrin, she will finally succumb and ask the prohibited question. In the production of this general feeling of fear lies the only necessity for a third act in which the fear is realized."[12]

---

[10] **Ibid.**, 193.

[11] **Communication,** 347.

[12] Wagner to Liszt, 8 September 1850, **Wagner-Liszt Correspondence,** 1:95.

So far there is something absurd and/or psychological significant in Wagner's assumptions about the women in his dramas. Senta, Venus, Elisabeth, Ortrud, and finally Elsa, all represent aspects of "woman." Yet, his strangely egocentric desire to find the "woman of the future", and to penetrate into the "essence of femininity" gives the impression of a man possessing a remarkable contempt for women. As an artist he seems unable to accept them as they are while as a man Wagner certainly appreciated what they had to offer him.

Although love, or its absence, figure prominently in Wagner's first three works, there are other issues which add to the feelings of alienation running throughout these dramas. The Flying Dutchman represented an alienated man, but his needs went beyond love. Wagner's use of the word "mitleid", compassion, represents perhaps the most often used word in his vocabulary. It is used, and found, in every drama! The Dutchman is doomed to wander the "seas" of life not because he defied God, as in the fable, but to see if he can find the archetypal woman who would be capable of true empathy--compassion; not the type of condescending compassion represented by pity, but the feelings of a fellow soul that knew, understood, and empathized with another suffering soul.

The Dutchman knows what he needs and wants but whether or not he will find it is the operative question. Is Senta capable of offering true compassion? The Dutchman's adversary is Eric who offers Senta the normal day to day expectations of a trusty, honest, hard-working uncomplicated man. He is a totally socialized individual and marriage with Senta would find the couple well accepted into society. Eric's cravings and desires are, in all respects, that of the normal man in a typical social setting. Wagner presents him as so uncomplicated that it is unknown if he has any inner strength. He views, without sympathy, her dreamy, sensitive nature while her originality and uniqueness is a definite threat to him. He is "stormy, impulsive and somber, like every man who lives alone (particularly in northern highlands)." Despite the fact that she loves him--"do you doubt my heart? Do you doubt my affection?", Eric doesn't satisfy her needs. He has not asked enough of her! The Dutchman wants more than love and marriage and it is this elusive "more" that Wagner relates to: "The figure of The Flying Dutchman is a mythical creation of the Folk: a primal

181

trait of human nature speaks out from it with heart-enthralling force. This trait, in its most universal meaning, is the longing for rest from amid the storms of life."[13]

But at the age of twenty-eight Wagner did not seem to know how to resolve the issue of compassion nor even how to end the drama. Senta sacrifices her life in the name of compassion, thereby redeeming the Dutchman and ending his wandering. Several years later, when Wagner revised the drama, he changed the death ending and added a theme of redemption. This time Senta's sacrifice of life permits them both to ascend, to live presumably in heaven, or some other such place. The two were not reconciled with society but, in the revised version, neither were they damned. Regardless of which ending is presented, Wagner really offers no message for modern man. Either way the drama ends with alienation remaining both the cause of the problem and an unresolved issue.

In **Tannhäuser** Wagner again confronts issues regarding the relationships between the sexes and between man and society. Although one aspect of the drama is based on sexuality and animalistic passion as depicted in Tannhäuser's relationship with Venus and the grotto of love, a second more spiritual relationship is portrayed by Tannhäuser's love for Elisabeth and through her love for him. Tannhäuser, like all men, is drawn toward both the spiritual and the animal lure of sexuality, and this is Wagner's thesis. He portrays sexuality as both animalistic and insensitive toward acting rationally, and as romantic or capable of great sensitivity, control, and beauty. But problems of alienation go beyond the question of love and sexuality.

Tannhäuser, for reasons that Wagner never explains, willingly left the real world where he found nothing but frustration and loneliness, despite his love for Elisabeth and hers for him. Wagner seems to be articulating the theory that alienation is a component part in this particular singing-artist and poet. Perhaps Tannhäuser is Wagner, a man who all too often experienced the pain of alienation. Regardless, Tannhäuser is unable to accommodate himself to society. It was his desire and decision alone which prompted him to leave the world of man for the joy of the Venusberg.

---
[13] **Communication**, 307.

Interestingly enough, after spending a considerable amount of time wallowing in sexuality, Tannhäuser perceives that there is something missing in his life. Sexuality may make it possible to temporarily replace alienation but, as he now knows, it can never be a permanent substitution. Although Tannhäuser desires to see the sun, stars, and flowers, and to experience the smells of nature, never once does he mention a desire to return to the world of society. His alienation is so intense that he has willingly forgotten the world of man or even why he left it.

When Tannhäuser is reintroduced to his former friends they ask him the meaning of his return. Is it for "reconciliation, or renewed strife?" or as one of them expresses it, "Do you come to us as friend or foe?" It is apparent from their queries that they feel somewhat neutral toward him, neither pleased nor angry, but certainly puzzled. If he will indicate that he returns as a friend, accommodation to society apparently can be immediate; but if he returns as a threat to society they want to know. Hearing mention of the name Elisabeth causes all of Tannhäuser's hostility toward society to dissipate. Life will again become meaningful through the love of the right woman: "Wholly and entirely mastered by this latest, this impression never felt before, he shouts for very joy of life, and rushes forth to meet the loved one. The whole Past now lies behind him like a dim and distant dream; scarce can he call it back to mind: one thing alone he knows of, a tender gracious woman, a sweet maid who loves him; and one thing alone lies bare to him within this love, one thing alone in his rejoinder,--the burning, all-consuming fire of Life."[14]

Ultimately, as with the Dutchman, accommodation to society is thwarted by social pressure and peer expectations. Tannhäuser, the innovative singing-artist poet can not be reconciled with society for his perceptions, and theirs, are irreconcilable. Wagner, like Tannhäuser, was so far unable to find his place within society.

In **Lohengrin**, Wagner underscored the nature of alienation by not dealing with it as a central element within the drama. Although Elsa is reconciled with society at the end, it is not on terms that are acceptable to her since Lohengrin departed for good.

----
[14] "On the Performing of **Tannhäuser**," 199.

She is, however, the first major character in a drama to live.

Since there are other issues in **The Ring** which are of greater importance to him, Wagner deals with problems relating to sexuality and compassion only incidentally and not in great detail. Nevertheless, even if treated briefly he manages to make several important comments and his central point is expressed forthrightly by Loge: "In vain I searched, and see now full well that in the whole wide world nothing is so rich that a man will accept it in lieu of woman's beauty and delight." It is in contrast to this thesis that both Wotan and Alberich are to be measured.

Driven to renounce love because of sexual denial and frustration, Alberich opts for world mastery although in doing so he recognizes that he is sinning against himself. The expedient of having renounced and cursed love alters him to such an extent that his physical ugliness becomes merely the outward sign of his inward ugliness. Wotan, although unwilling to renounce love, appears more enamored with political power and domination and even goes so far as to bargain away love for security and the retention of his domain. Neither has a healthy attitude toward the subject nor is either seriously concerned with examining the consequences of his actions.

Despite his assumed concern for law, and disregarding the code of morality imbedded in the runes on his spear, Wotan is indifferent to his transgressions. Only Fricka advances arguments questioning his improprieties while warning of the dire social consequences of his indifference: "Unloving, most unpleasant man! For the idle toys of might and dominion would you, in blasphemous scorn, stake love and a woman's worth?" Despite his argument that "I prize women even more than it pleases you!" that is exactly what Wotan had planned to do. He would probably have succeeded had Fricka not interceded. Curiously enough, but in the name of love and to keep Wotan at home, Fricka will join in the plot to secure wealth and dominion.

Contemporary man's willingness to compromise the leveling effect of love, especially when power is sought, is a problem of monumental proportions. By illustrating Wotan's indifference toward the imperative of love, Wagner seeks to correlate him with other

184

political figures who will compromise love for power. It is, of course, a timeless problem. And yet Wagner's own sexual digressions made it difficult for him to sermonize. Wagner's relationship with his wife was often so tenuous that one aspect of the duologue between Fricka and Wotan in the second act of **Die Walküre** could well have been spoken by Minna and Richard Wagner. After Fricka talks about the sanctity and holiness of marriage, Wotan comments: "Unholy I consider the vow that unites without love." This point is quite out of keeping with the social codes of nineteenth century European thought and culture and it is quickly refuted by her appeal to law, the sanctity of contracts, and the necessity for maintaining established order together with social customs and conventions. Fricka is a superb archetypal representation of conscience, morality, and reason, and her arguments can not be dismissed lightly.

But in the entire **Ring** cycle only one of the participants expresses a true capacity for compassion. Wotan, driven by power, exhibits but little genuine concern for anyone other than himself, expressing tenderness only while reflecting upon the losses incurred by his own behavior. Alberich displays bitterness, hatred, and a total inability for compassion. Only Brünnhilde grows in character as the work unfolds. At times Wagner seemed surprised at how often people overlooked the centrality of compassion in her character: "Always Tristan, they never talk of anything but Tristan; all the tender overflowing love that lies in Brünnhilde's reflections--nobody has noticed that."[15]

There are several occurrences in **Die Walküre** where Wagner gives Brünnhilde an opportunity to reflect on the meaning of love and compassion. Although capable of displaying genuine concern for the welfare of her father, it is in the scene where she has come to escort Siegmund to Valhalla that Brünnhilde is given the opportunity to reflect on the transcendental nature of the power of love. Siegmund refuses to go with her unless accompanied by Sieglinde. Never having experienced anyone questioning her annunciation of death, Brünnhilde is momentarily flustered, more by surprise than anger: "So little do you value everlasting bliss? Is she everything to you, this poor woman who, tired and sorrowful, lies limp in your lap?

----
[15] **CW's Diaries**, 2 December 1881, 2:759.

185

Do you think nothing else glorious?" Although Brünnhilde does not understand his behavior she is struck by Siegmund's emotions. His expression of love for Sieglinde is so new to her that it comes as a revelation. But she learns quickly, as Wagner pointed out: "Can you not see that it was for love's sake that Brünnhilde sundered herself from Wotan and from all the gods, because where Wotan clung to schemes, she could only--love? ... that for Love she has renounced her godhead. She knows also[16] that one thing alone is godlike, and that is Love."

Prompted by her first feeling of genuine compassion, Brünnhilde is determined to challenge fate itself. She does this, in the name of love: "I saw his eyes, heard his words; I realized the hero's solemn distress; I heard the sounds of this brave man's lament. Unbounded love's terrible sorrow, sad heart's grandest defiance. These fell upon my ears, and my eyes beheld what deep in my breast my heart sensed with noble throbbing. Shy, astonished, ashamed I stood. How best to serve him I could still imagine."

In **Götterdämmerung** Wagner again displays the intensity of her feelings for both love and compassion. When Waltraute tries to persuade her sister to return to Wotan the ring given her by Siegfried as a token of his love, Brünnhilde exclaims: "More than the heaven of Valhalla, more than the glory of the gods, is this ring to me.... For from it shines Siegfried's love on me like a blessing--Siegfried's love! ... I will never renounce love, and they shall never wrest love from me, though Valhalla's sublime splendour collapse in ruins!" In the name of love, and desirous of being reunited with Siegfried after his death, Brünnhilde immolates herself. In the original version her spirit is then reunited with Siegfried and both ascend to Valhalla. "Love, its complete unfolding and its power--that has never been expressed in music as it is in Brünnhilde and Isolde."[17]

During the twelve year interruption between the time Wagner completed composing the second act of **Siegfried** and began the third, he wrote and orchestrated both **Die Meistersinger** and **Tristan und**

[16] Wagner to Röckel, 26 January 1854, Roeckel, **Letters**, 105.

[17] **CW's Diaries**, 8 August 1879, 2:352.

Isolde. Both contain important personal statements regarding society, alienation, and accommodation.

While composing **Die Walküre** Wagner's relationship with Mathilde Wesendonck was so intense, though not necessarily sexual, that numerous references to Mathilde appear in the marginalia of the score. As Curt von Westernhagen illustrated, "The first act of **Die Walküre** is a particularly good example of the circumstances of a period in Wagner's life impinging on what he was working on at the time: the sketch includes sixteen easily decipherable allusions[18] to his relationship with Mathilde Wesendonk." Numerous examples abound whereby Wagner used abbreviations to reflect his growing feelings for her: "'L.d.m.M?' ('Liebst du mich Mathilde?'--Do you love me Mathilde?') is written above the solo oboe part," and again later on in the first act Wagner in "expressing Sieglinde's 'profoundest sympathy', with the marginal note 'D.b.m.a!!' ('Du bist mir alles'--You are everything to me.'"[19]

Although Wagner's personal and intimate relationships with women belong more properly in a biography, the influence of Mathilde Wesendonck on **Tristan und Isolde** relates directly to his social ideas and significantly influenced this music-drama. The story of their meeting and Wagner's move into the little house occupying part of the Wesendonck property in Zurich has been told before. What is significant is that Mathilde apparently offered Wagner what Minna did not: compassion.[20] She was perhaps the first woman who

----
[18] Curt von Westernhagen, **The Forging of the 'Ring'**, Arnold and Mary Whittall, trans., Cambridge Univ. Press, 1976, 67.

[19] **Ibid.**, 69-70.

[20] The role played by compassion as one of Wagner's personal needs also extended to his feelings for animals. A vegetarian who also opposed scientific experimentation on animals, he riled against contemporary vivisection studies and against those religions which agreed with the Old Testament idea that God gave the animal world to man for his use. While man should have compassion for his fellow man he should also have pity for animals: "But, that we have not the courage to set our only motive, this of Pity, in the forefront of our appeals and admonitions to the Folk,

truly understood him and this had a profound impact on both the orchestration of **Die Walküre** and the writing of the poem and prose to **Tristan.** As indicated, compassion as contrasted with pity was the major ingredient in the relationships between Senta and the Dutchman, Elisabeth and Tannhäuser, Brünnhilde and Siegmund, and Brünnhilde and Siegfried. Out of all the women he had met thus far in his life, only Mathilde was able to offer this to Wagner. There is no evidence to indicate that their love involved a sexual relationship and a good deal of evidence to suggest that it did not. Indeed, the special transcendental nature of their love seems to correlate with that of Tristan and Isolde but it would be fundamentally incorrect to view Tristan as Wagner or to assume that Mathilde was represented by Isolde. In every respect **Tristan** is both allegory and metaphor and not any specific individual.

Even before he had completed orchestrating **Die Walküre,** both Mathilde and Tristan had intruded so forcefully into his life that it interfered with his work. He was in love with Mathilde and she with him, despite her happy marriage to Otto Wesendonck. But the likely non-sexual nature of their relationship may have intensified the internal conflicts. For years Wagner had written and talked about the nature of compassion. Now that it was a reality but not destined to be fulfilled, either in a sexual relationship or through marriage, it stimulated him to a new project while forcing him to temporarily postpone work on the **Ring.** There may have been other reasons and considerations, both artistic and financial, for delaying further work on the **Ring,** but the emotional turmoil felt at this time represented an imperative that Wagner had never before experienced. And the resolution to his emotional conflict produced **Tristan and Isolde.** This towering work represents a transcendental discourse relating the nature of compassion to both erotic and spiritual love.

----

is the curse of our Civilisation, the attestation of the un-God-ing of our established church-religions." His impassioned conclusion: "That **Human Dignity** begins to assert itself only at the point where Man is distinguishable from the Beast by pity for it, since pity for man we ourselves may learn from the animals when treated reasonably and as becomes a human being." See "Against Vivisection, An Open Letter to Ernst von Weber," October 1879, **PW,** 6: 197, 210.

The first indication of Wagner's new feelings may be observed in the now famous letter sent to Liszt: "As I have never in life felt the real bliss of love, I must erect a monument to the most beautiful of all my dreams, in which from beginning to end, that love shall be thoroughly satiated."[21] There is something that is both pathetic and revealing in this unbelievably frank but not completely true statement. Years before and passionately in love with Minna, he had persuaded her, almost against her will, to marry him. Less than six months later he initiated divorce proceedings when she ran off with another man. They were reconciled and remained affectionate toward each other for over twenty-five years of marriage. Whatever their relationship, Minna temperamentally could not and did not offer what Wagner needed most--compassion. She undoubtedly loved him. Even many years later, after they permanently separated, she worked on his behalf to obtain his political amnesty. Her attempts to intercede on his behalf could not be faulted.

But Wagner needed more from her than love. A mutual friend of theirs once wrote: "his wife was so little suited to him that she was not capable of lifting him above the many trials and difficulties of his material situation, not to alleviate them with soothing feminine charm and generosity ... a woman who understood how to mediate between the genius and the world by realizing that the two were bound to be eternally apart. She tried to mediate by demanding concessions towards the world from the genius, which the latter could not and must not make."[22]

Nevertheless, Wagner apparently loved Minna and she appears to have been a good wife. Even a cursory examination of the dozens of letters written to Minna throughout the stormy course of their lives, even after he had met Cosima, reveals the depth of his affection, if not love for her. After they separated Wagner continued sending her whatever financial support he could afford while asking his friends to display both sympathy and kindness toward her. As her health

---

[21] Wagner to Liszt, undated but written between mid-September and mid-December, 1854, **Wagner-Liszt Correspondence**, 2:54.

[22] Malvida von Meysenbug, **Memoiren einer Idealistin**, 2nd. ed., Stuttgart, 1877, Vol. 3, 286-8, as quoted in Barth, 188.

deteriorated Wagner increased his written contacts. The nature of their incompatibility, from his perspective, is clearly revealed in an amazingly frank and stark letter:

> Our essential unlikeness of nature has given pains, sometimes slight, sometimes intense, to me--and especially to you--all the time we have known each other. ... What bound me nevertheless so irresistibly to you at those times was love; a love that looked beyond all differences, a love which you did not share, at least not in the degree in which it dominated me. You really only submitted perforce to my urgent desire for union. Perhaps you felt for me all that you were capable of feeling, but as regards that essential by the help of which every trouble is smilingly faced, love unqualified, the love whereby we love another for what he really is and **as** he is, **that** love you could not feel, for you did not understand me even then, and were always imagining me to be something other than I really am... You came [after Wagner arrived in Zurich in the aftermath of the Dresden revolution]--how happy I was! And yet, how unhappy! For you had not come to me, to share joy and sorrow with me as I was, but to **a Wagner,** who, you believed, **was about to compose an opera for Paris!** ... at least I felt **infinitely lonely** beside you, for I saw it was impossible to win you for me.[23]

---

[23] Wagner to Minna Wagner, 17 April 1850, Altmann, 1:174-5. Wagner had to plead with Minna to join him in exile in Zurich. For a while it appeared that she would not leave her home, friends, and life-style in Dresden but eventually she decided to join him after Wagner asked her to prove that she still loved him. Her reply: "in coming to you I make no slight sacrifice. What sort of a future do I face?" See Minna to Richard Wagner, 18 July 1849, Burrell, 251. Immediately after receiving this reply Wagner wrote Liszt requesting that he send Minna some money so she could immediately travel to Zurich. He did so promptly. Before Minna left Dresden she sent Wagner one further message regarding the receipt of the travel money: "it is very doubtful whether you will ever be able to pay it back, since you never adapt yourself to the world as it really is but demand that the whole world adapt and form itself according to your ideas." See Minna to Richard Wagner,

This was the beginning of Wagner's series of estrangements and reconciliations with Minna. Their friends were well aware of his "loveless life", but it appears that it may have been more a case of Minna's inability to reciprocate the extent and kind of his love. Obviously their needs were different. Two years later Wagner sounded a note of desperation: "since I can no longer seek fame or 'recognition' in art, but simply the satisfaction of a need which life denies me--the need of love--so too, I can no longer cheat myself into believing that, under conditions of public Art which are a true reflection of my love-denying life, this need can be satisfied even approximately."[24] Wagner's desperation is further reflected in a letter to his sister: "So I go on living in the old loneliness, but in the end I shall succumb to this heart starvation."[25]

At precisely this moment Wagner met Mathilde Wesendonck. But before their friendship developed and blossomed into intimacy Wagner's despondency deepened: "The truth is that I have come to my thirty-fifth year before realising that up to now I have not lived at all. It was my art that first disclosed to me what a wretched life, barren of love and joy, I have lived hitherto. What will you say when you learn I have never yet enjoyed the true happiness of love?"[26]

After his intimacy with Mathilde deepened, Wagner's letters changed remarkably. They now began to reflect a newly-awakened feeling of life, passion, and tenderness. Writing to his friend Röckel, Wagner commented: "The highest satisfaction and expression of the individual is only to be found in his complete absorption, and that is only possible through love. ... It is only by love that man and woman attain to the full measure of humanity."[27]

----

3 August 1849, Burrell, 256.

[24] Wagner to Robert Franz, 25 September 1852, Altmann, 1:232.

[25] Wagner to Cecilie Avenarius, 30 December 1852, Altmann, 1:241.

[26] Wagner to Liszt, 30 March 1853, Altmann, 1:245.

[27] Wagner to Röckel, 25 January 1854, Roeckel, **Letters**, 84.

While Wagner maintained that "it is only in the union of man and woman, by love (sensuous and super-sensuous), that the human being exists ... so the transcendent art of his life is this consummation of his humanity through love", it is possible to suggest that he had been so infatuated with the illusion of love that so long as it remained unfulfilled by either sexuality or marriage their love could be elevated beyond the realm of the physical. On her part, it appears that Mathilde remained faithful and loving to her husband and family, although she informed Otto about the intensity of her feelings toward Wagner.

Writing about her to his sister Clara, Wagner commented: "Yet we recognized forthwith that any union between us could not be so much as thought of, and were accordingly resigned; renouncing every selfish wish, we suffered, endured, but--loved each other!" It was a relationship "which on its side never violated morals."[28]

Considering the unlikelihood of any further relationship beyond that of genuine love, friendship, and compassion, it seems that both were aware that the intensity of their feelings might not be sustainable unless elevated into an almost mystical realm where it could then grow and flourish without fear of destruction. In this respect Wagner's relationships with Minna and Mathilde influenced his mental attitude and conditioned the milieu from which **Tristan und Isolde** would emerge. The compassion and understanding which Mathilde offered him was depicted not so much by the characters of Tristan or Isolde but through the symbolism which lay beneath the surface. Writing a short program note for a Vienna concert which featured the prelude and the ending to the drama, Wagner described what might have best expressed his thoughts about Mathilde:

----

[28] Wagner to Clara Wolfram, 20 August 1858, Wesendonck, **Letters**, ix. Even after Wagner and his wife separated, he continued denying any sexual liaison with Mathilde, assuring his wife of "the purity of these relations." Even Mathilde's husband Otto "was always able to bear himself to me with dignity and friendliness, just **because** he was convinced of the innocence of our relations." See Wagner to Minna Wagner, 23 April 1858, Altmann, 1:345-6.

Tristan und Isolde
a) Prelude (Liebestod)

Tristan as bridal envoy conducts Isolde
to his uncle king. They love each other.
From the most stifled moan of quenchless
longing, from the faintest tremour to
unpent avowal of a hopeless love, the
heart goes through each phase of
unvictorious battling with its inner
fever, till, swooning back upon itself,
it seems extinguished as in death.

b) Conclusion (Verklärung)

Yet, what fate divided for this life, in
death revives transfigured: the gate of
union opens. Above the corpse of
Tristan, dying Isold sees transcendent
consummation of their passionate desire,
eternal union in unmeasured realms, nor
bond nor barrier, indivisible![29]

Three years earlier he had described the final
transformation scene in these words: "the heart sinks
back to pine of its desire--desire without attainment;
for each fruition sows the seed of fresh desire, till
in its final lassitude the breaking eye beholds a
glimmer of the highest bliss: it is the bliss of
quitting life, of being no more, of last redemption
into that wondrous realm from which we stray the
farthest when we strive to enter it by fiercest force.
Shall we call it death? Or is it not Night's wondrous-
world, whence--as the story says--an ivy and a vine
sprang up in lockt embrace o'er Tristan and Isolde's
grave?"[30] The mysterious ether where the souls of
Tristan and Isolde may forever intertwine represented
the only acceptable illusion that could satisfy the
transcendental nature of Wagner's relationship with
Mathilde Wesendonck.

---

[29] Translated from the **Bayreuther Blätter**, 1902, from
the program notes written by Wagner for the Vienna
concert of 27 December 1863, see William Ashton Ellis,
The Life of Richard Wagner, Being an Authorized English
Version of C. F. Glasenapp's **Das Leben Richard
Wagner's**, 6 volumes, London, 1908, Vol. 6, 307.

[30] "Prelude to Tristan und Isolde," **PW**, 8:387. This
was written by Wagner for the Paris concert of 1860.

In **Tristan** Wagner continues to ask several important social questions that had been formulated in his earlier music-dramas while adding several significant new ones: What is the relationship between sexuality and spirituality? Can passion encompass compassion? Can one express genuine compassion when confronted by sexuality or does the power of the sexual urge consume everything in its path? All of the polarities that had intrigued Wagner for so long are to be found in this drama: day and night, life and death. passion and compassion, sexuality and spirituality, honor and dishonor.

The extent to which he answered these questions depends on one's personal interpretation. While Minna Wagner once referred to Tristan and Isolde as "a much odious and slippery couple", Wagner tried to illustrate "a being utterly consumed by love." It is in that consummation that Wagner tried to illustrate the antisocial nature of Tristan's actions, whereby honor and friendship can be compromised, albeit unintentionally, by the urgency of the power of passion. Tristan acted as a knight should act, purposely refusing to see Isolde when conveying her to his uncle; but Wagner's imperative required that the power of love not be restrained by rational attempts to deny its existence. Overcome by a force of nature which he is powerless to control, Tristan betrays Marke, thereby paving the way for his own undoing. It is, as[31] Wagner well describes it, "eros who holds sway."[31] In the grip of passion Tristan is "no longer himself." In the critical second act scene between Tristan and Isolde, Wagner portrays the frenzy of their emotions by depicting how neither is any longer in control of their passions. Constantly interchanging the words between them, it matters little who is talking. Seldom had Wagner found a more perfect way to express irrationality, and that is exactly his intention. The passion of love can express and encompass rage and violence as well as heroism and courage. It is one further aspect of human nature which society must seek to accommodate. As Cosima recorded: "in the second act he wanted ... to describe happiness, the feeling that there are no more barriers and all else is forgotten, and the desire to perpetuate this condition through death. 'How lovely it is that this happiness of total oblivion can only be felt by two alone!'"[32] Wagner

---

[31] **CW's Diaries**, 9 April 1870, 1:208.

once referred to Tristan as his most tragic subject because "in it Nature is hindered in its highest work."

Sexual frustration when combined with Isolde's loveless marriage to King Marke, prompts even friendship to be compromised. Wagner has skillfully portrayed in this drama the disintegration of a microcosm of society. Not only did these forces come into collision with each other but they left death and chaos in their aftermath. In explaining the Prelude Wagner seemed to imply that Tristan's willingness to escort Isolde to Marke was in itself wrong. Although playing the role of the valiant disinterested knight, Tristan refused to acknowledge to himself his love for Isolde, thereby precipitating the catastrophe: "Love's goddess, jealous of her downtrod rights, avenged herself: the love-drink destined by the careful mother for the partners in this merely political marriage, in accordance with the customs of the age, the Goddess foists on the youthful pair through a blunder diversely accounted for."[33]

Whether or not this scheme involving the love-potion exonerates Tristan's behavior toward the king's future wife, is debatable; but regardless of whether the couple had the free will to resist expressing their love toward each other, it sets into motion a series of events that--as Wagner implies--can not be restrained: "Henceforth no end to the yearning, longing, bliss and misery of love: world, power, fame, splendour, honour, knighthood, loyalty and friendship, all scattered like a baseless dream; one thing alone left living: desire, desire, unquenchable longing forever rebearing itself,--a fevered craving; one sole redemption--death[34] surcease of being, the sleep that knows no waking." The ferocity of their love can only be ended by death, the "bliss of quitting life." Only in death is their love to be redeemed. But is this the answer to King Marke's question: "Whither has loyalty fled now that Tristan has betrayed me? What price now honour and honesty, now that the champion of all honour Tristan, has lost it?" Angered, shocked, and hurt, Marke asks for an explanation. There is no answer.

----

[32] CW's Diaries, 20 November 1878, 2:206.

[33] "Prelude to Tristan und Isolde," PW, 8:387.

[34] Idem.

Wagner's social attitudes as reflected in his original perception of **Tristan** became modified over the next twenty-five years, especially after he met and fell in love with Cosima. Originally portraying in the drama the frustration and destructiveness of erotic love, he later tended to deny that the action represented a supersensual longing of two individuals who permitted no one to get in their way. Years later Wagner preferred to see in the pair the reflection of a transcendental rather than an erotic love, one which would remain unfulfilled during their physical life. Through no design of plot or situation could that pair become part of society.

Written at the time when Wagner's passionate involvement with Mathilde was at its zenith, having been forced to leave Zurich when Otto temporarily forbade his wife from seeing him again, forced by loneliness to complete the third act of the drama in a hotel room in Venice, **Tristan** represented a singular moment in Wagner's life: "The Tristan will cost me much still; but once it is quite ended, meseems a vastly important period of my life will have been rounded off, and I shall look with new senses, calmly, [35] clearly and with deep consciousness into the world." In no way, other than by death, could either couple hope to find redemption through each other; in no way could either find social accommodation.

----
[35] Wagner to Mathilde Wesendonck, 16 September 1858, Wesendonck, **Letters**, 41. Wagner's relationship with the Wesendonck's was never broken; however, it was strained somewhat during his last few months in Zurich after Minna intercepted a love letter written to Mathilde. Mathilde apparently explained to Otto the nature of her relationship with Wagner. Otto apparently forgave them when convinced that their relationship was platonic. It was Wagner's idea to leave the "Asyl," the cottage provided him by the Wesendonck's which bordered their property on the outskirts of Zurich. Letters between all of them continued over the next few years. When Wagner returned briefly to Zurich in 1859 he stayed as their house-guest: "The husband is very devoted to me and admirable in the truest sense of the word. A beautiful and certainly very rare relation has been evolved there, and has proved what true sincerity can do..." See Wagner to Hans von Bülow, 7 October 1859, Altmann, 2:75. There is, of course, supreme irony when one considers to whom this letter was sent.

Some see in Wagner's constant talk: of death; an
end to longing; reunification by denial of the world;
and other similar thoughts relating to life and death,
the reflection of Schopenhauer's pessimism, and in
particular that philosopher's concept relating to the
release of the will through death. But although Wagner
was genuinely impressed with and influenced by
Schopenhauer, he borrowed the verbiage more than the
philosophy. Denial of the will by death was reversed
and transformed by Wagner into the denial of the will
by love: "For it is a matter of demonstrating a path of
salvation recognised by none of the philosophers,
particularly not by Schopenhauer,--the pathway to
complete pacification of the Will through love, and
that no abstract love of mankind, but the love which
actually blossoms from the soil of sexual love... It
is conclusive, that I am able to use for this (as
philosopher,--not as poet, since as such I have my own)
the terminology which Sch. himself supplies me."[36]

Wagner's own sense of propriety and value
structure intruded into his professional work and no
amount of rationalization made it possible to see
anything commendable in the relationship between
Tristan and Isolde: all values were "scattered like a
baseless dream." It is understandable why Wagner, later
in life, attempted to place a milder interpretation on
his drama. Although musically significant, the poem was
proving to be an embarrassment. Kurvenal may have
expressed it best when in referring to the power of
love he called it, "the world's loveliest delusion",
----
[36] Wagner to Mathilde Wesendonck, 1 December 1858,
Wesendonck, **Letters**, 41. Some biographers tend to
stress the indebtedness of Wagner to Schopenhauer.
While certainly true that Wagner expressed nothing but
the highest admiration for him, and indeed, out of all
the philosophers who ever wrote his works alone were
selected as required reading for the education of his
son Siegfried, nevertheless it appears that
Schopenhauer merely reflected best what Wagner
believed. In a letter to Schopenhauer, never sent, he
stated: "You alone supply me with the terminology
whereby my views may be imparted philosophically..."
See Wesendonck, **Letters**, 77n. Subsequently in a further
letter to Mathilde Wagner comments about his "amendment
of some of his [Schopenhauer's] imperfections." Still
later: "Thus I did a lot of philosophy, and arrived at
some big results supplementing and correcting my friend
Schopenhauer." See, Wesendonck, **Letters**, 93.

but Wagner expressed it better: "Love as fearful agony."

Ultimately the questions of importance to Wagner in **Tristan** were psychologically-oriented and therefore more difficult to resolve. Nevertheless, they had to be acknowledged. Although the passions represent a reality that sometimes precludes social accommodation, society must learn how to deal with the problems caused by sexual alienation. It may well be that Wagner tried to illustrate a transcendental and spiritual relationship between Tristan and Isolde, perhaps as a corollary to his feelings for Mathilde Wesendonck. But in actuality, the antisocial behavior of Tristan and Isolde toward Marke vividly expressed the reality of a contemporary social problem. While Wagner and Mathilde may have agreed to a self-sacrifice of their love, the actions of Tristan were more in keeping with the urgency of the moment than was the romantic and transcendental illusion of love whereby Wagner and Mathilde willingly agreed to separate from each other. How society handles passion is not resolved in **Tristan,** but in **Die Meistersinger** Wagner illustrated how it is recognized and dealt with by one who is aware of its potential for mischief.

In **Die Meistersinger** one may observe the most completely thought-out combination of causes and forces at work regarding Wagner's theories on progress, society, social accommodation, and social alienation. Not only does this drama contain a microcosm of several of the social issues personally facing Wagner throughout his life, but it attempts to deal with the interplay of forces so prevalent in all interpersonal relations. It is therefore a vital document in terms of any understanding of Wagner's attitude toward man in society.

In the first act, Walther's trial song is initially reminiscent of **Tannhäuser.** By choosing as his subject the theme of love rather than the expected and more appropriate sacred theme, Walther comes dangerously close to becoming a threat to society by his willingness to so freely express his feelings and emotions:

> I felt it rising deep within me as if it were waking me from a dream;

my heart with its quivering beats filled my
whole bosom: my blood pounds all powerfully,
swollen by this new feeling;
from a warm night and with superior strength
this host of sighs swells to a sea in a wild
tumult of bliss: the breast -- how soon it
answers the call which brought it new life:[37]
strike up the majestic song of love!

His outspoken brazenness shocked the reputable
members of Nürnberg society. Determined to defend the
norm of conventionality in the wake of such blatant
sexual expressiveness, Walther fails his initial song
contest. But after learning the necessity for social
propriety and the value of stability, and being made
aware of the potential mischief that his liberality
might bring to a conservative but tranquil city, he
becomes socialized to the point where he learns how to
feign compromise in order to find acceptance.

The song contest toward the end of the drama
stands in sharp contrast to the earlier one. Taking
full measure of his instruction from Sachs, Walther now
raises love to its highest level. Instead of the
earlier celebration of sensual love, Walther uses
allegory to disguise, but not deny, its erotic imagery.

Most gracious day, to which I awoke from a
poet's dream!
The Paradise of which I had dreamed in
heavenly, new-transfigured splendour lay bright
before me, to which the spring laughingly now
showed me the path;
she, born there, my heart's elect, earth's most
lovely picture, destined to be my Muse, as holy
and grave as she is mild, was boldly wooed by
me;
in the sun's bright daylight, through victory
in song, I had won Parnassus and Paradise.

For the moment, through Walther's song, Wagner has
bridged the gap between spiritual and erotic love.

----

[37] English translation by Peter Branscombe, 1974, which
accompanies the Deutsche Grammophon recording of **Die
Meistersinger von Nürnberg** (2740 149). All uncited
quotations are from this translation; however, on
several occasions the author has preferred his own
translation of certain words.

In **Die Meistersinger** Wagner attempted to portray both an actual and an idealized way in which one society might have worked. Containing many of Wagner's social theories, together with many of his philosophical assumptions regarding the nature of economics and politics, this music-drama is more personal than many of his other works. Not only does he attempt to deal with real people in realistic situations, but he also expresses some important aesthetic ideas relating to the nature of music. When aesthetic ideals are correlated with his more important social theories regarding the nature of the thinking man in society, Wagner makes a powerful personal statement.

Unlike the earlier thirteenth century "Minnesinger" who was an upper-class knight of noble birth and a Catholic, the "Mastersinger" of the sixteenth and early seventeenth centuries represented one of the newly-emergent group of middle class Protestant businessmen. They were skilled craftsmen who established guilds to maintain the professional quality and integrity of their products and to insure that only those who were the most capable could become a master. But in addition to their professional skills the mastersingers were also musicians and literary figures whose badge and banner were symbolized by King David and his lyre. This movement declined in the seventeenth century.

Nürnberg in the sixteenth century was a free walled city of approximately thirty thousand inhabitants, in which the mastersingers played a significant role. The masters generally met after church on Sunday, and from time to time established song competitions with prizes to be awarded to the successful candidate. Rigidly-prescribed rules were maintained through which candidates might seek to advance from class to class along the road toward becoming a master. Broadly speaking, there were five designated classes: scholar, friend, singer, poet, and master. The rules determining the song contest were contained on the "tablatur" and these were inviolate. Once a year a new master might be initiated although the maximum total number was frequently set at twelve.

Wagner incorporated large sections from Wagenseil's **Nürnberg Chronicle** to illustrate how the procedure worked. A newly-arrived knight is taught the rules by an apprentice who has occupied the lowest rung on the ladder for a full year. Through a duologue all the details of the procedure and what is required at each level are clearly established, often in bewildering detail: the singer must perfectly execute each note with the finest musicality not to mention beauty of voice; the poet is required to correctly join his words and rhymes to a song composed by a master; the master singer is one who writes his own words and rhymes and adds them correctly to a new song of his own composition, all according to the defined rules as imprinted on the tablatur. Although all the masters vote on whether to admit a candidate to the rank of master, one from the group is chosen to serve as the "marker", a position of distinction. The marker, separated from his colleagues, independently records on a slate the faults made by the contestant. A maximum of seven errors are permitted, after which the candidate is disqualified, or in this music-drama, "un-sung."

During the time-period of the drama's setting the most outstanding master of the day was Hans Sachs (1494-1576). Wagner provides him with an apprentice, and in the year of his studies Sachs has been teaching David to be a "scholar, shoemaker, and a poet" and in that order. It is this combination which most appeals to Wagner. Representing the integration of the physical, the aesthetic, and the spiritual, the fully-integrated personality learns how to combine these elements for the benefit of the community. Consequently, Nürnberg has been enjoying a worldwide reputation as one of the more desirable cities in Europe in which to live. It was a city where the culture and artistry of the Renaissance combine with the Protestant qualities of skill, industry, and honesty brought in by the Reformation. During his lifetime, Sachs wrote over four thousand master songs, two thousand fables and several morality plays. His best-known song, "The Nightingale at Wittenberg", championed Martin Luther's cause and, historically-speaking, helped advance the cause of Protestantism. Part of this song is included in the third act.

By going into such great detail over the types and kinds of singing, the parts and characteristics of each song, the pitfalls to be avoided, and the painstaking method by which candidates are graded, Wagner establishes an intimate feeling and understanding regarding this aspect of life in sixteenth century Nürnberg. After describing the rigidity of the entire enterprise, and the value system of its most distinguished ruling class, Wagner illustrates how it is manifested in the public reading of the "Leges Tabulaturae", an event which actually took place:

> Each unit of a Mastersong shall present a proper balance of its different sections against which no one shall offend.
> A section consists of two stanzas which shall have the same melody; the stanza is a group of so many lines, the line has its rhyme at the end.
> Thereupon follows the Aftersong which is also to be so many lines long and have its own special melody which is not to occur in the stanza.
> Each Mastersong shall have several units in this ratio; and whoever composes a new song which does not for more than four syllables encroach upon other Master's melodies--his song may win a Master's prize.

By establishing all that is so rigidly-prescribed in Nürnberg society, Wagner permits his audience to understand and reflect upon the issues involved in the two major conflicting viewpoints of the drama; on one side, the clear-thinking and dedicated craftsmen who have established and defined a set of values which appear eminently sensible and correct; on the other, the stranger to Nürnberg, a newcomer, one who attempts to confront and even challenge absolute and seemingly inflexible values. It is a classic situation, the new and different represents a serious threat to all that seems important to the old and entrenched.

Hans Sachs stands as the pivotal figure between the established order and the perceived threat to it represented by the newcomer. Standing in sharp contrast to every other personality created in his music-dramas, perhaps no figure comes closer to Wagner's own temperament and way of thinking. As an archetypal figure representing the ideal wise man, he possesses all the qualities of "the thinking man." He is noble, righteous, and just, and possesses a keen sense of dignity. Nevertheless, he believes in the need to maintain a clearly-established system of moral, economic, political, and spiritual values for the best functioning of society. Being a conservative he is unwilling to see that which he feels to be right threatened or challenged, unless there is a solid and acceptable social base upon which the challenge is rooted. In this respect Sachs is a progressive; not a reformer for the sake of reform, he is an open-minded realist. By recognizing that mankind sometimes requires a belief in harmless illusions, and that self-deception is not always bad, Sachs becomes part-God, part-Jesus, part John the Baptist, and part Wagner. He is the personification of the ideal man of the sixteenth century.

As the wise man Sachs assumes the major role in the drama. He may reluctantly manipulate people and events when he perceives it to be necessary for the betterment of society or to achieve especially-desirable ends. He is confident enough in his own values to argue that he has a social responsibility to act on behalf of others when his own perception of right or wrong demands intercession to gently nudge people or events forward. Wagner's fondness for Sachs becomes more evident as the drama unfolds. Gradually it becomes clear that Sachs possesses ideas, attitudes, and a value system which transcends time and place.

There is, of course, an obvious danger in this glorified archetypal depiction. Portraying an ideal figure such as Sachs in a music-drama may be acceptable. But if this were reality, what are the implications? What would prevent Sachs from becoming the prototype of a fascist, one whose sense of values, on behalf of society, may enable him to arbitrarily determine all that people should believe and how they should act. If he personifies the one wise person, his value system becomes an absolute. An ability to manipulate others for the betterment of society may be appealing as a romantic depiction of a bygone society. But an actual person who is able to manipulate real people to help them attain what he believes they need, but which they can not attain for themselves because of their illusions or inabilities, borders on a totalitarian system that appears to be uncheckable. Any monopoly on wisdom, even if acknowledged by others, could represent an even greater threat to society than an entrenched inflexible conservatism. Wagner's ideal "thinking artist" may represent the greater danger to the society that he is determined to help.

Although the mastersingers emerge as a collective unit representing a conservative defense of the status quo, the ideals they defend are important and worthwhile. Sachs recognizes, appreciates, and cherishes these values, but perceives that there are times when permanence may preclude creativity. To automatically assume that the status quo is desirable and that values should be permanent and unchanging may provide stability but perhaps at the expense of growth and progress. A delicate balance between contending forces may provide the right amount of energy which could serve as a device for infusing new life into society. Society's beliefs are often both threatened and reinforced by art, love, and illusions, thereby creating both unavoidable conflict and desirable change. The highest and noblest purpose of art is to offer man values, even if they can not always replace illusions. Sachs accepts this as a truism of life. Sachs is therefore an enlightened man, altruistic, thinking always of society, concerned with both ends and means, and willing to help man do what he can not do for himself.

Several other interesting character vignettes appear in the drama and each is assigned a particular role to depict both social ideas and aesthetic values. Walther von Stolzing is one of the more significant. An outsider who is unfamiliar with the rules governing the guilds and their initiation procedures, he is determined to enter the song contest despite his lack of formal training. In the process he challenges the order and stability of society and this is one major purpose of the drama. Two conflicting viewpoints are presented: first, those who believe it imperative to maintain the status quo as if truth, once found and accepted, is a permanent and fixed absolute; second, those who seek to examine, question, challenge, and ultimately replace these assumptions. Both viewpoints are persuasive and each has merit; there is no point that is unequivocally right or wrong which would simplify the action. Before the drama comes to a close Wagner will carefully examine both viewpoints and will present compelling arguments supporting each side, before finding an acceptable method for bridging the gap.

To keep the important issues clearly in focus only two other mastersingers are given differentiated characterizations, Pogner the goldsmith, and Beckmesser the town clerk. The mastersingers are a guild comprising men of talent, ability, and taste. They created and maintain a system of economic, cultural, and social values to which they are committed but within this guild are to be found men of differing attitudes and points of view. Even among conservatives there are wide varieties of personalities.

Never personally sympathetic toward the business and commercial elements in society and often considering them to be parasites and corrupters of taste, Wagner presents Pogner as an exception. Perhaps he may even represent the archetype of the truly enlightened businessman in pre-industrial Germany for Pogner recognizes both the important position he occupies in Nürnberg society and the social role he is required to play. Representing the Protestant and capitalistic work-ethic which makes him willingly assume a stewardship role as protector and defender of society and its institutions, he automatically, perhaps unthinkingly, assumes the need for the existence of social control. In befriending Walther he is not opposed to the knight's entering the trial song contest which is to be held momentarily, and he will even bring Walther's name forward for admission to the guild, but only if all the rules are followed.

Beckmesser stands in sharp contrast to Pogner. The town clerk is a scholar and a pedant. Knowledgeable in Latin, he handles the minutiae of legal details so necessary in the performance of his duties. His pedantic nature proves highly useful since someone needs to grasp all the rules and regulations of society in order to provide answers to questions which might arise in the normal course of social intercourse. Because of his expertise and painstaking attention to detail, Beckmesser is frequently called upon to serve as the Marker in the song contest; if anyone knows the rules of the tabulatur it is he. In artistic terms Wagner seems to have been of two minds regarding how he should be portrayed. Advising that he should never appear as a caricature for he is called upon to play a deliberately important and philosophically significant role in the drama, Wagner does not wish Beckmesser depicted as a comic figure and most decidedly not a clown. Yet, twice he is given both the music and the setting which turns him into a buffoon-like character if not an outright buffoon.

There are Beckmesser's within all societies and although often mentally equipped to play significant roles they are, nevertheless, too often single-minded, intransigent, and incapable of flexibility or change. Often emerging as reactionaries they are so set against any form of change that progress itself becomes a threat to their security. Because of the love factor that Wagner places into the drama, Beckmesser will act irrationally and as part of his fever will commit a serious and unexpected moral transgression.

The romantic element involving Pogner's daughter Eva, in love with the newcomer Walther but loved by Beckmesser, gives Wagner an opportunity to create a social situation with wide implications. When Pogner suggests his daughter's hand in marriage to the winner of the song contest, a linkage is created between marriage and art. Questioning the propriety of tying these two elements together brings forth the first commentary by Sachs.

Sachs now raises a question with wide-ranging ramifications: once a year why not permit the people the right to comment on the substance of the rules? Neither advocating democracy nor suggesting that the masses be permitted to vote, Sachs merely raises the question of whether or not they should be permitted to "test the rules themselves, to see whether in the dull course of habit their strength and life doesn't get lost: and whether you are still on the right track of Nature will only be told you by someone who knows nothing of the table of rules." Introducing Sachs as not merely a quasi-liberal but a man possessing a fresh, dispassionate mind, Wagner is implying that "society" may rightfully extend beyond the masters and the guilds; perhaps the "people" might possess a vitality which could also enrich and nourish society.

These suggestions, inclining toward establishing a dangerous precedent, are too innovative for the moment. Fearful of the consequences of his suggestion they express concern that public participation would likely result in the debasement of both art and the high standards set by the guilds: "Farewell then Art and Master-tones." In pandering to the masses "Art is constantly threatened with downfall and disgrace if it runs after the favours of the people." The matter is not pressed further although Beckmesser glibly expresses suspicion at anyone who likes to curry favor with the public. Wagner has raised his first significant point regarding the potential divisiveness between established traditions and innovative alternatives. But at the same time he has made Sachs the "last of the folk's heroes."

Questioning Walther's eligibility to enter the trial song contest and fearful that if he did he might introduce discordant elements into society, the masters are suspicious when informed of his highly unusual learning approach: "what the wondrous power of the poet's song tried in secret to disclose to me ... if I must exchange life's highest prize for song, in my own words and to my own melody it will flow into a unity for me as a Mastersong." Choosing love as his subject, rather than the more appropriate and expected sacred theme, Walther not only feels free to express himself but also proves that he is an outsider unaware of and unconcerned with their traditions.

Returning to the theme and sentiment of the singing-contest in **Tannhäuser,** Wagner's perspective this time will be considerably different. Through **Tristan und Isolde,** Wagner said all that he wanted to regarding the extremes to which the delusion of love could carry unthinking and impressionable people. Now, in **Die Meistersinger** the theme of love and marriage will ultimately find its proper method of expression. In the polarity between unbridled passion and the sobering reality of man's responsibilities within existing society, a delicate balance will finally be achieved. Erotic love may exist within the freedom of the psyche but not as a viable expression of action within a highly structured and socialized collection of individuals. Sensuality may be an integral part of man, but its permissible method of expression is acceptable only within the orbit of marriage. Even when Walther and Eva attempt to elope, Sachs prevents it. Actions of this type are viewed as antisocial and unthinkable. Selfishness and egoism pit the individual against society and this would be unacceptable.[38]

----

[38] The marriage contract, fidelity, and monogamy, seemed to mean little to Wagner, the man. It is therefore ironic that the last article he worked on, dated 11 February 1883, two days before he died, was entitled, "On the Womanly in the Human." Intended for publication in the **Bayreuth Blätter** it was to be a supplement to "Religion and Art." Only a fragment was written but Wagner attempted to prove why mankind was heading for ultimate destruction: "If it is Marriage that raises man so far above the animal world, to highest evolution of his moral faculties, it is the abuse of marriage for ulterior ends that is the cause of our decline below the beasts." Categorically asserting that the superiority of the white race rested

Blithely exploiting a worldly subject while disregarding all the rules as enunciated so carefully by the reading of the tabulatur, Walther seems oblivious to events around him, seemingly enjoying himself at the expense of the masters. In addition to faulty construction, improper notes, obscure meanings, lack of melody--and the errors are unending--the song is interpreted as a personal affront to the masters. Is an anarchist trying to flout the rules? In all respects Walther represents a real, not an imagined threat to all values that the guilds hold sacred. Speaking not only on Walther's behalf, but for Wagner as well, Sachs expresses an important part of the thesis promulgated by Wagner in **Opera and Drama:** "The knight's song and melody I found new, but not confused; if he left our paths he at least strode firmly and surely. If you wish to measure according to rules something which does not accord with your rules, forget your own ways, you must first seek **its** rules."

What Sachs had to say related directly to Wagner's present personal circumstances. In the middle of composing the **Ring,** not knowing how or when it would be finished and more than uncertain where it could be performed even if he did manage to complete it, Wagner had incurred an artistic and an aesthetic problem attempting to produce **Tristan und Isolde.** Originally scheduled to have its premiere in Vienna, it was canceled as unplayable, after fifty-four rehearsals. Finally, when **Tristan** did have its premiere in Munich, Wagner was accused of breaking all the traditionally-accepted rules of music. Some critics bitterly complained that he was incapable of composing either true melodies or of consistency in maintaining key integrity. That Wagner was "inventing" new rules to suit himself was undeniable, even by Wagner, but was this invalid? Did not his own rules permit the music to receive a fair hearing?

Precisely this situation now faces Walther! The first positive words which Sachs utters are remarkably similar to those expressed toward the end of **A Communication to my Friends,** and in both cases they represent a plea not to reject that which is new,

----

with its advocacy of monogamy, Wagner admitted that polygamy might be more consistent with nature. But monogamy would more likely produce genetic superiority. See **PW,** 8:396-7.

unless and until it is first given a full, impartial hearing.

But Wagner attempts to deal quite objectively with the core of the argument even though he is not sympathetic with Beckmesser's counter-argument regarding Sachs' willingness to open a "loophole for bunglers who come and go as they please and follow their own frivolous course." Replying, "God forbid that what I ask should not be according to the laws!", Sachs nevertheless wants to hear the song in its entirety before determining whether or not it is frivolous. Insisting on objectivity the two uncharacteristically enter into a series of personal thrusts against each other, until the masters finally put a stop to it.

Fearful of Walther's intrusive and irregular behavior, the masters are determined that Walther should not succeed in applying for admission to the guild: "Is everyone of us not at liberty to decide whom he wishes as a colleague? if every stranger were welcomed what worth would the Masters then have?" This is more than a conservative defense of the status quo. It is a plea that rules which have been carefully devised should not be arbitrarily suspended just to meet new and possibly temporary circumstances. Clearly puzzled by the song Sachs can not yet determine whether it was as bad as the others thought. It had a "spirit" to it, and a "glow of inspiration", even though it broke the rules.

Obviously every society requires rules lest there be anarchy. But are there times when rules are so absolute that they inhibit creativity? If so, is there a practical solution? At what point are rules, or standards, to be rigidly and absolutely maintained and when might they become flexible and changing? How is this determination to be made and by whom? If rules can be conveniently modified to meet changing circumstances is this not likely to debase the standards they were designed to maintain? Is change to be encouraged or might it be a threat to stability? How does one deal with new thoughts which might encourage progress although at the possible expense of entrenched ideas? These are but a few of the significant questions that Wagner has been raising for many years, and each is to be found in this drama.

Struck by the enormity of these questions, Sachs reflects on them and perceives the agonizing implications in attempting answers. As a master shoemaker he is secure in knowing that he can measure the quality of his product and can tell if the workmanship is flawless; but with poetry and song the criteria are not always so objectively verifiable and there is the possibility for error: "I feel it and cannot understand it; and if I grasp it wholly, I cannot measure it!--But then, how should I grasp what seemed to me immeasurable?" By what objective yardstick can one measure art? Clearly perceiving that the "value" that one can place on aesthetic endeavors is seldom capable of being predicated in advance, nor is any decision on its merits final, Sachs hears certain elements within Walther's words and song that elude an immediate understanding. Most certainly it does not conveniently "fit" the rules, but can the song be dismissed arbitrarily as worthless: "No rule seemed to fit it, and yet there was no fault in it.--It sounded so old, and yet was so new." Reflecting further Sachs is finally forced to conclude that the song is innovative, but good!

Perhaps again Sachs is rallying to Wagner's cause; "he who was born a Master has among Masters the worst standing." Being as objective and as dispassionate as possible when confronting the new, the untried, and the untested, and after having carefully examined and analyzed his thoughts, Sachs sees in the song a relationship to nature itself: "sweet necessity placed it in his breast: then he sang as he had to; and as he had to, so he could."

Not unexpectedly, Walther's response over having failed the trial contest is one of hostility: "But these Masters! Ha, these Masters! The gluey, sticky nature of these rhyming laws! ... Away, to freedom! That's where I belong, where I'm Master in the house!" Determined that important issues need to be faced which will provide a satisfactory way of resolving the artistic impasse, Sachs persuades Walther not to leave Nürnberg. Departing now would be tantamount to yielding to selfish, egocentric desires while remaining and fighting for his aesthetic freedom would be more worthy of a thinking man.

Gradually establishing Sachs as the archetypal thinking artist, Wagner gives him the responsibility for bringing a clarity of vision and a depth of perception to those around him. In **The Art-Work of the Future** Wagner commented on the special thought patterns which some poets possess. Serving as a receptacle through which those elusive transcendental values can emerge for the betterment of society, Hans Sachs, the poet and artisan is in the process of becoming the politician. His purpose is not to expose man's illusions or delusions for these are sometimes necessary, but to serve as a catalyst that will permit change or progress to occur. Sachs will try to remove some of the impediments hindering man's vision.

While Walther yearns for his freedom of expression, even if it means challenging the system, the apprentice David represents the more typical hard-working pupil who seeks advancement by working within the system through traditional means. Diffident, obedient, well-socialized, and under Sachs' guidance and supervision, David is learning his trade in combination with the art of master-singing. Eventually he will take his expected place in the hierarchy of society and will likely become a staunch defender of traditionally conservative values. It is doubtful if he would ever become a threat or embarrassment to those around him.

Reflecting on the way events so often get out of hand, Sachs introspectively analyzes man's nature to determine how the future can be shaped to yield a satisfactory solution: "Illusion! Illusion! Everywhere illusion! Wherever I look searchingly in city and world chronicles, to seek out the reason why, till they draw blood, people torment and flay each other in useless, foolish anger!" Undoubtedly these questions are important, but assuming that all questions can be resolved only creates additional illusions.

Sachs assumes a predominant role through his ability to understand that while unable to resolve all issues he might be able to direct or redirect society in ways which could ameliorate some of the more stressful problems that arise through the normal course of events. Willingly, but cautiously, the thinking artist acknowledges reality: "who will give it its name? It is the old illusion, without which nothing can happen, nothing whatever." Man is so often capable of self-deception that when "driven to flight, he thinks he is hunting; hears not his own cry of pain"; but this truism is not necessarily incorrect; it is a recognition and an acceptance of reality.

Although perhaps only God knows why certain events happen, only man can "quench the fire of anger." As the new day dawns Sachs assumes responsibility for shaping and guiding the immediate course of events. The thinking artist will intercede on behalf of society: "Now let us see how Hans Sachs manages finely to guide the illusions so as to perform a nobler work: for if illusion won't leave us in peace even here in Nuremberg, then let it be in the service of such works as are seldom successful in common-place activities and never so without a touch of illusion."

By trying to view himself in a dispassionate and detached manner, almost as if he were outside his own psyche, the thinking artist is presumably capable of becoming an objective entity. If this were true it may even facilitate his ability to manipulate, in the best sense of the word and but moderately, those around him. But leadership is fraught with the danger of excess. In this idealized setting of reality, Sachs will not permit himself to get too far ahead of the masters or the townspeople, otherwise he would either fail in his task or else exert more power than is desirable. Wagner somehow assumed that those who will follow the role model of Sachs would know how, where, and when to draw the line so as to maintain the delicate balance between leadership and arbitrary control.

Walther is perhaps a younger and less disciplined reflection of what Sachs was like when he became a crusader on behalf of Martin Luther and a fighter in the cause of turning Nürnberg Protestant. He may even become a creative poet, and possibly a thinking artist; for the moment, however, he needs to learn how to work within the parameters established by society if he hopes to gradually make his ideas acceptable to them, a lesson that Wagner himself had trouble learning.

If the mastersingers are staunch defenders of the status quo who deliberately and persistently reject all change, then Walther's hostile attitude toward them might be understandable and may perhaps even be justifiable; but they are sincere and honorable men who have found a noble way of life and share a keen sense of values and traditions that have been tried and tested by experience: "You are dealing with men of honor; they make mistakes and are content that one takes them on their own terms. ... Your song made them uneasy; and rightly so." Presenting a rational and balanced argument in favor of establishing a clear

212

perspective between the differences of love and lust, Sachs in a few well-chosen words rejects the entire central theme of **Tristan und Isolde** and clarifies the point made so imperfectly by Tannhäuser.

Without rules there is anarchy, and no individual can achieve happiness and find the meaning of life outside of society. Wagner has now come to the heart of both his fictional story and his life history. Often alienated from society, forced to stand by himself for what he believed, an outsider more than an accepted insider, Wagner articulated through Sachs the ideal relationship between the thinking artist and society. But however he tried to make the necessary correlation, Sachs was a vital part of Nürnberg society while Wagner remained mostly on the periphery of German society. Sachs urges Walther to do what Wagner could not do: to work with and not against the masters and to accept life as a compromise in which one's range of options is not always unlimited. By accepting reality rather than the illusion of freedom, Walther would not be untrue to himself nor would he betray his sense of personal identity; yet he would achieve security and comfort and that would not exist if he maintained his romantic delusions.

Few answers to important questions are ideal and even at this stage of his life, Sachs is "a troubled man." If Walther could look within his soul he might find both the poetry and the appropriate rules. The wise man has finally found his worthy apprentice while the young man is to be taught by the one and only person capable of seeing him as possessing qualities of true leadership, the poet who might become the politician.

Although careful to keep Sachs as the mediator between the liberal Walther and the conservative Beckmesser, Wagner changes the balance in the scales when Beckmesser pockets a poem seemingly written by Sachs, thereby demonstrating the extent to which the twin emotions of love and jealousy can sometimes create unexpected and antisocial behavioral patters. Cleverly surmising how to achieve two necessary objectives-- discrediting Beckmesser for attempting to steal the poem while championing Walther's cause--Sachs presents Beckmesser with the poem, "so that people don't think evil of you, keep the sheet, let it be a present to you... So that you're no thief."

When homage is paid to Nürnberg's most outstanding and respected Master, "Sachs stands up before the whole assemblage, and is greeted by the people with a mighty outburst of enthusiasm, whereon they chant with clarion tongue the first eight lines of Sachs' ode to Luther." Demonstrating his admiration for the real Sachs, and as a tribute to him, Wagner included several lines from a poem written in 1523:

> Awake! the dawn is drawing near;
> I hear a blissful nightingale
> singing in the green grove,
> its voice rings through hill and valley;
> night is sinking in the west,
> the day arises in the east,
> the ardent red glow of morning
> approaches through the gloomy clouds.[39]

Adapted from "Wacht auf", the nightingale is an allegorical reference to Martin Luther whom the lion, the Catholic church, would like to chase away. The nightingale awakens the erring sheep who--no longer oppressed--become unafraid.

Toward the end of the drama Wagner reinforces two major points: first, that "art" is an end in itself and "he who cleaves to it for its own sake esteems it above all prizes"; second, whoever becomes a master should be "pure and noble, in wooing as in singing", a clear rebuke to Beckmesser who is attempting to use art as a means to an end, and even in that capacity, in a dishonest manner.

This time Walther's song receives a fair hearing by both the judges and townspeople alike. Having learnt lessons in diplomacy and tact from Sachs, the young knight uses allegory to disguise, but not deny, the eroticism of sensual love.

Interestingly enough, although the song is immediately acknowledged as a Master song, its meaning is still obscure to most of them: "Lulled as if in the most beautiful dream I hear it well, but scarcely grasp it." Likewise, the rules followed do not correspond to those established by the tabulatur. Wagner appears to be establishing Walther as a likely successor to Sachs, not only as an archetypal thinking artist, but as a

----
[39] Wagner to Mathilde Wesendonk, 22 May 1862, Wesendonck, **Letters**, 302.

214

poet-politician as well. Although Sachs had "thought it out excellently!" what exactly has transpired? Through the use of illusion Walther, like Sachs before him, manipulated the rules of society to achieve his ends. No harm was done. But the implications are horrendous!

Wagner seems to have recognized these implications as he tried to place the issues in a sharp perspective. Walther is a unique exception to the rules. An outsider who desired freedom above all restrictions, he began to realize, through the efforts of Sachs, that one could gain entrance to society by learning how to work within the structure. Although this exception should not necessarily become the rule, the system could be made to work. The masters had modified their rules to accommodate an exception: "What speaks high in their praise fell richly in your favour. Not to your ancestors, however worthy, not to your coat-of-arms, spear, or sword [but] to the fact that you are a poet, that a Master has admitted you." Unlike the Dutchman, Tannhäuser, Elsa, Lohengrin, Tristan, or Isolde, Walther can be accommodated to society if each side agrees, in principle, to a non-verbalized compromise.

The masters acknowledge him worthy of membership in the guild despite the fact that the song-poem did not really adhere to the rules of the tabulatur. Representing both change and stability, Sachs has been instrumental in managing events without assuming direct power or control over anyone. By gently nudging each party, a stalemate has been averted. The rules remain, as before, but accommodation became possible.

Perhaps this is Wagner's final answer to the question of man in society. Certainly some feelings of tension and frustration are just as likely in the future as in the past. Undoubtedly the thinking artist will still find it difficult to accommodate himself to the will of society. But in many of Wagner's dramas alienation resulted from a total dislocation whereby no relationship was possible between the contending forces, while in **Die Meistersinger** neither Sachs nor Walther remain alienated. The relationship between man and society is solvable.

In a fascinating statement to Liszt, Wagner summed up his basic attitude regarding the nature of society:

> I have faith in the future of the human race and that faith I draw simply from my inner

necessity. I have succeeded in observing the phenomena of nature and of history with love and without prejudice and the only evil I have discovered in their true essence is **lovelessness.** But this lovelessness also I explain to myself as an **error,** an error which must lead us from the state of natural unconsciousness to the **knowledge** of the solely beautiful necessity of love. To gain that knowledge is the task of history.[40]

----
[40] Wagner to Liszt, 13 April 1853, **Wagner-Liszt Correspondence,** 1:278.

CHAPTER 6

SPIRITUALITY AND THE NATURE OF THE SOUL

Unwilling to take the most convenient path by accepting his Lutheran heritage, Wagner seemed intrigued with questions that went beyond the more obvious, "Who put me here, and Why"? By intellect, temperament, or by disposition, Wagner's religious and spiritual ideas evolved over a lifetime of often intense questioning both as to the nature of religion and to its sometimes conflicting conceptions of God.

Since Wagner was concerned with so many questions relating to politics, economics, aesthetics, and man in society, one would expect that religion too might come under his scrutiny, and it did; but it is doubtful whether any other aspect of his mental processes caused him more frustration or anguish. It is a curious but interesting fact that in matters relating to religion, Wagner's thoughts about God, the nature and meaning of spirituality, and the hypocrisy of institutional religion, represented a cluster of thoughts that remained more clearly central throughout his life than any other subject. Even musical theory and composition did not require so much of his time, energy, and attention as thoughts on religion. From his earliest days in Paris until the final years of his life he talked, conversed, and wrote more often about religion than almost any other subject. It seemed to be both the starting point and the logical ending to his intellectual quest. But whether his spiritual questioning and restlessness ever brought him the solace that religious thoughts usually bring to people is debatable.

Although born into a Lutheran family Wagner did not seem to take religion very seriously until shortly after he moved to Paris in 1839 to embark on a career as an opera composer. The starting point was a performance of Beethoven's Ninth symphony by the Paris Conservatory Orchestra. Wagner had heard the Ninth many times, especially in Leipzig, but without experiencing anything more than "mystic constellations and weird shapes without meaning." In Paris, when he heard it played by a first-rate orchestra, he suddenly perceived it in a different and new dimension: "I now found, flowing from innumerable sources, a stream of the most touching and heavenly melodies which delighted my heart." According to Wagner this produced an "inner

217

change" and an "upheaval" which resulted in a renewed dedication to music and, more importantly, to a new belief in himself: "The direct result of this was my intense longing to **compose something that would give me a feeling of satisfaction,** and this desire grew in proportion to my anxiety about my unfortunate position in Paris, which made me despair of success. In this mood I sketched an overture to Faust..."[1]

Since he was still composing **Rienzi** one might have thought that Wagner would change direction or style as he proceeded with that work. But instead he decided to begin work on a symphony based on Goethe's **Faust.** Only the overture was eventually completed but it marked Wagner's first original composition. The strength to compose the overture came from within, an "inner change" as he had remarked. It was not Wagner's first mystical experience but it was an important one. Wagner wrote the piece for himself, as a necessary tonic to all the other music he had previously written. It is not surprising that he soon found it necessary to begin working on **The Flying Dutchman** even before he completed **Rienzi,** for the **Dutchman** would become his liberating force.

The importance of this event may be understood more clearly if one examines the brief preface that Wagner wrote to the **Faust** overture in 1846.

> The God that dwells within my breast
> Can stir the utmost of my being,
> Holds all my powers at his behest,
> Yet naught without, marks his decreeing:
> And so my whole existence is awry
> Life hateful, and my one desire to die.[2]

A new feature entered Wagner's life for the first time--spirituality, and with it the knowledge of the existence, not just belief, of God. But exactly what was meant by "heavenly melodies" and "inner change" remains uncertain.

It appears that Wagner had some form of mystical experience--and this would be only the first of several throughout his life--which seemed to permit him to intuitively posit some form of knowledge transcending

---
[1] **My Life,** 1:215.

[2] Ellis, **Life of Richard Wagner,** 1:287.

perception by the senses. Experiencing what might be called "a religious awareness" but one not connected with a specific religion, it appeared as if Wagner's soul was in harmony with something that existed beyond physicality. He could not articulate his feelings beyond certain symbolic catch phrases, almost all of which related to an "inner" something or other. This mystical event, whatever it was, or whatever Wagner thought it was, proved so decisive, and so all-embracing that it left a permanent imprint on his mind. Mysticism and intense spiritual questioning would be found in, and sometimes dominated, almost every subsequent work. "The God that dwells within my breast" is not just Faust, it is now Wagner.

Rienzi's prayer in the last act of that opera include lines similar to the ones Wagner used in the preface to the **Faust** overture. Bulwer's novel contained several references to God, one in particular when Rienzi first examined his thoughts before an impending battle: "But oh, Providence! hast thou not reserved and marked me for great deeds? How, step by step, have I been led on to this solemn enterprise! How has each hour prepared its successor!"[3] Still later when Rienzi commented on the accidental as opposed to the divine in nature: "'Fate!' cries Rienzi, 'there is no fate! Between the thought and the success, God is the only agent; and (he added with a voice of solemnity) I shall not be deserted.'"[4] When preparing his own libretto for **Rienzi** Wagner went one step beyond Bulwer. Recognizing the origin and nature of his mission, Rienzi comments:

> Almighty Father, look down upon me! Hear me as I plead in the dust! Do not let me lose that power which your miracle wrought in me.
> You strengthened me, gave me supreme power, gave me sublime qualities; to bring light to those whose thoughts were lowly, to raise up what had fallen into the dust.
> You transformed the people's shame into greatness, splendour and majesty!
> Oh God, do not destroy what has been erected to your glory!

----

[3] Lord Lytton, **Rienzi, The Last of the Tribunes,** London, 1874, 79.

[4] **Ibid.,** 202.

Oh Lord, dissolve the dark night which envelops
men's souls!
Let shine upon us the eternal refection of your
power! Lord and Father, look down upon me!
Lower your gaze from your lofty heights!
O God, who gave me such mighty strength, give
ear to my fervent pleas![5]

One line, in particular, will become a trademark
of Wagner's developing religious mysticism: "Oh Lord,
dissolve the dark night which envelops men's souls!"
The sentiments behind this thought dominates both **The
Ring of the Nibelung** and **Tristan and Isolde**. Wagner was
not yet in control of his perceptions but while still
in Paris he managed to summarize some of his thoughts
toward the end of an article entitled "An End in Paris"
which he wrote for the **Gazette Musicale** in early 1841.
It was his version of the Apostolic Creed.

I believe in God, Mozart and Beethoven, and
likewise in their disciples and apostles; -- I
believe in the Holy Spirit and the truth of the
one, indivisible Art; --I believe that this Art
proceeds from God, and lives within the hearts
of all illumined men; --I believe that he who
once has bathed in the sublime delights of this
high Art, is consecrate to Her forever, and
never can deny Her; --I believe that through
this Art all men are saved, and therefore each
may die for Her of hunger; -- I believe that
death will give me highest happiness; -- I
believe that on earth I was a jarring discord,
which will at once be perfectly resolved by
death. I believe in a last judgment, which will
condemn to fearful pains all those who in this
world have dared to play the huckster with
chaste Art, have violated or dishonoured Her
through evilness of heart and ribald lust of
senses; --I believe that these will be
condemned through all eternity to hear their
own vile music. I believe, on the other hand,
that true disciples of high Art will be
transfigured in a heavenly fabric of sun-
drenched fragrance of sweet sounds, and united
for eternity with the divine fount of all

----
[5] English translation of Wagner's **Rienzi** by Kenneth
Howe, London, 1976. Enclosed in EMI-Angel recording of
Rienzi (SELX 3818), 33.

Harmony.[6] -- May mine be a sentence of grace! -
-- Amen![6]

Despite a certain irreverence and a somewhat flippant
attitude in this parody of a familiar religious
statement of confession, Wagner was actually revealing
his own creed for the first time. In a curious way the
existence and presence of God would ultimately become
the most singular element permeating Wagner's thoughts.
God was at the center of man: He was the core and the
heart of man. And man related to him through the soul.

Believing in a God who was both transcendental and
imminent, Wagner was never disturbed that each of these
configurations was usually thought of as being mutually
exclusive. He visualized God as an impersonal force
operating in the universe yet one whose hidden meanings
could be revealed to man through some transcendental
process if and when it suited God's purpose. The age of
prophecy may be over, a claim made by both the Jewish
and the Christian traditions, but prophetic insights
were still possible. Truth, or the knowledge of good
and evil, could be apprehended through intuition: "my
God who moves me and through whom I act is the inner
necessity; ... At all times men have recognized God as
the highest being, the strongest emotion they have in
common, the mightiest conception which we all share ...
If men recognize--not because they are taught, but by
feeling it in their inner being--the good, noble, true,
beautiful as the highest principle, then this becomes
their God; and what denies this in the egotistic
nature of a single man rightly passes as damnable,
godless."[7]

Since life now held special meaning and value as
part of a divine plan, Wagner gradually began to assume
that the manipulation of man by his fellow man might be
alien to God's purpose. A deeply spiritual man in the
general sense of the term, Wagner clearly understood
the essence of religion but tended to reject its
particularization. He accepted Jesus as the son of God
but not necessarily the only son of God, and had strong
reservations about Christianity or any institutional
religion.

----
[6] "Death in Paris," **Wagner writes from Paris**, 101.

[7] Wagner to Ferdinand Heine, 4 December 1849, Burrell,
270-1.

221

Beginning with **The Flying Dutchman** religious allegories became one of Wagner's major obsessions. His music-dramas were not designed to enable man to return to Eden nor to offer truths and salvation to a waiting world. His works do not reveal mystical truths relative to man's place in the cosmos, nor do they offer definitive statements, solutions, or explanations of how man should live in the universe. But Wagner did present an amalgam of ideas to his readers and listeners in the guise of metaphor and allegory, and within these he touched upon, analyzed, and gave expression to a set of truly important questions: what is the meaning of life, and what role should the creative individual play in the drama of living?

Within Wagner's world of metaphor and allegory can be discerned the spiritual keys that might enable man to unlock some of the mysteries of life. Wagner's tapestries make it possible for certain individuals to see themselves and society more clearly, not by being given the answers but by being offered intuitive awareness. With self-knowledge comes the necessary insights for acting out the freedom of choice given by God. The relationship between God and man and man and God is a personal spiritual one that is not contingent upon man-made religious institutions.

Intrigued by and often obsessed with religious questions, early in life Wagner rejected Christian denominationalism, and all religious institutions, as perversions of truth. Through dogma and ritual they interposed themselves between man and God and interfered in direct contact: "Man will never be that which he can and should be, until his Life is a true mirror of Nature, a conscious following of the only real necessity, the inner natural necessity. The first will man become a living man--whereas till not he carries on a mere existence, dictated by the maxims of this or that religion, nationality, or state."[8]

The maxims of particular religions, whether Judaic or Christian (with all its component and denominational parts), troubled Wagner's sense of man's relationship to the divine force. Reacting against religious institutions he called for a "religion of universal Manhood", a not too uncommon thought in nineteenth century liberal European thought. But "this religion of the future, we wretched ones shall never clasp the

---

[8] **The Art-Work of the Future, PW,** I:71.

222

while we still are lonely units."[9] True religion would be universal for God operates in and through the world, sometimes interfering in the processes of the world but more often permitting man to remain in control of events. Anything that compromised the belief in God's universality tended to undermine the great principle of creation: the role intended for man in the great cosmic scheme. Only religious institutions, by preaching particularism, compromised God's universality. A universal is, by its nature, incapable of being divided, delimited or particularized.

It would be relatively easy to criticize Wagner's often simplistic and limited perspective and perceptions when he comments about and discusses both Christianity and Judaism. In all too many ways Wagner's thoughts and writings about both religious systems revealed a considerable lack of precise knowledge about either of them. By necessity it is beyond the scope of this study to illustrate just where and when Wagner went wrong in his perceptions of the Judaic-Christian systems or to discuss all of his mistaken or erroneous ideas. Suffice to say, he saw religion as he chose to see it, not necessarily for what it was but for what he thought it to be. When commenting about "primitive Christianity" Wagner knew what he meant--the belief in God held by Jesus before Christianity became institutionalized and established with its sundry dogmas and rituals. While Christianity may have seen God and Jesus as one, Wagner did not. In this and numerous other examples of the way he chose to believe, Wagner must be accepted for the beliefs he entertained and not for the mistaken ideas which he may have held. He saw spirituality in its simplest and universal purity, as a personal and direct relationship between man and God. Although his concept of Christianity was not inconsistent with this belief, it differed considerably from established doctrine.

The two most particularistic of all Western religious systems were Judaism and Catholicism, especially as practiced by orthodox Jews and Jesuits. In both systems a rigidly-defined code of behavior required that each be detached from the main body of society. Orthodox Jews often preferred to live away from their Christian neighbors lest they become corrupted and unable to perform the commandments required of them. The Jesuits too were unwilling to

----
[9] **Ibid.**, 90.

223

accommodate themselves to even traditional Catholic society. To the Jew and the Jesuit isolation from society was necessary both for survival and salvation; but to Wagner both viewpoints were offensive for they held to a limited and an exceptionally narrow concept of God. But by the nineteenth century Judaism had fallen into a rigid system based more often on the oral law and the Talmud than on the transcendental metaphors and allegories of the Old Testament.

Christianity, on the other hand, was no better. The great universal man Jesus was transformed into an unrecognizable deity by organized religious institutions which perverted his message while betraying the purpose of his life. Christianity had rejected the real Jesus. Buddhism attracted Wagner at different times, but this belief seemed to reject the importance and value of life. While this appealed to him at certain moments, it represented a tenet which Wagner finally found unacceptable.

Wagner recognized that something within man as a social being seemed to require him to create systems and institutions. Existence was so overwhelmingly complex that man sometimes had an almost instinctive need to deal concretely with the unanswerable in order to stabilize his flux. Illusions too were sometimes necessary to resolve the vagaries within life. Wagner never believed that institutional religion ought to be eliminated, but as far as he was concerned it tended to limit God.

Wagner's ideas on religion evolved but were in part shaped by mysticism, which appeared to include a knowledge of both Jewish and Christian kabbalistic thought; the teachings of the Buddha; his belief in a pure, primitive, and spiritual Christianity; a knowledge of both the Old and New Testaments; and by his reading of contemporary philosophers of religion, most notably Feuerbach and Schopenhauer.

Although Wagner did not possess a messianic belief that he was one of God's prophets who had been called upon to deliver the special word or truth about man and God, nevertheless he did believe that the creative artist could become the receptacle into which some special intuitive insights may be found. This theme is brought out more clearly in **Tannhäuser** and **Lohengrin**. Never indicating that he had something to say that came directly from God, it appears that Wagner believed that he possessed certain spiritual ideas although he did not know where they came from. Regardless of where they may have emanated, it gave him a unique perspective regarding religion.

Interestingly enough, Wagner's mysticism, and his belief in a transcendental relationship between God and man, was very similar to the attitudes held by many German Hasidic Jews, ideas which were actually quite uncharacteristic of traditional Christian thought. It is also curious how Wagner was able to quote from the Talmud, a work which was not well-known outside orthodox Judaic circles. Christian theology seeks to elevate man from the physical world to the spiritual but Wagner's transcendental views attempted to assert the exact reverse thereby associating him with orthodox Judaic thought which sought to bring spirituality to the physical world.

The philosophical question of how one arrives at knowledge is as old as man. Mystics sometimes claim to discover certain "truths" in the universe but Wagner did not seek to spiritualize man, although spirituality permeated his music-dramas. If God had intended man to be a spiritual entity, there was really no need for man to have been given a physical existence in the first place. Indeed, the physical is what separated man from God, and to enjoy and make use of matter is part of man's destiny. Since God gave man everything necessary for survival and comfort, man's holiness grew in proportion to the way and manner by which he uses God's gifts.

During the 1840's, and before he became aware of the writings of Feuerbach and Schopenhauer, Wagner wrote his first three music-dramas, **The Flying Dutchman, Tannhäuser**, and **Lohengrin**. In each, questions pertaining to religion, spirituality, death, and redemption, figure prominently. Exactly why Wagner was so intrigued with these subjects must be left to the psycho-historian, but at this point it is fair to say that Wagner was fascinated over the nature of the soul, that undifferentiated part of man's psyche which seemed to exist on its own, often even uncontrolled or uncontrollable by man. Wagner had been drawn to the legend of the Dutchman even before he had completed **Rienzi**, as if some inner force were urging him on to subjects that he had not previously considered working on.

Wagner's poem of **The Flying Dutchman** contains a mixture of elements from the well-known myth, his nearly disastrous sea experiences on the **Thetis** (the small ship on which he had sailed to Paris in 1839), and one or two thoughts from Heinrich Heine's **Memoir of Herr von Schnabelwopski** (in which the legend of the Dutchman is described in but two pages). One of Heine's major additions was the theme of redemption whereby a woman, faithful unto death, was able to rescue the Dutchman from an eternity of wandering. Heine's short account contains but three lines of actual dialogue but Wagner had an entirely different purpose in mind when he wrote the libretto and composed the opera.

In the character of the Dutchman Wagner portrayed the agony of an alienated man who yearns for death and seeks oblivion but is forced to endure a relentless search for something that seems illusive and unattainable. "He's curst to all eternity to hunt the desert seas for spoils that yield him no delight, but ne'er to find the only thing that could redeem him!"[10] What is to be the nature of the Dutchman's redemption? Wagner uses the theme of redemption in an expanded form, going well beyond Heine's treatment of the myth. He is not overly concerned with the questions most likely to intrigue one who comes to the drama for the first time: What is the reason for the Dutchman's predicament? Why is he forced to sail the seas but permitted to land once every seven years? What is his crime? Who determined this fate? Will redemption come automatically once he finds a woman who will be "true unto death", as Heine describes? For Wagner these questions were secondary.

Wagner was fascinated with the soul of the Dutchman and with the themes of guilt and redemption. Each thought struck a responsive chord in his mind. Clearly, Wagner's starting point is God. It is a religious perception that pervades this work, making it possible for spirituality to fuse itself into the creativity of the artist as he finds meaning and purpose for existence. Wagner, unhappy with the lack of true personal fulfillment in **Rienzi,** or in any of his other operas, was discovering the meaning of his life. He would not interpret this direction as divinely-ordained, nor did it come easily. The "cry of revolt" was vented in both spiritual and artistic terms. At

----

[10] "Overture to **Der fliegende Holländer,**" **Neue Zeitschrift,** 5 August 1853, **PW,** 3:228.

this time Wagner was just beginning to be aware of the
mystical and transcendental influences underscoring his
actions. That he had previously experienced a "psychic
force" and that this had produced within him an "inner
demonic effect" were not yet associated with a special
calling. "I have just called it my good angel: this
angel was not sent down to me from Heaven;   it came to
me   from out the sweat of centuries of human
'Genius.'"[11]

Wagner treated and manipulated the fable so that
it   could   serve   as   a   catharsis--a   religious,
philosophical, and psychological treatise where the
alienated individual is pitted against the perceptions
and misconceptions of society. Obviously the archetype
of the Dutchman is of major importance: "The figure of
The Flying Dutchman is a mythical creation of the Folk:
a primal trait of human nature speaks out from it with
heart-enthralling force.   This trait, in its most
universal meaning, is the longing for rest from amid
the storms of life."[12]   Nothing could better describe
Wagner's intent.   The "storms of life" portrayed so
vividly by Wagner's description of the ocean and sea on
which the Dutchman travels represent yet another
archetype. Life is turbulent! and one often sails its
seas, over unchartered territory, with uncertainty and
sometimes a sense of foreboding.

The religious symbolism is clear and unmistakable:
who put me here and why represents the very life force
of existence.   The sea is a symbol of turmoil and
confusion, perhaps even a representation of the self
which is rough and uncertain. In this archetype there
is danger and confusion for the direction is by no
means sure, clear, or swift. The storms of life play
havoc with the human soul in its physical, earthly
existence, for only by fleeing physicality can the soul
enjoy the perfect calmness that it craves--to be
reabsorbed by the soul of God from which it emanated.
Death permits this, but it must be by God's design, not
man's. Man is forced to experience the storms of life
as part of God's plan. There is a reason for existence
and only God's grace can end it. Therefore, it is not
the Dutchman who destroys, or puts to ease, his plight;
nor is it the Dutchman who ultimately resolves his
fate. It can only be a combination of forces outside

---
[11] **Communication**, 305.

[12] **Ibid.**, 307.

and beyond the Dutchman which can provide the conclusion. The sea of life therefore represents a fusion of many prototypes at work, but always symbolizes the storm-tossed human soul in its earthly existence. As an archetype it depicts the life journey to discover the self.

The combination of the Dutchman and the sea represents the confluence of these two major archetypal forces. The creative human intellect is set on a turbulent life-path while trying to resolve the reason for existence. All the while it desires a final resolution through death, but is forced to wander in search of true meaning and value for the brief time span granted by the Creator. The reason for existence can be assimilated only by recognizing and absorbing transcendental values emanating from the spirit which, if integrated into the creative artist, might enable him to take his special place in society. Hans Sachs in **Die Meistersinger** discovered just the right key by which this can be accomplished.

The **Dutchman** was constructed not as a drama based on a fable but as an allegorical reflection on life, with serious religious overtones. Only as the work unfolds do we begin to glimpse part of what goes into the meaning of salvation, and it is an incomplete picture. It would take Wagner a lifetime to finally resolve the question of salvation. Many times has the Dutchman pleaded to God for death, an end to his constant futile search for a meaning to life, but the fated answer is predestined: "Never to find a grave! Never to die!" Death is too simplistic a solution. The Dutchman must live at least until he is better able to understand himself and until the audience understands the archetypal characters being presented. To wander aimlessly on the sea of life would be tantamount to never having lived. The Dutchman does not want a meaningless life! He wants and needs an empathic female soul who could verify that life does have meaning, one who by her love and compassion, could be faithful even unto death. That "woman of the future", to use one of Wagner's favorite phrases, signified not the hopelessness of the life-situation but what it could mean on a positive basis when shared by a woman motivated by an inner strength rather than by the triviality and superficiality of contemporary society.

Looking imploringly toward heaven the Dutchman declares, "Tell me, blessed angel of the Lord, to whom

I owe the terms of my salvation, was I the wretched plaything of your scorn when you held out to me that hope of grace?" In portraying this scene Wagner indicated how "we must see before us a 'fallen angel' himself, whose fearful torment drives him to proclaim his wrath against Eternal Justice."[13]

Wagner offers an interesting and unexpected twist to the Dutchman's introspective thoughts: "This gloomy flame that kindles in my breast, should I, unhappy creature, call it Love? Oh, no! But rather, longing after grace,--would that this were the angel to confer it." In this remark we find the deeper meaning behind the Dutchman's quest: he searches not for love, but for grace. Exactly what is meant by grace will become only slightly clearer later in the work. It remains for subsequent works before Wagner is able to develop a definitive statement. Suffice to say at this point, it includes love and compassion, both united into a mystical unit. Senta reflects to herself, "The grace for which you seek with longing heart, could I poor soul, be she who would confer it!" Going well beyond the myth, Wagner has now entered into an entirely novel dimension as he penetrates to the core of man's existence. It is Wagner's religious nature which again emerges.

In the context of religious harmony man and woman are as an entity, the logical fulfillment of God's purpose. Male and female were meant to be a harmonious unit, and in the perfect embodiment of this harmony the two would merge into a unity that exists quite independently of sexual union and procreation. Each would be given to the other but not in a selfish and egocentric manner as in **Tristan and Isolde.** On the contrary, in the personification of the ideal and attainable union each would understand the needs of the other, and take responsibility for fulfilling them. Through the grace of God each can be made aware of those transcendental truths that come from God, thereby permitting spiritual values to become incorporated into the physical world. The union is based on more than love--although it can not exist properly without it-- for love alone is too often egotism and passion; but "grace" extends to a combination of love, empathy, and compassion. In the mixture of these ingredients something larger than these three elements emerges

---

[13] "Remarks on Performing the Opera: **The Flying Dutchman**," **PW**, 3:211.

making it possible for one individual to intuit the needs of another.

So far, Wagner's ideas are partly based on his own romantic illusions and are perhaps psychologically revealing of his own peculiar needs. But if the Dutchman and Senta are to transcend the myth as two humans, then it is important that Wagner indicate that they are not lonely, alienated, and isolated misfits from society.

The Dutchman can hardly contain himself: "You are an angel, and an angel's love may, even to the outcast soul, bring solace!" Again, Wagner's meaning is clear: "... he scarce can master himself any longer; he sings with the utmost fire of passion, and at the words 'Immortal God, through this girl may it come' he hurls himself upon his knees."[14] The evidence of Senta's spiritual nature shines forth by her comment regarding a woman's "holy duties", which does indeed go beyond love. The idea of duty, rather than love, figures most prominently in the Bible.

When Senta talks about the "purest chamber" of her heart she indicates as indirectly as Wagner can, without stating it forthrightly, that there are two chambers to the heart: one, the pure one, is attuned to God and represents the spiritual values of one's holiness; the second chamber (also comes from God, but it is given to man to control) relates to the physical values and the senses and operates on a more earthly level. In a manner of speaking the physical chamber is closely attuned to man's animalistic nature. The ideal is reached when both chambers are united in a workable relationship so that the spiritual could elevate the physical side while the physical could utilize the spiritual values to do on earth all that man is capable of doing to elevate the earth on which man lives. This kabbalistic notion regarding the duality of the heart is brought out in simple terms in the **Dutchman** while it forms a more essential element in **Tannhäuser.**

It is at this point that Wagner most clearly reveals that what we are hearing and understanding is not a fable, or a story, but a religious experience: it represents the point when the transcendental processes operating on both Senta and the Dutchman work

----
14 **Ibid.,** 215.

in perfect harmony. The myth has now become reality and the Dutchman has "become a human being."

The Dutchman is so overcome by Senta that he displays "the full impress of human passion; as if felled to the ground, he falls before Senta ... so that Senta stands high above him, like his angel, as she tells him what she means by troth." The Dutchman has been reborn and all the internal agitation is now externalized as he contemplates salvation.

What does all this mean? Has the Dutchman been redeemed? Is he now human and a part of society? Are they both to enter society? Is he to become a new archetypal figure? If so, what role is he to play? At this point in his life and career Wagner does not have the answers. Toward the end of the drama, thinking that he has been betrayed again, the Dutchman voices his intense disillusionment for "all is lost! Grace is lost forever!" Since Senta swore to be faithful only to him, and not to God, she had not committed blasphemy and was not doomed as were the other women in his past. One can not fail to notice that the Dutchman himself now plays the role of God's agent.

In the original ending her suicide redeems the Dutchman. His ship sinks and presumably his eternal struggle comes to an end as God permits him to die. His wandering has finally come to an end. In 1853 Wagner modified the ending to include a partial theme of redemption. When Senta throws herself off the cliff: "A heart has opened its unending depths to the unmeasured sorrows of the damned: for him must it make offering, to end alike his sorrow and its life. At this divinest sight the fated man breaks down at last, as breaks his ship to atoms; the ocean's trough engulfs it: but he, from out the waves he rises whole and hallowed, led by the victress' rescuing hand to the daybreak of sublimest love."[15]

In Paris, during 1860, Wagner once again modified both the overture and the ending to the music-drama. Instead of Senta and the Dutchman dying, both are redeemed and both ascend, presumably to heaven. The myth becomes modified, but not the archetypes. Nevertheless, the new ending indicated a positive, rather than a negative resolution, even if the reconciliation scene was somewhat contrived.

----
[15] "Overture to **Der fliegende Höllander**," PW, 3:229.

In **The Flying Dutchman** one finds several of the religious ingredients that will be found in Wagner's subsequent works, though it would take the rest of his life to mold them into a meaningful synthesis. Perhaps one of the most fascinating aspects of Wagner's personality is revealed in a letter sent to Mathilde Wesendonck: "there is a voice in me that cries with yearning after rest,--that rest which long, long years ago I made my Flying Dutchman yearn for. It was the yearning after 'home,'--not after the seductive joys of love: only a grandly faithful woman could gain for him that homeland."[16]

With **The Flying Dutchman** Wagner embarked on a lifelong path to achieve spiritual knowledge and truth. In the **Dutchman** he raised significant questions that he could not answer, but he was convinced that they were the right questions, and they reappear in all his future works. As each succeeding work was completed both the questions and their answers become more clarified and refined. Unlike other composers the role of ideas in Wagnerian music-drama is paramount, often playing a larger role than the music. Indeed, it is surprising how often music is called upon to play an ancillary role, as the means for conveying the ideas.

Wagner was often frustrated over his imperfect perceptions. Like most thinkers he sought a unified synthesis which would include religious answers devoid of ambiguities and loose strands. This was not a simple task. Wagner was concerned with conveying to society, as best he could, the spiritual values which he perceived. He recognized that not everyone would understand him, and those who did might well reject or ignore his ideas. Nevertheless, the artist had a responsibility to elevate art, and with art society itself would be elevated. Humanity was important to Wagner and the common man could be made to realize, understand, and appreciate spiritual values. But mankind had been debased by those in control of his political, economic, and religious institutions. Society had been continually thwarted by the wrong values, those imposed on mankind by the power-entrenched controllers of his destiny. Through no fault of his own man had become corrupted. But freedom from error was a possibility if the spiritual values that were available to the artist could be shared with

----
[16] Wagner to Mathilde Wesendonck, 6[?] July 1858, Wesendonck, **Letters**, 28.

society. The artist had the responsibility and the opportunity to help man free himself.

These are some of the religious issues that Wagner tackled in **The Flying Dutchman,** and in all the music-dramas after **Dutchman.** The values that were so important to him--the spiritual elements that had been subverted by society in its craving for economic, and political power--were love, compassion, tenderness, and the recognition of the worth of the individual and his true relationship with God.

Wagner's newly-acquired but deepening interest in philosophical and spiritual questions is immediately apparent in **Tannhäuser.** Tannhäuser became a creation quite unlike the Dutchman, and Wagner was aware of the nature of the change: "... the figure of Tannhäuser revealed itself to my inner eye... from the inmost heart. ... the eye of the Folk has plunged into its inner soul, and given it the artistic mould of Myth."[17] Of special interest is Wagner's perception of an "inner" element. He mentions the "inner eye", the "inmost heart", his "inner wish", and finally, the "inner soul." Wagner's elementary knowledge of psychology developed an immediacy about Tannhäuser which required nothing of him but to "follow the dictates of instinctive feeling." He soon became "overpowered" by **Tannhäuser** for it had become too personal an undertaking.

The foremost question that attracted Wagner related to the concept of the "inner soul." Wagner's good Jewish friend Samuel Lehrs had discussed with him questions relating to death, life after death, and the soul, and these questions had a profound and an immediate impact on Wagner's thoughts: Was there life after death? What is the nature of the soul? Surprisingly, Wagner again seemed to accept many of the ideas of the Jewish kabbalists regarding the duality of the soul: man's physical body comes from the human reproductive processes but God breathes life into man and gives him a soul at the moment of birth. God is therefore a copartner in the creation of man. The soul incorporates two distinct parts: one may be called the "divine soul" which seeks harmony, spirituality, and a return to its source; the second part is often referred to as the "animal soul" which relates to man's lower, physical, and more base side. God gives man free will

----
[17] **Communication,** 315.

233

to exercise control over the divine soul, the animal soul, both together, or neither. The truly "spiritual" person recognizes the existence of the animal soul and accepts its strength, but channels its force into a positive good by elevating the animal soul to the service of the divine soul. Through the existence of free will man directs the parts of the soul to positive or negative purposes. Although Wagner and Lehrs were very close friends, there is no evidence to suggest that kabbalistic matters were part of Lehrs' Jewish background.

The idea of the duality of the soul is clearly discernible in **Tannhäuser,** although where Wagner got his ideas from is still unknown. Early in the drama the animal soul pervades, soon to be replaced during the first act by the divine soul which dominates the first half of the second act. By the middle of the second act the divine soul loses out in its battle with the animal soul. In the third act Wagner seems unable to reconcile the duality and shifts to a different method: he transfers the battlefield from the soul to religion itself! Institutional religion--in this case Catholicism--is then pitted against God. The essential questions raised by Wagner in the **Dutchman** now take on a clearer form in **Tannhäuser.**

Shortly before the opening night performance in Dresden, members of the orchestra asked Wagner to explain what he envisioned as happening in the overture, so that by understanding the action they could play it better. In a short but clear statement Wagner responded that in the thirteen or so minutes necessary to play the overture we are witness to two extremes: spirituality as expressed in the Pilgrims' chant, and sexuality as expressed by the sensuous theme of Venus. The overture begins with the Pilgrims expressing their love of God. It is day and all is clear. As night approaches the Pilgrims' chant grows fainter, to be replaced by the "Whirlings of a fearsomely voluptuous dance ... These are the 'Venusberg's' seductive spells, that shew themselves at dead of night to those whose breast is fired by daring of the senses."[18]

Because Wagner is remarkably clear in his description one is aware that the sensuous music of the

----

[18] "Overture to **Tannhäuser,**" **Neue Zeitschrift,** 14 January 1853, **PW,** 3:230.

Venusberg scene is a mental image of Tannhäuser's sexuality. As an archetype Tannhäuser represents man's constant mental battle between the physical or animal soul as expressed by Venus, and the divine, or spiritual soul, as represented by the Pilgrims. These two forces will dominate Tannhäuser's mind throughout the music-drama and at various times each will have the dominate power. The archetype of sexuality is Venus herself and she makes an orchestral appearance of great beauty, so captivating Tannhäuser that he willingly succumbs to her offerings: "Then heart and senses burn within him; a fierce, devouring passion fires the blood in all his veins." Throughout the night Tannhäuser enjoys the state of "being-no-more" with sex as an end in itself, serving no other purpose than to gratify his primitive desires.

At the approach of dawn and with the light of day, reason and control return and once more the theme of the Pilgrims' chanting is heard. This time the theme grows louder as Wagner juxtaposes this music with the searing melody of Venus, symbolizing the battle in Tannhäuser's mind as he tries to unify the duality of his soul. Through the use of free will he begins to control the situation

> so that when the sun ascends at last in splendour, and the Pilgrims' Chant proclaims in ecstasy to all the world, to all that lives and moves thereon, Salvation won, this wave itself swells out the tidings of sublimest joy. 'Tis the carol of the Venusberg itself, redeemed from curse of impiousness, this cry we hear amid the hymn of God. So wells and leaps each pulse of Life in chorus of Redemption; and both dissevered elements, both soul and senses, God and Nature, unite in the atoning kiss of hallowed Love.[19]

Apparently the two aspects of the mind are capable of reconciliation, and within man's power to control.

When Wagner later revised **Tannhäuser** for its Paris premiere, seventeen years later, the final theme of reconciliation is missing. Instead of ending the overture, Wagner permitted it to run directly into the Venusberg scene of the first act, thus eliminating this

----
[19] **Ibid.,** 231.

early recognition of the redemptive process. The actual
ending of the drama remains unchanged.

Tannhäuser has been indulging in his animal lust
for some time, but sex for the sake of sex is losing
its singularly powerful hold on him. There is a void in
his present life-style and the unbridled enjoyment of
his passions can not fill it: "For no more do I see
sunlight, no more the friendly stars of heaven; I see
no more the fields which, freshly green, herald a new
summer; no more I hear the nightingale, harbinger of
spring."[20] Tannhäuser misses not the world of human
society, but the ethereal and spiritual world as a
balance to the animalistic world. His animal soul has
been satisfied, but not his divine soul! He misses all
of God's creations--trees, colors, birds, the seasons-
-except one, man! Although he is an incomplete person
in the Venusberg, Tannhäuser does not mention society,
his friends, or the civilization of which his society
is a part. The inference seems clear. In some way
society or civilization has played a role in
Tannhäuser's decision to enter the world of the
Venusberg and although he now craves a desire to leave,
he does not acknowledge, at this point, an interest in
returning to human society.

Venus is made to personify the animal soul and in
her counter-arguments she displays a realism as valid
as the power and lure of her sexuality. Forcing
Tannhäuser to recognize why he ventured to the
Venusberg in the first place, the dissatisfaction he
had felt in the world from which he had come, how he
could not cope with society and in desperation had
sought her out, she lures him into ignoring the divine
nature of his soul. Here, with her, he had found
happiness and had not been made to suffer. Having won
the goddess of love should he really desire more?

The arguments presented by Venus are well-grounded
and Tannhäuser knows it. He momentarily agrees and
again extols her praises; but the existence of the
divine soul can not be permanently unacknowledged and
again sends out signals that can not be ignored. He
declares that "my heart yearned, my soul thirsted for

----

[20] For the most part the excellent English translation
by Lionel Salter which accompanies the Deutsche
Grammophon recording of **Tannhäuser** (2711 008) has been
used. All subsequent unnumbered quotations are from
this translation.

joy, ah! for Divine pleasure", and in this perception
Tannhäuser clearly recognizes that even the animal soul
comes from God. But has it been used properly?

Wagner is not yet prepared to make a value
judgment at this point. The choice of moral or immoral,
good or bad, right or wrong, does not enter into his
consideration. By following only the dictates of his
animal soul Tannhäuser had denied to himself the
possibility of realizing his fullest potential. He has
failed to think about the origin of his existence: who
put me here, on earth, and why? There is nothing
immoral or evil in the Venusberg itself, except when it
serves egocentric or selfish purposes and denies the
higher element for which sexuality can be employed--as
a means to an end, either for procreation ("Be fruitful
and multiply" was God's first commandment to man), or
to deepen the relationship between a man and a woman
who love, care, and empathize with each other. In
neither case does this describe the relationship
between Tannhäuser and Venus.

One further point needs clarification. Nowhere
does Wagner postulate that Tannhäuser's sexuality is
ruled by a force greater that Tannhäuser himself. There
is no "devil-image" in possession of Tannhäuser's soul.
He is in command of himself and it is his free will
which controls the entire situation. He is not in hell
nor is he being tormented. Tannhäuser tells Venus, as
he perceives himself more clearly, "I have at heart not
pleasure alone, and in my joy long for suffering." He
finally realizes that there are other aspects to life
which, as a human being and not a god, he must
acknowledge.

Tannhäuser asks Venus to see him free but if this
were to happen then Venus would become the instrument
of his regeneration, and Wagner has no intention of
permitting this to happen. Ultimately Tannhäuser's own
free will must take the initiative. He must set himself
free! The exercise of free will is God's greatest gift
to man but it requires that man pursue an active not a
passive role. Absolute happiness as an end in itself is
self-defeating for it offers neither opportunities nor
challenges, "but I must hence to the earthly world,
with you I can only be a slave: for freedom I am
consumed for longing, for freedom I thirst; to strife
and struggle will I go, even though it be to downfall
and death!" Venus tries to maintain her hold on him,
entreating him to ignore the spiritual elements which

now interfere with her powers, but ultimately she fails. Wagner again implies that what Tannhäuser seeks is the power to control Venus, not the reverse as in the present situation. If he can gain the dominant hand then sexuality can be elevated and become a means rather than an end. The animal soul, however, works to defeat this objective. Determined that he will never return even if the entire world repulsed him, Tannhäuser temporarily conquers that part of his soul. His spiritual needs lie not with her: "My salvation lies in Mary!" The Virgin now becomes, for the moment, the symbol of Tannhäuser's newly-found spirituality. As a polarity to Venus, the Virgin will assume physical form in the archetype of Elisabeth.

In 1861 Wagner expanded the ending to this scene. Since he wrote the original poem, seventeen years earlier, his perspective had evolved. Now it was necessary to modify both the character and archetype of Venus: "I left the Venusberg with an altogether tame and ill-defined impression, consequently depriving myself of the momentous background against which the ensuing tragedy is to upbuild its harrowing tale."[21] In her new form her personality is milder for Wagner realized that he had made her original polarity too animalistic, and one dimensional. "The only scene I mean to recast entirely is that with Venus; I found Frau Venus; a few good features but no true life. Here I have added a fair number of verses; the Goddess of Delight herself becomes affecting and Tannhäuser's agony real, so that his invocation of the Virgin Mary bursts as a cry of anguish from his deepest soul."[22] By the Paris version Venus herself was capable of this love.

Tannhäuser's "final cry 'My salvation lies in Mary!' This 'Maria!' must come with such force that the miracle that at once occurs, of release from the Venusberg enchantment and of rapture in his home valley, should be understood from it as the needful fulfillment of an irresistible demand by feelings driven to extreme decision. With this cry he adopts the attitude of one lost in the most exalted ecstasy and

----

[21] Wagner to Mathilde Wesendonck, 10 April 1860, Wesendonck, **Letters**, 220.

[22] Wagner to Hans von Bülow, 22 July 1860, Altmann, 2:107.

thus he is now to remain, motionless, his gaze rapturously directed toward heaven."[23]

Tannhäuser returns to human society hoping to find both salvation and a renewed meaning to life: "with fullest unreserve he gives himself to the overpowering impression of reentered homely Nature, to the familiar round of old sensations, and lastly to the tearful outburst of a childlike feeling of religious penitence; the cry: 'Almighty, Thine the praise! Great are the wonders of Thy grace!' is the instinctive outpour of an emotion which usurps his heart with might resistless, down to its deepest root."[24] Through "pain and toil" Tannhäuser now seeks redemption for his sojourn in the Venusberg and for the moment he enjoys the illusion of a religious experience. This lasts only momentarily.

During the song contest in the second act, as Wolfram, Walter, and Biterolf try to deny the existence of eroticism within man, Tannhäuser's thoughts of his own animalistic nature becomes increasingly more intrusive. As he listens to the illusions of others he is once again mentally transported to the Venusberg, and the "dark oblivion" begins to surface. As the unreality of Wolfram's message becomes ever clearer, the animal soul begins to intrude consciously into Tannhäuser's mind. This battle becomes the psychological crux of the scene and Wagner was very much aware of its urgency: "Tannhäuser, who is capable of nothing but the most direct expression of his frankest, most instinctive feelings, must find himself in crying contrast with this world; and so strongly must this be driven home upon his Feeling, that for sake of sheer existence, he has to battle with this his opposite in a struggle for life or death. It is this one necessity that absorbs his soul, when matters come to open combat in the 'Singers'-tourney."

Tannhäuser's open admission of his recent sexual fling and his glib suggestion that if his friends were to gain some experience for themselves perhaps they would become more learned about the reality of life, prompts a violent confrontation among his friends who by now are unwilling and unable to accommodate any of his radical ideas. They immediately equate Venus with

---

[23] "Recollections of Ludwig Schnorr," **The Brown Book**, 137.

[24] "On the Performing of **Tannhäuser**," 198-9.

239

hell and use such words as "Abominable! Monstrous! Damnable!" to describe what he proclaims. Only the sudden interference of Elisabeth prevents bloodshed: "he must be saved. Would you rob him of eternal salvation?"

At this point Wagner had to resolve the issue regarding the nature of the soul without capitulating to theatrical devices which would weaken the importance of his argument. Wagner appears to be in a stalemate situation. Tannhäuser could never convince the others of the rightness of his argument that the animalistic nature exists in every soul, and yet to have him leave society with Elisabeth would keep mankind in a state of illusion. As a way out the scenario is shifted to the question of whether or not Tannhäuser can achieve religious salvation after having experienced the delights of the animal soul. The entire remainder of the drama now concerns this question, and the words previously uttered by Venus, that Tannhäuser would never be accepted by the world of men, prove to be resoundingly true.

The knights try to dissuade Elisabeth from asking mercy on his behalf, imploring her to let Tannhäuser leave with "the curse of heaven" on him, for never could he win salvation. It is at this point that Wagner set the stage for the important third act confrontation between institutional religion and God. Elisabeth indicates that only God, not the knights, can be Tannhäuser's judge: "What, may he never find salvation through repentance and atonement in this world? ... I plead for him, I plead for his life, let him contritely turn his steps to atonement."

Elisabeth's arguments are so persuasive that all are affected. Tannhäuser now experiences a renewal of his earlier religious illusion. He had left Venus determined to place reliance on Mary, but reentered society as a consequence of his love for Elisabeth. Her love for him has given him the courage to go on, and if God could forgive him then all would be well. It is axiomatic that if God does forgive Tannhäuser this in itself would prove the divine origin of the duality of the soul and would validate all of Tannhäuser's arguments. With utmost sincerity Tannhäuser proclaims that "to lead the sinner to salvation an angel was sent down to me from heaven!"

These words, with the expression lent them by this situation, contains the pith of Tannhäuser's subsequent existence, and form the axis of his whole career. ... If we have not been here at least attuned to deepest fellow-suffering with Tannhäuser, the drama will run its whole remaining course without consistence, without necessity, and all our hitherto-aroused awaitings will halt unsatisfied.[25]

Although he is to be banished there remains one way open to him. A group of pilgrims is leaving for Rome to seek absolution for their sins. If Tannhäuser joined them perhaps the Pope would extend God's mercy to him as well as to the other sinners. This solution finds favor with the assemblage. Elisabeth indicates that from that moment on she will spend her time praying for Tannhäuser's soul. Overwhelmed Tannhäuser beats his breast and begs Elisabeth's forgiveness. Gladly will he "kneel in the dust" and gladly will he set forth, as a penitent, to Rome. "We must believe him, that never did a pilgrim pray for pardon with such ardour."

Tannhäuser's return is preceded by a group of pilgrims expressing joy over the success of their pilgrimage to Rome. They atoned for, repented, and were absolved from their sins, and now in song they praise the glory of God for giving them the strength to do battle with hell and death. Tannhäuser's return and his appearance is in sharp contrast with the pilgrims and even Wolfram, his closest friend, does not immediately recognize him: "... a being from whom those who meet him shrink fearfully away, who has scarcely eaten for months and whose life is preserved only by a tiny flame of half-mad longing."[26] Wolfram is shocked when Tannhäuser asks him the way to the Venusberg, but Wagner makes it clear that it is not Venus who is drawing Tannhäuser back to her but life itself which is trying to push him back again: "not from any thirst for joy or pleasure, seeks he once more the Venusberg; but despair and hatred of this world..." At first angered, but now puzzled, Wolfram asks for an explanation.

----

[25] **Ibid.,** 179.

[26] Wagner to Albert Niemann, 21 February 1861, Altmann, 2:120.

Tannhäuser's commentary to Wolfram is the longest piece of narrative prose yet to appear in a Wagner music-drama. It represents a graphic depiction of Tannhäuser's religious, psychological, intellectual, and emotional state. After Elisabeth had come to his rescue and had shed tears for him, Tannhäuser's entire demeanor underwent a transformation. From that moment the "sin of pride" and the arrogance he formerly displayed which strained all his relationships with his friends had disappeared. All that he now sought was to be spiritually reunited with Elisabeth. On his journey to Rome Tannhäuser was contrite in body, spirit, and mind, and in all his actions, thoughts, and deeds he sought to atone for the unhappiness he had caused others. In vivid detail Tannhäuser explains the lengths to which he had gone to physically inflict himself so that when he appeared before the Pope he would be the contrite penitent sincerely ready to atone for his misdeeds. Tannhäuser gives Wolfram five specific illustrations:

> When at my side the heaviest laden pilgrim took the road, his burden seemed to me too light; when his foot trod the soft ground of the meadow, my naked sole sought thorns and stones; when he refreshed his lips at some fountain, I drank in the sun's scorching heat; when he offered up his pious prayers to heaven, I shed my blood in praise of God; when in the hospice he eased his weariness, I laid my limbs in snow and ice.

Like Francis of Assisi, Tannhäuser attempted to humiliate himself by self-infliction, deliberately seeking toil and suffering, for self-abnegation was his means to spiritual ecstasy. Only by total denial could he balance the heavy burden assumed by Elisabeth on his behalf. As he walked throughout Italy's countryside Tannhäuser had even refused to admire the beauty of nature and of God's creations lest they lighten his toil. Finally he arrived in Rome and went to St. Peter's. There, all through the night, Tannhäuser remained at prayer. Later, after day broke, the Pope arrived to bless the thousands. All received absolution. Tannhäuser approached the Holy Father and "beating my breast in sorrow, I confessed my sins, the evil desires that had filled my mind, the longing that no penance yet had stilled."

Wagner now reveals new information regarding Tannhäuser's psyche. Although all the actions that he had just described were sincerely motivated, nevertheless why was he doing them? In spite of all the trials that he had gone through, he still could not deny the existence of the physical within him. The duality of his soul remained and nothing that he did was able to destroy it. Wagner admitted much of this himself:

> But the more sincere and total his prostration, his remorse and craving for purification, the more terribly must he be overcome with loathing at the heartless lie that reared itself upon his journey's goal. It is just his utter single-mindedness, recking naught of self, of welfare for his individual soul, but solely of his love towards another being, and thus of that beloved's weal--it is just this feeling that at last must kindle into brightest flame his hate against the world, which must break from off its axis or ever it absolved his love and him; and these are the flames whose embers of despair scorch up his heart.[27]

Tannhäuser then proceeds to quote the Pope directly. In words that are clear but absolute the Pope proclaims: "If you have felt such sinful desires and warmed yourself at Hell's fires, if you have dwelt within the Venusberg, you are forever accursed! As this staff in my hand will nevermore put forth a living leaf, so from the burning brand of Hell salvation will never bloom for you!"

Wagner maintained that the Roman Catholic church represented a fixed and totalitarian system of irreligion. Through the Pope, its vicar on earth, the church practiced everything but compassion and love, as Wagner understood God's compassion and love for man. Unable or unwilling to understand the real nature of God's greatest creation, the church had established a rigid system of control which denied man's very biological nature. Living in Dresden, in the Lutheran kingdom of Saxony, Wagner was able to assert his religious ideas with relative impunity but one should not assume that **Tannhäuser** reflected a peculiarly Protestant point of view. Wagner went so far as to deny any specifically religious connection, at least in the

---
[27] "On the Performing of Tannhäuser," 201.

sense of any recognizable religious institution: "How absurd, then, must those critics seem to me, who, drawing all their wit from modern wantonness, insist on reading into my **Tannhäuser** a specifically Christian and impotently pietistic drift! They recognize nothing but the fable of their own incompetence, in the story of a man whom they are utterly unable to comprehend."[28]

Wagner would later have much more to say about religion, but in **Tannhäuser** he tried to establish one major point--that the Catholic church was a man-made institution and not a God-created institution and that it was incapable of understanding man's full nature as man. The Pope's words are precise. Just as a piece of dead wood could not blossom, so Tannhäuser's soul could not be saved. Before Wagner ends this drama God will overrule the Pope's pronouncement and intercede on Tannhäuser's behalf.

Tannhäuser is crushed by the intransigence of the Pope and as he listens to the songs of those who had been promised salvation their words appear perverse to him. The hypocrisy in man now drives him again to seek the Venusberg where at least the existence of the physical is recognized. "When he returns from Rome, he is nothing but embodied wrath against a world that refuses him the right of Being for simple reason of the wholeness of his feelings."

As pilgrims arrive with the coffin of Elisabeth, Wolfram announces that she is now appealing his case directly to God. Tannhäuser dies with the words "Holy Elisabeth, pray for me" and his "last breath goes up to her, in thanks for this supernal gift of Love. Beside his lifeless body stands no man but must envy him; the whole world, and God Himself--must call him blessed." Presently a second group of pilgrims arrive to indicate that a miracle has transpired: "The barren staff in the priest's hand He decked with fresh green: so to the sinner in Hell's flames shall redemption bloom anew!" The drama ends as all present proclaim that "the grace of God is granted to the penitent; now he enters into the bliss of heaven."

The words of the prose leave the impression that God has overruled the Pope and interceded on Tannhäuser's behalf as a result of Elisabeth's successful intervention. However, other interpretations

----
[28] **Communication**, 323.

are possible which are not so obvious, although there are references to them in Wagner's writings. First, by saving Tannhäuser God has acknowledged the existence of the entire soul as part of His gift to man. Tannhäuser achieved salvation not because of Elisabeth but on his own behalf; he learnt to balance, sometimes very delicately, both the animal and the divine souls rather than permit either to dominate. Tannhäuser did not betray the gift of life by dedicating himself to the exclusive service of the spiritual nor did he remain with Venus after perceiving that she represented a meaningless existence in and of itself. Unlike his friends Tannhäuser had come to grips with reality and in doing so he elevated himself. Elisabeth recognized this and loved him for it.

Secondly, Tannhäuser represents an archetype of the artist as the receptacle for transcendental knowledge. Tannhäuser is Wagner, the man who writes both word and music. He has a penetrating awareness of life even though he is misunderstood and ridiculed by others; he knows what others have yet to discover, and although he feels close to God he is as yet unable to relate to the world of man, and is as alienated from them as they are from him. He has acquired knowledge and truth but does not know how to use them properly because of deficiencies within his own personality. He is too instinctive and immature and can not accommodate knowledge within his being, therefore he is unable to teach or lead. It was necessary for Tannhäuser and Elisabeth to be removed from society, as in the case of the Dutchman and Senta, because it was not clear to Wagner how to enable Tannhäuser and Elisabeth to live as part of society. Nevertheless, Wagner's ideas on man and God are carried further than in the **Dutchman,** and in **Lohengrin** they are carried still further.

That Wagner made a distinction between traditional institutional Christianity and the ideas of Jesus may be observed in a comment made to his wife Cosima: "Yes, people ought to respect me for having expressed the spirit of Christianity in this--and, what is more, freed of all sectarianism."[29] Tannhäuser's redemption stimulated Wagner for he had expostulated a message that helped pave the way for a different religious approach in **Lohengrin.** God's love for man transcends religion, for God is ever willing to show compassion and mercy: "After I had thus seen it as a noble poem of

----
[29] **CW's Diaries,** 30 January 1880, 2:434.

man's yearning and his longing--by no means merely
seeded from the Christian's bent toward
supernaturalism, but from the truest depths of
universal human nature,--this figure became ever more
endeared to me, and ever stronger grew the urgence to
adopt it and thus give utterance to my own internal
longing; so that, at the time of completing Tannhäuser,
it positively became a dominating need, which thrust
back each alien effort to withdraw myself from its
despotic mastery."[30]

Wagner's religious ideas were now becoming clearer
to him, and several of them are touched upon in
Lohengrin and in subsequent dramas: first, Jesus,
whether as the son of God or not, is the perfect
embodiment of the altruistic man, one who possesses the
most perfect system of values. Jesus' love and
selflessness should serve as the model for man's
dealings with his fellow man; second, God's love is
demonstrated by the creation of man, and it is love
which should dominate man's actions; third, the lack of
love produces unhappiness but its permanent absence
augurs disaster, a point which he develops more fully
in **The Ring of the Nibelung**; fourth, God wants man to
live in harmony with his fellow man, but the Judeo-
Christian religious systems fragmentizes him, thereby
betraying the love of God for man.

Through religious means and possibly without fully
realizing what he is doing, man is actually trying to
manipulate God by dictating exactly what can and can
not be done in the name of God. The Judeo-Christian
tradition betrays God by postulating answers regarding
His "true" nature, as if this were possible or known.
Even Jesus is made the instrument of man's enslavement
instead of man's liberation. Wagner seeks to free Jesus
from the Judeo-Christian inheritance, permitting him to
emerge as God's means for man's redemption, regardless
of religious systems and irrespective of whether Jesus
is God in physical form. Wagner was more concerned with
Jesus as the ideal son of God than with God's need to
become corporeal. Jesus as Saviour need not be divine,
nor was a belief in his resurrection central to the
purpose of his life. Fifth, there was a deeper meaning
behind all myths which express man's universal need for
spirituality. By maintaining these beliefs Wagner has
all but divorced himself from Christianity. At no time

---

[30] **Communication**, 333.

does he mention the most central point within Christendom--the resurrected Christ.

Before the end of the 1840's Wagner will attempt to systematize his thoughts, but when he began **Lohengrin** he was well on the way toward a uniquely mystical concept of the soul. **Lohengrin** was a continuation of **Tannhäuser** in terms of the spiritual messages that are common to both, and when Wagner realized this interconnection he began immediately to work on it. **Tannhäuser** left Wagner with irreconcilable questions, some of which he tried to resolve in **Lohengrin**. In some ways Lohengrin and Tannhäuser are complementary personalities but in **Lohengrin** Wagner went one crucial step further: Elsa becomes the multidimensional woman who could share most, if not all, of Lohengrin's transcendental spiritual values. Although other problems develop which make their union just as irreconcilable as the one between Tannhäuser and Elisabeth, nevertheless, Elsa, unlike Elisabeth, remains within society, alive.

Once again the drama deals with love in the relationship between God and man, man and God, and man and his fellow man. In these matters **Lohengrin** establishes allegories and metaphors relating to the interconnection of the physical and spiritual. But just as Wagner denied that **Tannhäuser** was a specifically Christian drama, so too **Lohengrin** is not to be viewed in terms of the Jesus of Christianity:

> This **Lohengrin** is no mere outcome of Christian meditation, but of man's earliest poetic ideals; ... Not one of the most affecting, not one of the most distinctive Christian myths belongs by right of generation to the Christian spirit, such as we commonly understand it: it has inherited them all from the purely human intuitions of earlier times, and merely molded them to fit its own peculiar tenets. To purge them of this heterogeneous influence, and thus enable us to look straight into the pure humanity of the eternal poem: such was the task...[31]

While Wagner was not anti-Christian he did indicate that established systems of religion tended to inhibit the transcendental process. Whether as son of God or as messenger of God, Jesus was the perfect

---

[31] Ibid., 333-4.

embodiment of the transcendental process, and the "Holy Grail" into which his blood flowed was a divine receptacle, for Jesus was as divine as every son of God. The Holy Grail, however, was removed by God from its physical existence and became a purely spiritual symbol. "Devout imagination therefore set both source and bourne of this unfathomable love-stress outside the actual world, and, longing for the solace of its senses by a symbol of the Suprasensual, it gave to it a wondrous shape; under the name of the 'Holy Grail' this symbol soon was yearned and sought for, as a reality existing somewhere, yet far beyond approach."[32]

The blood of Jesus was the "fountain of imperishable Love", but until now God sought to remove the Holy Grail from "worthless Man." Borne by a "flight of angels" it now returned to the realm below heaven, though not necessarily earth, where man might ultimately receive again its message of "Love Eternal." The drama is vague in many respects perhaps to provide an allegorical rather than a complete and logical explanation. One can not assume that the Grail has now been physically returned to man on earth. But there is a connecting link between the spiritual and physical worlds. God, on occasion, uses special messengers to accomplish specific purposes. As illustrated in several Old Testament stories these messengers can assume properties that are spiritual, physical, or a combination of both.

The presence and existence of God's messenger is the key to an understanding of **Lohengrin**, for Lohengrin is the connecting link in the transcendental process. Through intuition man can communicate with God and through the transcendental process, sometimes by way of messengers, sometimes without their intercession, God can communicate with man: "This wonder-working Coming of the Grail, in escort of an angel-host, its committal to the care of chosen men, the tone-poet of **Lohengrin**--a Grail's knight--selected for the subject of a sketch in Tone, as introduction to his drama..."[33]

Wagner's final introductory comment revealed that not everyone could see or understand the meaning behind the Grail. The Grail is symbolic of God's love, but how each person interprets this is strictly up to the

---

[32] "Prelude to **Lohengrin**," 231.

[33] Ibid., 232.

individual. This idea removes the Grail yet further from its traditional Christian understanding. The Grail is available only to certain individuals but the reason why each had been selected is not indicated: "and when at last the Cup itself is bared in all the marvel of reality, and plainly set before the gaze of the elect, when the godlike fluid held within the 'Grail' sends forth the sunbeams of sublimest Love, like the shining of a heavenly fire, and every heart is set a-quivering with its radiance: then swoon away the seer's senses; to his knees he sinks in worship and annihilation."

The implication is that the chosen person is a seeker who now becomes a messenger. God therefore needs man as a means to an end. Man can do what an angel can not, and by recognizing the nature of the new relationship between the chosen seeker and God, the elect is temporarily transmuted into a state of such spiritual intensity that it appears as if his body no longer exists. The person has been chosen to accomplish a purpose known but to God: "the Grail now sheds its blessing, and consecrates him to its knightly service: the dazzling flames are softened down to gentler glory; like a breath of joy and ecstasy ineffable, it spreads across the earthly vale, and fills the supplicant's breast with happiness ne'er before."

The nature of the process by which the "dazzling flames are softened down" may be a reference to the kabbalistic doctrine of creation: God withdrew the blinding light of His radiance and through a process of withdrawal reduced the light of spirituality through contractions, until an absence of the blinding light appeared, making possible the physical creation of earth, and later that of man. When God first appears to an elect he may become temporarily blinded by God's presence, but through the grace of God this blindness is reduced until he is able to see the essence of God's existence: "he [God] exists in and for himself, but at certain moments in the life of nations or individuals, he is there, he awakens."[34]

Wagner ended the introduction by indicating: "Then, smiling as it looks down, the angelic-host wings back its flight to Heaven in tended gladness: the fount of Love, run dry on Earth, it has brought unto the world anew; it has left the 'Grail' in keeping of pure mortals, whose hearts its very Content now has drenched

----
[34] CW's Diaries, 2 November 1870, 1:291-2.

with blessing. In the clearest light of Heaven's aether the radiant host melts into distance as it came before."

The exact meaning of these words and the full nature of the Grail is, of course, open to interpretation. By implication the physicality that Wagner talked about might be viewed more clearly as the existence of a perception of the reality of spirituality rather than the metaphysical nature often associated with spirituality. The Grail need not be seen for it to have a concrete material existence. To the person who sees the "dazzling flames" the Grail exists. The Love, symbolized by the imagery of the Grail, is returned to earth by the person(s) chosen to act as God's messenger(s). The Love is the transcendental value made into a person. It is God's symbolic recognition that man can become worthy.

That God has not abandoned hope for mankind is evident by His continued willingness to send messengers to teach man to recognize higher priorities and values. In **Tannhäuser** Elisabeth prayed to God to intercede on behalf of Tannhäuser's soul, and God took recognition of her prayer. In **Lohengrin** God's love is manifested through an intermediary who is not mortal but assumes physicality in order to help man return to a state in which God and Love can be directly perceived by man. In all of Wagner's references to **Lohengrin** the subject is God and the object is man; in no way does organized religion play a role. The direction that Wagner took in **Tannhäuser** he continued in **Lohengrin**.

Elsa of Brabant, accused of fratricide, prayed so fervently that her prayers transcended time and space and were heard and acknowledged by God. The nature of prayer is such that one hopes that God will hear and acknowledge it. Normally the one who prays receives no immediate indication that God has heard and will act upon the request. There are some, however, who by praying with a special fervor and intensity are made to feel a direct spiritual link with God and emerge from the experience in a state of a mystically spiritual euphoria. Elsa's description of what happened in her praying goes beyond most levels of known prayer; she describes a kabbalistic experience in which one aspect of her prayer was so intense that it was received and immediately acknowledged by God. This is undisputed by Elsa although she had never discussed it before, nor was she able to understand the full impact of the experience. But all who see and hear her are aware that something of a religious aura surrounds her, although none can explain what it is.

Elsa's mystical experience did not end at this point. God acknowledged her plea for help and caused her to fall into a deep sleep, an experience described several times in the Old Testament. Once physically asleep she was able to enter into a direct spiritual experience. In a state of spirituality she rose beyond her body and was transported into a dimension somewhere above earth but below heaven, or by inference, to the domain of the Holy Grail. Here she saw the Grail-knight whom God had selected as His messenger for her defense. She sees and describes exactly how the knight will look: "In the shine of bright armour a knight then approached. Such virtuous purity I had never seen before. ... thus from the heavens he came to me, the worthy thane. His chivalrous bearing gave me consolation; I place my trust in the knight--he shall be my champion."[35] Completely assured that she will be vindicated, Elsa awakens from the mystical trancelike state in which she told her story.

In **Tannhäuser** God's physical presence was realized when the Pope's staff flowered, thus serving notice that Tannhäuser's soul was saved; but in **Lohengrin** God exists through a special messenger who is created solely to accomplish the purpose of saving Elsa--first from a wrong judgement; second, from the forces of darkness. It is Elsa who is responsible for Lohengrin's existence although it is by God's design that Lohengrin achieves physicality. Without Elsa this would not have come to pass. It is not enough to say that Elsa conjured up Lohengrin, although this is, in point of fact, true. We also see the nature of Elsa's kabbalistic experience and the emergence of Lohengrin as the means for her redemption. She places her complete trust in him despite her recognition that she encountered him only in a spiritual dimension; but the experience is fact, not belief, and she does not doubt that it will be verified in reality.[36]

----

[35] English translation by Karl Schumann which accompanies the Angel records recording of **Lohengrin** (3641). All subsequent unnumbered quotations are from this translation.

[36] Elsa was not the first of Wagner's characters to experience a mystical trancelike experience in which

Elsa places her trust in the ability of her spiritual experience to become corporeal, and offers herself as wife "to him whom Heaven sends." Now in her dire need, she asks for God's direct intercession to verify her innocence. God answers immediately! The "dazzling light" leaves no doubt that "a miracle had transpired." The incredulity of Lohengrin's arrival and his special mode of transportation was Wagner's way of illustrating that the event can be understood only in allegorical and metaphoric terms and certainly not by a simple literal story. Yet Wagner had to be rather careful not to transform the drama back to myth, for the story of Lohengrin and the swan was well-known.

Although the king is prepared to acknowledge that Lohengrin must have been sent by God, Lohengrin asserts only that he had come to champion Elsa's cause. The knight then takes total control of the situation. Would Elsa be prepared to leave unasked certain questions that might normally provide her with information? Lohengrin's questioning of Elsa is analogous to God's of man. In the Old Testament, God expects uncompromising loyalty and unquestioned obedience, and often asks if man will listen and obey Him without reflection or hesitation. Adam and Eve made just such a promise but it was soon broken, although when made both intended to keep it. Curiosity soon replaced trust, and both became subjected to the consequences of their actions when Eve succumbed to the temptations of the dark forces of doubt. Similarly, Elsa promises that uncertainty will not enter her mind.

Lohengrin's second question: if he proves her innocent would she become his wife? She gives her immediate consent. At first glance this question seems literal, but the intended wedding is an allegorical reference to a mystical union whereby Lohengrin would become the protector of Brabant, or its patron saint. Elsa must affirm three additional stipulations: that she will never ask where he came from, his name, or his race, and these questions will not enter her mind. A contractual relationship is established whereby both sides promise to fulfill important conditions. The
----
knowledge was acquired. In the **Dutchman** Eric foresees the imminent arrival of the Dutchman and what its effect will be on Senta. But at the time Wagner wrote the **Dutchman** his knowledge of mysticism was rudimentary. By the time he wrote **Lohengrin** his knowledge had deepened.

nature of the contract is similar to many made between God and the children of Israel and, as in the Bible, the contract is sometimes broken.

Some individuals who find religious institutions too restrictive search for other means to arrive at an understanding of the relationship between God and man and between man and God. For one who believes in the esoteric, organized religion may be seen as a direct impediment to knowledge. This possibility seems to be important in **Lohengrin** and Wagner acknowledges as much:

> He to whom there seems nothing comprehensible in **Lohengrin** beyond the category 'Christian-Romantic,' comprehends alone an accidental surface, but not its underlying essence. This essence, the essence of a strictly new and hitherto unbroached phenomenon, can be comprehended by that faculty alone whereby is brought to man, in every instance, the fodder for his categorical understanding: and this is the purely physical faculty of Feeling. But only an artwork that presents itself in fullest physical show, can convey the new 'stuff,' with due insistence, to this emotional faculty; and only he who has taken-in this artwork in that complete embodiment--i.e. the emotional man who has thus experienced an entire satisfaction of his highest powers of receiving--can also compass the new 'stuff' in all its bearing.[37]

For the average reader it was enough just to understand the words. Each could then work out for himself how best to accept them. But for Wagner the excitement and the truth of the drama was to penetrate to the hidden or esoteric layers.

These ideas are brought into sharp focus where Ortrud's presence may be viewed as political, pre-Christian, and yet fundamentally anti-Christian. It gradually becomes clearer that she is a powerful archetype, one whose scope is more complex than that of most of the other characters so far developed. She first dominates, and then manipulates her husband as the means to secure power over both him and Elsa. She is the antithesis to Elsa and epitomizes the forces of darkness. Wagner develops her as a significant character who wields black power, possesses prophetic

---

[37] **Communication**, 323.

insights and satanic strength, and is answerable only to the Teutonic gods. Serpent-like she plays a role similar to that force which tempted Eve in the Garden of Eden. But although Ortrud represents a powerful amalgam of forces she serves only as a foil to Elsa. Wagner did not present her as a viable alternative.

Ortrud's plan is brilliant: first, to convince Telramund that it was his cowardice, represented by Lohengrin's "black magic", and not God's wrath that was responsible for his losing the initial battle to Lohengrin; second, to make Elsa believe that her champion's power came not from God, but through sorcery. When her husband proclaims, "I thought I was defeated by God--but justice was cheated by trickery, through sorcery I lost mine honour!", Ortrud's machinations have worked so well that he doesn't realize that he is openly acknowledging the power of darkness. Both enter a solemn pact: "So swear upon the deed of vengeance from the darkness of my heart! You who are lost in sweet slumber shall know that evil is awake!"

In the typical God-loving, God-fearing individual the divine souls of Lohengrin and Elsa will dominate the negative, animal souls of Ortrud and Telramund; nevertheless, each exists. Whether Elsa is spiritually secure enough to take her place as a rightful partner in a mystical union with Lohengrin is yet to be determined. She has not yet been tested, but God eventually tests all to whom he shows special consideration. Only later is it revealed how and why Elsa ultimately fails the test.

As religious allegories, Elsa and Lohengrin are reflections of light. Both are aware of intuitive and transcendental values and the reality of God's love and compassion. Ortrud and Telramund represent the darkness that exists in each soul. They personify the murky side of man's nature, the animal soul, which permits evil and the satanic forces to emerge. Evil and the satan are viewed as part of man's soul. Neither exists outside of man. But free will determines whether the animal soul dominates or is dominated by the spiritual or divine soul. On several occasions Wagner refers to Ortrud in snakelike terms, usually calling her actions venomous. Angelo Neumann once described how Wagner directed part of this scene: "Then we went on to the second act, and where he showed us, in the great scene between Telramund and Ortrud, how the latter rises

254

snakelike from her prostrate pose on the Minster steps as she finds she has won Telramund for her purpose."[38]

As with Tannhäuser the force of light is in conflict with the force of darkness but in **Tannhäuser** the struggle was within one man who was trying to combat the animal side of the soul. In **Lohengrin** the conflict comes to its logical conclusion wherein woman becomes a part of the scenario. The drama therefore becomes a spiritual contest for dominance as Lohengrin and Elsa try to take power away from Ortrud and Telramund, the question being whether the divine soul possesses enough strength to win the battle.

The confrontation between Ortrud and Elsa pits the female animal soul against the female divine soul in a contest for supremacy. The biblical implication of this scene is again obvious. Adam and Eve succumbed to temptation when put to the test by the force of doubt. Doubt was personified by the illusion of a physical being engaging Eve in dialogue, but Eve had the gift of free will and possessed the power to win or lose the growing conflict within her soul. God was acting as the adversary in order to test them, but Adam and Eve, acting with God's greatest gift to man--free will-- betrayed him. From that moment the animal soul, the satan, became an integral part of mankind. The same situation exists between Elsa and Ortrud as between Eve and the satan. If Ortrud as the force of darkness can dominate Elsa to the point where Elsa's free will is confronted by doubt, both Elsa and Lohengrin would be the spiritual losers, as in Eden.

Reacting negatively to the sound of Ortrud's voice for it is alien to her soul, Elsa's spiritual strength never before permitted her to listen to any voices of doubt. But gradually Ortrud entices Elsa to acknowledge her presence. Talking in allegorical terms to test Elsa's awareness of the role of the satan, she comments on having lived a quiet and peaceful life in the forest, far away from Elsa and with no thought of doing harm. This metaphoric reference to the depth of the animal soul is unrecognized by Elsa who becomes confounded, giving Ortrud an indication that the conflict might not be too difficult to win. She now convinces Elsa that in her new-found happiness Elsa had become indifferent to the sufferings of others. Elsa's

---
[38] Angelo Neumann, **Personal Recollections** of **Wagner,** Edith Livermore, trans., Da Capo Press, 1976, 12.

255

innocence and naiveté cause her to overreact: "How ill would I repay your kindness, Almighty God, who gives me such joy, if I did cast aside the unhappy one who bends before me in the dust!" This reference to the dust in which Ortrud is to be found once again reinforces the mental image of Ortrud's serpent-like character.

In terms of physical action this scene is played with Elsa high on an outside balcony while Ortrud, symbolically-enough, grovels on the lower, ground level. When Elsa indicates, "Wait for me! I myself will let you in!", she enables Ortrud to enter both the house and her soul. Ortrud momentarily revels in her first flush of victory. Calling upon the "holy" gods to aid her in pursuit of her "sacred" cause, she calls upon the Teutonic gods to help her destroy Elsa, imploring them to bless her "deceit and trickery" so that her vengeance might triumph. It is a scene of immense musical as well as dramatic impact.

Demonology and the satan are directly pitted against spirituality. Pursuing this line of thought further, it almost appears as if Wagner is postulating the old Manichean heresy whereby the god of light is in perpetual battle with the god of darkness. Each is a spiritual force and both serve as co-rulers over man's destiny. There is also a kabbalistic interpretation that can be suggested. Ortrud calls upon the full power of the satan to take complete mastery over Elsa's mind by helping her undermine Elsa's spirituality. If Ortrud can gain sufficient strength she might be able to convince Elsa that her spiritual soul is an illusion. Once Elsa begins to entertain doubts this could lead to her damnation. The mind is now battling itself and the appeal of the animal soul is great enough to cause Elsa to yield to an element of spiritual doubt that will signal her defeat and Ortrud's victory.

Ortrud asks that her trickery be "blessed." Since God is in and of all things, what Ortrud asks is for God not to interpose Himself in the battle between the two souls. Her appeal is successful! The existence of God is His presence in all, and the satan exists as a necessary part of God's creation, as necessary to God as man. Free will is merely God's willingness to limit himself, thereby permitting the full interplay of these forces.

Ortrud's power is such that Frederick can not distinguish right from wrong or faith from doubt. Like mankind in general he sees events in a limited perspective, and for him matters appear black or white. Since he knows himself to be innocent God wouldn't permit wrong to win out; also, Lohengrin must truly have been involved in black magic for an honest man is not afraid to give his name and ancestry. In every respect Frederick's conclusions are non sequiturs. Through free will evil can and does win out, at least on earth; the true and honest can never be assured of victory. But it is not for Frederick, nor even for the king, that Lohengrin is prepared to answer, but only for Elsa. Wagner's intention is crystal-clear: the central issue of the drama is focused on Elsa's relationship to Lohengrin; the crux of that relationship pivots around whether Elsa's faith is stronger than the forces of doubt. Both Ortrud and Lohengrin know that Elsa is vulnerable but she still has the free will to win! Although Lohengrin can not help but ask God to strengthen Elsa's spirituality he knows that his request, in this case, is superfluous.

The drama of **Lohengrin** centers around Elsa's mental conflicts in much the same way that Tannhäuser relates to the conflicts within the male soul. If her faith, supported by Lohengrin's spirituality, can emerge in the dominant position, Elsa could become the embodiment of "woman", one who had been tried and tested. Elsa and Tannhäuser were not to be viewed as angels, nor as divine creations, but as "man" and "woman." But within their souls are contained all elements of God's transcendence in near-perfect balance. Both could be honed by free will, and they would then become receptacles for the light of the knowledge of the good.

The third act portrayal of the attempt at a mystical union between Elsa's physical body and Lohengrin's spiritual essence is profound and dramatically symbolic. Contained within this scene are several conflicts that are vital to the resolution of the drama. The duologue between Elsa and Lohengrin represents her final catastrophe for the mystical union fails. For the union to have achieved success, Elsa had to have control over all the negative mental influences that had been generated by Ortrud and Telramund. Faith--reinforced by free will--had to keep whatever doubt existed permanently subordinate. Wagner illustrated the spiritual rather than the literal nature of the union by a clever interchange of ideas which stressed the role of Lohengrin as an entity that

257

had transcended time and space. Because Elsa's spirituality was strong, divine grace made it possible for him to assume physicality in order to defend her cause. Prior to his arrival the two souls had already assumed a partial spiritual identification. Therefore, Elsa had been the receptacle through which Lohengrin's physicality could enter the earthly realm. Both of them recognize and acknowledge God as the means for having made this possible.

If Lohengrin were to assume permanent physicality it would undermine the entire concept of his being; nor must he be a Christ-like figure. The conclusion therefore had to center around Elsa's actions since she had been the one responsible for his arrival. By her own free will she would ask the prohibited questions. Like many she is pure in body and spirit, but her spirituality exists only on the surface. She possesses faith just so long as it is not seriously challenged, but once threatened, doubt would gradually assume power over faith.

Elsa's spirituality can not pass the test. Lohengrin tries to thwart her by warning of disastrous consequences if she continues to entertain doubt: "So cast aside thy doubts for ever, let thy love be my proud reward; for not from night and suffering, but from light and joy I came hither." This is a reference back to the darkness of doubt as opposed to the lightness of God's love, and to the joy of Lohengrin's previous spiritual form. Since this represents still another doubt, Elsa instead of recognizing the higher plane of which he speaks, is bound by her earthly role as woman. The animal aspect of her soul now becomes dominant and she expresses fear and anger that Lohengrin might desire to return to his higher plane instead of remaining permanently on the level of man. In her last prophetic insight she again sees the swan reappear. This time it will take Lohengrin back to the world from which he had come.

Wagner appears to have been intrigued with the character and personality of Elsa. He was attracted to her as an archetype for she personified the virginal and spiritual individual who ultimately succumbed to her earth-bound nature.

> I grew to find her so justified in the final
> outburst of her jealousy, that from this very
> outburst I learnt first to thoroughly

258

understand the purely-human element of love; and I suffered deep and actual grief--often welling into bitter tears--as I saw the tragical necessity of the parting, the unavoidable undoing of this pair of lovers. This woman who with clear fore-knowledge rushes on her doom, for sake of Love's imperative behest,--who amid the ecstasy of adoration, wills yet to lose her all, if so be she cannot all-embrace her loved one. ...

Elsa, the woman,--Woman hitherto un-understood by me, and understood at last,--that most positive expression of the purest instinct of the senses,--made me a Revolutionary at one blow. She was the Spirit of the Folk, for whose redeeming hand I too, as artist-man, was longing.-- But this treasure trove of Knowledge lay hid, at first, within the silence of my lonely heart.[39]

In the final scene, before the assembled crowd, Lohengrin relates how Elsa through "treacherous counsel" had been intimidated into asking him his name, ancestry, and place of origin. Lohengrin's narration represents a brilliant and skillful amalgam of the literal and the mystical. He comes from Montsalvat, a distant land where no one present has ever been--a reference to its non-earthly status. In its midst stood a temple unlike any known on earth. He goes on to explain, always in spiritual terms, how a host of angels returned the "Holy Grail" to the trust of specially-selected guardians. Those who had been chosen to serve the Grail were given supernatural powers. Once a year, perhaps on the Day of Atonement, perhaps on the day of Christ's resurrection, God sends a special dove from heaven to refresh the power of the Grail. The Knights of the Grail are neither physical nor spiritual beings, but they are capable of being either, and the angel of death is powerless to affect them. But if their mission or identity were to be revealed to any human then each would be required to leave for his special calling must be known only to God.

Lohengrin's father, Parsifal, recognized the swan's essence to be Elsa's brother Gottfried, the future protector of Brabant, who had been transformed mysteriously into a swan. But by whom? Some Wagner

----
[39] **Communication**, 347-8.

259

scholars assume that Ortrud, by throwing an enchantment on the boy, had transformed him into a swan. But this is only assumed when Ortrud later recognizes her chain around the neck of the swan when it reappears toward the end of the drama. One can speculate that she caused the transformation, but is it likely that black magic would transform Gottfried into a white swan? There is a second possibility which Wagner alluded to in an earlier prose sketch: that God freed the boy from his watery grave, transformed him temporarily into a swan, and would transform him back again into his human form at some later period of time. This kabbalistic reference was entertained by Wagner before he completed the final version. Lohengrin was specifically called a "God-sent hero."

Wagner deliberately chose to ignore both of these possible explanations at this time for either answer would have compromised the more important issues in the drama and would have detracted from the mystical allegories. Thus it became irrelevant how or why Gottfried became a swan, or who had been responsible for the transformation.

Wagner chose not to clarify the details of the Grail now how he interpreted this ancient legend. To have explained them would have destroyed the allegory. But twenty-five years later he shared a few thoughts with his wife Cosima:

> Richard explains ... that the Holy Grail can be regarded as freedom. Renunciation, repudiation of the will, the oath of chastity separate the Knights of the Grail from the world of appearances. The knight is permitted to break his oath through the condition which he imposes on the woman--for, if a woman could so overcome a natural propensity as not to ask, she would be worthy of admission to the Grail. It is the possibility of this salvation which permits the knight to marry. The Knight of the Grail is sublime and free because he acts, not in his own behalf, but for others. He desires nothing more for himself.[40]

Wagner had as much difficulty resolving **Lohengrin** as he did with **The Flying Dutchman** and **Tannhäuser** for he could not handle both the literal and the
_____
[40] **CW's Diaries**, 1 March 1870, 1:194-5.

allegorical meanings with equal ease. Elsa, no longer able to see the light of spirituality but only the darkness of the "night" of uncertainty, nevertheless raises an interestingly provocative question: if Lohengrin is divine then surely God is capable of showing mercy to her for a seemingly slight transgression. Lohengrin rejects the argument. Elsa had broken her promise not to ask the questions, and for that she must be punished by his departure: "Cut off and parted--this we both must see: this is punishment, this is expiation."

After the music-drama was first produced friend and foe alike appealed to Wagner to change or modify the ending. Some believed that Lohengrin, having compromised his true identity should now be permanently relegated to an earth-bound existence; others believed that Lohengrin and Elsa should be reunited in heaven; a few believed that Lohengrin desired a return to a more comfortable existence in Montsalvat. If was painfully obvious to Wagner that most of those who criticized the work tended to view it as an opera, and were unaware of and unconcerned with the inner thoughts and meanings of the drama. It was equally obvious that he could not hope to answer all the criticism nor could he adequately explain meanings that could only be understood by those who possessed the "feeling" for self-understanding. He did try to deal with a few points of dissension, perhaps more for himself than for those to whom his answer was directed:

> It was clear to my inner sense, that an essential ground of misunderstanding of the tragical significance of my hero had lain in the assumption that Lohengrin, having descended from a glittering realm of painlessly-unearned and cold magnificence, and in obedience to an unnatural law that bound him will-lessly thereto, now turned his back upon the strife of earthly passions, to taste again the pleasures of divinity.

> ... this misinterpretation had simply sprung from a wilful interpretation of that binding law, which in truth was no outwardly-imposed decree, but the **expression of** the necessary inner nature of one who, from the midst of

lonely splendour, is[41] athirst for being understood through **Love**.

Elsa had been incapable of transcending the limits of her womanhood but she does not die at the end of the drama, as is often believed. Her death would destroy the point that Wagner had been trying to make--that Elsa's punishment must be seen and appreciated by her, and that punishment is separation from Lohengrin: "Neither chastisement nor death can form that punishment. Every other form of punishment would be arbitrary and would arouse indignation; but the punishment of **separation**--the hardest of all, indeed-- appears inevitable and does not appear too hard, for it is the most just, the most logical. Elsa has forfeited Lohengrin, their union can not stand, for once Elsa has asked the questions they are thereby cut off from each other. The parting, the idea of the parting seemed to me the very heart and essence of the whole matter."[42]

Wagner seldom revealed the inner meaning of his dramas to anyone, but one remarkable letter exists which captures much of the spiritual nature which lies at the bottom of this drama:

> The symbolic meaning of the fable I hold to be that contact of the supernatural with human nature cannot last. The moral would seem to be that God (I mean the Christian God) would do better to withhold supernatural revelations from us, since he may not annul the laws of nature, and nature--human nature in this instance--revenges itself and thus brings the revelation to naught. ...
> The endeavour must be, therefore, to make the ultimate moment of parting appear as a positive act and this can be done by making the ultimate fate of both the separated lovers perfectly plain to the audience.[43]

Several years later when Wagner briefly flirted with Buddhist ideas, he considered writing a music-drama to supplement **Lohengrin**. Temporarily absorbed as

----

[41] **Communication**, 345.

[42] Wagner to Hermann Franck, 30 May 1846, Altmann, 1:123.

[43] **Ibid.**, 124.

262

he then was with the idea of the transmutation of the soul he considered a work entitled **The Victors.** In describing its content Wagner commented: "the spotless purity of Lohengrin is that he is the reincarnate Parzival, who won to purity by his own efforts. In the same way Elsa would reach Lohengrin through rebirth. Accordingly, my theme for The Victors seemed to me to be the continuation and fulfillment of Lohengrin. In it Savitri (Elsa) achieves Ananda utterly. All the terrible tragedies of life are but due to the divisions inherent in time and space."[44]

After completing **Tannhäuser** Wagner recognized that he might be heading toward a very lonely path in life, but now the path had become even more obvious; nevertheless, "... only through my **completed Tannhäuser** and my **completed Lohengrin** did I gain perfect clearness as to the direction in which I had been impelled by unconscious instinct. ... nothing of this can be contained in my autobiography."[45]

Lohengrin always occupied an important place in Wagner's heart. It is a far-reaching work and contains implications that are expanded upon in **Parsifal,** written thirty-four years later. Cosima Wagner commented in her diary: "... we talk a lot about the tragic element in **Lohengrin,** which offers no reconciliation.--Love produces faith, life produces doubt, which is punished unatoned. The lovingly faithful Elsa has to die, since the living Elsa must put the question to him. And all the scenic splendour, all the glory of the music, seem to be built up to throw light on the unique value of this one heart."[46]

Toward the end of 1848 Wagner worked on a prose work entitled **Jesus of Nazareth.** Whether or not it was ever envisioned as a possible music-drama is unknown but the work served as an important dramatic vehicle for Wagner's religious as well as political and social ideas. Wagner's direct purpose in writing it may have been to make Jesus into a social revolutionary, much as he had himself been at that time. Nevertheless, this

----

[44] Wagner to Mathilde Wesendonck, early August, 1860, Altmann, 2:108.

[45] Wagner to Franz Liszt, 22 May 1851, **Wagner-Liszt Correspondence,** 1:151.

[46] **CW's Diaries,** 11 November 1880, 2:557.

prose sketch contains significant glimpses into Wagner's religious ideas as they had developed by 1848.

It is important to realize that Wagner still does not necessarily equate Jesus as the divine son of God, although he may be the Christ, the Leader: "Jesus knows and practices God's love through his teaching of it: in the consciousness of Cause and Effect he accordingly is God and Son of God; but every man is capable of like knowledge and like practice,--and if he attains thereto, he is like unto God and Jesus."[47] Jesus is the perfect man for he elevated himself by free will, to do God's will; but every man is capable of doing exactly what Jesus did. Wagner sought to elevate enlightened man, the one who recognizes what can and must be done to enrich society by constantly searching for truth and values that transcend time and place. It would be absurd to believe that Wagner tried to identify himself with Jesus except as they both represent thinking man.

Wagner's beliefs are also very basic to Old Testament thought regarding the relationship between man and God, insofar as both must work together: "but inasmuch as we know this law, we must practice it, and thus are co-creators with God at every moment, and through the consciousness of that are God himself."[48] Christian society, according to Wagner, was posited on the belief that happiness and comfort are rewards to be enjoyed not on earth but in some "posthumous state of endless comfort and inactive ecstasy." By promising happiness in the next world man is taught to accept every type of debasement on earth; but through faith, man will willingly tolerate the wrongs inflicted on him in society, supremely confident that in his future life it will all turn out to have been worthwhile.

But were these really the views of Jesus? Did he practice passive acceptance? Was he willing to permit the status quo while expecting some possible reward only in an indeterminate future? The answer to Wagner was obvious: "the humble son of the Galilean carpenter ... proclaimed that he had not come to bring peace, but a sword into the world."[49] Obviously Jesus was a

---

[47] "Jesus of Nazareth," **PW**, 8:301.

[48] **Idem.**

[49] **Art and Revolution, PW**, 1:37.

radical, a reformer who sought to change life on earth, not in heaven, and one who, when necessary, advocated violence as an instrument of reform.

Wagner seemed convinced that the ideas and ideals of Jesus were undermined when Christianity, and especially Roman Catholicism, became an organized religion. It is no surprise that "the **artist** perceives at the first glance: that neither was Christianity Art, nor could it ever bring forth from itself the true and living Art." Christianity failed because it betrayed, and then destroyed, the purpose of Jesus' life. Unlike the days of pre-Christian Greece when art was enjoyed, Christianity, by renouncing art, attempted to destroy a creation of God. Man's very creativity, undermined by Christianity, was a betrayal of God!

Wagner was certainly aware of the artistic splendors that would never have come about without the patronage of the Catholic church; nevertheless, he believed that artists paid too high a price for financial support. Without necessarily rejecting the art works which existed in Christian Europe--although many of the religious themes horrified him--Wagner raised the question of whether they might have been even better and more original had the artists been free to express themselves without restrictions. To his way of thinking Christianity determined every subject that was artistically acceptable and this fact represented the nature and origin of the problem. The artist was not free to express himself as he or God saw fit, but only as the Church saw fit.

Wagner's analysis led him to some striking observations: "Hypocrisy is the salient feature, the peculiar characteristic, of every century of our Christian era, right down to our own day."[50] Within two years Wagner would find it necessary to deal with Judaism, the foundation-stone upon which Christianity has been built. But while Christianity undermines art, it can not destroy it. There were some creative souls who just managed to keep alive certain transcendental values and ideas. Although the "Art of Christian Europe could never proclaim itself, like that of ancient Greece, as the expression of a world attuned to harmony", there are some still seeking harmony and beauty, artists capable of discovering the processes

---

[50] Ibid., 39.

whereby God enables man to seek, and find, universal values.

The Catholic church, as hard as it might try, could not destroy the idea of "physical beauty." Physical beauty, to Wagner, represented "the complete denial of the very essence of the Christian religion." In the follow-up companion piece to **Art and Revolution** Wagner continued his analysis of religion. In **The Art-Work of the Future** Wagner called for man to revolt against his Judaic-Christian inheritance. This tradition was too restrictive and limited the individual, making him only part of select groupings, whereas Wagner called for the "Religion of the Future, the Religion of Universal **Manhood**." Through "Art" man could become attuned to all that nature teaches, and in the final analysis liberated by living as a reflection of heaven. "But this bond of union, this **Religion of the Future**, we wretched ones shall never clasp the while we still are **lonely units**, howe'er so many be our numbers who feel the spur towards the Art-work of the Future."[51] Art, supported and reinforced by science, enables one to go from "error to knowledge, from fancy to reality, from Religion to Nature."

Wagner's verbiage may be clumsy but he perceived the beginning of his answer to two of the most important questions in life: Who put me here, and Why? Wagner postulated that God exists, and that Jesus among others was a divine manifestation of God's love and concern for man. But religion, race, class, and nationalism had conspired to dehumanize man's greatness. What was basic was common to all, an "unnational universal" force that needed to be freed from its restrictive and generic trappings. Wagner knew that man could have a relationship with God. This fact alone will give humanity an opportunity to build a new and better world. But it could not be built on a weak foundation. By 1849 the Judaic-Christian inheritance had become an intrinsic factor in the problems facing man.

---

[51] **The Art-Work of the Future, PW,** 1:90.

CHAPTER 7

THE OUTMODED WORLD OF THE JUDAIC-CHRISTIAN TRADITION

In the 1840's while writing **The Flying Dutchman, Tannhäuser,** and **Lohengrin** Wagner tried to understand the religious and spiritual forces at work within the universe and to reconcile them within him. That he felt the existence of an "inner light" is clear, but where did it come from, what did it mean, and what did it reveal? In an attempt to find some answers he concentrated on "Jesus of Nazareth" but the power of his newly-awakened political interests dominated his thoughts and undermined the urgency of the religious questions. Instead of developing a religious theory Wagner concentrated on creating a Jesus who was a political revolutionary. Nevertheless, one can detect a few glimpses that do reveal the religious struggles in Wagner's mind as he tried to find the answers to his questions together with his true purpose in life.

Finding it unacceptable to believe just for the sake of believing, Wagner examined organized religions in terms of dogma, practices, tenets and beliefs. He demonstrated a good working knowledge of both the Old and New Testaments (and surprisingly enough, could quote parts of the Talmud), and could discourse on the basic elements of other contemporary religious systems, such as Buddhism and Confucianism. Having been raised in a Christian society but with little concern for its trappings, Wagner's constant quest for the nature of God ultimately forced him to examine the man Jesus.

Wagner approached his study of Jesus by first considering the subject as a likely topic for either a play or a music-drama. Once into writing "Jesus of Nazareth" he immediately found himself caught in a dilemma. He had no problem delineating the overall plan. The five act drama would be based simply on elements of Jesus' life and crucifixion.[1] But behind the drama lay the problem of defining and understanding

----

[1] Perhaps the most revealing aspect of "Jesus of Nazareth," and indeed in Wagner's entire lifelong conception of Jesus is the absence of all comments regarding the resurrection. Many Christian theologians maintain that the essential element in determining one's Christianity is belief in the resurrected and living Christ, a doctrine not maintained by Wagner. "Jesus of Nazareth" ends with the crucifixion.

the rationale and philosophy upon which the work was to be built. Until he could mentally integrate such a philosophy with his religious quest, Wagner could not even begin to work seriously on it. Aside from a half-finished sketch, Wagner was unable to complete "Jesus of Nazareth" partially because he could not reconcile Jesus as an existential political revolutionary with the religious allegory that he was trying to make. But one aspect of Jesus did concern him—his presumably Jewish lineage.

Wagner had little choice but to admit the obvious. Nevertheless, he sought to turn Jesus into a universal symbol rather than one belonging exclusively to a specific religion. Envisioning the possibility of one universal society which transcended both religion and nationalism, he romanticized the possibility of a spirituality based on the moral precepts of Jesus as the enlightened teacher and not limited to any denomination or creed: "Jesus further teaches us to break through the barriers of patriotism and find our amplest satisfaction in the weal of all the human race. ... the greater enjoyment do I draw from universal human love by dedicating myself thereto with consciousness."[2]

Maintaining that the important ethical and moral principles propounded by Jesus had been distorted and even perverted by the establishment of Christianity (an event that would have been rejected most assuredly by Jesus the universal man of God), Wagner sought to find his source of religious inspiration in the Jesus of the pre-"Christian" era. He saw Jesus as a man who transcended his Judaic background; therefore although Jesus was acknowledged as born to the house of David, of Jewish extraction and lineage, "David's own lineage, however, went back to Adam, the immediate offspring of God from whom spring all men." Wagner tried to minimize the Judaic inheritance by linking Jesus not to David but directly to Adam; but while this view of Jesus as descended directly from Adam, the universal man, did not deny the Davidic linkage, it did expand Wagner's commitment to the principles of religious universality.

Wagner seemed to hypothesize that if Jesus the Jew succeeded in his message, he would be effective and influential mainly among his own people; if, however, "he went still deeper to the founder of his race, to

---

[2] "Jesus of Nazareth," **PW**, 8:316.

Adam the child of God: might he not gain a superhuman strength, if he felt conscious of that origin from God who stood exalted over Nature?"[3]   Since the power of God lay within all mankind, Jesus could say that "through Adam had he sprung from God, and therefore all men were his brothers."

According to Wagner's version of history, when Jesus spoke of himself as the "Redeemer of Mankind" he was not speaking as "the" son of God, but as a son of God. In actuality, of course, there were many "false prophets" and "messiahs" at the time, but when Jesus said he is the son of God and the "Saviour" he became a religious threat to the Jews of his time as well as a political threat to the power of Rome. Interestingly enough, Wagner did not blame the crucifixion on the Jews but on Pontius Pilate who could not afford the potential political threat to Rome by a "King of the Jews."

Jesus was the "symbol" of the brotherhood of all men because God created Adam without imposing on him dogma or creed: "God is the Father and the Son and the Holy Ghost: for the father begetteth the son throughout all ages, and the son begetteth again the father of the son to all eternity: this is Life and Love, this is the Holy Spirit." Jesus released man from the fetters of the Mosaic code which viewed life, according to Wagner, in negative terms--frought with sinful and evil desires. But emancipation from this tribal code meant that man and nature might finally become harmonious: "hence-forward there is no more sin, save that against the spirit; but that can only be incurred through ignorance, and therefore is no sin... this law is Love, and what you do in love can never be sinful." Love and compassion were the dominant motifs in **The Flying Dutchman**, **Tannhäuser**, and **Lohengrin.** The centrality of the theme of compassion, and belief in the inherent brotherhood of mankind, represent the two crucial elements in Wagner's final drama **Parsifal.**

Wagner sought to return to man his divinity. All men can be like Jesus--"co-creators with God at every moment." Jesus was the perfect embodiment of the perfect man: he elevated himself by doing God's will; yet every man was capable of this! Evil originated when man turned away from his true inner self and denied the brotherhood of man and the universality of God's love.

---

[3] Ibid., 298.

269

To love God required love of one's fellow man. What was so wrong with Judaism in general and the Mosaic code in particular? Wagner believed that Judaism had become too exclusively confined to dogma and ritual, sometimes even at the expense of love. Unless God existed within man's heart, prayer itself became hypocritical.

Since Wagner felt that Judaism no longer had a divine purpose and that it had corrupted both Christianity and the German spirit, a universal religion was needed in its place, one devoid of the narrowness of the past. Here again, Jesus serves as a model. For this reason "Jesus weds not any woman: 'The seed of David shall die out with me, that I may leave to you the seed of God.'"

There is, of course, a very thin line between the intellectual understanding which underlay Wagner's belief that Judaism being too narrow, particularistic, and exclusive was incapable of embracing mankind, and an emotional desire to see the end of Judaism as a religion and the Jews as a nation of people. The difficulty is compounded by the extent to which Wagner crossed this line.

At this time Wagner certainly based his analysis on what he considered to be rational grounds, but later in his life there were times when Judaism became so emotional an issue to him that one can not help but wonder if this early rationalistic approach might not have served as a convenient guise for a more sinister inner desire to rid the world of Jews. Although often quite critical of Christians, Wagner never suggested for them a similar fate, except perhaps for the Jesuits. But Christianity was not the answer! Replacing Judaism with Christianity solved nothing for it merely substituted one set of dogmas for another. But a return to the simple pre-Christian ideals of Jesus was the better way to proceed.

Wagner placed considerable emphasis on free will. Everything that man did was in consequence of his conscious decision. Nothing was predestined. But love, the greatest expression of free will, was the spiritual force which involved the truest relationship between man and man and man and God. The idea of redemption consistently and persistently reappeared as a dominant theme on Wagner's mind. Man needed to redeem himself through the exercise of free will. Too often God's existence within man goes unrecognized. The Mosaic

270

code, as understood by Wagner, placed primary emphasis on law (commandments) rather than on spirit; it stifled man's relationship to God. Near the moment of death Moses hid himself from the Jews, but first insisted that they agree to keep God's commandments forever; but Jesus died in full public view so that the Mosaic code would come to an end. Wagner was not trying to undermine the ethical and moral code of the Jews, but only their dependency on an outmoded tradition.

God placed a dual nature within man's heart but through free will man alone decided which nature to follow: "in the human heart the notion of the Harmful developed into that of the Wicked: this seemed to be the opposite of the Good, the Helpful, of God, and that dualism formed the basis of all Sin and Suffering of mankind.[4] But as it was within man's heart to suffer so it was within him to find the key to the good. Whichever path man chose, or deliberately decided not to choose, he arrived on it exclusively by his own effort or by a conscious decision not to make the effort. As Jesus said, "The kingdom of God is not without us, but within us."

Sometimes psychological barriers may inhibit man from loving his fellow man. The "I" was so powerful that it was often necessary to make a conscious effort to accept one's fellow man. Nevertheless, the existence of the spirit of God lay within the human heart and only by an outward action could man prove his love of God: "To the Me the Universal stands opposed: the 'I' is to me the positive, the Universal the negative, for each requirement of the Universal in my regard is a denial of my Me. While I am aughtsolver to myself, the universe is naught to me;--only in degree as I rid myself of my Me, and ascend into the universal, does the universal become a fact to me..." Love was the key to the process by which the "I" could become attuned to the universal, and only the universal enhanced the brotherhood of man.

Did contemporary Judaism or Christianity embrace these postulates? Did either religious system actively seek to accommodate the idea of the brotherhood of all mankind? Christianity preached the idea, in the name of Christ, but did not act it in the name of God; nor did it truly maintain the ideals of Jesus. But one cannot

----
[4] Ibid., 310-11.

271

be commanded to love: "The Law is lovelessness; and even should it command me to love, in keeping it I should not practice love, for Love deals only after itself, not after a commandment."[5] Wagner found the finest and clearest expression of this aspect in the Gospel of John: "I bring you not a new commandment, but the old commandment which ye had from the beginning; whosoever is born of God committeth no sin, for his seed remainest in him, and cannot sin, for he is born of God. But he that loveth not his brother, he is not of God." In the final part of "Jesus of Nazareth" Wagner selected various excerpts from the New Testament to illustrate the major themes that he had been propounding in the five acts of his drama.

Did Wagner really believe what he said? Intellectually he was in the mainstream of liberal religious thought, but did he emotionally accept the implications of his thoughts? The question begs a definitive answer. That Wagner saw God as existing primarily within the individual and not necessarily manifested in the outside world, made him seemingly indifferent to the Judaic-Christian tradition. Likewise, he hypothesized positively on the responsibilities and obligations of human beings toward one another, irrespective of race and religion. Yet, eighteen months after completing "Jesus of Nazareth" an entirely different aspect of Wagner surfaced.

On September 3 and 6, 1850 a two-part article "Das Judentum in der Musik" ("Judaism in Music") appeared in the **Neue Zeitschrift für Musik.** It was written by Wagner under the pseudonym K. Freigedank (Free-thought). Why did he use a pseudonym? "Lest my very seriously intended effort should be degraded to a purely personal matter, and its real importance be thereby vitiated."[6] In many ways it represented one of the most curious pieces ever written by Wagner. Why he chose this subject while writing his important theoretical prose works, is conjectural. He had already completed **The Art-Work of the Future** and was soon to

----
[5] **Ibid.,** 322.

[6] This article with but a few minor changes appeared in his collected prose works in 1869 under his own name. Wagner then claimed that he had used a pseudonym so as not to be labeled a "composer indubitably envious of the fame of others." See **My Life,** 2:564; also the Appendix to "Judaism in Music", **PW,** 3: 102.

begin **Opera and Drama.** He had few, if any, associations with Jews either in Switzerland where he was then living, or in the previous seven years in Dresden. Nevertheless, he was deeply fascinated with the subject and now sought to deal with it.

Wagner's focal point and his primary assumption appeared in the first paragraph when he asked: why do people have an "instinctive dislike of Jewishness?" He drew a distinction between Jews and Jewishness, and it was more than a subtle difference. In attempting to answer the question Wagner left out all discussion of religious or political factors for "in religion the Jews have long ago ceased to be our hated enemies, thanks to those Christians who have drawn people's hatred toward themselves."[7] Since part of Wagner's concern related to the often expressed belief that Jews held a disproportionately high power over finances, he assumed that with economic power they became a significant force in determining both the future of society and its culture: "What the great artists have toiled to bring into being for two thousand years, the Jew today turns into an art business."

Curiously enough, the first point that Wagner introduced after asking what people "hate in the Jewish character" related to their outward visual appearance. Did the Jew dress in a distinctive way that made him conspicuous? Conceivably orthodox male Jews were easily distinguishable by their beards and the visible fringes of their undergarment. While serving to remind him to keep and perform the commandments, the fringes also made him, and his religious views, highly visible.

However, Jewish distinctiveness in dress was nowhere as important as the Jewish penchant for mispronouncing the German language: "The Jew speaks the language of the country in which he has lived from generation to generation, but he always speaks it as a foreigner." Wagner's anti-Jewish tendencies may have originated in 1827 when the Wagner family moved back to Leipzig from Dresden. Richard was fourteen at the time and the Wagner family lived in the Jewish section of the city where he came into daily contact with Polish Jews who had only recently settled there: "With their shaggy pelisses and high fur-caps, strange faces, long

----

[7] "Judaism in Music," **Richard Wagner: Stories and Essays,** Charles Osborne, ed., Library Press, New York, 1973, 24.

beards and pendent curls, their jumble of Hebrew and bad German, and their wild gesticulations, they at once amused and terrified him..."[8]

The unwillingness of Jews to assimilate, indeed their desire to remain isolated from the mainstream of Germanic citizenry, made them outsiders and effectively removed them from the processes by which society evolved. What Wagner held most against the Jew was his unwillingness to assimilate and help Germany achieve a common identity and a single nationality. He blamed them for deliberately maintaining their distinctiveness and individuality which made it impossible for them to want to learn and speak the German language properly. Yiddish was about as imperfect a form of German as could be imagined: "When we listen to Jewish speech we are involuntarily struck by its offensive manner and so diverted from understanding of its matter."[9] Since the Jew was not being assimilated into European society he remained on its periphery; yet his financial influence not only involved him in society but sometimes gave him the ability to help shape its culture.

Up to this point one could still find a serious and not unreasonable intellectual basis to his article. But after presenting these themes, most of which have some degree of truth to them, Wagner changes direction and his emotional concerns begin to override the rational as he wonders why Jews are incapable of really deep emotional feelings in music and art? Not only is the question absurd but his immediate response to it was even more unusual; even if Jews could feel deeply he doubted whether they could express their emotions! In "Judaism in Music" Wagner singled out two musicians for special attention, Mendelssohn and Meyerbeer (whom he doesn't even deign to mention by name despite the aid and encouragement that he had extended to further Wagner's career, an example of one of the few times that Wagner's ingratitude was appallingly evident).

Mendelssohn was born into a family that had already converted to Christianity so that he was, in
_____
[8] Ellis. **The Life of Richard Wagner**, 1:97, translated from Glasenapp"s **Life**, Wagner's "official" biographer and the first to have access to the documents of the Wagner family. This is the source from which Newman and Westernhagen obtained much of their uncited material.

[9] "Judaism in Music," 28.

fact, born a Christian, but not to Wagner. Although Wagner admitted that Mendelssohn possessed great talent, it was really only a superficial ability at best, quite suitable for entertainment purposes but hardly likely to achieve immortality as in the case of Bach and Beethoven. In the final analysis Mendelssohn's talent was "obscure and [with] non-existent content." Meyerbeer, on the other hand, enjoyed a popularity because his operas were quite novel and provided "diversion from boredom... but that famous operatic composer had made the nurturing of that delusion his artistic aim in life."[10] One additional psychological aspect of Wagner's relationship with Meyerbeer was revealed in a letter to Liszt: "I do not hate him, but he disgusts me beyond measure. This eternally amiable and pleasant man reminds me of the most turbid, not to say most vicious, period of my life, when he pretended to be my protector; that was a period of connections and back stairs when we are made fools of by our protectors, whom in our inmost heart we do not like. This is a relation of the most perfect dishonesty."[11]

Wagner's dialectic was perverse: since "music is the language of passion" and Jews were incapable of true depth of emotional feelings, it stood to reason that Jews could never possibly become eminent in the arts. "The Jew ... has no true passion, certainly none that can draw him towards artistic creativity." Wagner was unaware of any first-rate Jewish sculptor, architect, painter, or musician, although nine years earlier he had made many complimentary statements about the French composer Halévy and the German composer Meyerbeer.[12]

---

[10] Ibid., 36-7.

[11] Wagner to Liszt, 18 April 1851, **Wagner–Liszt Correspondence**, 1:145.

[12] "The best and most imaginative leader of the new French school has, for a number of years, undoubtedly been Halévy." Wagner, "The Opera Lies Dying," (Report to the Dresden **Abendzeitung**, 23 February 1841), **Wagner Writes from Paris**, 114. In a subsequent article to that paper, 6 April, 1841, Wagner commented, "His [Halévy] creative impulse certainly stemmed from grand opera; the force of his personality and of the mixed blood that flows in his veins directed him straight away to the large arena and brought him immediate victory there." See Wagner, "Farewell Performances,"

In the case of Meyerbeer Wagner displayed both jealousy and an amazing sense of ingratitude. While Wagner was struggling to make a living, during his early years in Paris, Meyerbeer befriended him. Wagner acknowledged his indebtedness in a letter to his brother-in-law:

> I have now been a year in Paris. I soon recognized that I had endless difficulties to encounter and would certainly have left the place within the first few months had I not found a great friend and protector in Herr Meyerbeer, through whom I believed that I should attain my goal sooner than would otherwise be possible. Indeed, all my hopes of speedy success were based on my belief in Meyerbeer's steady support. ... the Theatre de la Renaissance, at which I had got an opera accepted by Meyerbeer's help went bankrupt. During his last short stay in Paris Herr Meyerbeer again helped my affairs forward, so that I now have a perfectly secure mutual agreement with the administration of the Grand Opera.[13]

Again, when writing to a friend about his early frustrations at trying to break into a musical career, Wagner admitted candidly: "Then by a miracle of fate I met Meyerbeer in Boulogne. I told him about myself and my composition and he became my friend and protector. ... Meyerbeer has remained tirelessly faithful to my interests..."[14]

Wagner's convoluted syllogism about Jews and music led to an interestingly-rationalized conclusion. The Jew cannot "feel" true musicality but his money had given him the power to determine and influence musical matters. Since Christianity had all but denied to the Jew avenues of employment other than financial, it was to be blamed for this predicament. Nonetheless, possession of money marked the entrance of "the cultured Jew" into society.

Wagner Writes from Paris, 122.

[13] Wagner to Edward Avenarius, 20 September 1839, Altmann, 1:55.

[14] Wagner to Theodor Apel, 20 September 1840, Altmann, 1:58.

Modifying his earlier thought about the need for the Jew to assimilate into society--without being troubled by problems of inconsistency he will return to this point at the end of the article--Wagner now admitted that even by converting to Christianity the "cultured Jew" yet remained an outsider; but now the Jew was even more pitiful and "ridiculous" for he no longer belonged to either group: he was no longer part of the orthodox community while but a foreigner in the Christian community! "The cultured Jew stands alien and alienated in the midst of a society he does not understand, with whose tastes and aspirations he is not in sympathy, and to whose history and evolution he is indifferent."[15]

In 1850, when Wagner wrote "Judaism in Music", emancipation was still far from complete. A halfhearted baptism was traditionally the minimum price that had to be paid for admission to Christian society and some willingly paid this price. Wagner seemed to have more respect for Jews who retained their orthodoxy than those who assimilated while secretly retaining their Jewish beliefs. When Wagner declared that "the Jew has never had an art of his own so his life has never had an artistic side", he was speaking in general terms. Except for religious literature, artistic matters were not viewed as important to Jews. Traditional orthodoxy was not responsive to the arts except in a minor way and usually only when related to prayer. Judaism did not accept art as an end in itself; indeed this idea would have been considered a profanation. Wagner's economic thesis was also partially correct. By 1850 some Jews did have a financial influence on the arts.

"Jewish music" was confined to the synagogue but Wagner theorized that the music had not evolved over thousands of years. Any visit to a synagogue would leave one with "feelings of repulsion, horror and amusement on hearing that nonsensical gurgling, yodelling and cackling which no attempt at caricature can render more absurd than it is."[16]

Wagner did find it possible to say a few kind words about Heinrich Heine whom he had met several

----

[15] "Judaism in Music," 30.

[16] **Ibid.,** 32. One wonders if Wagner ever did visit a synagogue. But, interestingly enough, on several occasions he quoted from the Talmud.

times when living in Paris: "He was the conscience of Judaism, just as Judaism is the defaming conscience of our modern civilization." This fascinating statement seemed to tie Judaism into a wider parameter, linking it to his often very critical remarks about Christianity. Wagner went further in praising Heine: "But when our poetry turned into a lie ... then it became possible for a gifted Jewish writer of poems to reveal in a most fascinating manner, the endless acidity and Jesuitical hypocrisy of our versifying which still thought of itself as poetry."[17]

Wagner ended his article on a positive theme even if it did include a series of glaring inconsistencies. If Jews would cease being Jews they might become true citizens of the countries in which they lived. Imploringly he urged them to look only to the future, and ignore the past. By self-denial and redemption they might yet be able to escape the "curse" that had been placed on them and all the peoples of the earth might become "one and indivisible." Redemption would not come easily but it was possible. Total assimilation would be the best means for solving the problem of Jewishness both in music and in society; it would be the rational way to solve the "Jewish problem."

Why did Wagner write this article? When it appeared Franz Liszt asked whether the "famous article on the Jews ... is by you?" Unashamedly Wagner replied: "You must know that the article is by me. Why do you ask? ... I felt a long-repressed hatred for this Jewry, and this hatred is as necessary to my nature as gall is to the blood. An opportunity arose when their damnable scribbling annoyed me most, and so I broke forth at last. It seems to have made a tremendous impression, and that pleases me, for I really wanted only to frighten them in this matter; that they will remain the masters is as certain as that not our princes, but the bankers and the Philistines, are nowadays our masters."[18]

On a personal level Wagner's article on the Jews led to an interesting altercation with his wife, one of the few times that Minna expressed herself on a serious subject: "But since two years ago when you wanted to

----

[17] Ibid., 39.

[18] Wagner to Liszt, 18 April 1851, **Wagner-Liszt Correspondence**, 1:145.

read me that essay in which you slander whole races which have been fundamentally helpful to you, I could not force myself to listen; and ever since that time you have borne a grudge against me."[19]

It would be convenient and not inaccurate to label Wagner's comments as the rantings and ravings of an anti-Jewish fanatic who looked for and found a satisfactory scapegoat. Maybe they were! But not many of Wagner's thoughts were different from those held by so-called liberals, and to dismiss all such thoughts as anti-Jewish, while true, would provide too simplistic an answer.

Heine once commented that Jews and Germans represented the two major ethical nations, both of whom together could create a "New Jerusalem in Germany." Although many, perhaps most, Jews considered themselves to be equally Jewish and German, many Christians tended to disagree, and the conflict between the viewpoints caused many problems in an age of intensifying nationalism. Neither the phrase German-Jew nor Jewish-German was satisfactory. Neither term, then or now, solved the question of identity.

Wagner's autobiography offered a second reason for his decision to write on this subject: "I had noticed for some time that such ill-sounding catch-phrases as 'Jewish ornamental flourishes,' 'Synagogue Music,' and the like were being bandied about without any rhyme or reason beyond that of giving expression to meaningless imitation. The question thus raised regarding the significance of the modern Jew in music stimulated me to make a closer examination of Jewish influence and the characteristics peculiar to it."[20]

Nineteen years later Wagner added an appendix to "Judaism in Music" in which he expressed surprise at the initial reaction it caused. He had hoped that it would lead to a general discussion of the problems relating to Jewish isolation and assimilation, but "no

----

[19] Minna to Richard Wagner, 8 May 1850, Burrell, 291. Minna attributed Wagner's anti-Jewish sentiments to the "destructive influence" of Bakunin and Röckel. Although there is no evidence to warrant this assertion, both of them certainly held views substantially the same as those held by Wagner.

[20] **My Life**, 2:564.

attempt had been made to bring about a rejoinder in any intelligent, nay even any decent fashion."[21] When he dictated his autobiography to Cosima, close to fifteen years after the article first appeared, Wagner expressed amazement at how many Europeans read and were offended by the article; perhaps, he speculated, it was because "almost all the newspapers of Europe are in the hands of Jews," a nonsensical retort that can be easily disproved. Wagner rationalized that instead of an onslaught against him on the basis of what he actually said in the article, many opponents decided to disguise their true intent of seeking revenge and attacked him on the basis of his other prose writings. Since some launched a full-scale assault on his theories, it would only be a matter of time before hostility became transferred to his music. If a Jewish press existed, controlled by his enemies, it was axiomatic that a diabolical and pernicious "Jewish" plot was rapidly advancing.

But Wagner's attitude was not unique. Many German writers and editors were accused of being Jewish even when their Jewishness was invented. Liberals sometimes accused conservatives of being Jewish while their conservative counterparts assumed, at times, that every liberal had to be a Jew or to have a "Jewish heart." The famed Austrian music critic Hanslick was a Christian until he expressed certain reservations about Wagner's music, at which time Wagner turned him into a Jew. Hanslick, however, expressed no displeasure at this association and indicated that he had no objection at being placed on the same pile as Mendelssohn and Meyerbeer, but for the record his ancestors were all Roman Catholic.

Although Wagner called for assimilation, his view even on this subject was contradictory. Any attempt to mix Jewish with German blood would likely produce a cultural mongrelization which would undermine both music and art. Even the good German musician was being corrupted by the Jewish influence, as was evident in the music of Robert Schumann. Wagner used him as an illustration of what was going wrong in Germany. Schumann's early music revealed a quality that was far superior to his later music. Because of the pervasive influence of Jews in the arts, Schumann's latter music betrayed his earlier genius and his career deteriorated. Schumann at one time had been the editor

---
[21] "Appendix to Judaism in Music," PW, 3:102.

of the **Neue Zeitschrift für Musik** and several of Wagner's articles appeared in that prestigious paper. But this was in the period when Schumann "held out his German hand", before he came under pressure from the Jews: "So he lost unconsciously his noble freedom, and his old friends--even disowned by him in the long run--have lived to see him borne in triumph by the music-Jews, as one of their own people!"[22]

In 1869 Wagner announced "the total victory of Judaism on every side; and if now once more I raise my voice against it, it certainly is from no idea that I can reduce by one iota the fulness of that victory." What caused this victory? With unparalleled self-confidence, even for him, Wagner concluded that the Jewish presence in the arts might never have come about had he not written "Judaism in Music" in 1850. Reaction against that article by Jews and their weak-willed sympathetic and greedy German allies served as a catalyst which spread throughout the Germanic-speaking world, and became the means through which Jews were launched into the mainstream of Germanic thought and culture. Wagner took it upon himself to accept a large part of the blame for the current deterioration in German culture which might never have occurred had he not written his article. But can anything now be done? Wagner doubted it: "whether the downfall of our Culture can be arrested by a violent ejection of the destructive foreign element, I am unable to decide, since that would require forces with whose existence I am unacquainted."[23] On the other hand, lacking any other way of dealing effectively with the situation, Wagner still favored assimilation as the more likely solution to the problem; he cautiously admitted that some Jews who had came under his influence actually became so thoroughly Germanic that they had even been rejected by their own people.

---

[22] **Ibid.**, 118.

[23] **Ibid.**, 121. Less than seventy years latter a clearer legal distinction would be made between the Jewish-German and the German-Jew and shortly thereafter Jews were labeled a foreign nation, and not a religion, thereby permitting their designation as an "alien presence." This permitted appropriation of "foreign" property, the first step along the path which led to the holocaust.

In article after article Wagner returned to the theme of the Jews, and the subject became an idée fixe of unparalleled dimension. Seldom did Wagner attack Judaism in religious terms and when he did his barbs were seldom stronger than those he thrust against Christianity. But in his belief that Jews represented a nation and a race, he was unsparing in his determination that they and the German people could not coexist. Time after time he talked about "the invasion of the German nation by an utterly alien element" and the Jew's capacity to financially and artistically exploit the German character. But no matter how often Wagner criticized Jews he often coupled his argument by placing blame squarely on the Germans. German incompetence was so pervasive and to be found in so many different areas that "the Jew set right this bungling of the Germans."[24]

The unification of Germany in 1871 extended Jewish emancipation spreading both assimilation and acculturation. Wagner watched, sometimes approvingly but more often in dismay, as Jews became firmly entrenched into German society: "In truth this world must now appear a wholly new, unprecedented world to the Jews, who--as a national body--still stood remote[25] from our cultural efforts just half a century ago." Again he raised an issue that appeared of fundamental importance to him: when a Frenchman became a German his children learned to speak German; when a Jew became a German his children spoke Yiddish. Why? "One might believe they went too hastily to work in the adoption of the wholly-alien, betrayed by just that unripe knowledge of our speech, their jargon." But several of his most intimate friends were assimilated Jews who spoke fluent and pure German and after they "turned entirely away from the modern world-conquerings of their former co-religionists, nay, have even made quite serious friends with myself, for example." Therefore, Jews should depart from the "teachings of the Talmud," lose their identity, and accept the German Spirit--"a kind of right-belief in our stock of German science, art and philosophy", although he admitted candidly that the task of adopting the German Spirit was just as elusive for the German as for the Jew.

---

[24] See Wagner, "What is German," **PW**, 4:159.

[25] "Modern," **PW**, 6:44. This article appeared March 1878 in the **Bayreuther Blätter**.

Much has been written about Wagner's attitude toward Jews, ranging from the apologists to those who can never see anything in Wagner other than his often stated anti-Jewishness. What Wagner said about Jews ranged from the grotesque to the ludicrous. To be sure Wagner expressed negative sentiments toward virtually every major religion, but the intensity of his remarks against Jews exceeded in virulence his caustic remarks about other denominations. But there was an additional difference between Wagner's remarks about Jews and non-Jews: unlike all other denominations, the Jew represented, in the eyes of many people including many Jews, a religion, an ethnic entity, a race, and even a nation. The presence of a race of people who not only resisted assimilation and integration into German society, but insisted on their spiritual, cultural, and above-all, physical separation from non-Jews, presented real problems.

Orthodoxy necessitated the separation of the Jew from gentile society both for his survival and so he might study the Torah and carry out God's commandments. But to German-speaking people who were struggling to achieve a sense of national identity, the Jew represented an alien element within their midst, one with a different language, culture, and set of values. By their refusal to integrate they tended to attract attention. Yiddish seemed an affront for it appeared to prove the inability of the Jew to properly assimilate. In thinking about the need to create a "German spirit" Wagner could not reconcile the presence of any group of people who would not contribute to his ideal. To Wagner one could not be a Jew and a German at the same time. Although the Talmud required Jews to accept and obey the laws of the country they inhabited, this only begged the question as far as Wagner was concerned.[26]

----

[26] After 1830 waves of liberalism spread to several of the German states and Jews slowly but gradually began to find acceptance. With toleration came assimilation and acculturation, gradually weakening the fabric of orthodoxy. Shortly after Austria provided for the legal emancipation of Jews in 1848--it would take another generation before this became a reality--the Frankfurt Assembly debated the issue, and passed legislation calling for the establishment of "Basic Rights of the German People" which would implement civil and political privileges for all people, irrespective of religion. The failure of the Assembly to unite the German states delayed full emancipation of Jews for

Wagner expressed many cruel, ugly, silly, and even preposterous thoughts about the Jews. In Cosima's Diary his negative attitude is evident on so many occasions that one is left wondering why he had to spend so much time thinking about them. Often his vituperative utterances were enunciated totally out of context with his existing train of thought. The sheer quantity of such anti-Jewish remarks compels one to believe that Wagner's obsession was of such strength and intensity as to border on paranoia. Only one skillfully trained in abnormal psychology might explain the unbelievable frequency of his derogatory remarks. Perhaps, as Nietzsche once expressed it, Wagner really did entertain the belief that Ludwig Geyer, his stepfather, may have been not only his true father but also of Jewish extraction. Apparently even Cosima once speculated on this point.[27]

Wagner had an unusually large number of close Jewish friends several of whom were important to his artistic life. He was not oblivious to men of talent but he also cultivated those with whom he could enjoy a meaningful friendship. In his autobiography Wagner singled out an early friendship with Samuel Lehrs as

---

another generation but under Bismarck the North German Confederation provided total emancipation by 1869. After the political unification of the second reich in 1871 emancipation rapidly spread. In point of fact, not until the advent of legal emancipation, and the emergence of reform Judaism later in the century, did many Jews assimilate and become absorbed into the mainstream of German culture.

[27] There is no evidence to support the contention that the Geyer family was of Jewish extraction; indeed, there is much to prove that it was not. Nevertheless, Peter Burbidge recently commented: "A Jewish actor, Ludwig Geyer, lodged in the household for some months before Richard's birth and, on the death of Karl Friedrich when Richard was only six months old, assumed responsibility for the family and married Johanna less than a year later." This led Burbidge to conclude: "... there is a curious irony in the possibility that Wagner, dedicated and persistent anti-Semite, might himself have been a Jew." Aside from offering no source or evidence the remark would be technically incorrect even if true, since by definition a Jew is one born from a Jewish mother. See Burbidge, **The Wagner Companion**, Cambridge University Press. 1979, 15.

"the most beautiful friendship of my life", one that was cut short only by Lehrs' early death. Nevertheless, Joseph Joachim, Karl Tausig, Angelo Neumnann, Hermann Levi, Heinrich Porges, and Joseph Rubinstein, to name but a few, all figured prominently in his life. Yet, it was still possible, although perhaps bizarre, for one to be anti-Jewish while having so many close Jewish friends. On the other hand, not one of his Jewish friends appeared to believe (or wanted to believe) that Wagner was anti-Jewish. Several of them even categorically denied this assertion! Of course, Wagner could easily appreciate the importance of people whose talent and friendship worked to his advantage, but to say that he befriended them only for what he might gain would be both callous and untrue.

Wagner's early friendship with Samuel Lehrs has already been mentioned. Lehrs' early death left Wagner with a deep emotional void which he remembered and thought about throughout his life. A second very emotional friendship developed in 1858 when Wagner met Karl Tausig the seventeen year-old prodigy of Franz Liszt. When Tausig first arrived in Zurich in 1858, bringing with him a letter of introduction from Liszt, Wagner was in a highly-agitated state of despair. A love-letter which Wagner had written to Mathilde Wesendonck had been intercepted by his wife Minna. Consequently the Wagner and Wesendonck households were in turmoil and Minna, physically as well as mentally sick, had to be confined to a hospital. Wagner was alone and unhappy and the arrival of Tausig was just the tonic he needed. What struck Wagner was "his amusing, half-childish, though very intelligent and knowing personality, and, above all, his exceptionally finished piano-playing and quick musical faculty."[28]

Wagner quickly developed a strong liking for the boy and "he afterwards came to live quite near us; he was my daily guest at all meals, and accompanied me on my usual walks..." Tausig livened-up Wagner's depression by introducing him to many of Liszt's compositions which he apparently played with brilliant precision. In return Wagner began to look upon the boy as the son he never had. The strength of his feelings were vividly described to Liszt:

> You have given me great pleasure with little Tausig. ... He is a terrible youth. I am

---

[28] *My Life*, 2:683.

astonished, alternately, by his highly developed intellect and his wild ways. He will become something extraordinary, if he becomes anything at all. When I see him smoking frightfully strong cigars, and drinking no end of tea, while as yet there is not the slightest hope of a beard, I am frightened like the hen, when she sees the young ducklings, whom she has hatched, by mistake take to the water. ... My childless marriage is thus suddenly blessed with an interesting phenomenon, and I take in, in rapid doses, the quintessence of paternal cares and troubles. All this has done me a great deal of good. ... Whatever subject I may broach with him, he is sure to follow me with clearness of mind and remarkable receptivity. At the same time it touches and moves me, when this boy shows such deep, tender feeling, such large sympathy, that he captivates me irresistibly. As a musician he is enormously gifted, and his[29] furious pianoforte playing makes me tremble.

Friendship continued between them and although Tausig pursued his own career as an accomplished pianist his absorption with Wagner's work was unceasing. It was he who prepared the first piano score of **Die Meistersinger.**

By 1871 Wagner had grown so fond of Tausig and was so impressed with his ability and dedication that he appointed him to manage and superintend the entire plan for the proposed Bayreuth Festival. For over twenty-one years Wagner had been involved with the **Ring** project and nothing was of greater importance to him than building the Festival House for its presentation. That he appointed a thirty year-old Jew to head the project indicated not only his personal feelings for Tausig but his willingness not to permit religion to stand in the way of their relationship. Of course one could still assert that Wagner would be willing to tolerate a Jew if it meant that his enterprise would have a better chance of success, but this would be a convenient rationalization and not a very honest assessment of their relationship.

---

29 Wagner to Liszt, 2 July 1858, **Wagner-Liszt Correspondence,** 2:236-7.

Three months later Tausig died of typhus. Wagner was visibly crushed. Inscribed on his gravestone in Berlin is an "Epitaph for Karl Tausig," written by Wagner:

> To be mature for death,
> life's slowly thriving fruit,
>   to win it early ripe
> in sudden blossoming flight of spring--
> that was your fate, and that was your daring,--
> your fate we must lament, so too your daring.[30]

In his report on "The Festival-Playhouse at Bayreuth", written after the laying of the foundation stone, Wagner singled out Tausig's name alone: "Only to a handful of more intimate friends did I express my views as to the precise mode in which a solid form might be given to the interest I asked for. The youngest of these friends, the exceptionally talented and energetic Karl Tausig, embraced the matter as a task peculiarly falling to himself... Hardly had he begun to set his scheme in motion, than a sudden death removed him from us in his thirtieth year. My last word to him was committed to his gravestone: the present seems a not unworthy place to repeat it."[31]

Tausig's name came up many times in Cosima's Diary, clearly indicating Wagner's thoughts about him. But the Diary also displayed the unbelievable callousness of Cosima whose own anti-Jewish attitude greatly exceeded that of her husband. When word reached them of Tausig's hospitalization in Leipzig with typhus and the likelihood that he would lose the battle, she recorded the following entry:

> A great shock. Even if he recovers, he is in any case lost to our undertaking; what a lesson to us! To us his death [it had not yet occurred!] seems to have a metaphysical basis; a poor character worn out early, one with no real faith, who, however close events brought us, was always conscious of an alien element (the Jewish). He threw himself into Bayreuth

---

[30] **The Brown Book**, 193,

[31] "The Festival-Playhouse at Bayreuth," 1 May 1873, **PW**, 5:321.

with a real frenzy, but can this outward
activity help him? He is too gifted not to be
weary of life. 'I have no further wish to live
in the world' R. says. 'Now I have you, all I
want is to care for the children and just look
on; for no matter what one puts a hand to,
ghosts arise. The Flying Dutchman was nothing
compared to me'[32]

After Tausig died Wagner was unable to work for many
days and fell into a melancholy where "I have no will
for anything but business matters and the children's
lessons."

Four other Jews, Joseph Rubinstein, Heinrich
Porges, Angelo Neumann, and Hermann Levi, also played
important professional roles and figured prominently in
Wagner's life. Porges and Levi were pallbearers at
Wagner's funeral. One year after Tausig's death, just
as Wagner was preparing to leave Tribschen for Bayreuth
he received an unusual telegram from the Russian
pianist Rubinstein in Kharkov. "I am a Jew. By telling
you that I tell you everything. ... could I not be of
some use to you in the production of the 'Nibelungs'? I
believe I understand the work, even if not perfectly
yet. I look to you, then, for help, for the help I
urgently need. My parents are rich. I would have the
means to go to you at once."[33] On 21 April 1872, the

----

[32] **CW's Diaries,** 18 July 1871, 1:391. No evidence
exists indicating that Wagner ever discussed matters
relating to Tausig's Jewishness with him, although on
the occasion of a particularly successful performance
of **Lohengrin,** in Berlin, Tausig sent him the following
telegram: "Huge success of **Lohengrin,** all Jews
reconciled, Your devoted Karl." See **CW's Diaries,** 7
April 1869, 1:83.

[33] Joseph Rubinstein to Wagner, March 1872, as quoted
in Curt von Westernhagen, **Wagner,** Cambridge Univ.
Press, 1978, Vol. 2, 443. Westernhagen does not cite
the location of this letter nor do the editors of
Cosima Wagner's **Diaries** who comment in the notes for 7
March 1872: "Joseph Rubinstein (1847-84): son of a
wealthy Russian Jewish family; his letter to Wagner was
prompted by a reading of "Judaism in Music" and he told
Wagner in it that the only alternatives for him were to
commit suicide or to seek deliverance from his 'Jewish
deficiencies' by serving the man who had so revealingly
defined them to him; Wagner's reply [not to be found

night before Wagner was to leave for Bayreuth, Rubinstein suddenly arrived! Wagner befriended him. "Richard is infinitely kind to the young man and advises him to take things easy, offers him access to Bayreuth."[34] For the next five years Rubinstein worked as a copyist of orchestral and vocal parts for the **Ring,** and was so devoted to Wagner's cause that he became second in command at Bayreuth. As desperately as Wagner needed money for financing the Festival he never suggested that Rubinstein ask his father for his support. After the first Festival season was over Rubinstein remained and prepared the piano score for **Parsifal.**

Apparently Rubinstein was a difficult man to get along with. From several sources he appeared to be both highly temperamental and psychologically troubled. Cosima blamed this on his Jewishness: "In the evening a slight argument with friend Rubinstein, revealing once more the unbridgeable gulf between people of his kind and ourselves. Richard uniquely kind and friendly, so touching in all the ways he tries to inspire trust in this poor distrustful man."[35]

Wagner apparently befriended him both emotionally and professionally. In 1882 when the elder Rubinstein suggested that his son should pursue his career as a pianist rather than as Wagner's assistant, Joseph appealed to Wagner to intercede on his behalf. Wagner sent Isaac Rubinstein a letter which revealed much about Wagner the man:

> Honoured Sir,
> Pray permit me to write to you briefly once more about your son Joseph, in the hope of persuading you to adopt an attitude towards the young man that I believe would be beneficial. ... Joseph's honourable efforts to comply with your wishes concerning the exercise of his talent to establish a position in life have been as honourable in intent as they have been rendered useless in effect by his own

----

mentioned in either the Diaries nor in Westernhagen's works] opened the way for a personal relationship which proved a strain on both men...." 1:1077.

[34] **CW's Diaries,** 21 April 1872, 1:479.

[35] **CW's Diaries,** 5 May 1879, 2:302.

temperament. Without doubt one reason for this lies in certain morbid dispositions, which, however, I believe I am right in saying, might lead to the most regrettable excess if he was obliged obstinately to persist in those efforts. In him the recognition of the essence and the value of true art has grown to a truly religious belief, rooted in his soul where it has engendered a sensitivity that amounts to a passion. If you will assure him, without opposition, of the modest means he needs for his exceptionally sober and temperate mode of life, you will support him contentedly in the service of a noble cause.[36]

Wagner asked the father to do for his son what Ludwig had done for him: give him the modest means to find his own destiny. Wagner died the following year. During the year after Wagner's death Rubinstein became a successful international pianist, but unable to relieve his fits of depression committed suicide in 1884 at the age of thirty-seven. He was buried in the Jewish cemetery in Bayreuth. In the eleven years that he was associated with Wagner he never came to feel any pressure or hostility relative to his religion nor were any doors closed to him because of his Jewishness. Nevertheless, in her Diary, Cosima constantly took note of his sometimes eccentric behavior which she attributed to his Jewishness, and on more than one occasion Wagner had to ask her not to treat Rubinstein with such coldness.

In the final analysis Wagner's attitude toward Rubinstein may be described as fatherly and protective, but behind his back he was sometimes horrendously inconsistent and even insincere. Rubinstein spent hundreds of hours at Wahnfried, albeit on his own accord, playing whist or entertaining Wagner by his expert piano-playing, but when he left it was just as easy for Wagner to comment on "The Jews as 'calculating beasts of prey.'"[37]

----

[36] Westernhagen, **Wagner**, Appendix I, 596.

[37] **CW's Diaries,** 8 September 1879, 2:362. Wagner once commented: "One adds fuel to these fellows' arrogance by having anything at all to do with them, and we, for example, do not talk of our feelings about these Jews in the theatre in front of Rubinstein, 400 unbaptized and probably 500 baptized ones." See 18 December 1881,

Wagner first met Heinrich Porges (1837-1900) in Vienna at the time of the ill-fated **Tristan** rehearsals. When Wagner received an invitation to conduct a concert in St. Petersburg, but didn't have enough money to make the trip, Porges managed to arrange a concert in Prague as a way to earn funds. Wagner never forgot this act of generosity. "Young Porges, an out-and-out partisan of Liszt and myself, pleased me greatly, [38]not only personally, but by his obvious enthusiasm." After moving to Munich in 1864 when befriended by Ludwig II, Wagner attempted to establish an inner circle of friends who--as his learned disciples--would help further his musical and artistic projects. Impressed with Porges as a sensitive and insightful musician, Wagner managed to convince him to move there to assume the post of chorus master at the Royal Opera:

> I need a secretary... He would have to be able to take my business correspondence off my hands, keep my MSS in order, both the literary and the musical, make arrangements of my scores, etc.--in short, be an all-round fellow. Would you take it on? ... The 'secretary,' you know, is my pretext for having a friend about me. If you will unite your life with mine, you will, I hope, **never** regret it. And how great a thing, how pleasant and comforting it will be for me to have an intelligent and friendly companion always beside me![39]

In addition, Wagner secured him work as a writer of musical articles. After Wagner's forced departure, Porges remained in Munich and served as coeditor of a newspaper jointly established by Ludwig and Wagner for the dissemination of liberal political ideas as well as for publishing and popularizing pro-Wagner articles. That Wagner never had second thoughts about Porges becoming coeditor is significant. Obviously Wagner's great indignation over the assumed existence of a "Jewish press" became a non-problem if the Jewish press were pro-Wagner.

773.

[38] **My Life,** 2:852.

[39] Wagner to Heinrich Porges, 28 May 1864, Altmann, 2:201.

In 1871 Porges was appointed musical director in Munich but was soon criticized for his conducting of a performance of **Lohengrin**. Wagner, however, forgave him: "I can never forget it when someone has behaved well toward me. He arranged the concert in Prague very well for me, and in the evil days in Vienna he was the only one to whom I could turn, so he can go on sinning for quite a while before I strike him off my good books."[40] Porges was associated with the Bayreuth project right from its inception. After writing an article on Wagner's conducting of the Beethoven Ninth, at the laying of the foundation stone, he was asked to become Wagner's assistant, "an office of the very greatest future importance ... to follow all my rehearsals very closely ... and to note down everything I say, even the smallest details, about the interpretation and performance of our work, so that a tradition goes down in writing."[41]

Porges became Wagner's principal production assistant for the first **Ring** performances. His first major article on the **Ring** production, "Die Bühnenproben zu den Bayreuther Festpielen des Jahres 1876 (Rehearsals for the Bayreuth Festival of 1876)", appeared in the **Bayreuther Blätter**, May 1880, and proved to be an important guide for understanding Wagner's intentions. Porges indicated right at the outset that his purpose was to help Wagner create an original German work of art, to be presented in a new style, and "in the first German stage festival." Porges' "Germanness" revealed no trace of his "Jewishness" thereby further disproving Wagner's thesis that Jews and Germans can never truly coexist. According to Porges, "it has been Wagner's decisive achievement to liberate us from the witches' brew of modern opera by creating a genuinely German dramatic-musical art."[42]

While working on **Parsifal** Wagner requested that the King release Porges from his Munich obligations so that he might coach the forthcoming production. It was

----

[40] **CW's Diaries**, 24 June 1872, 1:503.

[41] Westernhagen, **Wagner**, 2:489.

[42] Heinrich Porges, **Wagner Rehearsing the 'Ring'**, An Eye-Witness Account of the Stage Rehearsals of the First Bayreuth Festival, translated by Robert L. Jacobs, Cambridge, 1983, 4.

ironic--and one sometimes wonders if it might not have been deliberate--that a work like **Parsifal,** which so many still consider as a sublime reflection of the mystic mysteries of the Holy Eucharist, and Christianity, should be entrusted to Porges, Rubinstein, and Levi!

Porges was not oblivious to Wagner's occasional eccentricities nor to the drives behind Wagner's psyche. Despite recognizing and appreciating his shortcomings, Porges knew and understood the inner Wagner: "Such demoniac personalities cannot be judged by ordinary standards. They are egoists of the first water [sic], and must be so, or they could never fulfill their mission."[43]

At the time Wagner met Porges in Vienna in 1862, Angelo Neumann (1837-1909) became baritone soloist with the Royal Opera company, and participated in the countless rehearsals of **Tristan** before the company decided that it was "unplayable." Neumann "belonged to the few who had fallen under the spell of the music," and appeared in several of Wagner's concerts. He also sang the Herald in a performance of **Lohengrin,** conducted by Wagner. Three years later when **Die Meistersinger** was to be presented the pro and anti-Wagnerites managed to disrupt the performance toward the end of the second act and "just before the Night-watchman's second entrance, such a hullabaloo arose in the audience that I could scarcely sing my final lines."[44]

In 1872 Wagner again returned to Vienna for performances of **Rienzi** and in 1875 for **Lohengrin** and Tannhäuser. Neumann fell further under his "spell": "These rehearsals convinced me that Richard Wagner was not only the greatest dramatist of all time, but also the greatest of managers and a marvellous character actor as well." Shortly before the opening of the first Bayreuth festival season Neumann became co-director of the Leipzig Theatre, a position he occupied for the next six years. During the time that Neumann lived in the city of Wagner's birth he spent considerable time in a one-man effort to see that all of Wagner's operas and music-dramas would be seen and heard. Neumann's

----

[43] Porges to Richard Batka, 15 May 1898, as quoted in Ernest Newman, **The Life of Richard Wagner,** 4:103n.

[44] Neumann, **Personal Recollections of Wagner,** 7.

co-director at Leipzig August Förster attended the
opening **Ring** cycle while Neumann attended the second
cycle:

> At the close of that performance of "Rhinegold"
> I was incapable of speaking to a soul, so
> deeply sunk was I in all that I had seen and
> heard. To be sure, I had known Richard Wagner
> as a stage manager in Vienna, and admired his
> methods; but in this performance I realised
> that a new field had been opened by the
> greatest of the world's stage directors; that
> it was an epoch-making performance, and from
> now on our work lay along altogether different
> lines."[45]

Neumann quickly determined that the **Ring** had to be
seen everywhere in Germany, but first at his Leipzig
Theatre: "I conceived the idea of transplanting this
whole colossal undertaking to Leipsic [sic] and giving
it there next year in a complete cycle." In January
1878 Neumann traveled to Bayreuth and talked Wagner
into giving him the rights to perform the cycle. After
his departure from Wahnfried Cosima commented in her
Diary: "A curious interruption in our sublime life is
provided by the visit of the opera director Angelo
Neumann from Leipzig and Israel. He has come for the
Ring but would also like to have **Parsifal**! Coaxes R.
out of half the royalties [in actuality the standard
ten percent] for the subscription quota--in short, is
just what such gentlemen always are."[46] Neumann's
successful production, attended by Liszt, brought an
immediate telegram from Wagner after the performance of
Die Walküre:

> All hail the town of Leipsic, beloved native
place,
> And hail its great conductor--the bravest of
his race!

After this initial endeavor the relationship
between Wagner and Neumann grew to the point where
Neumann was judged the right man to be placed in
complete charge of producing Wagner's musical works
outside of Germany (and in several cases, most notably
in Leipzig and Berlin, within Germany). For his part

---

[45] **Ibid.,** 21.

[46] **CW's Diaries,** 21 January 1878, 2:21.

Neumann felt that he had a mission to perform: "I feel called of spreading the fame of your wonderful works throughout the musical world--in foreign lands and even across the seas." It was Neumann who first brought the **Ring** to St. Petersburg and London, and toured it throughout Germany, Italy, and France.

Although their relationship was primarily a business arrangement, Wagner soon grew personally fond of Neumann, or as Cosima expressed it, "R does not dislike him." So highly respected was his talent and musical sensitivity that Wagner felt totally confident in Neumann's casting and conducting abilities, although he never hesitated to interfere if he felt that the wrong artistic decision might be made, especially where it concerned the hiring of singers. He would then express himself forcefully and even threateningly.[47] Neumann's personality seemed equally forceful which sometimes brought severe and angry letters from Wagner as happened when Neumann requested that **Parsifal** be performed at Leipzig before its premiere in Bayreuth. But Wagner obviously appreciated his talents more than his weaknesses, as Cosima begrudgingly noted in her Diary. This was demonstrated in August 1882 when Wagner felt so depressed about the future of Bayreuth and his ability to successfully produce **Parsifal** that "he even talks of handing over **Parsifal** and the festival theatre to Herr Neumann."

Neumann's most ambitious project for Germany was to superintend a **Ring** cycle in Berlin. Problems

----
[47] Once Wagner made up his mind on any artistic matter it was not likely that he would change it. When he arrived in Berlin for the first **Ring** cycle and discovered that the baritone Emil Scaria would be singing Wotan, Wagner demanded that Neumann pay him off and send him away. Neumann refused. According to Neumann's **Recollections**, Wagner threatened: "No, no never! I tell you plainly--either you dismiss him at once,--or else I leave" (p. 36). Neumann apparently was able to calm him down and Wagner eventually but reluctantly agreed to listen to him rehearse, unseen by the artist. After the rehearsal Wagner "flew down the steps, and tore on to the stage at such a frantic pace that I could scarcely follow; shouting, 'Where is he? Where is Scaria? That was glorious! Man alive, where did you get that voice!" (147). Two years later Wagner personally selected Scaria to sing Gurnemanz in the Bayreuth premiere of **Parsifal.**

developed from the beginning. Berlin contained a significantly large Jewish population and Wagner's "Judaism in Music" was fairly well-known there. In addition, an anti-Jewish ground-swell had developed by the later 1870's into one of the first notable examples of overt anti-Semitism. Added to these problems were those caused by internal bickering among the Berlin theatres and among the pro and anti-Wagnerites. Neumann wrote Wagner that the Jews would probably stay away from the **Ring** and "R is advising him to abandon Berlin and go straight to London; the ordinary citizens have no money, the aristocracy and the Court will stay away ... and the Jews on account of the agitation."[48] Although Wagner strongly urged that the Berlin project be canceled, his letter to Neumann also attempted to disassociate himself from the current anti-Semitic outbreak: "Nothing is further from my thoughts than this 'anti-Semitic' movement; see the Bayreuth papers for my article which will prove this so conclusively that people of sense will find it impossible to connect me with the cause."[49]

Whether Wagner's reluctance to exploit the current anti-Jewish sentiment growing in Germany was sincere or merely good business-sense, is impossible to answer. As theories of racial superiority were becoming more fashionable Wagner displayed a curious disinterest in associating himself with them. Neumann refused to consider canceling the planned cycles and they were performed, as scheduled, and successfully. Wagner attended the final cycle and agreed to say a few words at its conclusion but when Neumann started an ovation for Wagner at the end of the performance he promptly

----
[48] **CW's Diaries**, 23 February 1881, 630.

[49] Wagner to Neumann, 25 February 1881, Neumann, **Recollections**, 132. Wagner is referring to his forthcoming article "Religion and Art." This statement seems to have been only partially altruistic. The day before Wagner wrote to Neumann he was visited by Hans von Walzogen, the editor of the **Bayreuther Blätter:** "R. tells him that we cannot champion special causes such as vegetarianism in our **Blätter,** but must always confine ourselves to defining and demonstrating the ideal, leaving those outside to fight for their special cause; for the same reason we cannot join in the anti-Jewish agitation." See **CW's Diaries**, 24 February 1881, 2:631.

and discourteously walked off the stage. Cosima found something "disconcerting about this Israelite affair."

Neumann continued his close business and artistic relationship to Wagner's music even after Wagner's death in 1883. Wagner called him "my friend and benefactor" and the last signed contract provided for his exclusive rights to Wagner's works, except **Parsifal** (which Wagner was originally prepared to give to him but after her husband's death, Cosima decided that **Parsifal** should be done only at Bayreuth), in Berlin, Leipzig, Dresden, Breslau, Prague, Belgium, Holland, Sweden, Norway, Denmark, England, Italy, Austria, and North America. Cosima seemed pleased that Neumann went about his noble task with "Semitic earnestness" while Wagner had previously commented on Neumann's enormously successful role in "disseminating the whole work abroad. 'How curious that it should have to be a Jew!' he says."[50] On 11 February 1883, two days before Wagner died in Venice, he sent a letter of appreciation to Neumann in which he expressed both astonishment and pleasure at Neumann's devoted service to him. Wagner ended his letter: "And now may all the good blessings from Heaven be with you, to which I add my heartiest greetings and ask you to bestow them further as you see fit."[51]

Hermann Levi (1839-1900) studied music in Leipzig and Paris and in 1864 was appointed principal conductor at the Karlsruhe Opera. Five years later he first came into contact with a Wagner music-drama when he conducted a highly successful performance of **Die Meistersinger.**

In that year King Ludwig II insisted that Wagner's already completed but never performed prelude to the Ring, **Das Rheingold,** should be premiered in Munich. Wagner did not desire a piecemeal approach to his lifelong project and unsuccessfully tried to prevent the performance. But although angered he recognized that if the king were determined that it must be done, a refusal would be impossible. Since the king had paid Wagner for the exclusive property rights to **Rheingold, Walküre,** and **Siegfried** (unfinished at this date) he could order that they be performed. Forced to go along

---

[50] **CW's Diaries,** 17 October 1882, 932.

[51] Wagner to Neumann, 11 February 1883, Neumann, **Recollections,** 269.

with this decision, Wagner expressed his displeasure in
a poem entitled "Rhinegold."

> Just play with The Ring, you dwarfs of mist,
> well may it serve as wages for your folly;
> but have a care: for you The Ring's a noose;
> you know the curse: see if it's kind to
> thieves!
> Never, the curse wills, shall the work
> succeed,
> save for him who, fearless, keeps the gold.
> But your timid game of cardboard and of glue
> will soon be covered by the Nibelung's
> Tarnhelm.[52]

Wagner reluctantly agreed to the performance and
was initially prepared to supervise the production. But
when the conductor Hans Richter (who would later
conduct the first Ring cycle at Bayreuth) and several
of the lead singers urged a postponement because of
inadequate preparation time, Wagner urged that the king
accept this artistic decision. Ludwig refused. Richter
thereupon declined to conduct and was summarily
dismissed by an angry king. Hermann Levi was one of the
conductors who was then asked to replace him. His
refusal lost him a minor spot in musical history but
earned him Wagner's gratitude.

A few months later Ludwig insisted that the also
completed follow-up drama, **Die Walküre**, should also be
performed immediately at Munich and again calls went
out to all conductors. Once again Wagner tried to
dissuade the king and in a six stanza poem entitled,
"To the King, Last Effort", he tried desperately to
have the performance postponed:

> May you once more give ear to the voice
> that from within you once did speak to me;
> let me once more conjure forth the magic
> by which once my sorrow broke your heart:
> how should timid fear delude me now
> if I can reawaken voice and magic
> which poured forth upon me once from you
> when the spring-time of your love unfolded to
> me?
>   . . .
> O Sweet One, give then ear to your own voice
> as my heart echoes it to you today,

---
[52] "Rhinegold," 25 September 1869, **The Brown Book**, 173.

that ne'er for you the noble fire shall die,
nor your hearth in my heart grow ever cold!
And while, in patience, I ascend my height,
oppose to rash impulse your authority!
And this eminence I shall ascend:
then lead off your godly round dance there.[53]

Despite this effort, the king was adamant. Once again Levi was asked to conduct the world premiere of **Die Walküre**, but this time he wrote Wagner asking for his opinion. Explaining why the individual parts of the cycle should not be done in isolation and urging him not to conduct the performance, Levi earned Wagner's growing appreciation and respect by going along with his request. Wagner was pleased and commented to Cosima, in passing, "I respect him because he really calls himself Levi as in the Bible, and not Löwe, Lewy, etc." Shortly after this episode Levi and Wagner met for the first time.

In 1872 Levi was appointed court conductor at Munich a post which would automatically link him with Wagner since Ludwig's patronage and the Munich orchestra were indispensable for the Bayreuth project. He occupied this position until 1896. After the first **Ring** cycles at Bayreuth, Levi and Wagner began to cultivate their friendship, but it was initiated by Levi. After conducting a performance of **Die Meistersinger** in Munich in January 1877, Levi impetuously journeyed to Bayreuth without an invitation. Arriving there he sent Wagner a note indicating "that he could no longer bear not visiting R. here! We are astonished."[54]

Levi and the Wagners gradually developed a mutual rapport and Levi became a regularly invited visitor to Wahnfried. The two men took long walks together and solidified what appeared to be a genuine fondness for each other. As might be expected religion was a favorite topic of conversation but Levi's "Jewishness" seemed, at times, to upset him more than Wagner. According to Cosima, Wagner was very touched when Levi referred to his Jewishness as a "walking anachronism" to which Wagner replied that "if the Catholics considered themselves superior to the Protestants, the Jews are the most superior to all, being the eldest."

----

[53] **The Brown Book**, 174-5.

[54] **CW's Diaries**, 20 January 1877, 941-2.

It sounded good but it was doubtful if either knew what Wagner meant.

By early 1879 Levi was so affected by Wagner's charisma that he appeared to develop a good case of Jewish self-hatred. Levi had been born in Giessen where his father was currently the rabbi. His grandfather, also a rabbi, served in the Sanhedrin created by Napoleon. Several years later after visiting the cathedral at Bamberg, Levi told the Wagners that he was "leaning" toward Catholicism. Whether or not he was serious is unknown but the Wagners talked him out of it. If he were to become a Christian, as Wagner explained, he should become a Protestant because of the simplicity of the rituals. When he confided to Wagner, in positive terms, about the rising spirit of anti-Jewishness developing in Germany, Wagner appeared surprised: "The conductor speaks of a great movement against the Jews in all spheres of life; in Munich there are attempts to remove them from the town council. He hopes that in 20 years they will be extirpated root and branch, and the audience for the **Ring** will be another kind of public."[55] Cosima later remarked to her husband: "We know differently!"

It is difficult to know what Wagner really thought about Levi's critical remarks made against his own religion but it appeared to prompt Wagner to explain how he felt about the problem of Jews vis-a-vis Germans. His stand, as it had been for many years, was largely confined to the belief that Germany was a young country conspicuously lacking in unity. There was, as yet, no cohesion through which means a disparate Germanic peoples could be bound together into a single unit. The large influx of Jews, especially from culturally dissimilar Eastern Europe who emigrated to Germany in the early decades of the century, only compounded the problem. Without the integration of the Germans into a composite identity, the Jews could not hope to be properly assimilated. Wagner saw it not as a religious problem but as a cultural dilemma, but one with serious political overtones.

Opposition to Jews on the basis of this seemingly rational and intellectually defensible viewpoint could have been a convenient subterfuge to conceal Wagner's emotional dislike of the Jews. If so, he displayed a remarkable degree of consistency by so often expressing

---
[55] **CW's Diaries**, 13 January 1879, 254.

this viewpoint, and he maintained this opinion both in private discussions with Cosima, and with other intimate friends. In his constant harangue over the necessity for creating a "German spirit" nothing could get in Wagner's way, least of all Jews.

Now that "pet Israelite" Levi had been admitted to the inner circle at Wahnfried, Wagner found it both amazing and amusing how he was able to attract so many Jews: "Wahnfried will soon turn into a synagogue!" Cosima, usually far more anti-Jewish than her husband, seemed to develop a special fondness for Levi referring to him in her Diary as "our friend." While Wagner was composing **Parsifal**, Levi spent many nights at Wahnfried listening to or playing excerpts from the score as Wagner finished them: "While Rubinstein is playing, even singing quietly, and Levi listening with great emotion, R. says to me, 'what touching figures they are!--Beatific high spirits following our ecstatic bliss.'"[56]

No later than April 1880, ten months before he completed the final score of **Parsifal** and over two years before it was first performed, Wagner came to the conclusion that Levi would conduct its world premiere at Bayreuth (although he did not inform him of this fact until January 1881). However Wagner was concerned over Levi's Jewishness: "I cannot allow him to conduct **Parsifal** unbaptized, but I shall baptize them both [Rubinstein, as well], and we shall all take Communion together";[57] a peculiarly glib or even enigmatic casual remark, although perhaps Wagner thought that he himself might indeed perform the sacrament! Whether this attitude related to the supposed religious message of **Parsifal** is highly conjectural, but the idea of baptism was mentioned on several occasions and Wagner seemed confident of being able to find some way to accomplish it.

There are other possible explanations for Wagner's gratuitous remark. He may have been concerned that some would view Levi's appointment as a betrayal of his lifelong principals regarding the Jews and a serious mellowing to his often expressed belief in the need for Germans to develop a "German spirit." It might even be viewed by some as if Wagner were willingly compromising

----

[56] **CW's Diaries**, 10 April 1879, 290.

[57] **CW's Diaries**, 28 April 1880, 471.

his ideals in the name of self-interest. Baptism may well be an expedient way out of the dilemma. Either way, several months later Wagner remarked to Cosima that "as a member of the orchestra he would not like to be conducted by a Jew." It was somewhat ironic that while Wagner was worried about the inability to be both Jewish and German for Levi there was no problem. As early as 1864 he refused to consider an orchestral post in Paris: "I am rooted, as **musician,** in Germany with my whole being. ... Up to now no **real** German musician (I take this attribute as my own not for my ability but for my aspiration) has felt comfortable on foreign soil."[58]

By all accounts Levi was visibly shaken when Wagner told him in January 1881 that he would be conducting **Parsifal.** There were many others who Wagner could have selected and the appointment of this particular Munich conductor was not a requirement (in 1876 Wagner chose Richter to conduct the **Ring** when only a few years earlier Ludwig had ordered his dismissal from Munich for refusing to conduct **Rheingold**). Contrary to popular belief Wagner was not forced by the king to accept Levi or lose the Munich orchestra. His decision in favor of Levi was made almost three years before the performance. However, as a ploy and a way out of an embarrassing predicament Wagner would have enjoyed the popular rumor that it was Levi or no Munich orchestra.

A touch of scandal almost ended Levi's association with **Parsifal** when a rumor began to circulate that he was having an affair with Cosima. When Wagner showed him an anonymous letter to this effect, criticizing his relationship to the Wagners and his Jewishness, (according to Glasenapp the official biographer from whom both Newman and Westernhagen took their accounts of this incident), Levi was so hurt that he packed his bags and left Wahnfried and Bayreuth. Wagner sent a telegram imploring him to return, but to no avail; finally a follow-up letter ended the breach:

> Dear, best friend! I have the greatest respect for your feelings, but you do not make anything

---

[58] Peter Gay, "Hermann Levi, A Study in Service and Self-Hatred," **Freud, Jews, and Other Germans,** Oxford, 1978, 213. According to Gay "Wagner became the agent of Hermann Levi's fame and his misery, his self-esteem and his self-hatred." (p.194).

easy for yourself or for us. It is precisely your proneness to gloomy introspection that might make our relationship with you a little oppressive! We are quite agreed on telling the whole world this sh--, and your part will be not to run away, leaving people to draw completely nonsensical conclusions. For God's sake, turn round at once and get to know us properly at long last. Do not lose any of your faith, but gain the courage to go on with it! Perhaps--it will be a turning point in your life--but in any event--you are my conductor for **Parsifal**![59]

Levi returned the following day and Wagner called for "Hebrew wine" at lunch.

Shortly before the premiere of **Parsifal** Levi received a letter from his father which expressed certain reservations about Wagner. His reply to the rabbi is informative:

He is the best and noblest of men. Of course the rest of the world misunderstands him and slanders him... Goethe fared no better. But one day posterity will recognize that Wagner was as great a man as he was artist, which those close to him know already. Even his fight against what he calls "Jewry" in music and modern literature springs from the noblest motives, and that he's not just narrow-mindedly anti-Semitic ... is shown by his attitude to me and Joseph Rubinstein and by the close friendship he used to have with Tausig, whom he loved dearly. The most wonderful thing I have experienced in my life is the privilege of being close to such a man, and I thank God for it every day.[60]

---

[59] Wagner to Levi, 1 July 1881. Letter appears in Westernhagen, **Wagner**, 570. According to Cosima the incident started innocently, "but when the letter is shown to the poor conductor, he cannot master his feelings, it seems that such instances of baseness are something new to him!" See **CW's Diaries**, 29 July 1881, 2:681.

[60] Bayreuth Festival program, **Parsifal**, 1959, 9, as quoted in Westernhagen, **Wagner**, 571-2.

It would be relatively simple to dismiss Levi's reassurance to his father as either blind devotion or a further example of Jewish self-hate. It may be!

Wagner's closest Jewish friends did not see him as anti-Jewish, and most assuredly not anti-Semitic when that movement began to develop in earnest in the 1870's and 1880's. Yet the **hundreds** of derogatory remarks made against the Jews, filling the pages of Cosima's Diary, seems to represent a greater reality. The printed English edition of her Diary, in two volumes of small print, exceeds two thousand pages. Cosima began her Diary on Friday, 1 January 1869 and the last entry was recorded on the day before Wagner died, Monday 12 February 1883. Cosima's and presumably her husband's caustic and negative remarks against Jews appeared in the very first entry, and continued with regular frequency right up to the last day of his life. In the introduction Geoffrey Skelton (who brilliantly translated the massive project) commented that not only did Wagner read her Diaries but he actually wrote some of the entries himself, the first time being when their son Siegfried was born. Therefore Wagner seemed to be aware of what Cosima had written.

Were all his Jewish friends operating under illusions? Self-hatred? Were they so mesmerized by his aura that they could not or would not see him for what he was? This may be true. Or perhaps Cosima's Diary did not accurately reflect Wagner's true ideas. That Wagner was a complex, even contradictory man, was undeniable. On the other hand, perhaps his Jewish friends were so loving to the man, his works, and his artistic worth, that they were willing to put up with the irrational aspects of his personality. In some cases, they may even have agreed with him! There are many possibilities.

Levi was one of the last friends to see Wagner alive. He arrived in Venice on 4 February 1883 for a week's stay and "was most welcome to all of us." Yet, even then, only a few days before he died "R. observes that Jewishness is a terrible curse ... the Jews, the good ones, are 'condemned to a gently resigned asceticism.'"[61] Levi, together with Porges, were pallbearers at Wagner's funeral.

---

[61] **CW's Diaries**, 9 February 1883, 1007.

In the last five years of his life Wagner occasionally showed signs of mellowing although perhaps more out of frustration than conviction. When it appeared unlikely that the German people were going to develop into that very special type of country that Wagner envisioned in his more romantic days he lost all hope for the future. Now, all around him, he could find nothing but "Philistines, Jews, and Jesuits, but never a man." If the Germans were being taken over and exploited the fault rested with them, and not with the Jews. Perhaps Germany deserved its fate. In desperation he sometimes expressed the belief that "Germany is finished" as a country, but the Jews were really not to be blamed for this: "Oh, it is not the Jews--everybody likes to further his own interests--it is we ourselves who are to blame; [62] we the nation, for allowing such things to happen."

But even in his more reflective moments Wagner's thoughts sometimes tended toward the simplistic. Regardless of his Jewish friendships he remained impervious to the Germanness of Tausig, Porges, and Levi, still thinking it possible to view them not as Germans but as Jews, a rival nation who descended too quickly on the defenseless Germans. [63] Several years after Wagner's death Cosima told Levi that if he converted he could die a Christian but not a Teuton, and she made it clear which was higher, despite her own non-Teutonic birth.

Nevertheless, Wagner did not embrace the anti-Semitic movement which began to develop in earnest in the closing decades of the nineteenth century nor was he willing to sign his name to a popular anti-Semitic petition which asked Bismarck to take "emergency laws against the Jews."

Shortly after the publication of Darwin's theories, doctrines of racial superiority, aryanism,

----

[62] **CW's Diaries**, 13 November 1879, 395.

[63] Except on one occasion when he read a statement in Disraeli's **Tancred** that "all significant people are Jews." Momentarily modifying his belief that Jews and Germans were distinct entities he retorted to Cosima: "Most of them are German Jews and Disraeli overlooks the fact that it is German talent which is being used in this way." See **CW's Diaries**, 20 February 1881, 2:628.

and the germ theory regarding the supposed superiority of the Teutonic peoples, began to appear in great intensity, first among intellectual circles, but shortly thereafter in popular magazines and newspaper articles. But Darwinism only reinforced the already widely popular irrational and unscientific ideas of Count Joseph Arthur de Gobineau (1816-82). That Frenchman achieved fame and some notoriety for his monumental and extremely influential opus **The Inequality of the Human Races** which appeared between 1853-56. Wagner read Gobineau's work in early 1881 and later that year Gobineau visited Bayreuth. Although impressed with his thesis regarding the superiority of the Nordic and aryan races, Wagner believed that Gobineau "did not look deep enough." He was too intransigent and inflexible in his conclusions and his rigidity did not permit the spirit of Christianity to ameliorate the condition of race.

Wagner enjoyed Gobineau's company but this did not prevent several heated arguments: "at lunch he [Wagner] is downright explosive in favor of Christian theories in contrast to racial ones."[64] Although Gobineau's influence on Cosima was significant, his ideas received especially-favorable consideration by her future son-in-law Houston Stewart Chamberlain. Gobineau's theories, applied especially to the Jews, were expanded and amplified by Chamberlain becoming the theoretical and intellectual basis for the racial theories of National Socialism.

After the enormous success of the **Ring** and with Wagner's name now well-known throughout Europe as well as in Germany, he felt less inclined to speak out as forcibly on certain issues as in previous years, but not for long. Although the **Bayreuther Blätter** was the instrument for the expression and dissemination of Wagner's thoughts and ideas, he felt it necessary (or financially prudent) to be more circumspect when dealing further with the Jews. Nevertheless, while working on **Parsifal,** religion constantly occupied his mind.

In 1880 Wagner again returned to writing prose. "Religion and Art" was his last major religious statement. This article, to which was added two important supplements in 1881, taken together synthesized Wagner's lifelong thoughts on the subject

----
[64] **CW's Diaries,** 3 June 1881, 2:672.

of religion. He considered them to be among his best writings. Although his thoughts regarding the religious beliefs of Jews cannot be abstracted without destroying the integrity of his argument, certain aspects can be summarized here, although the subject will be dealt with at greater length in connection with **Parsifal.**

"What has given the Jews their now so dreaded power among and over us...?" asked Wagner. The answer was brief and to the point--the "nature and civilization" of the Germans! Wagner now takes pride in having been one of the few Germans to have seen this coming. For over thirty years he had warned his fellow countrymen that the emancipation of Jews would seriously dislocate German society and culture. The Jewish problem was a German problem which predated emancipation. By permitting Jews to acquire property, after the proclamation of the empire, Germans were responsible for their acquisition of wealth, influence, and power; and yet the Jew always remains an alien: "Without a fatherland, a mother-tongue, midst every people's land and tongue he finds himself again, in virtue of the unfailing instinct of his absolute and indelible idiosyncrasy: even commixture of blood does not hurt him; let Jew or Jewess intermarry with the most distinct of races a Jew will always come to birth."[65] Wagner was often blatantly inconsistent about whether conversion and intermarriage "cured" a Jew of his Jewishness. At times he insisted that only through intermarriage and conversion could Jews become Germans while at other times he denied the Christianity of Jews whose fathers or even grandfathers had converted. Mendelssohn was the classic example of a "Christianized Jew."

Yet all was not lost. A glimmer of hope still existed for deep within the German breast was a spark that may yet be ignited: "So let us save and tend and brace our best of forces, to bear a noble cordial to the sleeper when he wakes, as of himself he must at last. But only when the fiend, who keeps those ravers in the mania of their party-strife, no more can find a where or when to lurk among us, will there also be no longer--any Jews."[66] Seven years later Adolf Hitler

----

[65] "Know Thyself," being a continuation of "Religion and Art," **Bayreuther Blätter,** February-March 1881, **PW,** 6:271.

[66] **Ibid.,** 274.

was born.

Ultimately Wagner's attitude toward Jews was remarkably inconsistent but psychologically significant. Anti-Jewish although not necessarily anti-Semitic, befriending Jews yet he talked about them behind their backs, fascinated with the Old Testament and highly conversant in it, he condemned its God who was not his God. His anti-Jewishness often seemed to be a remarkably convenient crutch which helped to mitigate his sometimes very intense feelings of depression and frustration. One is reminded of how often he talked of suicide in his letters to Franz Liszt. It soon became extremely convenient for Wagner to blame his lack of success on a "Jewish plot" even where none existed. During the first performance of **Die Meistersinger** in Berlin he talked about the "distinctive physiognomies" who were ready "to take their revenge on the author of 'Judaism in Music.'"

Franz Liszt perceptively recognized that Wagner "needed" Jews. When he once wrote, "reviling the Jews,[67] a generic term with him, of most elastic meaning," he seemed to take recognition that anytime a newspaper printed an article against Wagner it automatically meant that its editor was Jewish; or if someone criticized his prose, or music, it reflected Jewish taste or Jewish values. How well Liszt understood him.

----
[67] Ellis, **Life of Richard Wagner**, 3:138.

CHAPTER 8

THE ARCHETYPAL MAN: JESUS AND PARSIFAL

Shortly after Wagner first met King Ludwig II in 1864 he was asked if his current religious ideas differed substantially from those held in 1849-51 when he wrote most of his significant theoretical works. That question forced Wagner to reexamine his beliefs.

In answering the king Wagner assumed two postulates: first, one can intuit the existence of a non-earthly spiritual world; second, "since this world [the physically earthly one] is the source of our unhappiness, that other world, of redemption from it."[1] The spiritual world redeemed man but man could prepare for it through "voluntary suffering and renunciation." In referring to the spiritual world Wagner was not postulating an afterworld, an afterlife, or a belief in bodily resurrection; indeed, one of his major criticisms of Judaism related to its persistent optimism, especially in maintaining a belief in the world to come, a simplistic idea which Christianity adapted and made even more absurd by vivid depictions of heaven and hell.

Wagner discussed religion in broad terms, mentioning the "Christian religion" but twice, and never indicating any particular denomination. Not once was Jesus mentioned! Although some of his assertions were now camouflaged through the use of Schopenhauer's rhetoric, his focal points emerged clearly: the religious spirit existed "within the deepest, holiest, inner chamber of the individual ... for this is the essence of true religion... it shines in the night of man's inmost heart, with a light quite other than the world-sun's light, and visible nowhere save from out that depth." An orthodox Jew could not have said it better.

This statement appears to be analogous to the struggle endured by Tannhäuser when his spiritual soul vied for supremacy over the animal soul. Wagner's mystical bent and his awareness of kabbalistic thought postulated a belief that God "revealed" himself by means of an inner light; both the essence of God and man's own spirituality were to be found within the individual. Nevertheless, there may be exceptional,

----
[1] "On State and Religion," 24.

309

although rare circumstances, when God's imminence sets
aside free will, thereby permitting his actions to be
witnessed in the physical world. Spirituality involved
a deeply personal inner relationship between man and
God. No obeisance to any religious denomination was
needed. Therefore, organized religious institutions and
the existence of a religious spirit within man, may
each exist independently of the other, inasmuch as both
differ in terms of means. But within the spirituality
of the individual lay the possibility for an intuitive
mystical linkage between the earthly and the
metaphysical worlds. Some individuals were capable of
linking the two.

The corollary to the mystical intuitive
relationship between man and God is found in the
transcendental, which established the connection
between the spiritual and the earthly world, or between
God and man. Wagner did not dwell on this aspect
perhaps fearful that Ludwig might not be responsive.
Since Wagner had not yet established a friendly
relationship with the eighteen year-old monarch, he was
unfamiliar with the king's personally-held religious
views. As he was indebted to the king for his present
and future economic well-being he tended to generalize
his religious thoughts. Ludwig was known to be a
practicing Catholic and if his upbringing had been
limited exclusively to exposure to Catholic dogma
Wagner might be wise to be circumspect.

The most important element in Wagner's exposition
related to the "inner chamber of the heart" and the
"light quite other than the world sun's light."
Returning to the themes implicit in both **Tannhäuser** and
Lohengrin, Wagner reintroduced them twenty years later.
Because of the extreme brightness of the internal light
man is incapable of perfect vision; he sees only
diluted reflections of God's spirit. It is incumbent on
those who have the ability to perceive the spiritual
insights emanating from the diffused light of God to
act in accordance with the message inherent in the
revelation. Spirituality precipitated and required
action. It necessitated creating a positive effect on
the earthly world: action justified the gift of
insight.

Although it was both possible and desirable, very
few people actually have the ability to find their
spirituality exclusively from within. The majority
prefer to relate to an established religious

institution. Without intending to minimize either the intelligence or the spiritual depth of the "volk", Wagner believed that the average man was not capable of metaphysical speculation nor of deep and profound philosophical inquiry; likewise, the average person needed the psychological and emotional crutch of religious tradition and dogma. Man needed religion to enhance his spirituality. Even the Catholic belief in saints was sometimes useful. Since there were few differences in morality among the various religious systems all points of view should be tolerated.

Returning to the meaning of Jesus' life, Wagner reasserted his opinion on how often man perverted his message and ideals. Who was Jesus and why was he so important? "The humble son of the Galilean carpenter ... who preached the reign of universal human love--a love he could never have enjoined on men whose duty it should be to despise their fellows and themselves. ... Thus would **Jesus** have shown us that we all alike are men and bothers."[2] While Wagner may not have objected to being called a Christian, the designation served only as a convenient label rather than as a measure of his religiosity. His ideas were strongly reinforced by Feuerbach and Schopenhauer but neither philosopher can be held responsible for generating the thoughts that he expressed, even though, at times, he may have borrowed some of their verbiage.[3]

Feuerbach was the first major philosopher whose views and ideas reinforced those already held by Wagner. This comforted him for it confirmed that his ideas were neither arbitrary nor whimsical. Although married to a Jewess, Feuerbach maintained that Judaism as a religion was too exclusive and this "egotism" gave it limited scope for Western man. Christianity removed some of this exclusivity but it too was narrow. Since the universality of spiritual matters was a cardinal

----

[2] **Art and Revolution**, 37, 65.

[3] In the "Translator's Preface" to the first volume of the **Prose Works of Richard Wagner**, William Ashton Ellis commented that Wagner's first mention of Feuerbach did not occur until January 1850 which was after he had already completed both **The Art-Work of the Future** and **Art and Revolution**. His argument is not persuasive. Wagner dedicated **The Art-Work of the Future** to Feuerbach and one is hardly likely to dedicate a major work to a man unless influenced by him.

aspect of Wagner's ideas he shared with Feuerbach a perception of the limited nature of the Judeo-Christian tradition.

Although displaying intense spiritual yearnings even early in life, Wagner never seemed to hold much importance for traditional religion. While writing his autobiography he reflected back to his first Communion:

> At the time of my confirmation, at Easter, 1827, I had considerable doubt about this ceremony, and I already felt a serious falling off of my reverence for religious observances. ... How matters stood with me spiritually was revealed to me, almost to my horror, at the Communion service, when I walked in procession with my fellow-communicants to the altar to the sound of organ and choir. The shudder with which I received the Bread and Wine was so ineffaceably stamped on my memory, that I never again partook of the Communion, lest I should do so with levity. To avoid this was all the easier for me, seeing that among Protestants such participation is not compulsory.[4]

Wagner's personal revulsion for dogma, tradition, and ceremony, remained fairly consistent throughout his life.

Although Wagner never developed a systematic or coherent philosophy of religion, he was fairly consistent in promulgating certain beliefs. He tended to assume that Christianity never failed because it was never tried. Right after the death of Jesus his followers began to distort his spiritual message, corrupting it in the process by turning it into a system. Christianity was optimistic, especially in the doctrine of a world to come, and optimism was at the core of Wagner's problem. Judaism posited the existence of a world to come, a belief which Christianity accepted from the beginning and without serious examination. However, since neither the Old Testament Bible nor the Talmud clearly described heaven or hell

---

[4] **My Life**, 1:23-4. In the 1870's, after he married Cosima, Wagner occasionally took communion with her, though possibly more for her sake than for his soul. Nevertheless he once admitted to her that prayer was "unknown to me."

as actual places, Christianity remedied this deficiency by adding colorful descriptions for both.

Neither the Bible nor Judaic law clearly defined an afterworld, only postulating who might or might not enjoy a portion of it; it was assumed that some form of afterlife existed where souls, at least of the pure, were reunited with the divine soul from which they emanated. This attitude offered hope and reinforced the belief that man had a divine purpose to play in the world. Presumably, the extent to which man assumed his "rightful" role in life, through what he did with the exercise of free will, determined whether or not he was to be rewarded with a portion of the world to come. Judaism attached its greatest import to what man did with his life while on earth. As a religion and a social system it tended to be optimistic.

Perceiving "life" primarily as a means to an end, Christianity not only accepted this Judaic idea of optimism, but extended it. By viewing the world to come as even more desirable than the earthly physical world, Christianity "imprisoned him [man] in a loathsome dungeon: so as, in reward for the self-contempt that poisoned him therein, to prepare him for a posthumous state of endless comfort and inactive ecstasy."[5] Christianity was responsible for "this deepest and unmanliest degradation", by viewing life as corrupt and sinful. But what is faith other than "the confession of its [mankind's] miserable plight, and the giving up of all spontaneous attempts to escape from out this misery; for the **undeserved Grace** of God was alone to set it free." Christian optimism "set man's goals entirely outside his earthly being" and this denied both the value of life and the importance of living: "Thus sighs the smug adorer of the heavenly kingdom in which--at least as far as himself is concerned--God will make good the inexplicable shortcomings of this earth and its human brood." Although this bleak view of Christianity was propounded shortly after his flight from Dresden, at a time when he was most desperate, it was a view that remained consistently active in his thoughts.

In many ways Wagner's ideas were analogous to those of other contemporary romantic transcendentalists and similar in certain respects to Karl Marx. When Marx postulated that religion was an "opiate" he too

----
[5] **Art and Revolution**, 37.

assumed, as Wagner had said earlier, that the optimism associated with an afterlife prevented man from aggressively changing the often miserable nature of society. Man was all too content to wait passively for some reward in the assumed world to come: "The misleading problem in these questions is always How to introduce into this terrible world, with an empty nothing beyond it, a God Who converts the enormous sufferings of existence into something fictitious, so that the hoped-for salvation remains the only real and consciously enjoyable thing."[6]

In one facet of Wagner's thoughts the passage of time did produce a change of opinion. In 1849 he was highly critical of Christian dogmas calling them "not realisable" because "they were directed against life itself, and denied and cursed the principle of living." Presumably Wagner was thinking of original sin or, as he called it, "the worthlessness of human nature." The exclusivity of Christian dogma was so restrictive that it served only to perpetuate the narrowness of Judaism, its parent religion. It did little for the brotherhood of man. Therefore Christianity was incapable of becoming a universal religion.

Later in life Wagner modified his attitude toward dogma, believing it to be both useful and necessary for the internal peace of mind of many people:

> I am becoming more and more convinced on the truth of Voltaire's saying that religion cannot be too absurd for the common people, and that Christianity cannot be separated from its Jewish roots. The Father in Heaven belongs to that idea, and a religion must remain naive, childlike, and simple; the benevolent god who has arranged everything properly even when we don't understand it, is for the common man the only consolation, the only inducement to resignation. Of course, once this faith is shattered, it can never be restored.[7]

Mid and late nineteenth century religious thought was greatly influenced by the application of the scientific method to Biblical criticism. The

---

6 Wagner to Liszt 7 June 1855, **Wagner-Liszt Correspondence**, 2:94.

7 **CW's Diaries**, 27 January 1875, 1:822.

introduction of this methodology sent shock waves throughout conservative circles. Wagner was a product of this period. He read Ernst Renan's **Life of Jesus** and followed closely the arguments made by liberal thinkers and religious reformers. For some of them the relationship between Christianity and the life, ideals, and message of Jesus remained two disparate elements. Jesus was the archetypal universal man who knew and understood the spiritual meaning behind life and the role to be played by man. Stressing universality, the brotherhood of all men, and a creedless, undogmatic and remarkably simple "religion", Jesus cut through the often complex verbiage of Judaic legalities, substituting stark simplicity for the often cumbersome and ritually-oriented Mosaic code.

By carefully selecting, paraphrasing, and rewriting certain sections from the Old Testament and the Gospels, Wagner enabled Jesus to stress the ideas of love, service to God (without the need for animal sacrifice), the divinity of all men, and a recognition of "the God that dwelleth in him [man]":

> 'No longer shall ye think to serve God by going to the Temple, saying prayers, and making sacrifice of things it pains you not to miss: another offering shall ye henceforth bring your whole life through, so long as e'er ye move and breathe: your body shall ye offer daily and hourly, that it may live in the love of God; i.e. in the love of your breathren, that ye now may no more live according to the law, which shielded your unlovingness, but after the commandment which I have brought you: when ye have recognised it in your heart as true, ye shall let your body do according to the heart: this is the sacrifice that liveth forever, holy and well-pleasing unto God--this is Life itself, which is the most reasonable service of God.--
>
> Everyone who walketh in Love, is King and Priest over himself, for he is subject unto no man, but to God, who dwelleth in him; but he who walketh without love, is a slave and subject unto every mighty man of earth, for in him dwelleth Sin, and Sin ruleth him.'[8]

----
[8] "Jesus of Nazareth," 305.

Jesus was a pure and simple man who was unafraid to live because he worked in the service of God. Through free will all mankind had the strength and ability to submerge the egoism of the self. By working actively for the betterment of the community, thinking only of the group and not of the self (egoism), man can even lose his fear of death. The thought of death was selfish, crass, destructive of personal happiness, and hostile to the betterment of humanity. But "Death is swallowed up in love." Anticipating a theme in the **Ring,** Wagner found in the fear of death a component in the perpetuation of lovelessness: "the loveless constantly abides in egoism, and in death he founders utterly. ... Only he who brings his free will to the divestment of his life-stuff, passes consciously into the universal, and thus lives on therein a multiple and broader life."

Too often "the Christian left the shores of Life" anticipating and yearning for the promised reward of salvation in the after-world: "The **Word,** the word of **Faith,** was his only compass; and it pointed him unswervingly toward Heaven." Christianity denigrated both life and man. Life became an endless ocean voyage with man waiting pathetically for death as the hopeful means for redemption from an ugly, sinful existence. Tracing the centrality of the death ethos to the voluntary martyrdom of Jesus, this represented to Wagner "the liberation of the Individual through redemption into God. The enthralling power of the Christian myth consists in its portrayal of a **transfiguration through Death."**[10]

Themes of death and redemption figured prominently in most of Wagner's music-dramas; yet he considered death as only part of the life process, not the sought-after goal. Critical of those who feared death, he was equally critical of those who were obsessed with the theme: "To the Christian Death was in itself the object. For him, Life had its only sacredness and warranty as the preparation for Death, in the longing for its laying down." Christianity introduced a "swarm of fables" which converted life into a religiously-oriented view which all but abnegated the sacredness and importance of living. Therefore the common man,

----

[9] **The Art-Work of the Future,** 114.

[10] **Opera and Drama,** Part 2, "The Play and Dramatic Poetry," 159.

through no fault of his own, had become indoctrinated through a theological conspiracy into a life of "inaction." When Christianity became a temporal force and evolved into an institution with political strength as well as religious power, the concept of death became even stronger: "The Christian Church had also striven for unity: every vital manifestation was to converge in her, as the centre of all life. She was not, however, life's central, but the terminal point, for the secret of the truest Christian essence was Death."

Wagner was intrigued with Christianity but remained critical of what he perceived to be its misguided direction when it turned away from the simplicity of its founder. In doing so the history of many Christian churches became infused with fundamental errors in theology: "The error (christianity [sic]) is necessary" but while science has the power to destroy error when its thinking proves incorrect, Christianity can not: "the great folk's-error of christianity first had the prodigious ponderance to slay itself" but instead became "dishonest, hypocritical, as theology."[11] Jesus had broken with the dogma of his ancestry, castoff the exclusivity of Judaism, and embraced God in a simple, direct fashion, with no need for intermediaries, rituals or complex institutional strictures.

Conveniently overlooking every statement made by Jesus contrary to what he wanted him to say, Wagner perceived that the ideals of Jesus stressed community--which Wagner consistently called "communism"--but this spirit decayed, to be replaced by a "religion of sufferers--Christianity. Error, triumph and corruption of Christianity: as the nature-religion of the first folk foundered in a tyrannical democracy."[12] Once institutionalized, Christianity soon outgrew and perverted the moral, ethical, and spiritual teachings of Jesus; in its place were introduced a corruption of his ideals, replacing community with "unbounded egoism" while promising a "contract" whereby individual salvation, happiness, and life in the future, were guaranteed "on condition of abstinence and free-willed suffering in this relatively brief and fleeting life."[13]

---

11   "Sketches and Fragments," PW, 8:350-1.

12   "The Genius of Communism," PW, 8:358.

317

For over twenty years Wagner's thoughts remained consistent. When writing that "profoundest knowledge teaches us that only in the inner chamber of our heart, in nowise from the world presented to us without, can true assuagement come to us", he recapitulated the theme of Tannhäuser's conflict between the two chambers of the heart. Yet by the time he reached his early fifties, Wagner became more appreciative of human frailty and man's need for security. Now he recognized that what profound spiritual insights he intuited for himself would not necessarily be accepted or understood by others. Religious conventions were obviously needed and important for the average person who seldom thought deeply or read widely in matters of religion. This did not give Wagner a sense of superiority but it did make him more responsive to the limitations of man's spiritual nature.

Recognizing the need to believe, he even went so far as to be highly critical of a friend for not having her ward baptized:

> This was not right, he said, not everyone could fashion his religion for himself, and particularly in childhood one must have a feeling of cohesion. Nor should one be left to choose; rather, it should be possible to say, 'You have been christened, you belong through baptism to Christ, now unite yourself once more with him through Holy Communion.' Christening and Communion are indispensable, he said. ... People who evade religion have a terrible shallowness, and are unable to feel anything at all in a religious spirit.[14]

Although he quite often commented in private that "religion is dying: it only keeps going by making fools of the people", yet for the common unsophisticated and non-philosophically oriented man, religious illusions were necessary; nevertheless, "religion is for those who can neither read nor write."[15] Wagner was not being hypocritical, merely psychologically realistic. Sometimes the need to believe is more compelling than

----

[13] "On State and Religion," 25.

[14] CW's Diaries, 9-13 December 1873, 1:707.

[15] CW's Diaries, 15 June 1872, 499; see also 17 July 1871, 390.

any act of faith: "If Christ for us is in the end even still merely a most noble poetic fiction, then it is at the same time more realizable than any other poetic ideal..."[16]

In **Die Meistersinger** Hans Sachs was the archetype of the self-contained man who reconciled the duality of his heart, understood the mystical and transcendental relationships possible between man and God and God and man, yet sympathized with and outwardly accepted the familiar dogmas of faith shared by the burghers and common folk of Nürnberg who found solace and comfort in Lutheranism. Sachs, like Wagner, never outwardly rejected these trappings but inwardly felt them to be unnecessary. Unlike the Dutchman, Tannhäuser, or Lohengrin both Sachs and Wagner became "socialized" and lived as part of society, Sachs more comfortably than Wagner. While seemingly conformist, both found spirituality within, rather than through religion.

Cleverly, Wagner began to make use of familiar religious thoughts and phrases. It was far safer to talk about the "fulfilment of Christ's teachings" than to discuss the "hypocrisy of Christianity." Ultimately this would lead to the brilliant outward Christian appearance of **Parsifal,** while inwardly Wagner's message and its real meaning had little if anything to do with nineteenth century Christianity. The important inner meaning of Parsifal's life related to his spiritual growth outside of Christianity, and was not related to anything currently existing within the institution of Christianity. Parsifal, like Jesus and Wagner, acquired spirituality without the need for formal religion.

Despite the inability of the common man to delve deeply into metaphysical subtleties, Wagner maintained that society had a responsibility and an obligation to universalize Christianity so that its more basic essentials might be understood and accomplished. But in the middle and later decades of the nineteenth century when both Italy and Germany were attempting to unite into states, nationalism and Christianity often served mutually exclusive ends. Veneration of the State, as an end, sometimes prevented the universal application of the brotherhood of man and this dilemma Christianity could not solve. But "the Christian religion belongs to no specific national stock: the Christian dogma

---

[16] "Thoughts on the Regeneration of Mankind and of Culture," **The Brown Book,** 202.

addresses purely-human nature. Only in so far as it has
seized in all its purity this content common to all
men, can a people call itself Christian in truth."[17]

Throughout the course of German history and
especially since the later middle ages and the
Reformation, Wagner saw graphically demonstrated the
conflict between the "German spirit and the un-German
spirit of the German Reich's supreme controller [the
Catholic Church]. Since that time--cleavage of
religion: a dire misfortune! None but a universal
religion is Religion in truth: divers confessions,
politically established and ranged beside or over one
another by contact with the State, simply confess that
Religion is in act of dissolution. ... The sequel we
may see in our public State-life of to-day." Since
institutional Christianity seemed unable to get across
the message of Jesus, perhaps another medium--art--
might succeed where religion failed.

Wagner first became familiar with the legend of
Parsifal in the 1840's while working on **Lohengrin**, the
mythical son of Parsifal. Although not mentioned by
name in Wagner's drama, it was Lohengrin's father, the
keeper of the Grail, who interceded on behalf of Elsa
and sent out his son to prove her innocent of
fratricide. The legend had been fairly well-known since
the thirteenth century. Attributed to Wolfram von
Eschenbach (c.1170-c1220) it was a courtly romance
based on the story of the Grail by Chrétien de Troyes.
For twelve years Wagner thought of Parsifal. After
moving into the "Asyl", his small cottage outside
Zurich, in April 1857, his mind again returned to this
subject. In his autobiography Wagner greatly
romanticized and embellished the occasion: "the little
garden was radiant with green, the birds sang, and at
last I could sit on the roof and enjoy the long-
yearned-for peace with its message of promise. Full of
this sentiment, I suddenly remembered that the day was
Good Friday, and I called to mind the significance this
omen had already once assumed for me when I was reading
Wolfram's **Parsifal**."[18]

----

[17] "What is German," 155.

[18] **My Life**, 2:661. Wagner was in error for he did not
move into the Asyl until after Good Friday. "Yesterday
evening, thinking about various dates in his life, R.
felt he had made a mistake in his biography, and that
it was only the stillness of the Asyl garden which felt

But by 1859 he gave up the idea of **Parsifal**:
"Considered strictly, Anfortas [sic] is the centre and
principal subject. There you have a pretty tale at
once. ... He lives, re-lives, and more fiercely than
ever the fatal wound ravens him, **his** wound! Devotion
itself becomes a torture! Where is an end to it, where
redemption? ... And I'm to execute a thing like that,
to boot? make music for it too?--Declined with thanks!
Let him do it who likes; I'll keep it fairly off my
neck!"[19]

Twenty years later, toward the end of August 1865,
Wagner prepared the first draft sketch of the legend;
but work on **Tristan** and the **Ring** prevented him from
devoting more than passing attention to it. Over the
ensuing years his thoughts persistently returned to
Parsifal, although the Christian aspects of the legend
still bothered him. Finally, when Wagner's own
religious thoughts began to coalesce in the late
1870's, he understood how to make the drama work for
his purpose. Now the timing was ripe and he wrote a
second prose sketch which incorporated ideas he had
been mulling over during the previous thirty-five
years.

Parsifal offered both a sublime dilemma and a
unique opportunity. Wagner, like Hans Sachs, would try
to lead man toward a nobler conception of human
----
in his memory like a Good Friday, it had not been Good
Friday in fact." See **CW's Diaries**, 13 January 1878,
2:18. Far more revealing was the diary notation for 22
April 1879, p. 295: "R. today recalled the impression
which inspired his 'Good Friday Music'; he laughs,
saying he had thought to himself, 'In fact it is all as
far-fetched as my love affairs, for it was not Good
Friday at all--just a pleasant mood in Nature which
made me think, 'This is how a Good Friday ought to
be.'" Nevertheless, the hyperbole served a useful
purpose and Wagner never corrected his autobiography.
Aside from the Good Friday reference Wagner claimed
that "his text has in fact no connection" with
Wolfram's **Parzival** although "when he read the epic, he
first said to himself that nothing could be done with
it, but 'a few things stuck in my mind--the Good
Friday, the wild appearance of Cundrie. That was all
it was.'" See 20 June 1879, 327.

19 Wagner to Mathilde Wesendonck, 30 May 1859,
Wesendonck, **Letters**, 140-1.

nature--in this case, a greater understanding of brotherhood, spirituality, and God. But Wagner recognized that he would have problems. A music-drama attacking Christianity for failing to follow the ideals of Jesus would be unthinkable. Yet by subtly manipulating the religious metaphor Wagner might be able to offer spiritual insights that were capable of transcending Christianity without being hostile to any denomination. To succeed he would have to use familiar Christian symbols; but underneath the surface he would try to depict a non-institutional religious allegory.

After years of struggling to be heard and understood, Wagner had now developed the musical and prose methodology to accomplish his goal. Finally he recognized how to express what he had himself been struggling to understand for so many years. **Parsifal** would portray an obviously Christian milieu complete with the sublime dogma of the Holy Eucharist. Underlying this, but readily available to all who were spiritually inclined to see it, would be found a larger and more universal theme stressing the love of Jesus and God for mankind, a message of far greater import than the narrowly-restricted doctrines and dogmas of institutional Christianity.

Wagner decided to call this work a "stage **dedication** play" ("Ein Bühnen**weih**festspiel" rather than "Ein Bühnenfestspiel" as the **Ring** was called), a word invention of his own choosing which indicated that it represented not only a newer development in his artistic career, but a type of drama not identical in method and scope as his other works. It was designed exclusively for his Bayreuth theatre because nowhere else did conditions exist which would permit a satisfactory performance. When other theatres could treat the subject artistically, dramatically, and professionally, then it might be released for general performances. Wagner did not view the festival house at Bayreuth as a shrine, as Cosima did after his death, nor did it represent the church of the new religion as some, including his one-time friend Friedrich Nietzsche, called it.

Parsifal was to be a dramatically-artistic philosophical presentation representing several spiritual metaphors and allegories, and not a theological set of dogmas set to music. Wagner's clear intent may be observed in his introduction to "Religion and Art" which appeared in the **Bayreuther Blätter** in October 1880, two years before the premiere:

> One might say that where Religion becomes artificial, it is reserved for Art to save the spirit of religion by recognising the figurative value of the mythic symbols which the former would have us believe in their literal sense, and revealing their deep and hidden truth through an ideal presentation. Whilst the priest stakes everything on the religious allegories being accepted as matters of fact, the artist has no concern at all with such a thing, since he freely and openly gives out his work as his own invention.[20]

Parsifal represented Wagner's "own invention", his final dramatic statement to be expressed in a musical form, although not his last prose word regarding the meaning of spirituality.

Unlike Wolfram's semi-Christian legend of Parzival where the Grail was a sacred stone, Wagner's Holy Grail incorporated a different legend, one which portrayed the spear that pierced the side of Jesus and the cup into which drops of his blood had been collected. The spear and the grail can be viewed as metaphoric male-female symbols which allegorized the birth or creation of a new covenant, although one renewing the love of God (and Jesus) for all mankind. The Knights of the Grail, in Wagner's drama, were the guardians of both relics. As long as the relics were properly venerated by the knights through service, and administered through love, its guardians successfully fulfilled their holy office. Since the knights were expected to serve God and mankind by participating actively in the earthly world, they were neither celibate nor oblivious to secular matters.

In traditional Catholic thought the physical counterpart to the mystical Holy Trinity was faith, hope, and charity, but in discussing the short Prelude to **Parsifal** Wagner indicated that the basis of Jesus' message was "Love--Faith: Hope? First theme: 'Love.'"[21] Love represented the key additional element necessary

---

[20] "Religion and Art," **Bayreuther Blätter**, October 1880, **PW**, 6:213.

[21] "Prelude to **Parsifal**", **PW**, 8:388.

for understanding the historical Jesus and the non-historical Parsifal. For close to two thousand years the absence of love had been characteristic of Christianity, thus betraying the simplest and most basic message of Jesus.

Roman Catholics and especially the Jesuits had preached the love of Jesus for man but ignored or denied it in practice. Once again, as it became obvious when viewing Wagner's intransigence toward Jews, one can see how harsh, myopic, and incorrect he became when trying to make certain points that were important to him. Second only to his intense hostility against Jews, Wagner condemned Catholicism in general and the Jesuits in particular. Out of all the Catholic orders to criticize, Wagner's attitude toward the Jesuits was all the more surprising since they shared some of his intellectual and mystical interests; but he continually and irrationally blamed them for many serious historical offenses, including the absurd charge that they retarded the growth and development of both music and man's religious freedom: "For Religion had vanished from the Church with Palestrina's music, and the artificial formalism of Jesuit observance had counterformed Religion and Music alike."[22] Especially evident was "the damaging effect of the Catholic church in Germany's development" which only the advent of Lutheranism was able to stem.

Prior to the reformation Catholicism had succeeded not simply because of its spiritual message but through its superb organizational techniques. By establishing a hierarchy with both spiritual and temporal power and by uniting the two swords through a well-constructed organizational structure which followed rigidly-prescribed rules, the Catholic church had developed into a formidable institution. Wielding its power it stifled culture and the intellect while at the same time it inhibited--by force of arms as well as through threat of excommunication--the development of potentially rival competing institutions, especially nationalism. For centuries the Church had manipulated man and his life on earth. Protestantism challenged that formidable structure and man as a thinking and feeling being finally emerged as the center of God's creation.

---

[22] Beethoven, 84.

In this analysis of Catholicism Wagner blended elements of historical accuracy with a considerable flair for invention. Usually his anti-Catholic remarks were said in private. But even his closest personal friend, Franz Liszt, did not escape unscathed: "The pious man does not love: what matters to him is simply domination. I know what I am saying. To me all this Catholic rubbish is repugnant to the very depths of my soul: anyone who takes refuge in that must have a great deal to atone for."[23]

No religious institution escaped his critical eye. Yet, behind his caustic hatred and condemnation can be found other themes that served to unify his religious framework. First, mankind needed a linkage with some religious institution and however regrettable this may be, it was a factor that could not be ignored. Second, religion was all-embracing and not limited only to spiritual matters. It contained elements of acute psychological necessity as well as social organization. When Moses brought down the Torah from Mount Sinai it represented more than the institutionalization of monotheism. This event marked the beginning of a totally new and highly significant organizational structure which embraced every aspect of man's activities and thoughts, and no element of life or death existed outside this system. Through the institution of the Papacy and by means of its superb bureaucratic structure, the Catholic Church continued the Mosaic structural model although it modified both means and ends. For centuries man accepted this model "as if it were a sort of magic, as if the Pope had the means of getting us to Heaven one way or another."[24] Although no one would deny the glory of Rome as a city, "all the monuments there bore witness to infamous and enslaved human beings from the Roman emperors to the

---

[23] **The Brown Book**, 65. Wagner was lonely and ill when he wrote this. Liszt had taken Cosima with him to Hungary and Wagner was angry that she had gone: "Your father is repugnant to me.--and when I was able to bear him, there was more Christianity in my blind indulgence than in all his piety." **Idem.** Several years later, after marrying Cosima, Wagner became more circumspect: "How can I possibly write for the **Bayreuther Blätter** when out of consideration for the King and your father I am unable to state my opinion of the Catholic Church." See **CW's Diaries**, 19 November 1878, 2:205.

[24] **CW's Diaries**, 4 September 1878, 2:142.

Jesuit churches and cardinals' palaces." Not until the Protestant Reformation did man finally emerge from the shackles imposed by a religion which acted as the exclusive agent of God, totally controlling the power of life and death.

Although some understanding of Wagner's religious predilections and assumptions is fundamental to grasp the primary message contained in **Parsifal**, behind all the complex allegories and metaphors stands one essential point: love and compassion could and does transcend religion. Parsifal, like Jesus, went beyond all religious institutions. It was unmistakably Wagner's intent to correlate Parsifal with Jesus, although not to turn Parsifal into Jesus. Even going so far as to use a conspicuously Christian framework as the means through which the events of the action were to be depicted, **Parsifal** was designed to circumvent the limitations of Christianity: "For me Christianity has not yet arrived, and I am like the early Christians, awaiting Christ's return."[25]

Continually fascinated with the "isms" which introduced "hypocrisy" into the world, "Judaism, Catholicism, and Buddhism ... Christianity can still be rescued for future ages" for up to the present time the world "has only experienced its barbarian epochs." The fundamental and irreconcilable problem is still the fact that "The Christian teaching is, however, derived from the Jewish religion and that is its dilemma. Christ's suffering moves us more than the Buddha's fellow suffering, we suffer with him and become Buddhas, through contemplation. Christ wishes to suffer, suffers, and redeems us. Buddha looks on, commiserates and teaches us how to achieve redemption."[26] Through the Torah and the Gospels the Judaic-Christian tradition possessed a record of historical continuity which offered distinct advantage over Buddhism. However, while "the Buddhist emerges as a most noble figure ... the Jewish religion has been grafted on to Christianity and has completely spoiled it." But, and this was of fundamental importance to Wagner, "it is a bad thing to deprive the people of their religion." Therefore, one must accept the existence of the Judaic-Christian tradition, work within this tradition, but try to free it from

----

[25] **CW's Diaries**, 15 July 1879, 339.

[26] **CW's Diaries**, 28 October 1873, 1:691.

restricted boundaries which man, not God, imposed. Protestantism represented the best and only currently available means to achieve this goal, for it "can only be understood as a **protest** against every confession in favor of the true core of religion, which lies in its nature."[27]

Despite a variety of personal inconsistencies in which he even occasionally argued against his own beliefs, Wagner constantly postulated that love, compassion, and the brotherhood of man, were the fundamental transcendental values. True spirituality linked man's soul to God: "The mystic is the man for me, even if he is mistaken--the man who feels the urge to ignite for himself the inner light in contrast to the outer brightness which shows him nothing."[28] The soul emanating from God was breathed into man at the moment of birth, and returned to God at the time the physical body died. Perceiving the need for "religion" as a necessary illusion, Wagner came to appreciate why dogma might have to play an important role to buttress man's spiritual stability. In practical terms religion had proved to be the logical means through which most people could achieve some semblance of spirituality, even if it is misguided or an illusion.

The psychological necessity which required man to invent religious systems tended to frightened Wagner. The sometimes arbitrary and capricious God of the Old Testament should have been softened and modified by the message of Jesus, but this had not been done. Protestantism, like Catholicism before it, had painted some graphic pictures of God's wrath. The fault was not in Jesus but what mankind did in his name. Christianity should have been rooted on the reform ideas of Jesus, by which a stern and vengeful God had been softened and remodeled into a loving and caring God, one who did not cruelly toy with man's fate. Without needing rituals, dogmas, or elaborate procedures Jesus brought man closer to a loving God. But Wagner seemed to have serious reservations about the disciples: "Considering his disciples' lack of understanding he could not have kept going for long ... but his great bitterness later, that was due to the company he kept."[29] When

---

[27] **CW's Diaries,** 23 June 1870, 236-7.

[28] **CW's Diaries,** 16 March 1873, 609.

[29] **CW's Diary,** 2 July 1879, 2:333.

Christianity became entrenched it betrayed the simplicity and beauty of Jesus, distorting and even perverting his message until it became self-serving. Protestantism only modified the extremes, but it did not go back to the basics.

What was Wagner's alternative? That he really had none was the dilemma and frustration which he shared with many nineteenth century religious romantics. But Wagner flatly rejected the radical assertion that "God was dead", a view becoming somewhat fashionable in intellectual circles after the rise of social Darwinism. A Darwinist himself, Wagner believed that "Godhead is Nature, the will which seeks salvation and, to quote Darwin, selects the strongest to bring this salvation about." Although this view did not necessarily negate an imminent God, it made it less likely: "These donkeys who do not believe in God and who think that such figures as Jesus of N. or of a great creative genius move according to the ordinary processes of Nature! They cannot understand that what prevails here is a special urge, a noble need which in the end produces something good. But one must not think in this connection of the old Jewish God."[30]

Shortly after the birth of Wagner's son Siegfried a plan for his education was drafted. In terms of required reading the one and only philosopher to make the list was Schopenhauer, while in matters of religion two names were listed: Meister Eckhart (c. 1260-c.1328) and his pupil Johannes Tauler (c.1300-61), two Catholic mystical theologians whose writings were sometimes considered heretical. Wagner's unbounded admiration for Schopenhauer related not to the entire body of his philosophy--much of which was too pessimistic even for him--but to certain religious points of view. Undoubtedly Wagner accepted many of Schopenhauer's attitudes regarding the will, but found God as the "inborn antidote to the will." Giving Schopenhauer credit as the one "who revealed Christianity to me," Wagner acknowledged his indebtedness; in actuality, Wagner's assumptions about the Judaic-Christian tradition were expressed well before he had first read the works of the philosopher.

Schopenhauer perceived how Christianity needed to replace Judaism "whose rude dogma was sublimated and tacitly allegorized in the Christian. Christianity is

---

[30] **CW's Diaries**, 11 June 1878, 91.

in general definitely of an allegorical nature: for what in profane matters is called allegory is in religions called mystery."[31] To Schopenhauer, as to Wagner, the mixture of the Old Testament with the New Testament represented an absurdity which tended to undermine Christianity, and all but certainly limited its effectiveness. But the greatest limitation is that: "Christianity possesses the peculiar disadvantage that, unlike the other religions, it is not a pure **doctrine,** but essentially and above all a **history,** a succession of events, and it is this history which constitutes the dogma belief in which redeems."

Schopenhauer compared the realistic and optimistic qualities of Judaism to the idealistic and pessimistic qualities of Buddhism, and found Christianity more indebted to the latter than the former, much to its disadvantage. Perhaps the closest point of contact with Wagner may be found in Schopenhauer's comment that: "The reason civilization is at its highest point among **Christian** peoples is not that Christianity is favourable to it but that Christianity is dead and no longer exercises much influence: as long as it did exercise influence, civilization was at a very low point among Christian peoples. All **religion** is antagonistic towards culture." Wagner would not agree that "Christianity is dead" since he had made the point that it had never been created.

Schopenhauer observed that "mankind is growing out of religion" but Wagner not only doubted this tendency but denied the need for it to happen. Nevertheless, religion had to be modified so as to be capable of embracing spirituality, a point which Schopenhauer had Demopheles make in "On Religion: A Dialogue": "Religion is no deception: it is true and is the most important of all truths. But because, as I have already said, its doctrines are of so lofty a kind that the multitude could not grasp them directly; because, I say, its light would blind the common eye; it appears veiled in allegory and teaches that which, while not strictly true in itself, is true in respect of the lofty meaning contained within it: and thus understood, religion is truth."[32]

----

[31] Arthur Schopenhauer, "On Religion," **Essays and Aphorisms,** R. J. Hollingdale (ed., and trans.), Penguin Books, 1970, 182.

[32] **Ibid.,** 107.

Forever concerned with man-made as opposed to spiritual values, in each of Wagner's music-dramas he confronted several issues relating directly or indirectly to man's spirituality: in the **Dutchman** the forces of light were in opposition to the powerful forces of Satanism and darkness; in **Tannhäuser** man faced the issue of spiritual as opposed to animalistic pleasures; in **Tristan** Wagner juxtaposed romantic love with erotic love; finally, in the **Ring,** political and economic power existed in a godless setting devoid of all spirituality. In each drama man was pitted against himself, and the universe. In almost every case, an unending battle took place between mutually exclusive polarities. Man often lost the battle, yet behind the polarities appears a constant and persistent dual theme, often overlapping and sometimes used interchangeably: compassion and spirituality. Even when Wagner had difficulty articulating the nature of the spiritual, he always assumed that compassion was intrinsic in the man-God continuum. This was, of course, easier said than done.

Several of Wagner's most interesting characters, Senta, Tannhäuser, both Lohengrin and Elsa, and Tristan and Isolde, were somehow incapable of relating to God. Each was so intricately involved with illusions that compassion was either difficult or impossible. Aside from Hans Sachs, Wolfram in **Tannhäuser** was perhaps the one character who most successfully displayed true nobility in compassion. The relationship between values and illusions reached its fullest summation through the character of Hans Sachs. Realizing that illusions could not be dissipated but were not necessarily dangerous, Wagner recognized in **Die Meistersinger** that illusions could coexist with both compassion and spirituality. It was an important statement. Sachs was the first mature and stable character to perceive this reality, and being himself free from illusions he could use them as the means for achieving certain values beneficial to society. In essence he manipulated illusions as a psychologically useful device to serve socially desirable ends. Since his values were not self-serving, society reaped the benefit. Sachs became the receptacle through which society might recognize those values which came from God. Without the illusion of religion, society might never come to appreciate this reality.

In **Parsifal** Wagner would go even further. He utilized religious allegories and metaphors "not strictly true in itself" to enable the message of

Christianity to transcend its institutional limitations. If the drama were understood it would enable his listeners to perceive the value of compassion and love. Universal spiritual forces would be encompassed within a Christian series of metaphors, none more so than the celebration of the Eucharist; but those attuned to an inward spirituality would perceive the non-specifically Christian allegory.

Hypothesizing that spiritual and religious values might be mutually exclusive, Wagner theorized that religion further separated man from God while pretending to bring him closer through dogma and ritual. But was there an alternative? Would it not be worse to eliminate all considerations of God from man's perceptions, thereby making man even more brutish? If but an illusion, religion at least kept alive the ideals of love and compassion even if it did not practice them in fact.

Parsifal became Wagner's most important music-drama. It was a more personal statement than his other works. But in retrospect, and from a vantage point of one hundred years, no other work left his listeners with more questions. Whether **Parsifal** is or is not a religious work continues to be debated.[33] Wagner had finally attempted to deal with the dichotomy separating religion from spirituality and in a drama which encompassed both illusions and transcendental values. If successful **Parsifal** would emerge as both a religious allegory and a spiritual experience. Christian symbolism would became the means, the necessary illusion, through which spiritual insights might be

----
[33] For an excellent discussion of this issue and the work in general see Lucy Beckett, **Richard Wagner's Parsifal**, Cambridge University Press, 1981. Beckett discusses the sources of the legend, how Wagner utilized them, and reactions and critical assessments by several important contemporary scholars. With specific regard to the issue of whether or not **Parsifal** is an inherently Christian work she comments (p. 139): "It is easier, perhaps, to decide with Chamberlain, Dahlhaus, Tanner and many others that Wagner uses the trappings of Christianity only to exploit the symbolic charge they retain from the past; that it is not only possible but correct, since 'Art was the only idea in which Wagner believed' (Dahlhaus), to sit through a performance of the work without feeling to any degree threatened or persuaded by the ideas it embodies."

gleaned; and yet since spirituality was universal, it would have to transcend the Christian symbolism of the drama. Spirituality is achieved but not because of Christianity! **Parsifal**, as a drama, became an artistic device by which the metaphysical sphere was made more accessible to man's insights and feelings.

The characters involved in the action portray fascinating archetypal roles. The knights of the Grail are elemental to the course of the action but they are neither monastic nor celibate. They marry, raise families, and pass on certain chores to their descendants. In the first complete prose sketch, written in 1865, the brotherhood of the Grail were specially-selected individuals who would be sent forth by Titurel, the original "winner" of the Grail, to serve those in need. Through a miracle Titurel had been informed of the Grail's mysterious powers. Into this cup the blood of Jesus had flowed. It was therefore one of the most sacred relics in Christendom, one which was capable of bringing redemption to man:

> Titurel had gathered about him a body of holy knights to serve the Grail, and build, in wild, remote and inaccessible mountain forest, the Castle of Monsalvat, which none unworthy to care for the Grail may find. The relic has proclaimed its miraculous power chiefly by freeing its custodians from earthly care by supplying the community with food and drink; and by mysterious writing which, comprehensible only to the Keeper of the brotherhood of knights, appears upon the glowing surface of the crystal, making known the worst afflictions suffered by the innocent of the world, and issuing instructions to those of the knights who shall be sent forth for their protection. ... But only he who preserves himself from the allurements of sensual pleasure retains the power of the Grail's blessing: only to the chaste is the blessed might of the relic revealed.[34]

When Wagner rethought the drama twelve years later the brotherhood now served as an archetype which illustrated the impotence of religion. The knights mechanistically go through their rituals and dogmas, going about their business with neither energy nor a

----

34   "Parzival," **The Brown Book**, 27 August 1865, 47.

sense of purpose. Despite participating in the celebration of the Eucharist at the end of the first act, and again in the third act, the knights are incapable of acting out their spirituality in any way other than through the celebration of the mass and by attending to Titurel and his son Amfortas. They appear to be spiritually impotent and are constantly threatened by sexual seduction. Many of them, including Amfortas, have yielded. Close to the Grail, they are neither nourished by its spiritual legacy, nor seem capable of bringing salvation and redemption to themselves or others. Led by one who is spiritually impotent to lead, the decline of the brotherhood is spectacular, and they seem incapable of changing direction by themselves. Amfortas not only offers no moral leadership, he has to be forced against his will to celebrate the Eucharist; he does so in anger!

By the third act the decline is complete. The knights have grown old; they lead meaningless and empty lives; the grass around the Grail castle is unkempt; and "we send out no more on messages." Like animals in the forest they now have to forage just to survive: "herbs and roots each finds for himself." Seldom has Wagner portrayed a more aimless or pathetic collection of individuals! Yet they personify a community whose greatest distinction is purity and dedication to mankind through Jesus.

As originally conceived, the Grail endowed each of the knights "with Divine power, rendering them everywhere victorious. From its votaries it banishes death: he who sets eyes on that Divine vessel cannot die." Only by yielding to sensual desires would this exalted status alter. When Wagner wrote the second prose sketch he modified this point. Only Amfortas and not the remaining knights had transgressed, but his sin was bestowed on all of them. Not until he found redemption would the brotherhood be redeemed. In Wagner's mind Christianity did not, and could not, bring redemption either to Amfortas or to the Grail brotherhood. This central point is crucial to Wagner's concept. The final words in the drama are "our Redeemer redeemed." But who would redeem the Redeemer? And how?

The spear and the cup as symbols were the two most sacred relics in Christendom. Although Titurel became the first king of the Grail, through age and infirmity he eventually found it difficult to carry out his

task.[35]   Bestowing the spear to his son, Amfortas lost
possession of it at the moment of his seduction by
Kundry.   Betraying his sacred trust, he brought
disrepute on himself and the brotherhood.   Receiving a
wound from the same spear that pierced the side of
Jesus, it is as much spiritual as physical, and will
not heal.   Titurel prayed for his son, that "in His
service you may expiate your sin!", but this was not to
be. Amfortas became king, "head of the race, a man here
chosen to protect the Grail: nothing was to distinguish
him from the other knights, save the mystic import of
the lofty office reserved for[36] him alone, and his
sufferings understood by none."[36]   All that Amfortas
pleads for is death, which is denied him. His exhalted
position "painful" for he endures the "torments of hell
in this Office." Pleading for salvation, Amfortas
implores: "by the repentance of my inmost soul must I
reach Him." Momentarily he feels "the fount of divine
blood pour into my heart", but it is an illusion. No
physical or spiritual relief is forthcoming: "Amfortas
alone feels worse than before: he has again to be
carried off in the litter; his wound has reopened: the
Redeemer has remained silent."[37]

Some may view this scene as a reflection of a
state of sin while others may interpret it as a searing
indictment of the impotence of Christianity. Wagner's
intent is clear: a belief in Christianity and the
practice of its dogmas and rituals is not necessarily
enough to sustain or redeem man even if, as in this
case, they represent the brotherhood in possession of
the "Holy Grail."

Neither a belief in God nor faithfulness to Jesus
will redeem Amfortas since he is performing a ritual
that has become mechanical and therefore without a true
‾‾‾‾‾‾‾‾‾‾‾‾‾‾‾‾‾‾
[35] "Who is Titurel?" Wagner asked his wife on 19
February 1878.   Before she replied he gave her the
answer: "Wotan. After his renunciation of the world he
is granted salvation, the greatest of possessions is
entrusted to his care, and now he is guarding it like a
mortal God. ... Titurel, the little Titus, the symbol
of royal standing and power, Wotan the God-King." See
CW's Diaries, 2:29.

[36] "Parsifal at Bayreuth," **Bayreuther Blätter**,
November-December, 1882, **PW**, 6:309.

[37] **The Brown Book**, 54.

inner meaning. He is looking to religion to find his
spirituality,   but   belief   in the blood and body of
Christ is not enough. Salvation and redemption are not
to be found there. The Grail has denied him both
physical death and spiritual nourishment. Wagner's
focal point is becoming clearer: the god whom Amfortas
and the Grail brotherhood serve is the Judaic-Christian
god, a cruel one who apparently enjoys the agony of
sinners for he offers no consolation; perhaps a god
who is not even listening! Amfortas pleads: "Take back
my inheritance, heal my wound, that I may die holy,
pure and whole for Thee!", but his prayer is in vain.
He calls to his dead father to "call to Him: 'Redeemer,
grant my son repose!'", but that too is useless.

Wagner paints an unbelievably bleak picture.[38]
When Amfortas lost the spear he also lost power over
himself. While he possessed both relics together he
retained the symbolic unity of the male-female
continuum, the mystical force of creation through which
he fulfilled his duty: to elevate the physical into the
spiritual thereby serving God, and to bring
spirituality into the physical world thereby serving
man. By losing the spear the mystical continuum had
been broken. Dogma and ritual, the spear and the grail,
were not enough. More was required. Wagner now comes to
the point of the drama. What was missing? The answer is
simple: inner love and compassion in addition to the
external performance of the sacraments.

These were the principle values not to be found
within the realm of the Castle brotherhood. Instead
they must be taught to the knights by one who knows and
feels nothing about institutional religion, but one who
will grow to understand and know God. If Wagner
succeeded in getting this thesis understood by at least
a small percentage of those who saw it performed, then
he will have struck an uncompromising blow at the
illusions of religion. One sees clearly why Wagner
called "my work a stage **dedication** play; it would be
‾‾‾‾‾‾‾‾‾‾‾‾‾‾‾‾‾‾
[38] If one knew nothing about the complexities behind
the drama, and listened only to the music, one would
hear sounds that were so ethereal, sensual, and
alluring that it is made to appear as if one is having
a religious experience. This was deliberate. In
Parsifal as in **Tristan und Isolde** Wagner expressed in
the music an outer, external, and--in a curious way--a
superficial beauty while the internal disharmony of the
words revealed the more important messages.

unthinkable in our ordinary theatres, and it is very bold...." It is, indeed.

The nemesis and antithesis to all that Titurel and the Grail stand for is represented by Klingsor. Who he is, where he comes from, how he used magic both to raise his castle out of the dust and to ensnare the knights of the grail, are unstated, perhaps so as not to deflect from the focal point: "Perhaps Titurel has at some time forbidden him to speak. It is supposed that Klingsor is the same man who once so piously inhabited the place now so changed:--he is said to have mutilated himself in order to destroy the sensual longing which he never completely succeeded in overcoming through prayer and penance. Titurel refused to allow him to join the Knights of the Grail, and for the reason that renunciation and chastity, flowing from the innermost soul, do not require to be forced by mutilation."[39]

In this original prose sketch Klingsor castrated himself as expiation for his intense sexuality. Then, seeking to be admitted to the Grail's brotherhood, he was denied admission by a horrified Titurel who refused to condone the action. In the second prose sketch Klingsor was first rejected as unfit for the brotherhood, after which he castrated himself and swore vengeance on all of the knights. Using the Flower Maidens to sexually ensnare and forever damn the Grail's knights, Klingsor had captured the sacred spear while Amfortas was being seduced by Kundry, the most alluring of the creatures. Using the spear to inflict a wound which will not heal on Amfortas, "he planned for him the same disgrace that, in raving blindness, he inflicted on himself."

Klingsor represents the archetypal evil inherent when man falls prey to his animalistic nature. Unable to control his own intense sexuality despite a sincere desire, thwarted by man from serving God, Klingsor will seek to destroy the spirituality of God's noblest creation while forcing them to serve sinfulness: "once deprived of purity you will remain my slave." In several key respects Klingsor continues where Venus left off in **Tannhäuser**. Ultimately, of course, his plans are thwarted but the archetype remains.

----

[39]   **The Brown Book**, 48.

Wagner intended to make Klingsor "very brutal", standing in sharp contrast to the Grail brotherhood. As Titurel represented a transformation of Wotan, Klingsor related to Alberich. "R. tells me that he once felt every sympathy for Alberich, who represents the ugly person's longing for beauty. In Alberich the naiveté of the non-Christian world, in Klingsor the peculiar quality which Christianity brought into the world; just like the Jesuits, he does not believe in goodness, and this is his strength but at the same time his downfall, for through the ages **one** good man does occasionally emerge!"[40]

Perhaps the most unique character of all is Kundry: "Who this woman is and where she comes from, no one knows. ... The brotherhood of knights treat her more as a strange, magical animal than a human being. ... many too are in doubt whether she should be considered good or evil. ... Never is she seen at any religious act."[41] Yet she performs service to the Grail's knights, and travels the world seeking a potion which might cure Amfortas of his wound. Wagner considered Kundry "his most original character; when he had realized that the servant of the Grail was the same woman who seduced Amfortas, he said everything fell into place." Once comparing her to the "Wandering Jew", it was Kundry who mocked Jesus on the cross. For that a curse was placed on her which "condemns her, in new shapes, to bring to men suffering of seduction; redemption, death, complete extinction is vouchsafed her only if her most powerful brandishments are withstood by the most chaste and virile of men."

Although Kundry is constantly found on the grounds of the Grail castle and aids and comforts the knights in time of trouble, she can also become an instrument for evil because she is not in control of her will. Freely she roams both the spiritual and animal worlds doing what is required by everyone claiming mastery over her. Capable of being manipulated to serve either good or evil, she possesses no identity of her own. She is knowledgeable about everything that has transpired in history but is able to influence nothing on her own.

In Kundry Wagner seems to be presenting a timeless, ageless "being." She may be an allegorical

----

40 **CW's Diaries**, 2 March 1878, 2:33.

41 **The Brown Book**, 50-1.

force, rather than a person. In metaphoric terms she is like a soul without a body, and can be used for animalistic or divine purposes depending exclusively on the wishes of her master. In a curious way Kundry seems to represent in a seemingly corporeal form, the incorporeal elements within man's psyche. Wagner indicated that she can assume many forms and personalities from the past, seemingly implying that she can become like Mary Magdalene, first a harlot and then a spiritual being. How she is used depends exclusively on the way in which she is mastered, which is why she declames honestly, "I never help." Who is her master? Man! Kundry is the divine bitch in whom both Amfortas and Klingsor will find their identity and their destiny.

As The Flying Dutchman could find redemption only by a woman who would be faithful even to death so too Kundry hopes to find redemption through one who is both pure of heart and able to resist her strong sensual appeal. She waits for one: he who though ignorant on matters of faith can learn the meaning behind love and compassion, thereby becoming a receptacle for transcendental values untaught to him by institutional religion. She awaits the archetype of Jesus, and it is to be found in the character of Parsifal.

Amfortas too, waits: "I await the one appointed to me: 'enlightened through compassion'--was that not it?" The Grail shines forth with but one hope for Amfortas, and this is couched in enigmatic terms: "'Aware, suffering in fellow-suffering, a fool will redeem thee! '--Who can it be who suffers only in fellow-suffering, and, without knowing, is wiser than others?"

Parsifal is the simplest character in the drama. He is, as Wagner once said, "the pure fool who dominates everything. ... It is all so **direct**!" Seldom has any archetypal character been presented in so clear a manner. Parsifal is so simple that he requires considerable effort to be understood. Throughout the course of the drama he is the most uncomplicated man since Jesus--the personification of one who embodied the godly virtues of love and compassion. No character in any of Wagner's other works approaches Parsifal in expressing the most elemental characteristics of humanity. Parsifal goes well beyond Sachs. The famed cobbler represented a fully developed sincere personality, the altruistic man who could exist in the world without the need for illusions, and was reluctantly willing to manipulate man in the best interests of society. Parsifal was less sophisticated but also less complicated. Sachs worked quietly and discretely within society to achieve his purposes while Parsifal ultimately represented a more radical approach: direct and overt intervention to transform the very nature of society.

Like Jesus, Parsifal was unsubtle, blunt, but above-all simple. Taking from the Gospels only the quotations that were self-serving to his religious views, Wagner assumed that institutional Christianity must not be attributed to Jesus but to those less well-intentioned men who were out for their own ends. This harsh indictment was not untypical of Wagner's distrustful attitude toward the Catholic church and all that he thought it represented. Parsifal is an allegorical being through whom Wagner symbolized, by his art, a spiritually divine archetype analogous to Jesus. Parsifal represented everything that Jesus represents, and in this connection Parsifal is as divine as Jesus: "One cannot paint Christ, but one can portray him in music."[42] Parsifal is not Jesus but Jesus was the archetype of Parsifal. By becoming receptacles for spiritual truths, both revealed their divinity.

Parsifal, a pure but uncomplicated man, is neither an intellectual nor a fool, and certainly not a simpleton. Who he is and where he comes from is unknown; he is unaware of religion and has no clear knowledge of his parents or upbringing. These factors are important for they illustrate that Parsifal belongs to no particular race, creed, heritage, or background. He is nobody and therefore everybody. While his original instincts are unrefined and seemingly undifferentiated, he possesses that uniquely sensitive internal capacity for growth and spiritual development. The divine soul is just waiting to burst forth. Once again we see Wagner's ever-present conception of the dualistic nature of man's soul. Having been breathed into man by God, all souls are divine. Man is inherently divine but this does not necessarily

---
[42] **CW's Diaries**, 22 October 1882, 2:935. After this comment Cosima wrote: "I see it as evidence of his great and so significant artistic sagacity that he abandoned the figure of Christ and created Parsifal instead: 'To have Chr. sung by a tenor--what a disgusting idea!' he says."

manifest itself. Man has the free will to do and to become evil. Therefore, what man does with his spiritual soul separates and distinguishes the power of his animalistic soul. If Wagner can succeed in illustrating the nature of this truism then "art makes religion eternal."...

Parsifal's entrance into the drama illustrates both his initial insensitivity and the dormant quality of the spiritual soul. After "trespassing" into the sacred land of the Grail castle he kills a swan in flight, not for food but for fun. Apprehended, he is castigated for his indifferent attitude toward animal life: "Unprecedented act! You could murder, here in the holy forest, where tranquil peace surrounded you?" Parsifal's original indifference is quickly transformed into an intense feeling of guilt as a feeling of unbearable compassion develops within. Acting impulsively and without thinking he breaks his bow and throws the arrows away. Wagner has made his initial but significant commentary on the character of Parsifal.

A potentially dangerous animal soul is only an external façade which disguises an internally beautiful but not fully developed spiritual soul. Parsifal is already showing signs that he possesses a great capacity for tenderness, a seemingly clear indication of the existence of a deeper capacity for feeling that now needs to be nourished. Is he the answer to the prophecy: "Enlightened through compassion, the innocent fool; wait for him, the appointed one."

The final lengthy scene of the first act in which Amfortas, in agony, performs the celebration of the Eucharist is portrayed in music of such great religiosity that Wagner's most important point is often easily overlooked. Having watched all the proceedings, Parsifal is unmoved! The celebration of the mass is strange, unknown, and without meaning. When Gurnemanz asks: "Do you know what you have seen?" Parsifal makes but a simple negative gesture. Observing the consecration of the host, the most holy sacrament within Christendom, is to him a matter of indifference, thereby illustrating the non-Christian nature of Parsifal. This point will become more crucial as the drama enfolds.

During the course of the second act the spiritual quality of Parsifal's divine soul gradually takes precedence over the animalistic soul, but not at first.

Finding himself in the domain of Klingsor's castle, importuned by the Flower Maidens to play with them, Parsifal finds them alluring; but when they begin to quarrel and fight among themselves he treats their seductiveness as a game. Unlike the Rhine Maidens they "do not play for gold" and Parsifal well understands what this implies. As Kundry tries to seduce him the nature of his spiritual soul begins to overpower that of his animal soul. When she kisses him a reaction of the greatest intensity takes place:

> Suddenly the youth springs up with an expression of utter terror. With this kiss a dreadful change has taken place in him: he puts his hand to his heart; there suddenly he feels the wound of Anfortas [sic] burning; hears rising from deep within him Anfortas' lamentation. 'The wound! The wound is bleeding here! Miserable one, and I could not help you!' To the horror and amazement of the beautiful woman he responds with a cold stare: the mysterious happening witnessed at the Castle of the Grail claims him entirely; transformed wholly into the soul of Anfortas, he feels Anfortas' enormous suffering, his dreadful self-reproach; the unspeakable torments of yearning love, the unholy terrors of sinful desire....[43]

By identifying so intimately with Amfortas, Wagner seemed to imply that Parsifal was actually able to enter his soul. If true, this raises yet further unanswered questions.

Perhaps Wagner was trying to indicate that genuine love and compassion enabled one to feel such a tenderness for others that one could even reach another's soul through empathy. Parsifal seems to become the spiritual person that Amfortas should have been when he was in this identical sexual encounter with Kundry: "O torment of love! How everything trembles, quakes and quivers in sinful desire," shouts Parsifal as he breaks away from her. Parsifal expresses his first direct knowledge of the spiritual soul in the process of confronting the animal soul. Had Amfortas done this he might never have lost the sacred spear. But does this relate to anything Christian?

----

[43] 29 August 1865, **The Brown Book**, 56.

Since Parsifal has never mentioned Jesus nor appears to be aware of any of the dogmas or rituals within Christianity, what is the meaning of his sudden awareness of sin?

In the first prose sketch Wagner was vague. Parsifal "invoked the Grail, the Blood of the Redeemer: he hears Divine lamentation over the fall of the Chosen One; he hears the Saviour's cry for the relic to be freed from the custody of besmirched hands." But what exactly does Wagner mean? Is Parsifal enacting a scenario that Amfortas should have performed? If so, as his surrogate? Or, assuming that the "Saviour" referred to is Jesus, is Wagner suddenly giving Parsifal some intuitive knowledge of Christianity? Some answers will come in the final act.

By permitting an indeterminate period of time to elapse between the end of the second and the beginning of the third acts, Wagner is able to vividly portray the further deterioration of the Grail brotherhood. The castle grounds have been poorly kept, the pious knight Gurnemanz now lives the life of a hermit on the edge of the castle grounds, and the Grail's knights no longer go forth to serve humanity. Unable to be refreshed by the Grail's nourishing gift of life, Titurel has died in agony, and Amfortas is both unwilling and unable to take communion. No penance seems adequate for any knight of this brotherhood; no one seems holy enough to achieve redemption; no acts of contrition are able to secure release from misery. It is as if God had abandoned them! Is Wagner deliberately making the point that Christianity can not save or redeem man?

Considering the unhappy state of the Grail Castle and its brotherhood, it is more than obvious that they have been forsaken by God; nothing they can do will secure redemption: "all are starving and demoralized." But Parsifal's arrival changes this. He will redeem the brotherhood and become the new Keeper of the Grail. But is this in any way related to Christianity? Parsifal meets Gurnemanz, a "childish old man" who berates him for his appearance: "Here you are in a hallowed place: no man comes here armed, with vizored helmet, shield, and spear; and today [Good Friday] of all days! Do you not know what holy day this is?" Parsifal's inability to answer is striking. In the first prose sketch Wagner was equally vivid: "Where does he come from then? He

can hardly have lived amongst Christians not to know
that today is most holy Good Friday?"[44]

This is Wagner's central point. Parsifal
possesses the holy spear that once pierced the side of
Jesus, but it means little to him; more precisely, the
religious significance of that spear is important only
to one who has been brought up within a specifically
Christian tradition. Since Parsifal transcended that
tradition its great religious significance is devoid of
meaning and of little concern to him. But the depth of
his feeling of compassion for Amfortas has made him
acutely aware of its importance to others. By rescuing
the spear and, through his spiritual love and
tenderness for others, he will now accommodate himself
to Christian illusions to bring salvation to these
miserably unhappy creatures. This can best be
accomplished not by circumventing Christianity which
would only destroy them further, but by using
Christianity as a means to help them achieve the grace
of God.

Living within a Christian milieu, and after years
of religious uncertainty, Wagner will now utilize the
illusions of Christianity to help Parsifal redeem the
knights. In his mature years Wagner recognized more
perceptively than in the past that his music-dramas and
prose could only allude to the problems that religion
brought into the world. Privately he was able to
express himself more freely: "Not until all churches
have vanished will we find the Redeemer, from whom we
are separated by Judaism. But his ideas are not easy to
grasp; God as the ending of the universe--that does not
allow for a cult, though perhaps monasteries, in which
people of similar beliefs could find a refuge and from
which they could influence the world, from the solitary
state--but within the world itself it is not
possible."[45]

Like Jesus, Parsifal was one with God: "Not the
light which illumines the world from without is God,
but the light which we cast upon it from within us:
i.e. perception through sympathy."[46] And like Jesus,

---

[44] **The Brown Book**, 59.

[45] **CW's Diaries**, 27 November 1878, 2:211-12.

[46] "Thoughts on the Regeneration of Mankind and of
Culture," **The Brown Book**, 200.

his faith was too simple to be accepted. Why did mankind need a complex institutional structure in which to find God? Salvation and redemption are universal but mankind is not yet ready to free himself to accept this simple truism. Parsifal adopts the Christian formalism previously irrelevant to him, brings salvation to the knights by nourishing their illusions, and commands them to "uncover the Grail, open the shrine!" It immediately begins to glow signifying a return of spirituality. Parsifal was the necessary intermediary: "the magic to which you succumbed is broken; strong is the magic of him who desires, but stronger is that of him who denies. 'Thanks be to your suffering: it has made me a fellow-sufferer; be thankful for my foolishness,[47] through which I was able to attain to knowledge.'"

Perhaps the most essential point Wagner desired to make in **Parsifal** is that service to God is service to man: "Man is the completion of God. The eternal gods are the elements for the begetting[48] of man. In man, therefore, creation finds its end." If the illusion of religion was necessary to make this point understood, this was acceptable; but to others for whom religion is not an absolute necessity, an inner spirituality may suffice. Although Parsifal's compassion transcended the Christian tradition, in the final analysis his service to mankind required that he utilize the trappings of Christianity to bring spirituality to the knights. Given the nature of the brotherhood and the character of their basic assumptions only Christianity would be a suitable means to achieve grace. Parsifal went further than Hans Sachs because of his expanded religious dimension.

In the final analysis Wagner's thinking was not especially profound, nor was it meant to be. Love and compassion were central to man's nature and part of the process by which man became a social being. Despite man's historical tendency to dehumanize life these values were recognized by, and given lip service through, the Judaic-Christian tradition. But, and this was a key point, merely to give lip service to certain basic values was not good enough. Obviously religion was not truly capable of teaching man how to behave toward one another. Since Christianity had "never been

---

47   **The Brown Book**, 61.

48   "Sketches and Fragments", **PW**, 8:367-8.

tried" Wagner searched for an alternate way of expressing what he considered to be the heart of the meaning behind the life of Jesus.

Parsifal was the one music-drama which actually pleased Wagner for he had said what he wanted to say. While chatting to Cosima he commented: "'... it is quite remarkable that I held this work back for my fullest maturity; I know what I know and what is in it;' ... He then hints at, rather than expresses, the content of the work, 'salvation to the saviour'--and we are silent after he has added, 'Good that we are alone.'"[49] Even before he completed the music Wagner published the prose copy. Before it went on sale to the public a local Protestant minister stopped him on the street, engaged him in conversation, and importuned him not to write anything further that might be against the Christian idea of morality. "Richard is good enough to give him a copy of Parsifal: 'In this you will see that I am more Christian than you are.' He: 'That we shall know when we stand at God's right hand.' R: 'Or at the Devil's left,' and with these words he dismissed the importunate man."[50]

At the work's premiere on 26 July 1882 the audience reacted very positively. At the end of the second act, amidst the "noise and calling" Wagner addressed the audience: although applause and curtain calls were important and highly appreciated both by the singers and himself, they all agreed not to "impinge on the impression, not to take a bow, so that there would be no curtain calls." Not fully understanding his intention, silence greeted the conclusion of the last act! Wagner "is vexed by the silent audience, which has misunderstood him; he once again addresses it from the gallery, and when the applause then breaks out and there are continued calls, Richard appears in front of the curtain and says that he tried to assemble his artists, but they were by now half undressed." Wagner wished that no applause should take place during each of the acts, a common habit in opera houses and one that continued even when the **Ring** was first performed. Wagner, ever the reformer, was trying to educate his audience by asking them to withhold applause until the very end of each act. The singers, however, agreed not

---

[49] **CW's Diaries**, 5 January 1882, 2:784.

[50] **CW's Diaries**, 16 September 1878, 150.

to appear before the audience until the very end of the work.

Out of this trivial and amusing incident an accidental precedent began, although one that Wagner tried unsuccessfully to stop. Word erroneously emerged that **Parsifal** was a religious work and not a drama, one to be treated with reverence as if one were in church. Nothing could have been further from Wagner's mind. At a subsequent performance Wagner broke his own rules when he shouted out "bravo!" in the middle of the Flower Maiden's scene "whereupon he is hissed by the outraged audience." To this day many opera houses request that applause be withheld at the end of the first and final acts; but applause and curtain calls[51] are usually permitted at the end of the second. During the second performance at Bayreuth no applause was heard at the end of the first act, making Wagner somewhat nervous although he found it "a pleasant effect. But when, after the second, the applauders are again hissed, it becomes embarrassing. At the end ... Richard makes a short speech, presenting his artists and asking the audience to express its gratitude toward them..."[52] Wagner was unsuccessful in getting his views understood or accepted. For better or worse a pattern became established: no applause at the end of the first and last acts. Mankind will have their illusions after all!

Whether Wagner's religious philosophy, as expressed in this drama, was or is understood is conjectural at best. Immediately after the initial performances he returned to his prose writing, continuing to clarify and refine his religious views and thoughts. In the period between the final prose sketch of **Parsifal** and the completion of the orchestral score many of his essays appeared in the Bayreuth **Blätter**. During the final years of his life he seldom

---

[51] At the Metropolitan Opera all the lights in the theatre and in the orchestra pit are extinguished before the conductor appears on the podium. He is then able to begin the music before the audience has the chance to applaud his entrance. That this absurd charade should take place in the 1980's would probably have amused Wagner, but it serves to prove how little understood the work enjoys even in the present day and age.

[52] **CW's Diaries**, 28 July 1882, 894.

wrote with such earnestness on any other topic. Neither
advancing age nor fear of death prompted his attention
for nothing in his prose related to such topics as
divine retribution, the existence of an afterworld,
heaven-hell polarities, or other metaphysical
speculations common to those who begin to think more
frequently of their mortality. As **Parsifal** advanced
toward completion Wagner seemed to need yet another
avenue by which he could express his thoughts, perhaps
for fear that this stage dedication play by itself
could not cover everything that he wanted to say; or
possibly because he realized how few would really
understand his intent and meaning.

Wagner's final religious thoughts focused more
precisely on areas that had been broached superficially
at an earlier age. By the late 1870's textual criticism
of the Bible engrossed many liberals and conservatives
in heated disputations. Keeping up with his reading of
newspapers and major religious publications, Wagner
incorporated the so-called "scientific findings" to
reinforce his views and opinions. In doing so he found
it necessary once again to reassert that as long as
Christianity emanated from Judaism it could not be
called Christian. "Who now knows Jesus?--Historical
criticism, perchance? It casts in its lot with Judaism,
and, just like every Jew, it wonders that the bells on
Sunday morn should still be ringing for a Jew once
crucified two thousand years ago."[53]

While at an earlier time Wagner considered the
Gospels as offering dramatic insights into the early
period of Christianity, he now began to view them as
not totally relevant, if not actually irrelevant. Since
historical criticism of the Bible tended to explore and
expose the inconsistencies and major textual and
translation errors within the New Testament, Wagner
often chose to accept these views as valid. As there
was now ever-increasing evidence that the Gospels were
erroneous in some areas and inconsistent in others,
Wagner felt more secure in again denying the Jewish
heritage of Jesus. He once even went so far as to
suggest that Jesus had not been born to a Jewess in the
Holy Land, but came instead from an Indian heritage and
migrated to the land of the Bible. This point he did
not press.

---

[53] "Public and Popularity," **Bayreuther Blätter**, August
1878, P**W**, 6:78.

Although the Gospels may have been partially incorrect, the important significance of the message of Jesus was not necessarily dependent on their accuracy. Wagner's point centered around a belief that the God of Jesus was not the god of either the Jews or the writers of the Gospels: "but from the beginning of the Church the God revealed to us by Jesus has been converted by the Theologians from a most sublime reality into an ever less intelligible problem. That the God of our Saviour should have been identified with the tribal god of Israel, is one[54] of the most terrible confusions in all world-history."[54] Unlike the god of the Jews and the Christians, Wagner's God, the God of Jesus, is substantially different: "By **God**, speaking strictly, man seeks to figure to himself a being not subject to the sorrows of existence (of the world), and consequently above the world--now this is Jesus (Buddha), who overcomes the world.--The world-Creator has never been truly currently believed in."[55] The expression "Saviour" also appears to have been narrowly construed.

In summary, Jesus was the son of God, but not the only son of God. He was the "Saviour" but only to the extent that he was able to show man the way to approach God and the way to live life. At no time did Wagner appear to believe in Jesus as God incarnate, nor that man could obtain universal salvation and redemption through Jesus. The message of Jesus was divine. But it was a universal message that transcended race, religion, and time. Those who called themselves Christian knew little, if anything, of what Jesus had been trying to say; and they practiced it even less. As for the most crucial element of all, the resurrection, Wagner was all but silent.

Warning that man did not have time on his side, Wagner returned to a theme first presented almost forty years earlier. Mankind must save itself from the religious tradition of its Western heritage. The perversion of human values began when Christianity was adopted as the state religion, toward the end of the Roman empire. Since then Western man had steadily become more corrupt while human values had become increasingly less significant and more irrelevant. Wagner shared with other frustrated romantics an ever-

----

[54] Ibid., 77.

[55] "Sketches and Fragments," 302.

deepening pessimism. Undeniably mankind was gaining in knowledge, but seemed unable to translate his learning into a better system of values. Few thinkers, and even fewer leaders, seemed concerned with the social and economic inequities of the world. Just as time had run out for the Roman Empire, Western Europe may also be facing an uncertain future: "Can one imagine the state of barbarism at which we shall have arrived, if our social system continues for another six-hundred years or so in the footsteps of the declining Roman world-dominion?"

Man's one hope remained a new revitalized Christianity, the "simplest of religion": "To the 'poor in spirit' no metaphysical explanation of the world was necessary; the knowledge of its suffering lay open to their feeling; and not to shut the doors of that, was the sole divine injunction to believers."[56] Being able to assert a direct linkage with God, Jesus transcended all religious thought existing at that time and was therefore a freethinker who became a danger to the Jewish establishment. But when Christianity emerged as a fully institutional religion, during the final days of the Roman Empire, then there began "the ceaseless struggle of the intellectually rich to rob the poor in spirit of their faith, to twist and model it anew to suit their own abstractions." In later years Christianity "accommodated itself to the brute violence of every ruling power in the world."[57] Wagner's simplicity was both convenient and exceptionally functional.

All of these disparate thoughts congealed while Wagner worked on **Parsifal**. His religious attitudes and observations became so important and so intrusive, that he sometimes interrupted his composing time to put them down on paper. "Religion and Art" appeared in the **Bayreuther Blätter** in October 1880. The timing is important for it demonstrates that a closeness exists between these explicit prose thoughts and those implicit in **Parsifal**. One fascinating example of this interaction may be observed by looking at the celebration of the Eucharist which closes the first act. At the time he composed this scene he wrote elsewhere:

---

[56] "Religion and Art," 214-5.

[57] "Know Thyself," **Bayreuther Blätter**, February-March 1881, **PW**, 6:269.

'Taste such alone, in memory of me.' This the unique sacrament of the Christian faith; with its observance all the teaching of the Redeemer is fulfilled. As if with haunting pangs of conscience the Christian Church pursues this teaching, without ever being able to get it followed in its purity, although it very seriously should form the most intelligible core of Christianity. She has transformed it to a symbolic office of her priests....[58]

With unabashed simplicity Wagner determined that Revelation meant nothing other than the belief whereby God "had called to Him", to Jesus, to preach the doctrine that all men were brothers for they all had in common one father. Jesus had successfully entered into a direct mystical and transcendental relationship with God, so powerful in its simplicity, that the soul of Jesus desired to achieve a return to its origin even before his death.

Wagner's ideas were not original. To be more precise, a remarkable similarity exists between many of his ideas and those of traditional Judaism. Indeed, many of his religious thoughts were more easily reconcilable with Judaism than to Christianity. One wonders, was Wagner aware of these similarities? One essential tenet of Judaism maintains that God breathes a soul into man at the time of birth. Man is therefore the son of God. God was automatically man's spiritual father, and Jesus would therefore be the son of God in the same way that all mankind have to be considered as children of God. But God granted more to Jesus: Divine Revelation! This represented the essential core of Wagner's thoughts of Jesus. Many times Wagner pondered on why it was so hard for man to understand this simple truth! Jesus was an archetype, the first--and there could be others--who entered into a direct and simple relationship with God. It could happen to anyone; it did happen, metaphorically, to Parsifal!

Perhaps the most controversial element of Wagner's religious philosophy related to his persistent assertion that Jesus had to be divorced from both Judaism and Christianity. Present-day Christianity was leading man to "Atheism" by "tracing back this Godliness upon the cross to the Jewish 'Creator of heaven and earth,' a wrathful God of Punishment who

---
[58] "Religion and Art," 231-2.

350

seemed to promise greater power than the self-offering, all-loving Saviour of the Poor."[59]

Wagner was left with one crucial question: through which means could mankind begin to understand how history had perverted the greatness and importance of Jesus? The answer, he thought, was simple: through "Art." If Wagner could link religion with Art then he might become a catalyst through which Jesus could be made more intelligible to the modern world. But first Wagner had to create his elemental image of Jesus. Once the archetype had been successfully established and imbued with the qualities that Wagner considered essential, then he could make Parsifal into an allegorical Jesus. Some believe he succeeded.

By maintaining that "music reveals the inmost essence of the Christian religion", Wagner clarified his focal point: first, he reiterated some of his earlier thoughts regarding the process of artistic creation and the mystic origin of man's inspiration; second, he reintroduced the"artist as the receptacle for the revelation of transcendental thoughts. Obviously Wagner could not prove that he was right, but never for one moment did he doubt that Divine Revelation could be made known to the world, as it had been to Jesus, by those who were spiritually attuned to God. This meant "some" but not all artists. To his credit never once did Wagner talk about, or think of himself, as divinely inspired, nor as one of those who had been chosen to enlighten the world. He wouldn't dare!

For those in the West who had assumed that religion meant only the Judaic-Christian world, Wagner had a different perspective: "But the ancient world has also **religion.** Who derides antique religiousness, let him read in Plutarch ... Our world, on the contrary, is irreligious."[60] But virtually every modern religion, including Brahminism and Buddhism, taught "alienation from the world and its passions", and thus betrayed God in whose image man was made and in whose name the world was given to man as a gift to be used and enjoyed.

---

[59] **Ibid.,** 217.

[60] "Shall we Hope", **Bayreuther Blätter,** May, 1879, **PW,** 6:118.

Wagner was convinced that Western man was witnessing the ever more rapidly "degeneration of the human race." The god of the Judaic-Christian-Islamic tradition, a bloodthirsty god of vengeance (and cruelty to animals!) offered mankind little hope for the future of the human race. Man's only possibility was that "Regeneration, can spring from nothing save the deep soil of a true Religion." But who will bring this about? Who will be the new Messiah, the new Savior? Wagner returned to one of his earliest thoughts: "This Poet priest, the only one who never lied, was ever sent to humankind at epochs of its direst error, as mediating friend: us too, will he lead over to that reborn life, to set before us there in ideal truth the 'likeness' of this passing show, when the Historians's realistic lie shall have long since been interred beneath the mouldering archives of our Civilization."[61]

Art may yet save mankind. Art through music can bring to man a "deep religious consciousness and the reason of its fall, and raising up itself therefrom to new development." Christianity tried to offer man a new soul; music as the principal aspect of art will elevate that soul into a new universal religion, one that will ennoble mankind and redeem the world.

Of course Christianity wasn't totally useless; it may yet be capable of modification! Calling friends and supporters to his side, Wagner announced a crusade: **"We recognize the cause of the fall of Historic Man, and of the necessity of his regeneration; we believe in the possibility of such Regeneration, and devote ourselves to its carrying-through in every sense."**[62] But he was equally quick to point out that all he was prepared to do was offer advice; action must be taken by others.

In **Parsifal** Wagner tried to illustrate one fundamental shift in emphasis which might offer some modicum of regeneration to the Christian world. Throughout historical Christianity one found three so-called "Theologic Virtues": "These are commonly arranged in an order that appears to us not quite the right one for the development of the Christian spirit; we should like to see 'Faith, Hope, and Charity'
----
61 "Religion and Art," 247.

62 "What Boots this Knowledge", **Bayreuther Blätter,** December, 1880, **PW,** 6:262.

352

transposed into 'Love, Faith, and Hope.'"[63] Parsifal represented the embodiment of the unification of Wagner's triad.

Wagner's last major religious article, "Hero-dom and Christendom", appeared in the **Bayreuther Blätter** in September 1881. According to Cosima "he considered his article ... which he read again today [four days before he died], to be his best."[64] Accepting part of Gobineau's thesis that the human family consisted of widely differing races, Wagner concluded that through intermixture "the blood of Christendom itself is curdled." He then raised a question--to which race did Jesus belong?--which he answered with a question: "The blood of the Saviour, the issue from his head, his wounds upon the cross,--who impiously would ask its race, if white or other?" Wagner thereupon gives his answer: "Divine we call it, and its source might dimly be approached in what we termed the human species' bond of union, its aptitude for Conscious Suffering."[65]

Wagner's answer was predominantly self-serving. It preached that the importance of Jesus transcended race, as it bypassed religion, thus conveniently denying his Semitic origin. While race may have precipitated a problem the question of color was simpler to deal with: "Thus, if we found the faculty of conscious suffering peculiarly developed in the so-called white race, in the Saviour's blood we now must recognize the quintessence of free-willed suffering itself, that godlike Pity which streams through all the human species, its fount and origin."

Unlike the ideals of the Brahminic religion, which Wagner called a "race-religion", Jesus went further. The blood of Jesus "shed itself on all the human family for noblest cleansing of Man's blood from every stain." Therefore, through the symbolic act of the Eucharist all mankind can be elevated, regardless of the present-day mixture of races. This sacrament could "raise the very lowest races to the purity of gods." Wagner's perception of the Eucharist was philosophical and metaphoric, and not essentially religious. It

---

[63] Ibid., 259.

[64] **CW's Diaries**, 9 February 1883, 1007.

[65] "Hero-dom and Christendom," **Bayreuther Blätter**, September 1881, **PW**, 6:280.

involved no physical or spiritual change. But in a special sense, through it man would become more closely attuned to his divinity. This would produce both a sense of equality among races and peoples and a fundamental perception of morality. Were this to happen man might even develop a "true aesthetic Art", and that could lead to his salvation.

CONCLUSION

WAGNER'S ROMANTIC NATIONALISM IN RETROSPECT

In 1834, at the age of twenty-one, and well before Wagner attained any serious recognition for his musical compositions, he published two articles regarding German music. In the first, "On German Opera", he speculated on several points which occupied his immediate attention. Since Germans were first-rate instrumentalists and wrote exceptional symphonic music, why did they not compose first-rate operas? Why were Germans still so far behind both the French and the Italians in the genre of opera? He came to one major observation: "but a German Opera we have not, and for the selfsame reason that we own no national Drama. We are too intellectual and much too learned, to create warm human figures."[1]

Wagner was not attempting to deprecate Mozart's operatic endeavors but since "it was the beauty of Italian Song that he breathed into his human beings" his operas could not really be considered as examples of a truly Germanic opera composer: "Mozart is the founder of German declamation ... when you consider the text [of **Die Zauberflöte**] ... and compare what was written before Mozart's time--on the one side the wretched German Singspiel, on the other the ornate Italian opera--one is amazed at the soul he managed to breathe into such a text."[2]

Although several of Wagner's contemporaries had made some notable contributions to the realm of opera, ᵢn the final analysis "the talents of the good German opera-composers of modern times, of Weber and Spohr, are unequal to the dramatic province."[3] The French were equally impoverished in their operatic endeavors. Despite a perception that "the dramatic poet intervened to far greater purpose than in Italy", in the final analysis French opera was "designed for a pathetic declamation of polished rhetorical phrases."[4]

----

[1] "On German Music," June 10, 1834, **Zeitung für die elegante Welt, PW**, 8:55.

[2] **CW's Diaries**, 29 May 1870, 1:225.

[3] "On German Music," 56.

[4] "Zukunftsmusik," 299.

But German music, from Bach to Beethoven was more notable in form than music emanating from Italy, France, or Spain. It was "universal" in importance. And yet Wagner had perceived that a specific quality existed within the Germanic disposition or temperament that he considered as an undesirable characteristic, one that "is an evil which, however ingrained in the character of the nation, must needs be rooted out." That "evil" which was so disturbing to Wagner helps explain why the average German does not respond to opera: Germans are unemotional! The inability of Germans to respond with passion and feeling produces an inhibiting quality which infects composers and audiences alike. This is the reason, thought Wagner, why so few first-rate German composers write for the opera. He speculated that part of the reason for this emotional inhibition related to an inbred Germanic intellectual tradition whereby erudition was viewed as the proper counterforce to that type of emotionalism so characteristic of the Latin peoples. But was this desirable? Was it good for Germany?

In another article entitled "Pasticcio", he again raised several questions relating to the German style of singing, and shuddered at the nonexistence of a true Germanic "training-shool for higher vocal culture." His conclusion: "our ordinary stage-performances in Germany pitch down from the height of rapt emotion to the depths of fussy dulness, and lack the outward stimulus of sustained artistic charm."[5] Coming to the heart of the problem as he perceived it, Wagner asked, "Why is it, that no German opera-composer has come to the front of late?" His answer went to the point: "Because none has known how to gain the voice of the Folk,--in other words because none has seized true warm Life as it is."

As instrumentalists, the peoples of no nation could approach the technical perfectionism to be found in the German musician. But German opera composers lack greatness precisely because they do not base their operas on the folk and their traditions. Believing that the only true spiritual reflection of the German folk at that time is to be found in Passion Plays, Wagner maintained that these "embody the whole essence and

----

5 "Pasticcio," **Neue Zeitschrift für Musik,** November 6 and 10, 1834, **PW,** 8:61.

substance of the German nation--the more so since [6] they stem from the hearts and customs of the people."

Part of Wagner's romantic nationalism was thus apparent even before he composed his first major musical work. Right from the beginning there existed within his psyche a mental association between the Germanic peoples and the need to create an authentic Germanic musical style. He felt certain that Germans would respond emotionally to a musical style rooted on the volk. Even before developing a coherent aesthetic philosophy, Wagner sensed that it needed to be rooted in the "volk", the people, the German people.

And yet, even in the intimate association between cultural nationalism and his belief in the future destiny of the German state, Wagner remained a universalist. His romanticism appeared to be rooted in a belief that although Germany was superior to Italy, France, and England, this truism was not to be viewed as an end in itself but merely as the best means whereby the human race could be elevated. Germany could help lead the nations of the world to achieve the most noble of all perceptions, the universality of man. Germany alone has the potential. Therefore in puffing up all that was German, Wagner saw Germanic exceptionalism only as a stepping stone. Nationalism could evolve toward internationalism providing one followed the Germanic model. For a German to compose and "be favourably received they had to denationalise themselves completely as artists." By assimilating Italian and French opera, the German would raise it to a higher level, making it capable of transcending "the limiting barriers of nationality."

Wagner's cultural nationalism was an incipient element within his larger vision of romantic nationalism but it formed an early part of his lifelong desire to see the creation of a unified Germanic State. Several elements were intimately bound to each other: Germanic music and the German State were both rooted in the German people. It is in this assumption that one can find the true beginning of Wagner's nationalism. Gradually as he grew older, he read, thought about, and speculated on the meaning and design of life. Soon other elements were added to Wagner's already

----

[6] "De la Musique Allemande," July 12, 26, 1840, **Gazette Musicale**, as translated in **Wagner Writes from Paris**, 44.

357

nationalistic outlook. But in the final analysis
Wagner's romantic nationalism was a composite
representing his aesthetic, political, economic,
social, and religious ideas, and all of these were
directly related to his sense of Germanness. Whatever
psychological forces or conditioning may have led to
this amalgam is left to others to determine. Suffice to
say, no understanding of Wagner, or his works, is
possible unless this element of his nationalism, the
crucial flux of his life, is clearly in focus.

While sometimes critical of the unemotional
responses of Germans toward artistic endeavors, Wagner
did believe that not only was this correctable, but it
may even reflect a national characteristic that would
bring a new element into the realm of traditional
opera: "The German wants not only to feel his music,
but to think it. The desire for mere sensuous pleasure
gives way to a longing for spiritual nourishment."
Since all romantic nationalists seem to involve
themselves with some significant belief in national
exceptionalism, Wagner saw the Germans as capable of
discovering their strength from within: "A German
prefers to withdraw from social life in order to seek
the sources of his inspiration inside himself, whereas
the Frenchman looks for inspiration to the remotest
reaches of society."[7]

It was while living in France in the early 1840's,
a struggling German emigré trying to achieve his
artistic niche in society, that Wagner's romanticism
first began to take on a more definite form. When the
Paris Opera decided to perform Weber's **Der Freischütz**,
Wagner speculated on whether the French were capable of
turning an essentially Germanic folk-opera into a
successful production.[8] He saw in this opera a
peculiarly distinctive Germanic saga that was foreign
to the French experience. The German loved and

----
[7] "Berlioz and Liszt," **Wagner Writes from Paris**, 131.

[8] His puzzlement took on even greater meaning and
concern when he learnt that Berlioz would not only
write additional recitatives for the opera, but would
also compose a ballet to be included in it! "Mournful
visions" began to enter Wagner's mind as he pondered on
whether the French would be capable of understanding
the "inward contemplative spirit which is bred in the
German nation as its birthright." See Wagner, "Der
Freischütz," **PW**, 7:182.

appreciated "surrounding Nature", and in this love of nature Wagner thought he saw a major difference between the German and French people. He had grave doubts whether the French could ever begin to either understand this opera or be able to present it properly. It was too German!

Incensed over an article which appeared in **Charivari,** a local paper, which erroneously asserted that the Paris Opera should be congratulated for "having granted asylum to this masterpiece from Germany after it had been disavowed by its composer's own fellow-countrymen and banned from performances on its native soil", Wagner saw this attitude as additional proof that Germans must be careful not to lose their own peculiar--and superior--national characteristics.[9]

Throughout his life Wagner would maintain a love-hate attitude toward the French. One of the more intriguing elements of Wagner's romantic nationalism was his capacity to feel such intense love for French culture and such hate for French cultural imperialism into Germany! In matters of literature, "the worst German book means more to me than the best French one- -in German some mystical chord is touched of which others show no trace."[10]

By the time he returned to Saxony, Wagner's romantic nationalism was inbred. It would not take long before it would be reflected in every aspect of his life and thought. Flawed though it was, Mozart's **Die Zauberflöte** was the first Germanic opera capable of becoming universalized. Weber in **Der Freischütz** took this one step further, but failed to follow it up in **Euryanthe** which Wagner perceived to be a backward step. However, it was Weber who first saw how Germans might elevate opera beyond the Italian model and for this his fellow countrymen should be indebted to him. Italian opera had been enormously popular in Germany but Weber single-handidly attempted to show how Germans could take a popular Italian art-form and transform it into something more than a collection of colorful tunes. By rethinking the nature of opera and by adding new dimensions of saga and nature, Weber demonstrated Germanic exceptionalism in opera. Wagner would continue

---

[9] "Le Freischütz," **Wagner Writes from Paris,** 152-3.

[10] **CW's Diaries,** 26 April 1882, 2:852.

in this tradition but would carry it to its logical conclusion in music-drama.

Not long after settling in Dresden, Wagner led a renewed effort to have Weber's remains brought back to Germany. Weber had died and was buried in London but in 1844 his body was re-interred on German soil and Wagner delivered the eulogy: "Ne'er has a **German-er** musician lived, than thou. Where'er thy genius bore thee, to whatsoever distant realms of floating fancy, it stayed forever linked by thousand tendrils to the German people's heart--and who shall blame us if we wished thine ashes, too, should mingle with this earth, should form a portion of dear German soil?"[11] Weber had "discovered" what the German had known all along, that opera was more than frivolous entertainment.

Since romantic nationalism is often a state of mind containing multifaceted psychological underpinnings, it was relatively easy for Wagner to rationalize and correlate seemingly unconnected or even disconnected elements. That Germanic exceptionalism in both instrumental music and opera could be created, was accepted as fact. When coupled with his assertion regarding the exceptionalism of the universal "German spirit", Wagner developed a mental axiom which led him to believe that just as Weber had reformed opera by introducing its higher form, so too the King of Saxony could reform the political state by altering its course and form. As Weber based **Der Freischütz** on the folk-tradition, rooted in both the people and nature, so too could the King, single-handedly, raise the dimension of Saxon political history. The King could utilize a workable political model from the past, from which the modern world had deviated, and restore to the free citizens of the State control of their political destiny. What could be more logical than to reintroduce the ancient concept of republicanism? Although his version of republicanism would substitute the folk over the nobility, as a process of government it represented a means to an end, one which could easily incorporate the monarchy without the slightest element of inconsistency. Wagner envisioned the king as the "First of the free Folk."

His romantic nationalism embraced a political society in which every citizen had the right to vote

----

11 "Speech at Weber's Last Resting Place," 1844, **PW**, 7:235-6.

and participate in the political process free from the fear of a standing army. Every member of society would have equal rights and privileges for all would be "united in the one great class of the free Folk."[12] And the king would become the "freest of the free." Wagner's dialectic contained many elements but he never doubted the rationality of his thinking and this is both the strength and the weakness of romantic nationalism.

In actuality there was nothing inconsistent in Wagner's model. He recognized, as did many, that republicanism was not rooted on a single political model but could indeed embrace a wide variety of forms of government: "Respublica means: the affairs of the nation. What individual can be more destined than the Prince, to belong with all his feelings, all his thoughts and actions, **entirely to the Folk's affairs**?" Man by himself was but an imperfect creature, an egocentric extension of the will, motivated by self-interest and potentially tyrannical. As an isolated unit, man, according to Wagner, was incapable of development in mind, body, or spirit. But the "aggregate of men" in the form of the folk, represented the best and only means by which society could arrive at a knowledge of the good and the beautiful, for "in combination man's strength increases."[13] Therefore men, not man, serve as the only consistent means to achieve the most desirable ends, the betterment of society. Since the evolution of the current political state had prevented men from exercising their freedom to better society, revolution was the only legitimate way to achieve a society of the folk: "I am the e'er-rejuvenating, ever-fashioning Life; where I am not, is Death! I am the dream, the balm, the hope of sufferers!"[14]

Therefore Wagner became a revolutionary both in terms of art and politics. One did not necessarily lead to the other for both were inextricably part of the scheme. In fact both were integral to his concept of romantic nationalism although in the early stages of his radicalism he did not associate all the elements as

---

[12] Appendix to "German Art and German Policy," **PW**, 4:138.

[13] "Man and Society," **PW**, 8, 229.

[14] "The Revolution," **PW**, 8:235.

belonging to a whole. Only gradually would this perception become clearer, but when it did it led directly to the **Ring,** and indirectly to the integration of art and politics with economics, religion, and society.

The constant association and interaction of ideas between the aesthetic and political worlds remained foremost in Wagner's mind throughout his life, imbuing his romantic nationalism with a clear sense of purpose as he tried, sometimes desperately, to fuse these two disparate elements. After fleeing Dresden in the aftermath of the unsuccessful revolution his ideas emerged with a greater clarity and sense of purpose than before. Aesthetic ideas may have precipitated his political awareness as he contemplated a restructured German state as the best likelihood for the emergence of a viable aesthetic spirit, but the aborted revolution only reinforced his political conviction that the artistic future of Germany went hand in hand with the destiny of the state.

After settling in Zurich, Wagner seemed so intrigued with the anomalies of history and the role played by man in the destiny of the world, that he was unable to concentrate on any musical subject. Instead his mind worked overtime as he postulated a whole series of questions that he felt had to be answered before he could return to composing. Two interrelated questions came to the forefront: who was the primary political figure of the day, and who was considered the major opera composer of Europe? The two answers were obvious: Metternich and Rossini (despite the fact that he was no longer composing). And Wagner sensed a relationship between them beyond the fact that both were reactionaries. Just as Gluck tried to revolt against the entrenched conservatism of Rossini so too did the liberal revolutionaries try to revolt against the entrenched conservatism of Metternich: "As Metternich, with perfect logic on his side, could not conceive the **State** under any form but that of **Absolute Monarchy:** so Rossini, with no less force of argument, could conceive the **Opera** under no other form than that of **Absolute Melody.**"[15]

But Wagner's starting point was not the monarchy nor the dominant political or artistic leaders of the

---

[15] "Part One: Opera and the Nature of Music," **Opera and Drama, PW,** 2:45.

362

day, but the folk--those who collectively represented
the German heart and soul.[16] It was they who would
"fulfil its mission of redemption." But for the folk to
lead mankind toward redemption they would need a common
focus, and this was missing in Germany. What would help
achieve a common focal point? An aesthetic endeavor
stemming from the common experiences of the folk, which
would be capable of uniting them into a collective
unit, a force possessing both aesthetic and political
power. The role that tragedy played in the life of the
ancient Greeks provided Wagner with just that type of
focal point. In the Greek world "tragedy flourished for
just so long as it was inspired by the spirit of the
Folk." When this "communal" spirit "shivered into
fragments" the core behind Greek society was
undermined, and eventually decay set in.
Individualism, the "I", soon replaced the folk. Egotism
destroyed both the Greek and the Roman worlds and now
threatens nineteenth century Europe.

The antithesis to egoism, the collective will of
the folk, must reassert itself for man's very survival
is at stake: "This consciousness of self, or better,
this becoming conscious of ourselves in the universal,
makes our life creative, just because by our
abandonment of self we enrich the generality, and in it
ourselves."[17] Only through the reemergence of the folk
could Europe's redemption be achieved. Only they could
reestablish art, politics, and society along the right
path from which modern civilization had deviated. The
establishment of this type of mental nucleus was the

----

16 See George L. Mosse, **The Crisis of German Ideology,
Intellectual Origins of the Third Reich,** New York,
1964. Mosse perceives that historians have tended to
underplay the great influence of "Volkish ideology" on
German history. As Germans sought to find national
roots, the Volkish ideas came to play an increasingly
more important role as the cement through which
"ideology was elaborated and diffused." According to
Mosse: "'Volk' signified the union of a group of people
with a transcendental 'essence.' This 'essence' might
be called 'nature' or 'cosmos' or 'mythos,' but in each
instance it was fused to man's innermost nature, and
represented the source of his creativity, his depth of
feeling, his individuality, and his unity with other
members of the Volk."(p. 4). In many ways, Wagner's
life and ideas reflects Mosse's thesis.

17 "Jesus of Nazareth," **PW,** 8:318.

primary basis behind Wagner's romantic nationalism. It was the beginning of the pathway which would lead man from Germanic exceptionalism to universalism. The goal of history would become the "gigantic march of evolution, from the fallen natural kinsmanship of national community to the universal fellowship of all mankind."[18] The evolution of art, politics, and society were entwined with that of the human race, and the end to be achieved was freedom: "There exists no higher **Power** than **Man's Community**; there is naught so **worthy Love** as the **Brotherhood of Man**. But only through the **highest power of Love** can we attain to **perfect Freedom**; for there exists no genuine Freedom but that in which **each Man hath share**."[19]

That art and politics were related did not mean that the two evolved together for clearly this was not the case in Italy. Rossini's music certainly bore no relationship to the Italian city-states currently in existence. Nevertheless, in Germany, Weber's **Der Fresichütz** "harked back to the **Folk**, and ... in the German **Folk** he found the happy attribute of naive heartiness without the cramp of national insularity."[20] Out of all the major countries within Western Europe only Germany still contained within its folk tradition certain elements that had been found in the Greek love for universals. The Greek world had attempted to discover all those fascinating component parts loosely described as inimical to human nature, but when Christianity ascended to dominance the search for human nature temporarily seemed to end.

Rather than discover the nature of man, Christianity attempted to dissect him in a search for his soul. In the process "Christianity had choked the organic impulse of the Folk's artistic life." Instead of looking at life, Christianity became obsessed with death: "To the Christian, however, Death was in itself the object." Christian art became symbolically expressed by the crucified Jesus while Christian music attained its highest end in the Passion Plays and in Catholic church music. The love of man and the value of life were all but obliterated. What did this do to man?

---

[18] **The Art-Work of the Future, PW,** 1:166.

[19] "Art and Climate," **PW,** 1:263.

[20] **Opera and Drama,** "First Part, Opera and the Nature of Music," II:54.

It placed his freedom in jeopardy. But not for long: "the first purely human stir of freedom manifested itself in warding off the bondage of religious dogma; and **freedom of thought** the State at last was forced to yield."[21]

Wagner now added another dimension to his romantic nationalism, the element of religion. Aesthetic freedom, political freedom, and religious freedom, were all intimately associated regardless of whether one element preceded or emanated from the others. Bringing religion into the amalgam was an imperative. Man was essentially religious but the nature of his religiosity, like that of his politics and aesthetics, needed to be examined. What was the nature of the religious experience and what did it mean for man? Once again Wagner thought in the broadest terms: "Religious Conscience means a **universal** conscience; and conscience cannot be universal, until it knows the Unconscious, the Instinctive, the Purely-human as the only true and necessary thing, and vindicates it by that knowledge."

Therefore, to the extent that religious institutions are external to man they are man-made and particularistic, whereas the mystical, intuitive, and transcendental is common to all for God is to be found within each individual soul. It is not within the province of man-made religious institutions to unlock the existence of God within the breast of the folk. Wagner assigns that task to the poet! He is the **"knower of the unconscious,** the aimful demonstrator of the instinctive."[22] The intuitive knowledge of the poet can become the necessary link between man and God, and the instrument for encouraging universality: "So long, moreover, shall we have states and religions, till we have but **one** Religion and **no longer any** State."

Finally, word fused with tone and transmitted by the orchestra will represent the art-work of the future. Based on the sagas of the folk, this new music could serve as the means by which the human race could be elevated. How? By showing and revealing man's true inner worth. The art-work of the future represented the

---

[21] **Ibid.,** "Second Part, The Play and the Nature of Dramatic Poetry," 147.

[22] **Ibid.,** "Third Part, The Arts of Poetry and Tone in the Drama of the Future," 265.

"unity of artistic Form" for it incorporated a "united content" of word-speech, tone-speech, and melody, becoming in the process the music of the future. The role of the orchestra is to express and reinforce the aim of the poet, for he alone is most attuned to the unconscious, the repository of the soul.

These ideas for the regeneration and redemption of mankind might have been the destiny of any nation, but as it turned out the art-work of the future "could only happen in the German tongue. ... It has been proved that the womb of German mothers could receive and bear the loftiest geniuses of the world; what remains to prove, is whether the receptive organs of the German Folk are worthy of the noble issue of those chosen mothers."[23] But this would not automatically occur, nor was it even destined to happen. In fact, there was little likelihood that it would or could happen unless the conservative and reactionary elements were eliminated from German politics, aesthetics, and religion.

It was the centrality of man acting to encourage this revolution that turned Wagner into a politically active romantic nationalist. Only by a total and all-embracing revolution--to achieve an entirely new way of thinking--could German exceptionalism emerge: "While pondering on the possibility of a thorough change in our theatrical relations, I was insensibly driven to a full perception of **the worthlessness of that social and political system which, of its present nature, could beget no other public art-conditions than precisely those I then was grappling with**.--This knowledge was of decisive consequence for the further development of my whole life."[24] The romantic nationalist hoped to become just the catalyst to start the process for "it is the **artist**, whose clear eye can spy out shapes that reveal themselves to a yearning which longs for the only truth--**the human being**. The artist has the power of seeing beforehand a yet unshapen world, of tasting beforehand the joys of a world as yet unborn, through the stress of his desire for Growth."[25]

----

[23] "Letter to an Italian Friend [Arrigo Boito] on the Production of **Lohengrin** at Bologna," November, 1871, **PW**, 5:288.

[24] **Communication**, PW, 1:354.

[25] **Opera and Drama**, "Third Part", 375.

These thoughts represented the embryonic core behind Wagner's perception of where man should go and the role to be played by the folk in helping to propel man forward to this goal. His ends were clear: a universal political state which transcended patriotism and nationality; a universal art form which encompassed all the arts; and a universal religious system which cut across Judaism and Christianity. Anything that interfered with this grand universal perception represented a threat to the folk.

By transcending Judaism and Christianity Wagner meant that man should emulate pure spirit, as exemplified by Jesus: "I do not believe in God, but in godliness, which is revealed in a Jesus without sin."[26] It was the simple purity of Jesus which defined true Christianity and not the "church", regardless of denomination. Exactly how far Wagner would be willing to go to resolve the "Jewish problem" is purely speculative. Although he declined to go along with the rising anti-Semitic movement, and refused to ask Bismarck to deal harshly with the Jews--thus earning considerable applause from the Jewish community--he could still confide to Cosima that he would like to "ban Jewish holidays on which they will not sell merchandise to Christians--also the boastful synagogue. 'What then will be the significance of our feast days.'"[27]

And it was the folkish tradition that Wagner looked to as the basis of action behind his all-embracing concept of reform for "that genuine Revolution could never come from Above, from the standpoint of erudite intellect, but only from Below, from the urgence of true human need."[28] It was they who would determine the future course of German and European civilization: "We know that it was the 'German Spirit,' so terribly dreaded and hated 'across the mountains,' that stepped into the field of Art, as everywhere else, to heal this artfully induced corruption of the European race."[29]

---

[26] **CW's Diaries**, 20 September 1879, 2:367.

[27] **Ibid.**, 30 November 1880, 564.

[28] **Communication**, 356.

[29] "Beethoven," Autumn, 1870, **PW**, 5:84.

Romantic nationalism is seldom consistent and Wagner was so prolific in his prose-writing, and so often emotionally involved in what he was striving to say, that he did not always carefully think out what he was stating, nor did he seem to know exactly where he was going. His essays sometimes ramble aimlessly and are too often endlessly repetitious and frustratingly contradictory. At one moment he could glibly expound on the as yet nonexistence of the "German Spirit" but could confidently predict that as long as the German Folk existed a true spirit would eventually reemerge: "How are we to conceive a state of things in which the German Folk remained, but the German Spirit had taken flight?"[30] Two years later he reversed and modified his thinking: "for demonstrably, as scarce another fact of history, the resurrection of the German Folk itself has emanated from the German Spirit..."[31]

Either way, a symbiotic relationship existed in his mind between the Folk and the Spirit. Once Germany was politically united in a truly national state both elements would play a major role in defining the characteristics and future qualities of that state: "Ever since the rejuvenation of European Folk-blood, considered strictly, the German has been the creator and inventor, the Romanic the modeller and exploiter: the true fountain of continual renovation has remained the German nature." Germany may be, at present, in a state of "suspended animation" but the day will come when the stage will be set for the rebirth of man; and Germany is destined to lead the way. The poet will eventually recognize that by utilizing the spirit to be found in myth, the Folk will find its future destiny linked to its assumed mythical past: "I therefore believed I must term the 'mythos' the poets ideal Stuff--that native, nameless poem of the Folk, which throughout the ages we ever meet new-handled by the great poets of periods of consummate culture."[32]

But how could the folkish tradition be reinvigorated so that Germany could play its role in leading man forward toward redemption? Through which means could Germany begin to tap the strength and

----

[30] "What is German," Autumn, 1865, **PW**, 4:164.

[31] "German Art and German Policy," Autumn, 1867, **PW**, 4:40.

[32] "Zukunftsmusik," 312.

resources of the Folk? Through theatre! "There lies the spiritual seed and kernel of all national-poetic and national-ethical culture, that no other art-branch can ever truly flourish, or ever aid in cultivating the Folk, until the Theatre's all-powerful assistance has been completely recognised and guaranteed."[33] Wagner was, of course, thinking in very broad terms. His idea of "theatre" was related to the observations and conclusions expressed in a variety of theoretical prose works in which he correlated theatre as being the reflection or amalgamation of all the arts. Theatre would be a reflection of drama "but in Drama glorified by Music, the Folk will one day find itself and every art ennobled and embellished."[34]

Since theatre would be the best means to achieve German and then universal art, Wagner's lifelong desire was to establish schools, academies, or conservatories that would accelerate the process of Germanizing the arts. Trying desperately in Dresden, Zurich, Vienna, Munich, and finally Bayreuth to establish those institutions which would teach Germans music, singing, acting, and the other attendant elements of art, he hoped to spark that special quality of "German originality" out of which would ultimately emerge a "universal Music-school." The relationship between Bach and Beethoven in music to Schiller and Goethe in drama, proved to Wagner just how far German art had already evolved. By the establishment of new conservatories the evolutionary process could be speeded up thereby hastening the advent of universalism: "Indisputably a great mission lies prefigured in the whole temper of the German, and a mission scarce within the cognisance of other nations... [which] when felicitously cultivated, it must be assigned the character of universalism"[35]

The reemergence of theatre, after it had been virtually destroyed by Italian opera, could best be accomplished by "applying Beethovenian Music to the Shakespearean Drama" which, if properly accomplished, might result in the "perfecting of Musical Form." Only the German could successfully accomplish this task. Italian opera's widespread popularity in Germany

---
[33] "German Art and German Policy," 69.

[34] "Introduction to the Collected Works," **PW**, 1:xviii.

[35] "A Music School for Munich," **PW**, 4:213.

temporarily stifled the creation of a "German national-art" but when the German composer reflected on the nature of the problem he would soon realize that the obvious solution would be for the German composer to inaugurate a new art-form more closely related to the German folk, and that would be in "the field of Musical Drama." The result would be novel in terms of what European thought and culture had envisioned as art, but it would be the clearest reflection of a unique quality of perception that is to be found within the German character itself, a perception of reality that could be shared with others. And this is the essence of Drama, that is no form of poetry, but the likeness of the world reflected by our silent soul."[36]

Wagner seldom doubted that the soul of the German made him uniquely qualified to make a major contribution to the history of the human race, providing what resulted was consistent with the inborn quality of the German Spirit. This apparently meant that the German had a unique capacity to intuit a reality of human values emanating from God. But it was not automatically available and it had to be cultivated with care and diligence. Perhaps this was one of the reasons why he was always so critical of Jews. Time after time Wagner was incensed over, but intrigued with, the idea that the Jews were the "chosen people." It riled him to think of this possibility. If ever a people were destined to be "chosen" it would have to be the German and certainly not the Jew who always remained but an alien in any country.

But the Jew had a tradition, a history, a fundamental sense of God-given morality, and a unity that transcended nation: "As we well know, Jews have no interest in the formation of a German empire but, on the contrary, are in favor of cosmopolitanism."[37] This reality formed an endless source of Wagner's discontent. If the Jews and their God could be undermined, there might be room left for the emergence of the German as the newly chosen people--but not if the basis of the German religion was that of the Judeo-Christian tradition. That would only tie the German nation in more closely with the desires of the

----

[36] "Letter to Heinrich von Stein," 31 January 1883, **Bayreuther Blätter**, 1883, **PW**, 6:327.

[37] **CW's Diaries**, 27 September 1870, 1:277.

Jews thus making it even more difficult for German exceptionalism to emerge.

The German nation was exceptional exactly because it had the opportunity to fulfill a unique mission. They could become the new chosen people, for destiny had singled them out from among all the peoples of Western Europe, if not the world, to lead mankind to a new and glorious future. Wagner actually believed that the fate of generations to come now rested in German hands. But--and this point was of the essence--unlike the Jews who at one point of time in history might have been selected by God to be his servants on earth, and specifically given the responsibility and duty of promulgating God's commandments, the German must earn the world's respect. No new divine covenant was being handed down. And yet, if Germans exercised their freewill they could bring about an entirely new series of political, economic, social, aesthetic, and religious values which would be emulated by all Europe. Mankind would then be on the way toward finding redemption, regeneration, and true happiness. This was Wagner's concept of romantic nationalism.

Wagner spent years trying to work out a scenario by which these thoughts could become reality rather than theory. In all respects it was a vivid, if potentially dangerous reflection of his romantic nationalism: "my belief in the German spirit, and the trust in its predestined place amid the Council of Nations ... took an ever mightier hold upon me as time rolled on. ... For myself, I feel assured that just the same relation which my ideal of Art bears to the reality of our general conditions of existence, that relation is allotted to the German race in its destiny amid a whole political world in the throes of 'Spontaneous Combustion.'"[38]

How to revive the "genuine Essence of the German Spirit" was the single most difficult question of Wagner's life. It was the one question that occupied hundreds and hundreds of hours of thought and discussion as he tried, sometimes desperately and irrationally, to answer it. He tended to assume that the Thirty Years War had a devastating effect on Germany for it buried the German spirit, henceforth making Germans the mockery of Europeans. But the

---
[38] "Introduction to Art and Revolution," 1872, **PW,** 1:29.

371

evolution of a "new community" emanating from the folk was still a distinct possibility. If this were inspired to happen then Germany's aesthetic, intellectual, political, and spiritual dimensions would go well beyond that of any other currently existing nation. This new community of the folk "belonging to no special section of society, but permeating its every class, in my eyes ... would represent the latent receptivity of German Feeling become responsive to original expression of the German Spirit on that domain which hitherto had been abandoned to the most un-German abuses."[39]

Nationalism traditionally embodies a wide variety of thoughts and an infinite cluster of ideas and feelings. While economic, or political, or cultural nationalists generally try to focus their energies on one major aspect of thought, Wagner attempted to paint a larger canvas and with broader strokes. He often found himself alone. Seldom was he able to influence a large share of the population although many were sympathetic with certain specific elements of his nationalism. Intuitively perceiving who the German was and where the nation might go, Wagner was not always able to articulate his views clearly enough, and never gained a wide or a broad audience for his non-musical ideas. For forty years Wagner's intense active life reflected his thoughts and feelings and gave him an energy that was undiminished with time. But having achieved so little success in his non-musical endeavors left him, especially in his last few years, often bitter and dejected.

After the unification of Germany Wagner's frustration only increased as he viewed all the lost opportunities: "Many an intelligent observer has been struck with the fact that the recent prodigious successes of German Policy have not contributed one jot toward diverting the sense and taste of the German people from a foolish hankering for the Foreign, toward arousing the wish to cultivate those native aptitudes still left to us."[40] Regrettably, the German yet wallows in the mediocre, "that which brings us no new

---

[39] Wagner, "Final Report on the Fates and Circumstances that Attended the Execution of the Stage-Festival Play, **Der Ring des Nibelungen** Down to the Founding of the Wagner-Societies," April, 1873, PW, 5:319.

[40] "The Festival-Playhouse at Bayreuth," April, 1873, PW, 5:339.

and unknown thing, but the known-already in a pleasing and insinuating form. ... No wonder the really good, the work of genius, is uncommonly hateful to these men of printed German intellect, for it so very much upsets them."[41] Of course some of these comments may have been precipitated by a national indifference toward him following the success of the first Bayreuth Festival. Wagner may have been smarting over what appeared to be a benign neglect by the country to which he dedicated his monumental **Ring**. But his chagrin extended well beyond personal pique even though that was obviously part of the overall picture:

> I am the most German being, I am the German spirit. Question the incomparable magic of **my** works, compare them with the rest: and you can, for the present, say no differently than that -- it is **German**. But what is this **German**? It must be something wonderful, mustn't it, for it is humanly finer than all else? -- Oh heavens! It should have a soil, **this German**! I should be able to find my people! What a glorious people it ought to become. But to this people only could I belong.--[42]

The essential problem remained a question: how to reach the German soul that lay buried deep within the German bosom? At this point of German history only the naivete of the folk was visible. He raised a plaintive cry: "Shall We Hope?" It was a good question, one which begged for an answer, but all that he could do was reiterate that "from a strong inner Must alone can spring the Necessity of Action; and without such Necessity no true or genuine thing can be set on foot."[43]

Wagner never gave up on his belief that the regeneration of man could come through the redemption of the German folk. But time was not on the side of Western Europe. Toward the latter decades of the nineteenth century several new factors seemed to be complicating the belief in the future course of German and/or human history. As "scientific evidence" began

---

[41] "Public and Popularity," March 1878, **PW**, 6: 56, 58.

[42] **The Brown Book**, 73.

[43] "Shall We Hope," **Bayreuther Blätter**, May 1879, **PW**, 6:130.

circulating which sought to assert, if not prove, not only the disparity between superior and inferior races but the likely prospect that the mongrelization of Europe was about to begin, fears arose over the purity and future of the white Anglo-Saxon-Teutonic race. Wagner, like many others, was sincerely concerned over a "decay in a depravation of those race's blood." As Darwin's hypotheses became bastardized by the social Darwinists and with Gobineau's racial theories gaining in prominence, Wagner began to believe more seriously that it would be only a matter of time before "Europe will be submerged by Asiatic hordes" and "our music playing would be the first thing to go by the board."

Ultimately it would be the folk who let Wagner down. They who were the backbone of Germany were unable to rise up to meet his expectations. They who were the ones who could "deal instinctively and of necessity" failed to act. Germany was "finished" partially because Jews gained equality and power before Germany had the opportunity to gain an identity, and partly because the German spirit, the spirit of the folk, failed to materialize. The Jew had a tradition, a heritage, a past, and found a common identity in the Talmud, while the German "had no civilization behind us." It was beginning to appear that Germany had no special or divine place in the world. The Jew had a soul and was worried about it, while the German did not possess even this; or if it did exist it was so dormant as to be all but nonexistent. The Jew and not the German would dominate the future of the Western world: "If our civilization comes to an end, what does it matter? But if it comes to an end through the Jews, that is a disgrace."[44]

At the end of his life Wagner remained skeptical and frustrated, but ever so slightly hopeful: "The theory of the degeneration of the human race, however opposed it seems to that of constant progress, might yet be the only one, in earnestness, to lead us to some hope."[45] But however much of a future mankind may possibly have, in the final analysis in terms of the present, "there's not a century--not a decade of history, that is not almost exclusively filled with the human race's shame." Only a romantic nationalist could

----

[44] CW's Diaries, 14 February 1881, 2:622.

[45] "Sketches and Fragments," PW, 8:394.

continue to maintain some faith in the possibility of man's redemption and regeneration.

But it was not to Germany that Wagner's very final thoughts centered. Now viewing Germans as "cruel and indifferent people", he all but gave up on them as the Western leaders capable of leading man forward toward redemption and regeneration. Finally, at the end of his life, he believed that man's only hope might be found in the two great empires of the future, Russia and America.

BIBLIOGRAPHY

Wagner, Richard: **The Diary of Richard Wagner. The Brown Book, 1865-1882.** Presented and annotated by Joachim Bergfeld. Translated by George Bird. London, 1980.

---**My Life.** N. Y, 1911. Reprinted 1977. Two volumes.

---**Richard Wagner's Prose Works.** Translated by William Ashton Ellis. Broude Brothers, 1966. Eight volumes. Reprinted from the London edition.

Volume 1 (1892):

Author's Introduction to the Collected Works.
Autobiographic Sketch.
Art and Revolution, with Introduction.
The Art-Work of the Future
Wieland the Smith.
Art and Climate.
A Communication to my Friends.

Volume 2 (1893):

Opera and Drama.

Volume 3 (1894):

Author's Introduction.
On the "Goethe-Stiftung."
A Theatre at Zurich.
On Musical Criticism.
Judaism in Music.
Mementoes of Spontini.
Homage to L. Spohr and W. Fischer.
Gluck's Overture to "Iphegenia in Aulis.
On the Performing of "Tannhäuser."
Remarks on Performing "The Flying Dutchman."
Explanatory Programmes:
  1. Beethoven's "Heroic Symphony."
  2. Beethoven's Overture to "Coriolanus."
  3. Overture to "Der Fliegende Holländer."
  4. Overture to "Tannhäuser."
  5. Prelude to "Lohengrin."
On Franz Liszt's Symphonic Poems.
Epilogue to the "Nibelung's Ring."
Preface to the "Ring" Poem.
A Letter to Hector Berlioz.

"Zukunftsmusik" ("Music of the Future")
On the Production of "Tannhäuser" in Paris.
The Vienna Opera-House.

Volume 4 (1895):

To the Kingly Friend (Poem).
On State and Religion.
German Art and German Policy.
Appendices:
  The Vaterlandsverein Speech.
  Letter to Von Lüttichau.
What is German?
A Music-School for Munich.
Ludwig Schnorr of Carolsfeld.
Notices:
  Introduction.
  W. H. Riehl.
  Ferdinand Hiller.
  A Remembrance of Rossini.
  Eduard Devrient.
About Conducting.
Three Poems:
  Rheingold.
  On the Completion of Siegfried.
  August 25th, 1870.

Volume 5 (1896):

To the German Army Before Paris (Poem)
A Capitulation.
Reminiscences of Auber.
Beethoven.
The Destiny of Opera.
Actors and Singers.
The Rendering of Beethoven's Ninth Symphony.
Letters and Minor Essays:
  1. Letter to an Actor.
  2. A Glance at the German Operatic Stage of Today.
  3. Letter to an Italian Friend on the Production of
     "Lohengrin" at Bologna.
  4. To the Burgomaster of Bologna.
  5. To Friedrich Nietzsche.
  6. On the Name "Musikdrama."
  7. Prologue to a Reading of the "Götterdämmerung"
     Before a Select Audience in Berlin.
Bayreuth:
  1. Final Report on the Fates and Circumstances that
     Attended the Execution of the Stage-Festival-

Play Der Ring des Nibelungen" Down to the Founding of the Wagner-Societies.
2. The Festival Playhouse at Bayreuth, with an Account of the Laying of its Foundation-Stone.

Volume 6 (1897):

Spohr's "Jessonda" at Leipzig.
Minor Bayreuth Papers:
   1. To the Presidents of Wagner-Vereins.
   2. Proposed Bayreuth "School."
   3. Introduction to the First Number of the Bayreuther Blätter.
   4. Introduction to a Work of H. von Wolzogen's.
   5. Postponement of "Parsifal."
   6. Introduction to the Year 1880.
   7. Announcement of "Parsifal" Performances.
   8. Introduction to a Work of Count Gobineau's.
Modern.
Public and Popularity.
The Public in Time and Space.
Retrospect of the Stage-Festivals of 1876.
Shall we Hope?
On Poetry and Composition.
On Operatic Poetry and Composition.
On the Application of Music to the Drama.
Against Vivesection.
Religion and Art.
  "What Boots this Knowledge?"
  "Know Thyself"
  Hero-dom and Christendom
End of the Patronat-Verein.
The Stipendiary Fund.
"Parsifal" at Bayreuth.
A Youthful Symphony.
Letter to Herr von Syein.
The Human Womanly (Fragment).

Volume 7 (1898):

Author's Introduction.
"Das Liebesverbot."
A German Musician in Paris
   1. A Pilgrimage to Beethoven.
   2. An End in Paris.
   3. A Happy Ending.
   4. On German Music.
  4A. Pergolesi's "Stabat Mater."
   5. The Virtuoso and the Artist.
  5A. Du Métier de Virtuose.

6. The Artist and Publicity.
7. Rossini's "Stabat Mater."
On the Overture.
Der Fresichütz in Paris.
1. To the Paris Public.
2. Report to Germany.
Halévy's "Reine de Chypre."
Author's Introduction to Vol. II of the Ges. Schr.
Weber's Re-internment.
  Report.
  Speech.
Beethoven's Choral Symphony at Dresden.
  Report.
  Programme.
The Wibelungen.
The Nibelungen-Myth.
Tercentenary Toast.
A German National Theatre.

Volume 8 (1899):

"Siegfried's Death."
Discarded:
  On German Opera.
  Pasticcio.
  Bellini.
  Parisian Amusements.
  Parisian Fatalities for the German.
  Letters from Paris.
  Halévy and "La Reine de Chypre."
  Jottings on the Ninth Symphony.
  Artist and Critic.
  Greeting from Saxony to the Viennese.
  On E. Devrient's "History of German Acting."
  Theatre-Reform.
  Man and Established Society.
  The Revolution.
  Invitation to the Production of "Tristan" in
  Munich.
Posthumous:
  "The Saracen Woman."
  Sketch for "The Apostle's Love-Feast."
  "Jesus of Nazareth."
  Sketches and Fragments

---**Wagner Writes from Paris.** Stories, Essays and Articles by the Young Composer. Edited and translated by Robert L. Jacobs and Geoffrey Skelton. London, 1973.

380

Letters and Other Primary Sources

Correspondence of Wagner and Liszt. Francis Hueffer, translator. Second edition revised by William Ashton Ellis. Two volumes. New York, 1897.

Cosima Wagner's Diaries. Volume 1, 1869-1877. Edited and annotated by Martin Gregor-Dellin and Dietrich Mack. Translated and with an Introduction by Geoffrey Skelton. New York, 1977.

---Volume 2, 1878-1883. New York, 1980.

Family Letters of Richard Wagner. William Ashton Ellis, translator. London, 1911.

Letters of Hans von Bülow to Richard Wagner and Others. Hannah Walter, translator. New York, 1979.

Letters of Richard Wagner. The Burrell Collection. Edited by John N. Burk. New York, 1950.

Letters of Richard Wagner. Selected and edited by Wilhelm Altmann. Translated by M. M. Bozman. Two volumes. New York, 1927.

Letters of Richard Wagner to Anton Pusinelli. Translated and Edited by Elbert Lenrow. New York, 1972.

Letters of Richard Wagner to Emil Heckel. William Ashton Ellis, translator. London, 1899.

Lippert, Woldemar. **Wagner in Exile, 1849-62.** Keeper of the Principal Public Archives of Saxony. Translated by Paul England. London, 1930.

Neumann, Angelo. **Personal Recollections of Wagner.** Edith Livermore, translator. New York, 1976.

The Nietzsche-Wagner Correspondence. Edited by Elizabeth Foerster-Nietzsche. Translated by Caroline V. Kerr. New York, 1921.

Porges, Heinrich. **Wagner Rehearsing the 'Ring'.** An Eye-Witness Account of the Stage Rehearsals of the First Bayreuth Festival. Translated by Robert L. Jacobs. New York, 1983.

Richard to Minna Wagner, Letters to his First Wife. William Ashton Ellis, translator. New York, 1909.

Richard Wagner's Letters to August Roeckel. Eleanor C. Sellar, translator. London, 1897.

Richard Wagner to Mathilde Wesendonck. William Ashton Ellis, translator. London, 1899.

Richard Wagner to Otto Wesendonck. William Ashton Ellis, translator. London, 1899.

Wagner: A Documentary Study. Compiled and edited by Herbert Barth, Dietrich Mack, Egon Voss. Preface by Pierre Boulez. New York, 1975.

Major Secondary Sources

Glasenapp, Carl Friedrich. The Life of Richard Wagner. Being an Authorized English Translation by William Ashton Ellis. Six volumes. Reprinted, New York, 1977.

Newman, Ernest. The Life of Richard Wagner. Four volumes. New York, 1933-46.

von Westernhagen, Curt. Wagner. A Biography. Translated by Mary Whittall. Two volumes. New York, 1978.

INDEX